THE POLITICAL ECONOMY OF AGRICULTURAL PRICE DISTORTIONS

Despite numerous policy reforms since the 1980s, farm product prices remain heavily distorted in both high-income and developing countries. This book seeks to improve our understanding of why societies adopted these policies and why some but not other countries have undertaken reforms. Drawing on recent developments in political economy theories and in the generation of empirical measures of the extent of price distortions, the present volume provides both analytical narratives of the historical origins of agricultural protectionism in various parts of the world and a set of political econometric analyses aimed at explaining the patterns of distortions that have emerged over the past five decades. These new studies shed much light on the forces affecting incentives and those facing farmers in the course of national and global economic and political development. They also show how those distortions might change in the future – or be changed by concerted actions to offset pressures from vested interests.

Kym Anderson is George Gollin Professor of Economics, School of Economics, University of Adelaide, Australia. During 2004–07, he was on extended leave at the World Bank's Development Research Group as Lead Economist, Trade Policy. Earlier, he spent 1990–92 at the Research Division of the GATT (now the WTO) Secretariat in Geneva. Professor Anderson has published approximately 300 articles and 30 books, including *The Political Economy of Agricultural Protection* (with Yujiro Hayami and others), which received the Tohata Memorial Award from Japan's National Institute for Research Advancement; *Disarray in World Food Markets* (Cambridge University Press, with Rod Tyers); *New Silk Roads* (Cambridge University Press); and *Agricultural Trade Reform and the Doha Development Agenda* (with Will Martin), which received the American Agricultural Economics Association's (AAEA) 2006 Quality of Communication Award and the Australian Agricultural and Resource Economics Society's (AARES) 2007 Quality of Research Discovery Prize. During 2006–09, Professor Anderson directed a large empirical research project for the World Bank on distortions to agricultural incentives, covering seventy-five countries. From this research project, four region-oriented books and two globally oriented books appeared in 2008–09 and 2009–10, respectively, in addition to the present book. His 2009 volume on *Distortions to Agricultural Incentives: A Global Perspective, 1955–2007*, received the AAEA's 2010 Bruce Gardner Memorial Prize for Applied Policy Analysis and the AARES's 2010 Quality of Research Discovery Prize.

The Political Economy of Agricultural Price Distortions

Edited by

KYM ANDERSON
University of Adelaide

CAMBRIDGE
UNIVERSITY PRESS

Shaftesbury Road, Cambridge CB2 8EA, United Kingdom

One Liberty Plaza, 20th Floor, New York, NY 10006, USA

477 Williamstown Road, Port Melbourne, VIC 3207, Australia

314–321, 3rd Floor, Plot 3, Splendor Forum, Jasola District Centre, New Delhi – 110025, India

103 Penang Road, #05–06/07, Visioncrest Commercial, Singapore 238467

Cambridge University Press is part of Cambridge University Press & Assessment, a department of the University of Cambridge.

We share the University's mission to contribute to society through the pursuit of education, learning and research at the highest international levels of excellence.

www.cambridge.org
Information on this title: www.cambridge.org/9780521763233

© Cambridge University Press & Assessment 2010

First published 2010
First paperback edition 2013

A catalogue record for this publication is available from the British Library

Library of Congress Cataloging-in-Publication data
The political economy of agricultural price distortions / [edited by] Kym Anderson.
p. cm.
ISBN 978-0-521-76323-3 (hardback)
1. Agricultural prices. 2. Agriculture and state. 3. Agricultural subsidies.
4. Agriculture – Economic aspects. I. Anderson, Kym. II. Title.
HD1447.P65 2010
338.1′3–dc22   2010022616

ISBN   978-0-521-76323-3   Hardback
ISBN   978-1-107-61627-1   Paperback

To Bronwyn, for supporting me in every way
throughout this project

Contents

Figures

Tables

Contributors

Kym Anderson is George Gollin Professor of Economics at the University of Adelaide and a Research Fellow of the Centre for Economic Policy Research in London. During 2004–2007, he was on an extended sabbatical as Lead Economist (Trade Policy) in the Development Research Group of the World Bank in Washington, DC.

Robert H. Bates is Eaton Professor of the Science of Government in the Department of Government and a member of the faculty of African and African-American Studies, Harvard University, Cambridge, MA. His latest books are *The Political Economy of Economic Growth in Africa, 1960–2000* (Cambridge 2007) and *When Things Fell Apart* (Cambridge 2008), the latter focusing on state failure and conflict in Africa.

David Blandford is a Professor in the Department of Agricultural Economics and Rural Sociology and in the School of International Affairs at the Pennsylvania State University, University Park. Before that, he was at the OECD in Paris, analyzing impacts of OECD policies, and he has chaired the International Agricultural Trade Research Consortium.

Steven Block is an Associate Professor of International Economics and head of the international development program at the Fletcher School of Law and Diplomacy, and Associate Professor at the Friedman School of Nutrition Science and Policy, both at Tufts University. His research concentrates on food policy, rural development, and nutrition.

Olivier Cadot is a Professor of Economics at the University of Lausanne, an Associate Scholar at CERDI and CEPREMAP, and a Research Fellow of the Centre for Economic Policy Research in London. His research interests are in the area of international trade and development with an emphasis in political economy determinants of trade policy.

Johanna Croser has been a short-term consultant with this project and is a PhD and law student at the University of Adelaide, having completed her doctoral economics coursework at the University of British Columbia in Vancouver, Canada.

Pushan Dutt is an Associate Professor of Economics at the Asia campus of INSEAD, Singapore. His research lies at the intersection of politics, institutions, and international economics.

Andres F. Garcia was an Assistant Professor in the Development Economics Research Group of the University of Copenhagen in Denmark after completing his PhD at Purdue University (when he contributed to this volume). He is now with the Young Professionals Program of the World Bank in Washington, DC.

Kishore Gawande holds the Roy and Helen Ryu Chair of Economics and Government at the Bush School of Government and Public Service, Texas A&M University at College Station, where he heads the International Economics and Development track.

Bernard Hoekman is Director of the International Trade Department and former Research Manager of the trade and integration unit of the Development Research Group at the World Bank in Washington, DC. He is also a Research Fellow of the Centre for Economic Policy Research in London.

Timothy Josling is Professor Emeritus in the Food Research Institute and Senior Fellow at the Freeman Spogli Institute for International Studies at Stanford University, CA. His research covers a wide range of agricultural trade policy areas, including the relationship between multilateral and regional trade agreements and domestic policies.

William A. Masters is a Professor and Associate Head of the Department of Agricultural Economics at Purdue University in West Lafayette, IN. He has also been a lecturer at the University of Zimbabwe (1988–1990). He is currently a coeditor of *Agricultural Economics*, the IAAE's journal.

Devashish Mitra is a Professor of Economics and the Gerald B. and Daphna Cramer Professor of Global Affairs at the Maxwell School of Citizenship and Public Affairs, Syracuse University in Syracuse, NY. He is also a coeditor of the journal *Economics and Politics* and associate editor of the *Journal of International Economics*.

John V. C. Nye is the Frederic Bastiat Chair in Political Economy and Professor of Economics at George Mason University in Fairfax, VA. He specializes in British and French economic history and the new institutional economics. He is the author of *War, Wine, and Taxes* and coeditor of *Frontiers in the New Institutional Economics* (2008).

Marcelo Olarreaga is a Professor of Economics at the University of Geneva and a Research Fellow of the Centre for Economic Policy Research in London. His research interests are in the areas of political economy of trade policy, barriers to developing countries' exports, and the impact of trade reforms on income inequality and poverty.

Alessandro Olper is an Associate Professor in the Department of Agricultural and Food Economics at the University of Milan in Italy. His research interests are in the areas of international trade, political economy, and agricultural policy analysis.

David Orden is a Senior Research Fellow at the International Food Policy Research Institute (IFPRI) in Washington, DC, and Director of the Global Issues Initiative, Institute for Society, Culture and Environment at Virginia Polytechnic Institute and State University in Alexandria. His research focuses on the economics and political economy of agricultural policies.

Valentina Raimondi is an Assistant Professor in the Department of Agricultural and Food Economics at the University of Milan in Italy. Her research interests are in the areas of international trade and the economics and politics of agricultural policies.

Gordon C. Rausser is the Robert Gordon Sproul Distinguished Professor in the Department of Agricultural and Resource Economics at the University of California in Berkeley. His research interests include a wide range of agricultural and resource economics areas and associated policy issues.

Gérard Roland is a Professor of Economics and Political Science at the University of California in Berkeley, where his research includes the political economy of transition economies, particularly in Europe.

Scott Rozelle holds the Helen Farnsworth Endowed Professorship and is Senior Fellow in the Freeman Spogli Institute of International Studies at Stanford University, having previously been at the University of California, Davis. His research focuses on all aspects of agricultural developments in China.

Damiano Sandri was a PhD candidate in economics at the Johns Hopkins University in Baltimore, MD, during 2006–2007, when he worked as a short-term consultant with this project in the Development Research Group at the World Bank in Washington, DC. He is now with the Research Department of the International Monetary Fund.

Johan F. M. Swinnen is a Professor in the Department of Economics and Director of the LICOS Center for Institutions and Economic Performance at the Katholieke Universiteit Leuven in Belgium, and a Senior Fellow of the Center for European Policy Studies in Brussels. He focuses on agricultural policies in both Eastern and Western Europe.

Jeanne Tschopp is a doctoral student in Economics at the University of Lausanne in Switzerland. Her research interests are in the area of international trade and development, including the political economy of trade policy.

Ernesto Valenzuela is a Senior Lecturer in the School of Economics and Director of the Centre for International Economic Studies at the University of Adelaide in Australia. During 2005–2007, he was an extended-term consultant at the Development Research Group of the World Bank in Washington, DC.

Foreword

For generations, the prices of farm products have been heavily distorted by government policies in both high-income and developing countries. True, many countries began to reform their agricultural price and trade policies in the 1980s, but a 2009 World Bank book, *Distortions to Agricultural Incentives: A Global Perspective, 1955–2007* (edited by Kym Anderson), shows that the extent of intervention is still considerable. In particular, policies still favor agricultural producers in high-income countries relative to those in developing countries – although, as they have become more affluent, some middle-income country governments also are beginning to support their import-competing farmers. This pattern of policies is of concern to the vast majority of the world's poorest households, who depend directly or indirectly on agriculture for their income. And even though low food prices may benefit the urban poor, a 2010 World Bank book, *Agricultural Distortions, Inequality and Poverty* (edited by Kym Anderson, John Cockburn, and Will Martin), finds that current price-distorting policies still contribute to global inequality and poverty.

If economists are to provide useful advice to national governments on how to reform those policies, a first step is to improve our understanding of why societies have allowed their governments to adopt them in the first place, and why some but not others have subsequently chosen to reverse those welfare-reducing measures. Prerequisites for improving our understanding are better political economy theories, plus better information on the evolving nature and extent of market interventions by governments. In recent years, there have been substantial developments in both pertinent theories and – thanks to the 2009 study mentioned earlier – in empirical measures of price distortions resulting from agricultural and trade policies. The distortion estimates involve more than seventy products that cover around 70 percent of the value of agricultural output in each of seventy-five countries that together account for more than 90 percent of the global economy. They also expose the contribution of the various policy instruments (both farm and nonfarm) to the net distortion to farmer incentives. Such a widespread coverage of countries, products, years, and policy instruments provides an opportunity to test a wide range of hypotheses suggested by the new political economy literature, including the importance of institutions.

The present volume draws on those new theories and new data to provide a set of analytical narratives of the historical origins of agricultural protectionism in various parts of the world, and also a set of *ex post* political econometric analyses aimed at explaining the patterns of distortions that have emerged over the past five decades. These new studies shed much light on the underlying forces that have affected incentives facing farmers in the course of national and global economic and political development, and hence on how those distortions might change in the future – or be changed by concerted actions to offset political pressures from traditionally powerful vested interests. It is hoped that this volume also will stimulate further studies, and that together they will shed light on how that improved knowledge can be utilized to bring about pro-poor, welfare-improving, and sustainable policy reforms.

Justin Yifu Lin
Senior Vice President and Chief Economist
The World Bank

Preface

This book is a product of an empirical research project, begun in 2006, aimed at improving our understanding of the extent, causes, and effects of government interventions in global agricultural markets over the past five decades. The first stage of the project generated analytical narratives of the evolution of policies for a sample of seventy-five countries that together account for between 90 and 96 percent of the world's population, farmers, agricultural output, and total GDP. In each country case study, the narrative was informed by the authors' new estimates of distortions to agricultural incentives caused by price, trade, and exchange rate policies. Annual estimates for nominal rates of assistance and consumer tax equivalents were provided for more than seventy different farm products, with an average of eleven per country that represented around 70 percent of the gross value of agricultural production in each focus country. Estimates of the overall rate of government assistance to agriculture relative to that for nonfarm tradable goods also were provided. The country studies are reported in four regional volumes and a global overview volume that were published by the World Bank in 2008–09, along with the global database of price distortions. They were followed by another volume, published in early 2010, that focused on quantifying the effects of current distortions on global welfare, inequality, and poverty.[1]

---

[1] The regional volumes cover Europe's Transition Economies (Anderson and Swinnen 2008), Latin America (Anderson and Valdés 2008), Africa (Anderson and Masters 2009), and Asia (Anderson and Martin 2009). The global overview book (Anderson 2009) includes four chapters covering high-income countries as well as summaries of the regional volumes. The core database of the distortion estimates (Anderson and Valenzuela 2008) is available at http://www.worldbank.org/agdistortions. The inequality and poverty volume (Anderson, Cockburn, and Martin 2010) uses national and global economywide models. See the references listed in Chapter 1 for full citation details.

The focus of the present volume is on explaining the historical origins of governments' distortions to agricultural markets and the patterns of intervention that have evolved over the past half century. The book's contributors draw on recent developments in political economic theory and econometrics, but they could not have undertaken their empirical analyses without the World Bank's new global agricultural distortions database. The contributors to the present volume are thus very grateful to the authors of the Stage 1 country case studies and to Ernesto Valenzuela and a team of very able assistants, including Johanna Croser, Esteban Jara, Marianne Kurzweil, Signe Nelgen, Francesca de Nicola, and Damiano Sandri, who helped compile the global megaspreadsheet of distortion estimates from the various national spreadsheets (all of which are accessible at the project's Web site at http://www.worldbank.org/agdistortions).

The contributors also have benefited from feedback provided by participants in a series of workshops at which draft papers were presented over the past three years. The first of those workshops was cosponsored by the team responsible for the World Bank's *World Development Report 2008: Agriculture for Development*, led by Derek Byerlee and Alain de Janvry. Our thanks extend also to the project's Senior Advisory Board, whose members have provided sage advice and much encouragement throughout the planning and implementation stages of the project. The Board consists of Yujiro Hayami, Bernard Hoekman, Anne Krueger, John Nash, Johan F.M. Swinnen, Stefan Tangermann, Alberto Valdés, Alan Winters, and, until his untimely death in March 2008, Bruce Gardner.

Finally, our thanks go also to the Development Research Group of the World Bank (with special thanks to Will Martin) for hosting this research project and the editor's extended sabbatical there in 2004–07, and to the governments of the Netherlands and the United Kingdom for providing Trust Funds that supported each author's participation. Their combined support made it possible for the study to generate estimates of price distortions for countries from all regions of the world except the Middle East (which accounts for less than 2 percent of global agricultural production). Thanks also to the Australian Research Council and the University of Adelaide's School of Economics for supporting the completion of the first two chapters and the Appendix, as well as the overall editing task.

Kym Anderson
December 2009

Abbreviations and Acronyms

CGE	computable general equilibrium (model)
CIS	Commonwealth of Independent States (of the former Soviet Union)
CPI	consumer price index
CSE	consumer support estimate (or earlier, consumer subsidy equivalent)
CTE	consumer tax equivalent
EU	European Union
EU15	the 15 Western European members of the EU as of April 2004
EU25	the 25 members of the EU as of May 2004
EU27	EU25 plus Bulgaria and Romania (joined on January 1, 2007)
EUR	Euro (currency)
FAO	Food and Agriculture Organization (of the United Nations)
GATT	General Agreement on Tariffs and Trade
GDP	gross domestic product
MFN	most favored nation
NAFTA	North American Free Trade Agreement
NRA	nominal rate of assistance (to an industry or sector)
NRP	nominal rate of protection (from import competition)
NTB	non-tariff barrier (to international trade)
OECD	Organization for Economic Cooperation and Development
PSE	producer support estimate (or earlier, producer subsidy equivalent)
RRA	relative rate of assistance
SPS	Sanitary and phytosanitary (trade restrictions)
STE	state trading enterprise
TBI	trade bias index
TBT	technical barrier to trade
TRI	trade reduction index

TRQ	tariff rate quota
URAA	Uruguay Round Agreement on Agriculture
WDI	*World Development Indicators* (published by the World Bank)
WRI	welfare reduction index
WTO	World Trade Organization

PART ONE

INTRODUCTION

ONE

Understanding Government Interventions in Agricultural Markets

Kym Anderson[1]

> Find out the cause of this effect,
> Or rather say, the cause of this defect,
> For this effect defective comes by cause.
> – Polonius, in Shakespeare's *Hamlet* (Act II, Scene 2)

Most of the world's poor still live in rural areas, a situation that is forecast to prevail for many decades to come if we continue with "business as usual." The absolute number of rural poor people living on $1 a day fell between 1993 and 2002 by an estimated 150 million, to 890 million globally, but if China is excluded, there has been virtually no net decline over that period (Chen and Ravallion 2008, Ravallion, Chen and Sangraula 2007). As well, many urban poor are recent emigrants who, perceiving bleak prospects in agriculture, moved to the city in search of a higher income. Thus higher rewards to farming in developing countries could help reduce both urban and rural poverty, a view that is confirmed by a recent set of simulation studies (Anderson, Cockburn and Martin 2010).

In the past, earnings of farmers and agribusinesses in developing countries often have been depressed by prourban and antiagricultural biases in own-country policies. While progress has been made over the past two or three decades by numerous countries in reducing those and associated antitrade policy biases, many price distortions remain intersectorally as well as within the agricultural sector of low- and middle-income countries. Some governments provide explicit subsidies to selected food consumers, but they are often offset by implicit distortions to consumer prices via border measures such as taxes or quantitative restrictions on imports.

[1] The author is grateful for helpful discussions with workshop participants and for funding from World Bank Trust Funds provided by the governments of the Netherlands and the United Kingdom, and by the Australian Research Council.

3

In addition to the impact of own-country policies, farm earnings in developing countries are depressed by agricultural protection measures in other (especially high-income) countries, which lower real prices of food, feed, and fiber in international markets. This issue has escalated in recent years because of the Doha Development Agenda of the World Trade Organization (WTO): Agricultural exporting countries are demanding large cuts to farm subsidies and barriers to food imports in protective countries, as well as the removal of nonreciprocal preferential market access arrangements for former colonies under the Cotonou Agreement.

WHY THIS ISSUE IS IMPORTANT

These distortions to incentives, which have characterized world agricultural markets for a long time (Haberler 1958, Johnson 1973, Bates 1981, Tyers and Anderson 1992), matter because they are wasteful of the world's resources and exacerbate global inequality and poverty. They are wasteful of resources not only at any point in time (reducing the allocative efficiency of both producers and consumers), but also in the sense of slowing national and global economic growth. Growth is slowed in part because many of the distortionary policies restrict imports, and in some cases exports, and so curtail the normal dynamic gains from trade. As well, the antitrade bias in those policies has a particularly debilitating characteristic that arises because those measures typically involve fluctuating trade restrictions that attempt to stabilize domestic food prices over time. Such market-insulating behavior of governments necessarily "thins" international food markets and so makes them less stable, which in turn encourages other national governments also to be market insulating.

Agricultural policies that support farmers in high-income countries and tax them excessively in developing countries necessarily add to income inequality across countries. They also add to within-country inequality of income and wealth because they most commonly operate through altering the prices of outputs (and sometimes also purchased farm inputs), and hence benefit farm households in proportion to the marketed output of their farm. In the case of tenanted farms, most of those benefits will accrue, in the form of higher rent, to the landowner, who is almost invariably wealthier than the tenant. In the case of farm outputs sold under contract to processors or retailers, some of those benefits will be passed from the farmer along the value chain, depending on the relative bargaining power of the processor or supermarket vis-a-vis the (typically much smaller and poorer) farmer.

In addition to being wasteful of resources and exacerbating inequality and poverty, trade-distorting agricultural policies impose another cost on the world economy in the sense that they have greatly slowed progress in multilateral trade negotiations. Since the signing of the General Agreement on Tariffs and Trade (GATT) in 1947, agricultural policies have been so contentious as to be left aside in the first seven rounds of multilateral trade negotiations. They were responsible too for the eighth one (the Uruguay Round) taking a mammoth eight years to complete; and they are the main reason for the difficulties in concluding the current round (the WTO's Doha Development Agenda). That difficulty, in turn, has contributed to a proliferation of regional and other preferential trading agreements that may well have added to global distortions to agricultural incentives. It also means a delay in or foregoing of the prospective gains from reductions of barriers to trade in nonfarm goods and services that the WTO might have delivered by now.

If distortions to agricultural markets are so pervasive, and the reform of farm protection measures so elusive, there must be strong political economy reasons for such widespread intervention by governments. Improving our understanding of the political economy forces at work is an important part of economic analysis because, as Stigler (1975, p. ix) says, "Until we understand *why* our society adopts its policies, we will be poorly equipped to give useful advice on how to change those policies." Greater understanding is also required if we are to provide more nuanced counterfactuals and hence more reliable projections of the likely economic effects of remaining and prospective price and trade distortions, using forward-looking national and global sectoral and economywide models.

WHY FOCUS ON THIS ISSUE NOW?

This area of political economy analysis was a focus of researcher attention in the 1980s, perhaps stimulated by the prospect of agricultural protectionism being taken more seriously in the Uruguay Round of GATT negotiations. As well, international financial institutions were concerned that agricultural and trade policies were inhibiting growth prospects in developing countries. Emerging political economy theories from the University of Chicago (Stigler 1971, Peltzman 1976, Becker 1983) and the influential work of Downs (1957), Buchanan and Tullock (1962), and Olson (1965) provided new conceptual frameworks for addressing this issue; and new time series estimates of price distortions, by Krueger, Schiff and Valdés (1988, 1991) for eighteen developing countries and by Anderson, Hayami and Others (1986) for a similar number of high-income and newly industrializing countries, induced a rich set of empirical studies in the 1980s and the first part of the 1990s (see the survey in de Gorter and Swinnen 2002, which is updated in Chapter 3 of this volume by Swinnen 2010a). More estimates of the extent of agricultural price distortions in high-income countries have been generated each year since 1986 by the Organization for Economic Cooperation and Development (OECD) (2008), but until recently there had been no comparable effort for monitoring developing country policies.

To generate a set of distortion estimates for non-OECD countries that are comparable to those for OECD countries requires careful domestic-to-border price comparisons for each product, so as to capture the effects on producer and consumer prices of such measures as export restrictions, nontariff import barriers, exchange rate distortions, and exceptions to the applied import tariffs such as duty drawbacks or preferential arrangements with certain trading partners. To get an indication of how distortions have changed over the course of economic and political development requires those price comparisons to go back in time.

A recent research project at the World Bank has addressed this lacuna (see http://www.worldbank.org/agdistortions) by developing a methodology for measuring the extent of distortions to agricultural incentives (Anderson et al. 2008) and applying it consistently to seventy-five countries spanning between 90 and 96 percent of the world's farmers, agricultural production, GDP, and population. The resulting database (Anderson and Valenzuela 2008) includes annual nominal rate of assistance (NRA) and consumer tax equivalent (CTE) distortion indicators for more than seventy crop and livestock products (an average of eleven per country) that cover around 70 percent of agricultural output of each of the focus countries for as many years as data allow since the mid-1950s (an average of 41 years per country). The database thus comprises a large panel dataset of around 30,000 NRA and CTE estimates. Moreover, it identifies several groups of policy instruments from which the price distortions arise (domestic farm output and input tax/subsidy equivalents, domestic consumer tax/subsidy equivalents, and import and export tax/subsidy equivalents including via the operations of multiple foreign exchange rates), and it includes, in the final aggregate national NRA, any non-product-specific payments. As well, a separate line identifies so-called decoupled payments that have been provided increasingly to farmers in some OECD countries since the late 1980s.

It is not possible to understand the characteristics of agricultural development with a sectoral view alone, so the World Bank research project estimated consistent time series not only of the extent of direct agricultural policy measures on farm prices, but also of distortions in nonagricultural tradable sectors, for comparative evaluation (with both including the differential effect on exportables and import-competing products of distortions in the domestic market for foreign exchange). Specifically, it provides a production-weighted average NRA for nonagricultural tradables, for comparison with that for agricultural tradables via the calculation of a Relative Rate of Assistance (RRA), defined as the percentage by which the price of farm relative to nonfarm tradables is above what it would be if the national government had not distorted prices in those goods-producing sectors. This measure is useful in that if it is below (above) zero, it provides an internationally comparable indicator of the extent to which a country's sectoral policy regime has an anti- (pro-)agricultural bias.

Moreover, the creators of each country's database have used the NRAs and CTEs to write an analytical narrative of national economic and policy developments, and those are now published.[2] Also, the database has been used to generate a set of agricultural trade- and welfare-reduction indexes for that same time period (Anderson and Croser 2009; Croser, Lloyd and Anderson 2010; Lloyd, Croser and Anderson 2010). The NRAs and CTEs also have been aggregated in a way that makes them usable to national and global economywide computable general equilibrium (CGE) modelers (Valenzuela and Anderson 2008) as a replacement to the tariff-only developing country distortion indicators in the GTAP global protection database; and that resource has been used already by modelers to analyze (a) market and welfare effects of reforms since the early 1980s and of remaining distortions globally (Valenzuela, van der Mensbrugghe and Anderson 2009), and (b) household income inequality and poverty consequences of recent distortions in various developing countries (Anderson, Cockburn and Martin 2010).

Meanwhile, in the past two decades, huge strides have been made in developing political economy theories for government intervention in markets, as well as econometric techniques for testing empirically between them.[3] While that recent theoretical and empirical work has not focused

---

[2] The working paper versions of those narratives and the associated national spreadsheets can be found at http://www.worldbank.org/agdistortions. A global overview of the results is provided in Anderson (2009), and the detailed developing country case studies are reported in four regional volumes covering Africa (Anderson and Masters 2009), Asia (Anderson and Martin 2009), Latin America (Anderson and Valdés 2008), and Europe's transition economies (Anderson and Swinnen 2008).

[3] See the survey in Swinnen (2010). Included in that literature are three new seminal studies of the long history of policy choices by governments and the role of institutions and conflicts in affecting those choices, by Acemoglu and Robinson (2006), Findlay and O'Rouke (2007), and North, Wallis and Weingast (2009). A short but pithy study of policy developments in the late 20th century in sub-Saharan Africa is available in Bates (2008).

on agriculture particularly, it is a rich source of inspiration for developing hypotheses as to why the pattern of global distortions to agricultural incentives has developed in the ways exposed in the new World Bank agricultural distortions database. One of the points of emphasis in the new political economy theories is the importance of political institutions. Partly as a result, the World Bank has also been developing global time series databases on political institutions (Beck et al. 2001, 2008) and on governance as it affects business incentives (Kaufmann, Kraay and Mastruzzi 2009).[4]

The economics profession is thus in a far better position now than ever before to develop and empirically test competing and complementary hypotheses as to why governments have done what they have done to agricultural markets and farmer welfare leading up to and since the 1950s in different parts of the world. Given the ongoing difficulty WTO members are having in being able to agree to multilateral reforms in agricultural and trade policies under the Doha Development Agenda, not to mention the continuing cost to national governments and most of their constituents of current farm policies, there is a potentially high social payoff from such research.

WHAT THIS BOOK SEEKS TO ACHIEVE

The present volume is the first attempt to use the World Bank's new agricultural distortions database to revisit the question of why governments intervene in the ways they do to distort incentives facing producers and consumers of farm products. It does so by making use of the new political economy theory which, in the light of the stylized facts that can be distilled from the new Database of Agricultural Distortions, provides a conceptual framework for better understanding the long history of agricultural export taxation and import protection growth, as well as for suggesting numerous testable hypotheses. The final section of the book contains several political econometric studies that begin to exploit these new frameworks and data.

What Still Needs to be Explained? Findings
from the New Database

Chapter 2 provides a comprehensive summary of the evidence from the new estimates of price distortions, from which twenty stylized facts

---

[4] The World Bank has also prepared an annual report of 200-plus pages each year since 2004 on doing business in around 180 countries, which provides indicators of the changing degree of government regulation in each national economy, including of its trade with the rest of the world. See http://www.doingbusiness.org.

are presented (Anderson et al. 2010). Some of those are familiar, being unchanged from the findings of the earlier empirical work on this topic in the 1980s. An example is that poor countries tax farmers, rich countries protect them, and as countries become less agrarian in the course of their economic development, their policies transition from the former to the latter – and to a greater extent and earlier the weaker a country's agricultural comparative advantage. The agricultural policy regimes thus also tend to have an antitrade bias. Other stylized facts are new, either because previous, less comprehensive databases were insufficiently detailed (e.g., in specifying contributions to assistance from different policy instruments) or because there are new policy developments requiring explanation (such as the slight reversal of agricultural protection growth in the European Union and the gradual increase in importance of decoupled payments to farm households).

Specifically, the additional stylized facts that political economists could seek to explain include the following:

- Within the agricultural sector of each country, whether developed or developing, there is a wide range of product NRAs. Despite the fall in average agricultural NRAs, the across-product standard deviation of NRAs around the national average each year is no less in the most recent decade or so than it was in previous decades for both developed and developing countries (see the national Box plots shown in Figure A.4 in the Appendix to this volume, Anderson and Croser 2010). Some product NRAs are positive and high in almost all countries (sugar, rice, and milk), others are positive and high in developed economies but highly negative in developing countries (most noticeably cotton), and yet others are relatively low in all countries (feedgrains, soybean, pork, and poultry).
- The antitrade bias in farm products has declined over time for the developing country group, but mainly because of the decline in agricultural export taxation and in spite of growth in agricultural import protection, whereas for the high-income group, the antiagricultural trade bias has shown little trend over time, mainly because the rise and then decline in agricultural export subsidies has been matched by a similar trajectory for import protection.
- Around the long-run trend for each country, there is much fluctuation from year to year in individual product NRAs, and while this tendency has diminished since the mid-1980s for most key products, it has increased for rice and wheat (see the national Box plots shown in Figure A.3 in the Appendix to this volume, Anderson and Croser

2010). Product NRAs tend to be negatively correlated with movements in international prices of the products in question and, on average over a sample of twelve key products, barely half of the change in the international price is transmitted to domestic markets within the first year.

- Even when decoupled payments are included in the measure of total support, trade policy instruments (export and import taxes, subsidies or quantitative restrictions plus dual exchange rates) account for no less than three-fifths of agricultural NRAs, and hence for an even larger share of their global welfare cost. Domestic subsidies to or taxes on farm output and food consumption have made only minor contributions. Subsidies to farm input use and support for public agricultural research have been common but have added little to overall farmer assistance in high-income countries and have done very little in the past to offset the effective taxation of farmers in developing countries.

- The fall in assistance to producers of nonfarm tradables has contributed to more than half the rise since the mid-1980s in the RRA for developing countries, and as much as two-thirds of the RRA rise for high-income countries. This suggests much of the reduction in relative prices faced by farmers over the past two decades can be attributed to general trade liberalization rather than to specific farm policy reform.

The penultimate section of Chapter 2 examines econometrically the extent to which the cross-country variation in nominal and relative rates of assistance can be accounted for by the explanatory variables used in the 1980s. It finds that two variables alone – per capita income and a relative factor endowment indicator of agricultural comparative advantage – explain a little more than half of the variation in the full panel's NRAs and RRAs (adjusted R^2 of 0.55 and 0.59, respectively). When those panel data are separated by region, however, there is a considerable range in the extent to which those two variables account for the variation across countries. In the case of RRAs, the adjusted R^2 is a high 0.72 for Asia, a moderate 0.33 and 0.42 for Latin America and high-income countries, respectively, but just 0.07 for Africa. Clearly there is a great deal more heterogeneity among countries to be explained outside of Asia, and especially in Africa.

The final question raised by the data summarized in Chapter 2 is whether or not more developing countries will follow the example of earlier industrializers and increase assistance to their farmers as their economies and polities develop. One might have hoped the Uruguay Round Agreement on

Agriculture would bring that tendency to a halt, but in reality, even newly acceding countries such as China, let alone earlier signatories to the GATT such as India, have bound their agricultural tariffs and subsidies at very much higher levels than currently applied rates. Moreover, there appears to be a strong reluctance on the part of most developing countries to sign on to a WTO agreement under the Doha Agenda that would tighten those bindings. Political economy analysis clearly is needed not only to address this question as to whether more developing countries will become more agricultural protectionist but also to suggest politically feasible ways of countering that tendency.

New Conceptual Frameworks

To begin the process of providing explanations for the half or so of the variation in NRAs and RRAs that is not due to differences in just income per capita and comparative advantage, Chapter 3 provides a survey of findings from the political economy literature to date (Swinnen 2010a). First it covers the active period of analysis of agricultural policies up to the early 1990s, and then it reviews the important new developments in other parts of the economics profession that are yet to be applied extensively to agricultural distortions. One of the findings from the new literature is that political institutions and ideology matter. This suggests that analytical narratives, based on detailed knowledge of the countries involved and of their policies, remain important. Specifically, they can assist in deciding on specifications of the political economy model to be applied, provide a complementary set of insights to those generated from econometric model results, and serve as a guide to interpreting the results. Thankfully, the providers of national NRAs and RRAs to the new Database of Agricultural Distortions each authored an analytical narrative that has since been published as chapters in a series of five books (see footnote 2 for this Chapter), which increases the prospects for sound political economy analysis using this database.

With that literature review as background, Chapter 4 provides a conceptual framework for moving forward (Rausser and Roland 2010). In seeking to explain public policy choices, it assumes vested interest groups are the units of analysis that compete by spending time, energy, and money on the production of pressure to influence both the design and tactical implementation of policies. Thus both public and private sector agents are involved. Modern economics has compartmentalized the links between them into at least four analytical dimensions. The oldest and

most common has focused on analyzing the incidence of existing policies and the consequences of alternative policy instruments. The second
involves relaxing the perfect implementation assumption, allowing the
application of mechanism design concepts while still maintaining no
feedback effects from interest group or coalition formation, and a given
governance structure. The third involves relaxing the assumption of no
feedback effects from interest group or coalition formation, but typically
still imposes a given governance structure. And the fourth focuses on
governance structures that delineate the boundaries on the negotiations
and bargaining that take place among public and private sector agents.
That is, in its most general form, it relaxes the assumptions of perfect
implementation, no feedback effects among interest group or coalition
formation, as well as given governance structures. It is then capable of
analyzing how the distribution of political power leads to alternative
governance structures.

In the context of this general framework, Chapter 4 isolates three principal policy instruments: redistributive instruments, national public good
expenditures, and local public good expenditures. In much of the work on
agricultural distortions, only a general distinction between national public good policies intended to correct for institutional and market failures
(e.g., agricultural research) and redistributive policies have been examined. What also needs to be recognized is that local public policies can be
treated like redistributive policies as transfer mechanisms, with associated
deadweight losses and wasteful political economic activities resulting from
rent seeking by private interest groups or policy-making authorities. All
three principal policy instruments are influenced by political institutional
structures, by the assigned authority for governmental decision making,
by market structures and other socioeconomic characteristics, and by sector mobility and asset diversification. The distinction between presidential
and parliamentary regimes, and between different electoral rules, also is
potentially important, as is the degree of decentralization of decision making. The rich conceptual framework of this chapter thus suggests numerous hypotheses that might be tested empirically.

Revisiting the Long History of Protection Growth

Before moving on to formal political econometric analyses, it is helpful
to reflect on the origins of agricultural protection. Detailed data are not
available to do the same type of empirical analysis that is now possible
with the new database for the past half century, but analytical narratives

can be valuable nonetheless, and the above conceptual frameworks provide fresh ways of revisiting that long history.

Not surprisingly, given the finding that assistance to farmers rises with per capita income, the first systematic emergence of farm protection policies is found in the first economies to industrialize, that is, in Britain, then in other parts of Western Europe, and then in Japan. Certainly there was much government intervention in agricultural trade before the industrial revolution, but it was aimed mainly at stabilizing domestic food prices and supplies and at raising revenue for those in authority. Prior to its industrial revolution – from the late 1100s to the 1660s – densely populated Britain used export taxes and licenses to prevent domestic food prices from rising excessively. But during 1660–90, a series of Acts gradually raised food import duties, making imports prohibitive under most circumstances; and export restrictions on grain were reduced. These provisions were made even more protective of British farmers by the Corn Laws of 1815. However, those laws were famously repealed in the mid-1840s. Schonhardt-Bailey (1991, 2006) attributes that reform in large part to the diversification of landowners' interests. Consistent with an idea stressed in Chapter 4, as capital markets emerged, landowners began to diversify their asset portfolios such that the share of their income from land rent declined relative to that from higher-yielding industrial capital.

The reform of the Corn Laws is often said to have heralded a period of relatively unrestricted food trade for Britain. However, Chapter 5 challenges this view (Nye 2010). It suggests that protection for grain producers was retained for another generation, albeit indirectly via restrictions on imports of wine and spirits that provided assistance to domestic breweries and distilleries. According to Nye, it was only after the passage of the 1860 Anglo-French Treaty of Commerce that Britain moved closer to freer trade than France, and that other European countries began to open up.

Agricultural trade reform was less difficult for countries such as Britain, with overseas territories that could provide the metropole with a ready supply of farm products, than it was for some of its continental neighbors. As explained in Chapter 6 by Swinnen (2010b), the fall in the price of grain imports from America in the latter 1870s and 1880s provided a challenge for all, but the governments' responses varied. Denmark coped well by moving more into livestock production to take advantage of cheaper grain. Italians coped by sending many of their relatives to the New World. Farmers in France and Germany successfully sought protection from imports, however, and so began the post-Industrial Revolution growth of agricultural protectionism in densely populated countries. Agricultural protection took a further jump in the 1930s and steadily increased over the next five decades. Indeed on the Continent of Europe, the period of freer trade in the 19th century was quite short for some countries, and agricultural protection levels in those countries throughout the 20th century were somewhat higher on average than in Britain.

That is, the growth of agricultural protection was not linear, but rather there were substantial fluctuations over the ten decades prior to the implementation of the Common Agricultural Policy of what is now the European Union. Factors that appear to Swinnen (2010b) to have played an important role are the decline of income for farmers in comparison with incomes from the rest of the economy, reduced share of consumer expenditures for food, structure of farms, political organization of farmers, growth in government administrative capacity for regulating markets, food shortages during the World Wars in Europe, and democratization. The impact of each of these factors was complex and almost always interrelated with other factors. Periods of substantial increases in agricultural protection were characterized by a combination of three conditions: Farmers had substantive political influence, strong political action by farmers was triggered by a crisis in agriculture or a growing income gap with the rest of the economy to influence governments, and the opposition to protection was sufficiently low. Such a combination of factors was present to some extent in the 1930s but especially in the 1950s, when protection grew strongly. Meanwhile, tariffs on West European imports of manufactures were progressively reduced after the GATT came into force in the late 1940s, thereby adding to the encouragement of agricultural relative to manufacturing production.

Japan provides an even more striking example of the tendency to switch from taxing to increasingly assisting agriculture relative to other industries. Its industrialization began later than in Europe, after the opening up of the economy following the Meiji Restoration in 1868. By 1900, Japan had switched from being a small net exporter of food to becoming increasingly dependent on imports of rice (its main staple food and responsible for more than half the value of domestic food production). This was followed by calls from farmers and their supporters for rice import controls. Their calls were matched by equally vigorous calls from manufacturing and commercial groups for unrestricted food trade, since the price of rice at that time was a major determinant of real wages in the nonfarm sector. The heated debates were not unlike those that led to the repeal of the Corn Laws in Britain six decades earlier. In Japan, however, the forces of protection triumphed, and a tariff was imposed on rice imports from 1904. That tariff then gradually rose over time, raising the domestic price of rice to more than 30 per cent above the import price during World War I. Even when there were food riots because of shortages and high rice prices just after that war, the Japanese government's response was not to reduce protection but instead to extend it to its colonies and to shift from a national to an imperial rice self-sufficiency policy. That involved accelerated investments in agricultural development in the colonies of Korea and Taiwan behind an ever-higher external tariff wall that by the latter 1930s had driven imperial rice prices to more than 60 percent above those in international markets (Anderson and Tyers 1992). After the Pacific War ended and Japan lost its colonies, its agricultural protection growth resumed and spread from rice to an ever-wider range of farm products. That history is now well known (see, e.g., Anderson, Hayami and Others 1986) and so we do not include a chapter on it in this volume.

The other high-income countries were settled by Europeans relatively recently and are far less densely populated. They therefore have had a strong comparative advantage in farm products for most of their history following Caucasian settlement, and so have felt less need to protect their farmers than Europe or Northeast Asia. Indeed Australia and New Zealand until the present decade – like developing countries – had adopted policies that discriminated against their farmers. Anderson, Lloyd and MacLaren (2007) and Anderson et al. (2009) explain that the unusual phenomenon of gradual removal of agricultural support there since the 1970s was tolerated by farmers because it was explicitly linked with manufacturing protection cuts that were bigger than the cuts in farm subsidies, and so their negative RRAs rose gradually to zero. By contrast, agricultural support has grown in the United States since the 1970s. Even since the Uruguay Round trade negotiations concluded in 1994 and established the WTO, the continued ability of the powerful farm lobby in the United States to elicit support in the political arena is evident from the analysis in Chapter 7 by Orden, Blandford and Josling (2010). While there have been some changes in policy that have reduced their distortionary effects, they show there have also been some setbacks to reform efforts. Prospective commitments under a new WTO agreement that might emerge from the struggling Doha Round could put further constraints on subsidies provided by some U.S. policy instruments, but Orden, Blandford, and Josling expect the strong capabilities of the U.S. farm lobby to ensure support programs in that large agricultural exporting country endure through 2012 and beyond.

An important set of countries where there have been dramatic agricultural and trade policy reforms over the past quarter century is the former communist bloc. In Chapter 8, Rozelle and Swinnen (2010) examine changes in distortions to agricultural incentives in the transition countries of East Asia (China and Vietnam), Central Asia (Kazakhstan, Kyrgyz Republic, etc.), the Central and Eastern European countries (ten of which joined the European Union in 2004 or 2007), and the rest of the former Soviet Union. Policy changes have been dramatic in all those regions, yet there were large differences between countries in their reform strategies and in the extent and nature of their remaining distortions. If market reform leads to economic growth, why did leaders in many transition nations not choose to implement a comprehensive reform program? Why was it that leaders in China decided to implement their reforms gradually while those in Europe did so all at once? Why did leaders in Europe's transition countries undertake a broad spectrum of reforms whereas those in many nations of the former Soviet Union did not? Even more fundamentally, why is it that the policies were implemented by the leaders of some Communist regimes while in others it took a major political regime shift for policy reforms to gain momentum? Rozelle and Swinnen provide several reasons for expecting these large differences between transition countries, including the change in political regimes (in China and Vietnam it occurred within the Communist party whereas in many other countries it occurred only when the Communist regime collapsed), the fact that in some countries but not others a broad approach to reforms was needed to introduce irreversible changes to the entire political system, and the differing influences of various international agreements (including accession to the EU or WTO) on agricultural distortions.

Political Econometrics: Testing New Hypotheses with New Data

The remaining chapters of the book provide a set of quantitative studies that begin the process of exploiting both the new developments in general political economy theory and the new Database of Agricultural Distortions by applying modern econometric methods to test hypotheses using those panel data.

Chapter 9, by Masters and Garcia (2010), builds on the analysis at the end of Chapter 2 by first showing not only that governments tend to tax agriculture in poorer countries and subsidize it in richer ones, tax both imports and exports more than nontradable farm products, and tax more/ subsidize less where there is more land per capita, but also that there are differences across continents in these tendencies. That study then tests a variety of political economy explanations. It finds that larger groups obtain more favorable policies, suggesting that positive group size effects can outweigh the negative influence from more free-ridership, and that demographically driven entry of new farmers is associated with less favorable farm policies. It also finds rent-seeking motives for trade policy in that countries with fewer checks and balances on the exercise of political power have smaller distortions, and time-inconsistency motives, as perennials attract greater taxation than annual crops. They find there is support for a revenue motive for taxation for importables, but not for exportables. An incidental result is that governments achieve very little domestic price stabilization relative to benchmark international prices, and in the poorest countries, governments appear to destabilize domestic prices of farm products: A given policy may achieve short-term stability, but on average these policies are not (or perhaps cannot be) sustained, leading to large price jumps when policies eventually have to adjust.

The point of departure in Chapter 10, by Gawande and Hoekman (2010), is the dominant use of trade measures to either tax or subsidize agriculture. This study explores institutional reasons for that policy phenomenon. It finds, for example, that exports of a crop are more likely to be subsidized than taxed the stronger the electoral competition for the office of executive and the more comfortable the majority of the ruling party(-ies). Greater electoral competition also makes import protection more likely; and the greater the proportion of land that is arable and of the population that is rural, the higher the probability that exports will be taxed.

In Chapter 11, by Dutt and Mitra (2010), both the political ideology of the government and the degree of income inequality are found to be important determinants of the relative rate of assistance to agricultural producers. In other words, even though government decision making has some partisan elements, the concerns of the majority are also important. Thus both the political-support-function approach and the median-voter approach can be used in explaining the variation in agricultural assistance/taxation across countries and within countries over time. These results are consistent with the predictions of a model that assumes that labor is specialized and sector-specific in nature, and are inconsistent with a model in which labor is assumed to be a general, intersectorally mobile factor. Some aspects of protection also seem to be consistent with predictions of a lobbying model in that agricultural assistance is negatively related to agricultural employment and positively related to agricultural productivity. Public finance aspects of assistance and taxation also seem to be empirically important, particularly for developing countries.

The subsequent two chapters have a regional focus. In Chapter 12, Bates and Block (2010) explore the pattern of distortions in sub-Saharan Africa. Historically, African governments have discriminated heavily against agricultural producers in general (relative to producers in nonagricultural sectors) and against producers of export agriculture in particular. While more moderate in recent years, these patterns of discrimination persist even though farmers comprise a political majority. Bates and Block explore the impact of three factors: institutions, regional inequality, and the need to generate tax revenue. They find that, in the absence of electoral party competition, agricultural taxation increases with the share of the population that is rural. In the presence of party competition, on the other hand, the lobbying disadvantage of the rural majority turns into a political advantage. They also find that privileged cash crop regions are particular targets for redistributive taxation, unless the country's president comes from a cash cropping region. One further finding is that governments of resource-rich African countries, while continuing to tax export producers, tend to tax their food consumers less than is the case in other African countries.

The region of focus in Chapter 13 is Latin America, although the global sample of NRAs is used to test if Latin America is different from the rest of the world. The issue addressed in that Chapter, by Cadot, Olarreaga and Tschopp (2010), is the impact of trade agreements (regional but also multilateral) on volatility of nominal rates of assistance to agricultural industries. Such volatility is important: It is likely to be welfare-reducing, because the welfare costs of distortions rise with the square of the wedge between domestic and world prices, and because policy uncertainty it generates harms investment and hence growth. Latin America is worth focusing on also because it is the region with the highest volatility in agricultural NRAs among developing countries, followed by sub-Saharan Africa, which has a degree of volatility that is 30 percent smaller. The authors find that participation in a regional trade agreement (RTA) significantly reduces the volatility of NRAs for agricultural goods, and the effect is quantitatively substantial (about 13 percent less volatility for each additional RTA) and is robust across a wide variety of model specifications. The WTO's agricultural agreement also contributed to reducing agricultural NRA volatility, in spite of the weak disciplines involved, but the effect is weaker than for RTAs. Among RTAs, those involving high-income country partners have more volatility-reducing effects, presumably because the latter have strong and stable domestic institutions which spill over to stronger RTA rules.

The final Chapter, by Olper and Raimondi (2010), deals with the effect of constitutional rules on agricultural policy outcomes. It highlights the important role played by the form of democracy and finds that transition to democracy tends to raise a country's agricultural NRA. Furthermore, what matters are transitions to proportional as opposed to majoritarian democracies, as well as to permanent, as opposed to temporary, democracies. Moreover, while they do not detect significant differences across alternative forms of government (presidential *versus* parliamentary systems), they provide evidence that the effect of proportional systems is exacerbated under parliamentary regimes but dampened under presidential ones. They also find that different constitutional rules affect the dynamic adjustment of agricultural NRAs. Overall, these results support the notion that rules-based institutions do matter in affecting the adoption of sectoral policies.

CONCLUSION

Conceptual and econometric studies reported in this volume are but a beginning to the process of using both the new developments in general political economy theory and the new set of panel data on agricultural distortions to improve our understanding of why governments intervene in agricultural markets in the ways they do in the course of national and global economic and political development. It is hoped that this will stimulate further studies and that together they will shed light on (a) how distortions might change for various types of countries in the future under "business as usual," and even more importantly, on (b) how this improved knowledge can be utilized to bring about pro-poor, welfare-improving, and sustainable policy reforms.

One obvious area for additional econometric analysis is to focus on individual commodity markets. Such analyses could explore why some product NRAs are positive and high in almost all countries (sugar, rice, and milk), others are positive and high in developed economies but highly negative in developing countries (most noticeably cotton), and yet others are relatively low in all countries (feedgrains, soybean, pork, and poultry).[5]

Another area worthy of analysis is to explore the "protection for sale" hypothesis for countries in which lobbying data are unavailable. Imai, Katayama and Krishna (2008, 2009) suggest a methodology for doing that, involving an instrumental variables quantile regression technique. A first

---

[5] A beginning has been made in the case of sugar, for example, by Rausser and Valenzuela (2009).

attempt to do that using our seventy-five-country agricultural distortions database, by Croser (2010), provides promising results.

The third area for further analysis could be to seek to explain the timing of major turning points in the extent of distortions to producer prices. The distortions database's annual assistance rate estimates for individual farm products, together with pertinent information in that database on international product prices, lend themselves to identifying when governments chose to begin reforms for one or more products and whether the policy reform was sustained. Even if the reform was part of the general tendency to reduce agricultural taxation in the course of economic development, was it triggered by, for example, a crisis event (see Alesina, Ardagna and Trebbi 2006) or by a new reformist government coming to power (see Krueger 1993)? In an econometric study using a much simpler index of distortions than used here but covering eighty-eight developing countries, Giuliano and Scalise (2009) find that the sudden and severe decline in international commodity prices, as in the mid-1980s, played a significant role in reducing agricultural taxation. Crises have been shown to be important triggers for structural reforms in high-income countries too (e.g., Hoj et al. 2006, OECD 2009). The new agricultural distortions database provides an opportunity to test this for a large sample of countries covering all per capita income levels.

Finally, the new agricultural distortions database identifies the relative contributions of the various domestic and border policy instruments to each NRA estimate (Croser and Anderson 2010). Explaining the variations in those instruments' relative contributions across products, countries, and years could be helpful for anticipating how governments might be expected to respond to shocks such as a spike in international food prices in 2008. It also could shed light on how governments respond to pressure (e.g., from other WTO members) to abandon border measures, as in the reinstrumentation of the EU's assistance to its farmers. This offers yet another way in which political econometrics could contribute to the fine-tuning of efforts of modelers seeking to provide a baseline projection of agricultural markets that does more than simply assume future policies remain unchanged from the base year.

References

Acemoglu, D. and J.A. Robinson (2006), *Economic Origins of Dictatorship and Democracy*, Cambridge and New York: Cambridge University Press.

Alesina, A., S. Ardagna and F. Trebbi (2006), "Who Adjusts and When: on the Political Economy of Reforms," *IMF Staff Papers* 53: 1–29.

Anderson, K. (ed.) (2009), *Distortions to Agricultural Incentives: A Global Perspective, 1955-2007*, London: Palgrave Macmillan and Washington DC: World Bank.

Anderson, K., J. Cockburn and W. Martin (eds.) (2010), *Agricultural Price Distortions, Inequality and Poverty*, Washington DC: World Bank.

Anderson, K. and J. Croser (2009), *National and Global Agricultural Trade and Welfare Reduction Indexes, 1955 to 2007*, Supplementary database at http://www.worldbank.org/agdistortions.

(2010), "Coverage and Distribution of Assistance across Countries and Products, 1955-2007," Appendix in this volume.

Anderson, K., J. Croser, D. Sandri and E. Valenzuela (2010), 'Agricultural Distortion Patterns Since the 1950s: What Needs Explaining," Ch. 2 in this volume.

Anderson, K., Y. Hayami and Others (1986), *The Political Economy of Agricultural Protection: East Asia in International Perspective*, London: Allen and Unwin.

Anderson, K., M. Kurzweil, W. Martin, D. Sandri and E. Valenzuela (2008), 'Measuring Distortions to Agricultural Incentives, Revisited', *World Trade Review* 7(4): 1-30, October.

Anderson, K., R. Lattimore, P.J. Lloyd, and D. MacLaren (2009), "Australia and New Zealand," Ch. 5 in Anderson, K. (ed.), *Distortions to Agricultural Incentives: A Global Perspective, 1955-2007*, London: Palgrave Macmillan and Washington DC: World Bank.

Anderson, K., P.J. Lloyd and D. MacLaren (2007), "Distortions to Agricultural Incentives in Australia Since World War II", *Economic Record* 83(263): 461-82.

Anderson, K. and W. Martin (eds.) (2009), *Distortions to Agricultural Incentives in Asia*, Washington DC: World Bank.

Anderson, K. and W. Masters (eds.) (2009), *Distortions to Agricultural Incentives in Africa*, Washington DC: World Bank.

Anderson, K. and J. Swinnen (eds.) (2008), *Distortions to Agricultural Incentives in Europe's Transition Economies*, Washington DC: World Bank.

Anderson, K. and R. Tyers (1992), "Japanese Rice Policy in the Interwar Period: Some Consequences of Imperial Self Sufficiency," *Japan and the World Economy* 4(2): 103-27, September.

Anderson, K. and A. Valdés (eds.) (2008), *Distortions to Agricultural Incentives in Latin America*, Washington DC: World Bank.

Anderson, K. and E. Valenzuela (2008), *Global Estimates of Distortions to Agricultural Incentives, 1955 to 2007*, core database at http://www.worldbank.org/agdistortions

Bates, R.H. (1981), *Markets and States in Tropical Africa: The Political Basis of Agricultural Policies*, Berkeley: University of California Press.

(2008), *When Things Fell Apart: State Failure in Late-Century Africa*, Cambridge and New York: Cambridge University Press.

Bates, R.H. and S. Block (2010), "Agricultural Trade Interventions in Africa," Ch. 12 in this volume.

Beck, T., G. Clarke, A. Groff and P. Keefer (2001), "New Tools in Comparative Political Economy: The Database of Political Institutions," *World Bank Economic Review* 15(1): 165-76.

Beck, T., P.E. Keefer and G.R. Clarke (2008), *Database of Political Institutions*, accessible at http://go.worldbank.org/2EAGGLRZ40

Becker, G. (1983), "A Theory of Competition Among Pressure Groups for Political Influence," *Quarterly Journal of Economics* 98: 371–400, August.

Buchanan, J.M. and G. Tullock (1962), *The Calculus of Consent*, Ann Arbor: University of Michigan Press.

Cadot, O., M. Olarreaga and J. Tschopp (2010), "Trade Agreeements and Trade Barrier Volatility," Ch. 13 in this volume.

Chen, S. and M. Ravallion (2008), "The Developing World is Poorer Than We Thought, But No Less Successful in the Fight Against Poverty," Policy Research Working Paper 4703, World Bank, Washington DC, August. Forthcoming in *Quarterly Journal of Economics*.

Croser, J.L. (2010), "Agricultural Protection for Sale at Different Stages of Development," Ch. 5 in her *Empirical Analysis of Global Agricultural Price Distorting Policies: 1955 to 2007*, unpublished PhD thesis, University of Adelaide, Adelaide.

Croser, J.L. and K. Anderson (2010), "Changing Contributions of Different Agricultural Policy Instruments to Global Reductions in Trade and Welfare," Paper presented at the Annual Conference of the Australian Agricultural and Resource Economics Society, Adelaide, February 10–12 (CEPR Discussion Paper 7748, London, March).

Croser, J.L., P.J. Lloyd and K. Anderson (2010), "How Do Agricultural Policy Restrictions to Global Trade and Welfare Differ Across Commodities?" *American Journal of Agricultural Economics* 92(3): 698–712, April.

de Gorter, H. and J.F.M. Swinnen (2002), "Political Economy of Agricultural Policies," pp. 2073–2123 in B. Gardner and G. Rausser (eds.), *The Handbook of Agricultural Economics, Volume 2*, Amsterdam: Elsevier.

de Gorter, H. and Y. Tsur (1991), "Explaining Price Policy Bias in Agriculture: The Calculus of Support-Maximizing Politicians," *American Journal of Agricultural Economics* 73(4): 1244–54.

Downs, A. (1957), *An Economic Theory of Democracy*, New York: Harper and Row.

Dutt, P. and D. Mitra (2010), "Impacts of Ideology, Inequality, Lobbying, and Public Finance," Ch. 11 in this volume.

Findlay, R. and K. O'Rourke (2007), *Power and Plenty: Trade, War, and the World Economy in the Second Millennium*, Princeton NJ: Princeton University Press.

Gawande, K. and B. Hoekman (2010), "Why Governments Tax or Subsidize Agricultural Trade" Ch. 10 in this volume.

Giuliano, P. and D. Scalise (2009), "The Political Economy of Agricultural Market Reforms in Developing Countries," *B.E. Journal of Economic Analysis and Policy* 9(1), Article 33.

Haberler, G. (1958), *Trends in International Trade: A Report by a Panel of Experts*, Geneva: General Agreement on Tariffs and Trade, October.

Hoj, J., V. Galasso, G. Nicoletti and T. Dang (2006), "The Political Economy of Structural Reform: Empirical Evidence from OECD Countries," OECD Economic Department Working Papers 501, Paris: Organization for Economic Cooperation and Development.

Imai, S., H. Katayama and K. Krishna (2008), "A Quantile-Based Test of Protection For Sale Model", NBER Working Paper 13900, Cambridge MA, March.

——— (2009), "Is Protection Really For Sale? A Survey and Directions for Further Research," *International Review of Economics and Finance* 18: 181–91.

Johnson, D.G. (1973), *World Agriculture in Disarray*, London: St Martin's Press (revised in 1991).

Josling, T. (2009), "Western Europe," Ch. 5 in Anderson, K. (ed.), *Distortions to Agricultural Incentives: A Global Perspective, 1955–2007*, London: Palgrave Macmillan and Washington DC: World Bank.

Kaufmann, D., A. Kraay and M. Mastruzzi (2009), "Governance Matters VIII: Aggregate and Individual Governance Indicators 1996–2008," Policy Research Working Paper 4978, World Bank, Washington DC, June. See also http://www.govindicators.org

Krueger, A.O. (1993), *Political Economy of Policy Reform in Developing Countries*, Cambridge MA: MIT Press.

Krueger, A.O., M. Schiff and A. Valdes (1988), "Agricultural Incentives in Developing Countries: Measuring the Effect of Sectoral and Economy-wide Policies," *World Bank Economic Review* 2(3): 255–72, September.

(1991), *The Political Economy of Agricultural Pricing Policy, Volume 1: Latin America, Volume 2: Asia, and Volume 3: Africa and the Mediterranean*, Baltimore: Johns Hopkins University Press for the World Bank.

Lloyd, P.J., J.L. Croser and K. Anderson (2010), "Global Distortions to Agricultural Markets: New Indicators of Trade and Welfare Impacts, 1960 to 2007," *Review of Development Economics* 14(2): 141–60, May.

Masters, W. and A. Garcia (2010), "Agricultural Price Distortions and Stabilization," Ch. 9 in this volume.

North, D.C., J.J. Wallis and B.R. Weingast (2009), *Violence and Social Orders: A Conceptual Framework for Interpreting Recorded Human History*, Cambridge and New York: Cambridge University Press.

Nye, J.V.C. (2010), "Anglo-French Trade, 1689–1899: Agricultural Trade Policies, Alcohol Taxes and War," Ch. 5 in this volume.

OECD (2008), *Producer and Consumer Support Estimates* (online database accessed at www.oecd.org for 1986–2007 estimates; and OECD files for estimates using an earlier methodology for 1979–85).

(2009), *Economic Policy Reforms: Going for Growth 2009*, Paris: OECD.

Olper, A. and V. Raimondi (2010), "Constitutional Rules and Agricultural Policy Outcomes," Ch. 14 in this volume.

Olson, M. (1965), *The Logic of Collective Action*, New Haven: Yale University Press.

Orden, D., D. Blandford and T. Josling (2010), "Determinants of United States Farm Policies," Ch. 7 in this volume.

Peltzman, S. (1976), "Towards a More General Theory of Regulation," *Journal of Law and Economics* 19: 211–40, August.

Rausser, G. and G. Roland (2010), "Special Interests Versus the Public Interest in Policy Determination," Ch. 4 in this volume.

Rausser, G. and E. Valenzuela (2009), "The Evolution of Sugar Market Distortions," Agricultural Distortions Working Paper 93, World Bank, Washington DC, May. Available at http://www.worldbank.org/agdistortions.

Ravallion, M., S. Chen and P. Sangruala (2007), "New Evidence on the Urbanization of Poverty," *Population and Development Review* 33(4): 667–702.

Rozelle, S. and J. Swinnen (2009), "Why Did the Communist Party Reform in China, But Not in the Soviet Union? The Political Economy of Agricultural Transition", *China Economic Review* 20(2): 275–87.

(2010), "Agricultural Distortions in the Transition Economies of Europe and Asia," Ch. 8 in this volume.

Schonhardt-Bailey, C. (1991), "Specific Factors, Capital Markets, Portfolio Diversification, and Free Trade: Domestic Determinants of the Repeal of the Corn Laws," *World Politics* 43(4): 545–69.

(2006), *From the Corn Laws to Free Trade: Interests, Ideas, and Institutions in Historical Perspective*, Cambridge MA: MIT Press.

Stigler, G.S. (1971), 'The Theory of Economic Regulation', *Bell Journal of Economics and Management Science* 2: 137–46, Spring.

(1975), *The Citizen and the State*, Chicago: University of Chicago Press.

Swinnen, J.F.M. (2010a), "Political Economy of Agricultural Distortions: The Literature to Date," Ch. 3 in this volume.

(2010b), "Agricultural Protection Growth in Europe, 1870–1969," Ch. 6 in this volume.

Tyers, R. and K. Anderson (1992), *Disarray in World Food Markets: A Quantitative Assessment*, Cambridge and New York: Cambridge University Press.

Valenzuela, E. and K. Anderson (2008), "Alternative Agricultural Price Distortions for CGE Analysis of Developing Countries, 2004 and 1980–84," *Research Memorandum* No. 13, Center for Global Trade Analysis, Purdue University, West Lafayette IN, December.

Valenzuela, E., D. van der Mensbrugghe and K. Anderson (2009), 'General Equilibrium Effects of Price Distortions on Global Markets, Farm Incomes and Welfare', Ch. 13 in Anderson, K. (ed.), *Distortions to Agricultural Incentives: A Global Perspective, 1955–2007*, London: Palgrave Macmillan and Washington DC: World Bank.

TWO

Agricultural Distortion Patterns since the 1950s

What Needs Explaining?

Kym Anderson, Johanna Croser, Damiano Sandri,
and Ernesto Valenzuela[1]

Among the most important influences on the long-run economic growth and distribution of global welfare are trade-related policy developments in individual countries and their combined effect on other countries via the terms of trade in international markets.[2] Some of the policy developments of the past half century have happened quite suddenly and been transformational. They include the end of colonization around 1960, the creation of the Common Agricultural Policy in Europe in 1962, the floating of exchange rates and associated liberalization, deregulation, privatization, and democratization in the mid-1980s in many countries, and the opening of China in 1979, Vietnam in 1986, and Eastern Europe following the fall of the Berlin Wall in 1989 and the demise of the Soviet Union in 1991. Less newsworthy and hence less noticed are the influences of policies that change only gradually in the course of economic development as comparative advantages evolve. This chapter is focused on summarizing a new database that sheds light on the combined impact of both types of trade-related policy developments over the past half century on distortions to agricultural incentives and thus also to consumer prices for food.

For advanced economies, the most commonly articulated reason for farm trade restrictions has been to protect domestic producers from import competition as they come under competitive pressure to shed labor as the economy grows. In the process, however, those protective measures hurt not only domestic consumers and exporters of other products, but also foreign producers and traders of farm products, as well as reduce national and global economic welfare. For decades, agricultural protection and

[1] The authors are grateful for helpful discussions with workshop participants and for funding from World Bank Trust Funds provided by the governments of the Netherlands and the United Kingdom, and by the Australian Research Council.
[2] See, for example, Anderson and Winters (2009) and the literature surveyed therein.

subsidies in high-income (and some middle-income) countries have been depressing international prices of farm products, which lowers the earnings of farmers and associated rural businesses in developing countries. The Haberler (1958) report to GATT Contracting Parties forewarned that such distortions might worsen, and indeed they did between the 1950s and the early 1980s (Anderson, Hayami and Others 1986), thereby adding to global inequality and poverty because three-quarters of the world's poorest people depend directly or indirectly on agriculture for their main income (World Bank 2007).

In addition to this external policy influence on rural poverty, the governments of many developing countries have directly taxed their farmers over the past half century. A well-known example is the taxing of exports of plantation crops in postcolonial Africa (Bates 1981). At the same time, many developing countries chose also to overvalue their currency and to pursue an import-substituting industrialization strategy by restricting imports of manufactures. Together, those measures indirectly taxed producers of other tradable products in developing economies, by far the most numerous of them being farmers (Krueger, Schiff and Valdés 1988, 1991). Thus the price incentives facing farmers in many developing countries have been depressed by both own-country and other countries' agricultural price and international trade policies.

This disarray in world agriculture, as D. Gale Johnson (1973) described it in the title of his seminal book, means there has been overproduction of farm products in high-income countries and underproduction in low-income countries. It also means there has been less international trade in farm products than would be the case under free trade, thereby thinning markets for these weather-dependent products and thus making them more volatile. Using a stochastic model of world food markets, Tyers and Anderson (1992, Table 6.14) found that instability of international food prices in the early 1980s was three times greater than it would have been under free trade in those products. During the past twenty-five years, however, numerous countries have begun to reform their agricultural price and trade policies. This has raised the extent to which farm products are traded internationally, but not nearly as fast as globalization has proceeded in the nonfarm sectors of the world's economies.[3]

---

[3] In the two decades to 2000–04, the value of global exports as a share of GDP rose from 19 to 26 percent, even though most of GDP is nontradable governmental and other services, while the share of primary agricultural production exported globally, including intra-European Union trade, rose from only 13 percent to just 16 percent (World Bank 2007 and FAO 2007, as summarized in Sandri, Valenzuela and Anderson 2007).

To what extent have reforms of the past two decades reversed the above-mentioned policy developments of the previous three decades? Empirical indicators of agricultural price distortions (called Producer Support and Consumer Support Estimates or PSEs and CSEs) have been provided in a consistent way for twenty years by the Secretariat of the OECD (2008) for its thirty member countries. However, there are no comprehensive time series rates of assistance to producers of nonagricultural goods to compare with the PSEs, nor do they tell us what happened in those advanced economies in earlier decades – which are of more immediate relevance if we are to see how the two groups of countries' policies developed during similar stages of development. As for developing countries, almost no comparable time series estimates have been generated since the Krueger, Schiff and Valdes (1988) study, which covered the 1960–1984 period for just seventeen developing countries.[4] An exception is a new set of estimates of nominal rates of protection for key farm products in China, India, Indonesia, and Vietnam since 1985 (Orden et al. 2007). The OECD (2009) also has released PSEs for Brazil, China, and South Africa, as well as several more East European countries. The World Bank's new Database of Agricultural Distortions (Anderson and Valenzuela 2008) complements and extends those two institutions' efforts and the seminal Krueger, Schiff and Valdés (1988, 1991) study. It builds on them by providing similar estimates for other significant (including many low-income) developing economies, by developing and estimating new, more comprehensive policy indicators, and by providing estimates of nominal rates of assistance (NRAs) for nonagricultural tradables.

The purpose of this chapter is to summarize the stylized facts that can be drawn from the Anderson and Valenzuela (2008) compilation that are worthy of the attention of political economy theorists, historians, and econometricians. These indicators can be helpful in addressing such questions as the following: Where is there still a policy bias against agricultural production? To what extent has there been overshooting in the sense that some developing-country food producers are now being protected from import competition along the lines of the examples of earlier-industrializing Europe and Japan? What are the political economy

---

[4]   A nine-year update for the Latin American countries in the Krueger, Schiff, and Valdés sample by the same country authors, and a comparable study of seven central and eastern European countries, contain estimates at least of direct agricultural distortions (see Valdés 1996, 2000). The Krueger, Schiff and Valdés (1991) chapters on Ghana and Sri Lanka have protection estimates back to 1955, as does the study by Anderson, Hayami and Others (1986) for Korea and Taiwan (and Japan, and much earlier in the case of rice).

forces behind the more successful reformers and how do they compare with those in less successful countries where major distortions in agricultural incentives remain? Over the past two decades, how important have domestic political forces been in bringing about reform relative to international forces (such as loan conditionality, rounds of multilateral trade negotiations within the General Agreement on Tariffs and Trade, regional integration agreements, accession to the World Trade Organization, and the globalization of supermarkets and other firms along the value chain) and compared with forces operating in earlier decades? What explains the pattern of distortions across not only countries but also industries and in the choice of support or tax instruments within the agricultural sector of each country? What policy lessons may be drawn from these differing experiences with a view to ensuring better growth-enhancing and poverty-reducing outcomes – including less overshooting that results in protectionist regimes – in still-distorted economies during their reforms in the future?

The new database includes estimates for seventy-five countries that together account for between 90 and 96 percent of the world's population, farmers, agricultural GDP, and total GDP (Table 2.1). The sample countries also account for more than 85 percent of farm production and employment in each of Africa, Asia, Latin America, and the transition economies of Europe and Central Asia, and their spectrum of per capita incomes ranges from the poorest (Zimbabwe and Ethiopia) to among the richest (Norway).[5] nominal rate of assistances (NRAs) and consumer tax equivalents (CTEs) are estimated for more than seventy different products, with an average of almost a dozen per country. In aggregate, the coverage represents around 70 percent of the gross value of agricultural production in the focus countries[6] and just under two-thirds of global farm production valued at undistorted prices over the period covered. Not all countries had data for the entire 1955–2007 period, but the average number of

---

[5] See Appendix for more coverage details. The only countries not well represented in the sample are those in the Middle East and the many small ones, but in total, the omitted countries account for less than 4 percent of the global economy (made up of 0.2 percent from each of sub-Saharan Africa and Asia, 0.9 percent from Latin America, and the rest from the Middle East and North Africa).

[6] Had seven key mostly nontraded food staples (bananas, cassava, millet, plantain, potato, sweet potato, and yam) been included for all instead of just some developing countries, their product coverage would have risen from around 70 to 76 percent; and had those staples had an average NRA of zero, they would have brought the weighted average NRA for all covered agriculture in developing countries only about half of one percentage point closer to zero each decade over the sample period (Anderson 2009, Table 12.10).

Table 2.1. *Key economic and trade indicators of focus countries, by region, 2000 to 2004*

	Share (%) of world				National relative to world (world=100)			Agric trade specialization index[b]
	Pop'n	Total GDP	Agric GDP	Agric worker	GDP per capita	Ag land per capita	RCA,[a] agric & food	
Africa	10	1	6	11	14	148	na	na
Asia	51	10	37	73	20	34	80	-0.03
Latin America	8	5	8	3	64	171	na	na
Europe and Central Asia	7	4	6	3	48	178	na	na
Western Europe	6	29	16	1	454	46	106	-0.03
United States and Canada	5	33	11	0.3	636	186	119	0.08
Australia and New Zealand	0.4	2	2	0.1	405	2454	354	0.62
Japan	2	13	5	0.2	610	5	12	-0.84
All focus countries	90	96	91	92	na	na	na	na
Other (nonfocus) developing and transition economies	10	4	9	8	na	na	na	na

[a] Revealed comparative advantage index is the share of agriculture and processed food in national exports as a ratio of that sector's share of global exports.

[b] Primary agricultural trade specialization index is net exports as a ratio of the sum of exports and imports of agricultural and processed food products (world average =0.0).

Source: Sandri, Valenzuela and Anderson (2007), compiled mainly from World Bank (2007) and FAO (2007).

years covered is forty-one per country.[7] Of the world's thirty most valuable
agricultural products, the NRAs cover 77 percent of global output, ranging from two-thirds for livestock, three-quarters for oilseeds and tropical
crops, and five-sixths for grains and tubers. Those products represent an
even higher share (85 percent) of global agricultural exports (see Appendix
for details). Having such a comprehensive coverage of countries, products, and years offers the prospect of obtaining a reliable picture of both
long-term trends in policies and annual fluctuations around those trends
for individual countries and commodities, as well as for country groups,
regions, and the world as a whole.

This chapter begins with an outline of the methodology used to generate
annual indicators of the extent of government interventions in markets,
details of which are provided in Anderson et al. (2008). A selection of stylized facts that can be gleaned from the distortions database is then summarized across products, sectors, regions, and over the decades since the
mid-1950s.[8] The chapter concludes with a list of political economy questions needing to be addressed, many of which are the subject of subsequent
chapters in this volume.

METHODOLOGY FOR MEASURING
PRICE DISTORTIONS[9]

The present study's methodology focuses mainly on government-imposed
distortions that create a gap between domestic prices and what they would
be under free markets. Since it is not possible to understand the characteristics of agricultural development with a sectoral view alone, not only are
the effects of direct agricultural policy measures (including distortions in

[7]   By way of comparison, the seminal multicountry study of agricultural pricing policy by
Krueger, Schiff and Valdés (1988, 1991) covered an average of 23 years to the mid-1980s
for its eighteen focus countries that accounted for 5–6 percent of the global agricultural
output; and the producer and consumer support estimates of the OECD (2008) cover
twenty-two years for its thirty countries that account for just over one-quarter of the
world's agricultural output valued at undistorted prices. Anderson (2010) reports that the
more limited product and country coverage of the Krueger, Schiff and Valdés study led to
it understating (by two-fifths) the extent of the antiagricultural bias of developing country
policies during 1960–84.

[8]   These estimates and associated analytical narratives are discussed in far more detail in a
global overview volume (Anderson 2009), and the detailed developing country case studies are reported in four regional volumes covering Africa (Anderson and Masters 2009),
Asia (Anderson and Martin 2009a), Latin America (Anderson and Valdés 2008), and
Europe's transition economies (Anderson and Swinnen 2008).

[9]   Only a brief summary of the methodology is provided here. For details, see Anderson
et al. (2008) or Appendix A in Anderson (2009).

the foreign exchange market) examined, but also are those of distortions in nonagricultural tradable sectors.

Specifically, the NRA for each farm product is computed as the percentage by which government policies have raised gross returns to farmers above what they would be without the government's intervention (or lowered them, if NRA<0). Included are any product-specific input subsidies. A weighted average NRA for all covered products is derived using the value of production at undistorted prices as product weights (unlike the PSEs and CSEs computed by OECD [2008], which are expressed as a percentage of the distorted price). To that, NRA for covered products is added a 'guesstimate' of the NRA for noncovered products (on average around 30 percent of the total) and an estimate of the NRA from non-product-specific forms of assistance or taxation. Since the 1980s, some high-income governments have also provided so-called 'decoupled' assistance to farmers but, because that support in principle does not distort resource allocation, its NRA has been computed separately and is not included for direct comparison with the NRAs for other sectors or for developing countries. Each farm industry is classified either as import-competing, or a producer of exportables, or as producing a nontradable (with its status sometimes changing over the years), so as to generate for each year the weighted average NRAs for the two different groups of covered tradable farm products. We also generate a production-weighted average NRA for nonagricultural tradables, for comparison with that for agricultural tradables via the calculation of a percentage Relative Rate of Assistance (RRA), defined as:

$$RRA = 100^*[(100+NRAag^t)/(100+NRAnonag^t)-1]$$

where $NRAag^t$ and $NRAnonag^t$ are the percentage NRAs for the tradable parts of the agricultural (including noncovered) and nonagricultural sectors, respectively.[10] Since the NRA cannot be less than 100 percent if producers are to earn anything, neither can the RRA (since the weighted average $NRAnonag^t$ is non-negative in all our country case studies). And if both of those sectors are equally assisted, the RRA is zero. This measure is useful in that if it is below (above) zero, it provides an internationally

---

[10] Farmers are affected not just by prices of their own products but also by the incentives nonagricultural producers face. That is, it is *relative* prices and hence *relative* rates of government assistance that affect producer incentives. More than seventy years ago, Lerner (1936) provided his Symmetry Theorem that proved that in a two-sector economy, an import tax has the same effect as an export tax. This carries over to a model that also includes a third sector producing only nontradables.

comparable indication of the extent to which a country's sectoral policy regime has an anti- (pro-) agricultural bias.

This approach is not well suited to analysis of the policies of Europe's or Asia's former socialist economies prior to their reform era, because prices then played only an accounting function and currency exchange rates were enormously distorted. During their reform era, however, the price comparison approach provides as valuable a set of indicators for them as for other market economies of distortions to incentives for farm production, consumption and trade, and of the income transfers associated with interventions.[11]

In addition to the mean NRA, a measure of the dispersion or variability of the NRA estimates across the covered farm products also is generated for each economy. The cost of government policy distortions to incentives in terms of resource misallocation tend to be greater the greater the degree of substitution in production. In the case of agriculture that involves the use of farm land that is sector-specific but transferable among farm activities, the greater the variation of NRAs across industries within the sector then the higher will be the welfare cost of those market interventions. A simple indicator of dispersion is the standard deviation of the covered industries' NRAs.

Anderson and Neary (2005) show that it is possible to develop a single index that captures the extent to which the mean and standard deviation of protection together contribute to the welfare cost of distortionary policies. That index recognizes that the welfare cost of a government-imposed price distortion is related to the square of the price wedge, and so is larger than the mean and is positive regardless of whether the government's agricultural policy is favoring or hurting farmers. In the case where it is only import restrictions that are distorting agricultural prices, the index provides a percentage tariff equivalent that, if applied uniformly to all imports, would generate the same welfare cost as the actual intrasectoral structure of protection from import competition. Lloyd, Croser and Anderson (2010) show that, once NRAs and CTEs have been calculated, they can be used to generate such an index even in the more complex situation where there may be domestic producer, or consumer taxes, or subsidies in addition to not only import tariffs but any other trade taxes or subsidies or quantitative restrictions. They call it a Welfare Reduction Index (WRI). Such a measure is the percentage agricultural

---

[11] Data availability also affects the year from which NRAs can be computed. For Europe's transition economies, that starting date is 1992 (2000 for Kazahkstan), for Vietnam it is 1986, and for China it is 1981.

trade tax (or uniform NRA and CTE) that, if applied equally to all agricultural tradables, would generate the same reduction in national economic welfare as the actual intrasectoral structure of distortions to domestic prices of tradable farm goods. They also show that, if one is willing to assume that domestic price elasticities of supply (demand) are equal across farm commodities, then the only information needed to estimate the WRI, in addition to the NRAs and CTEs, is the share of each commodity in the domestic value of farm production (consumption) at undistorted prices.

While most of the focus is on agricultural producers, we also consider the extent to which consumers are taxed or subsidized. To do so, we calculate a Consumer Tax Equivalent (CTE) by comparing the price that consumers pay for their food and the international price of each food product at the border. Differences between the NRA and the CTE arise from distortions in the domestic economy that are caused by transfer policies and taxes/subsidies that cause the prices paid by consumers (adjusted to the farmgate level) to differ from those received by producers. In the absence of any other information, the CTE for each tradable farm product is assumed to be the same as the NRA from border distortions, and the CTE for nontradable farm products is assumed to be zero.

To obtain dollar values of farmer assistance and consumer taxation, we have taken the country authors' NRA estimates and multiplied them by the gross value of production at undistorted prices to obtain an estimate in U.S. dollars of the direct gross subsidy equivalent of assistance to farmers (GSE). These GSE values are calculated in constant dollars and are expressed on per-farm-worker basis. Likewise, a value of the consumer transfer is derived from the CTE by assuming the consumption value is the gross value of production at undistorted prices divided by the self-sufficiency ratio for each product (production divided by consumption, derived from national volume data or the FAO's commodity balance sheets). These transfer values can be added up across products for a country, and across countries for any or all products, to get regional aggregate transfer estimates for the studied economies. That valuation is used to generate an estimate of the contribution of each policy instrument to the overall NRA, and the trade data that provide the self-sufficiency ratio helped each country author attach a trade status to each product each year.

Once each farm industry is classified either as import-competing, or a producer of exportables, or as producing a nontradable (its status could change over time), it is possible to generate for each year the weighted average NRAs for the two different groups of tradable farm industries. They can then be used to generate an agricultural trade bias index (TBI) defined as:

$$TBI = \left[\frac{1 + NRAag_x}{1 + NRAag_m} - 1 \right]$$

where $NRAag_m$ and $NRAag_x$ are the average NRAs for the import-competing and exportable parts of the agricultural sector (their weighted average being $NRAag^t$). This index has a value of zero when the import-competing and export subsectors are equally assisted, and its lower bound approaches -1 in the most extreme case of an antitrade policy bias.

Anderson and Neary (2005) show also that it is possible to develop a single index that captures the extent to which import protection reduces the volume of trade. Once NRAs and CTEs have been calculated, Lloyd, Croser and Anderson (2010) show how they can be used to generate a more general Trade Reduction Index (TRI), that allows for the trade effects also of domestic price distorting policies, and regardless of whether they (or the trade measures) are positive or negative. Such a measure is the percentage agricultural trade tax (or uniform NRA and CTE) which, if applied equally to all agricultural tradables, would generate the same reduction in trade volume as the actual intrasectoral structure of distortions to domestic prices of tradable farm goods. They also show that, if the domestic price elasticities of supply (demand) are equal across farm commodities, then again the only information needed to estimate the TRI, in addition to the NRAs and CTEs, is the share of each commodity in the domestic value of farm production (consumption) at undistorted prices.

Needless to say, there are numerous challenges in applying the above methodology, especially in less developed economies with poor-quality data. Ways to deal with the standard challenges are detailed in Anderson et al. (2008), and the country-specific challenges are discussed in the analytical narratives in the regional and global volumes listed in footnote 8 for this Chapter.

We turn now to summarizing the stylized facts that have emerged from Anderson and Valenzuela's (2008) compilation and aggregation of the NRAs and related estimates provided by the project's country case studies, and Anderson and Croser's (2009) estimation of the WRIs and TRIs, from which numerous questions emerge for political economy theorists, historians, and econometricians to address.

STYLIZED FACTS: GLOBAL AGRICULTURAL
DISTORTION PATTERNS

For the purposes of the present study, the world economy is divided into high-income countries (Western Europe, the United States/Canada, Japan, and Australia/New Zealand),[12] three developing country regions (Africa, Asia, and Latin America), and Europe's economies that were in transition from socialism in the 1990s, plus Turkey.[13]

North America and Europe (including the newly acceded eastern members of the EU) each account for one-third of global GDP, and the remaining one-third is shared almost equally by developing countries and the other high-income countries.[14] When the focus turns to just agriculture, however, developing countries are responsible for slightly over half the value added globally, with Asia accounting for two-thirds of that lion's share. The developing countries' majority becomes stronger still in terms of global population and even more so in terms of farmers, almost three-quarters of whom are in Asian developing countries. Hence the vast range of per capita incomes and agricultural land per capita, and thus agricultural comparative advantages, across the country groups in Table 2.1.

Asia has had much faster economic growth and export-led industrialization than the rest of the world: Since 1980, Asia's per capita GDP has grown at four times, and exports nearly two times, the global averages, and the share of Asia's GDP that is exported is now one-third above that for the rest of the world and for Latin America and far above that for Africa (Sandri, Valenzuela and Anderson 2007). Asia's GDP per capita is now half as high again as that of our focus African countries, although still only one-third that of Latin America (Table 2.1). However, in the earlier half of our time series, Asia was poorer than Africa and hence the poorest of the country groups in Table 2.1.

By 2000–04, just 12 percent of Asia's GDP came from agriculture on average. That contrasts with Africa where the share for our focus countries ranges from 20 to 40 percent, and with Latin America and Europe's

---

[12] Korea and Taiwan are categorized here as "developing" rather than high-income because at the beginning of the fifty-year period under study, they were among the poorest economies in the world.

[13] Turkey is included in this last group because it is in the same geographic region and, like others in that region, has been seeking European Union accession, which has influenced the evolution of its agricultural price and trade policies.

[14] The only countries not well represented in the sample are those middle- to high-income ones in the Middle East and the many small (often low-income) ones elsewhere that together account for less than 4 percent of the global economy.

transition economies where it is down to 6 percent (and to just 2 percent on average in high-income countries). The share of employment in agriculture remains very high in Asia, though, at just under 60 percent – which is the same as in Africa and three times the share in Latin America and Eastern Europe, although more farmers work part time on their farms in Asia than in other developing countries. By contrast, less than 4 percent of workers in high-income countries are still engaged in agriculture. Hence the much greater importance to developing country welfare, inequality, and poverty of own-country and rest-of-world distortions to agricultural incentives.

Regional NRAs and RRAs: Rising with Economic Growth and Industrialization

We turn first to the estimates of NRAs for covered products plus non-product-specific assistance and guesstimates of assistance to the roughly 30 percent of the value of farm products that have not been included in the study's explicit price comparison exercise. These are summarized in Table 2.2, from which (in combination with the right-hand half of Table 2.1) it is apparent that the NRAs are higher the higher a region's income per capita and the weaker its agricultural comparative advantage. The NRAs are also rising over time, and fastest for fastest-growing Asia and least so for slowest-growing Africa, with the exception of declines in Western Europe and Australia/New Zealand since the late 1980s. For developing countries as a whole, their average NRA has gradually moved from more than 20 percent below zero in the 1960s and 1970s to 9 percent above zero during 2000–04.

When the changes in NRAs to nonfarm tradable sectors are taken into account by calculating the RRA, the intersectoral changes in distortions are even starker. Table 2.3 shows that Latin America, Asia, and Australia/New Zealand all had high rates of manufacturing protection in the first half of the period that were dramatically reduced over the most recent three decades. As a result, the RRA for developing countries as a group has transformed from -50 percent prior to the mid-1970s to slightly above zero by the end of the 1990s. The RRA for Australia/New Zealand was also negative in the first half of the period (averaging more than 10 percent below zero) but, notwithstanding the decline in its NRA for farm products, the RRA has risen almost to zero because the manufacturing protection cuts were bigger than the cuts in farm subsidies (as explained in Anderson, Lloyd and MacLaren 2007). Even in the other high-income countries, the

Table 2.2. *NRAs for agriculture,[a] focus countries, 1955 to 2007 (percent)*

	1955–59	1960–64	1965–69	1970–74	1975–79	1980–84	1985–89	1990–94	1995–99	2000–04	2005–07
Africa	-14	-8	-11	-15	-13	-8	-1	-9	-6	-7	na
Asia	-27	-27	-25	-25	-24	-21	-9	-2	8	12	na
Latin America	-11	-8	-7	-21	-18	-13	-11	4	6	5	na
Europe and Central Asia[b]	na	na	na	na	na	na	na	10	18	18	25
Western Europe	44	57	68	46	56	74	82	64	44	37	18
United States and Canada	13	11	11	7	7	13	19	16	11	17	11
Australia and New Zealand	6	7	10	8	8	11	9	4	3	1	2
Japan	39	46	50	47	67	72	119	116	120	120	81
Developing countries	-26	-23	-22	-24	-22	-18	-8	-2	6	9	na
High-income countries	22	29	35	25	32	41	53	46	35	32	17
All focus countries (wted. average)	3	5	6	0	2	5	17	18	17	18	na

[a] Weighted average for each country, including non-product-specific assistance, as well as authors' guesstimates for noncovered farm products (but not decoupled assistance), with weights based on gross value of agricultural production at undistorted prices. Estimates for China pre-1981 and India pre-1965 are based on the assumption that the nominal rate of assistance to agriculture in those years was the same as the average NRA estimates for those countries for 1981–84 and 1965–69, respectively, and that the gross value of production in those missing years is that which gives the same average share of value of production in total world production in 1981–84 and 1965–69, respectively.

Developing country and world aggregates are computed accordingly.

[b] East European and Central Asian countries are not included in the high-income or developing country aggregates.

Source: Authors' derivation, using data in Anderson and Valenzuela (2008).

Table 2.3. NRAs for agricultural and nonagricultural tradables, and the RRA,[a] by region, 1955 to 2007 (percent)

	1955–59	1960–64	1965–69	1970–74	1975–79	1980–84	1985–89	1990–94	1995–99	2000–04	2005–07
Africa											
NRA agric.	na	−13.3	−19.6	−25.0	−22.1	−13.5	−0.3	−15.4	−8.7	−12.0	na
NRA nonagric.	na	3.7	2.7	1.5	5.7	1.6	9.2	2.7	2.0	7.3	na
RRA	na	−15.2	−21.4	−26.0	−25.9	−13.1	−8.3	−17.1	−10.4	−18.0	na
Latin America											
NRA agric.	na	−11.4	−9.3	−23.0	−19.0	−12.9	−11.2	4.4	5.5	4.9	na
NRA nonagric.	na	26.9	31.3	27.8	23.3	18.5	16.8	7.3	6.6	5.4	na
RRA	na	−30.2	−30.9	−39.8	−34.2	−26.6	−24.0	−2.7	−1.0	−0.5	na
South Asia[b]											
NRA agric.	na	4.1	4.4	9.7	−7.7	1.8	47.1	0.2	−2.4	12.7	na
NRA nonagric.	na	114.4	117.8	81.7	57.8	54.6	39.9	18.6	15.0	10.1	na
RRA	na	−51.5	−51.9	−39.8	−41.6	−33.3	5.1	−15.5	−14.9	3.4	na
China and Southeast Asia[b]											
NRA agric.	na	−43.6	−42.6	−40.1	−35.7	−34.5	−27.8	−12.0	4.9	7.1	na
NRA nonagric.	na	36.5	36.5	33.7	30.8	20.6	23.3	19.8	9.6	5.5	na
RRA	na	−58.7	−58.0	−55.2	−50.8	−43.4	−41.6	−26.4	−4.2	1.5	na
Japan, Korea and Taiwan											
NRA agric.	30.1	39.9	48.8	51.3	75.5	78.8	124.3	129.9	130.5	138.1	126.1

	1955–59	1960–64	1965–69	1970–74	1975–79	1980–84	1985–89	1990–94	1995–99	2000–04	2005–07
NRA nonagric.	8.6	8.3	6.1	4.2	3.5	2.4	2.5	1.4	1.1	0.6	1.0
RRA	19.7	29.1	40.2	44.9	69.6	74.6	118.7	126.7	128.1	136.7	123.7
European transition econs.											
NRA agric.	na	na	na	na	na	na	na	10.0	18.3	16.1	17.0
NRA nonagric.	na	na	na	na	na	na	na	9.8	5.5	4.6	2.7
RRA	na	na	na	na	na	na	na	0.1	12.2	11.0	13.9
Western Europe											
NRA agric.	43.8	57.0	67.5	45.7	56.3	74.4	82.0	63.4	43.6	36.8	18.5
NRA nonagric.	8.0	7.2	5.7	3.8	2.5	1.5	1.7	1.3	1.5	1.4	1.2
RRA	33.1	46.5	58.6	40.4	52.6	71.9	79.0	61.3	41.5	34.9	17.1
North America											
NRA agric.	12.5	10.5	10.9	7.5	7.6	13.8	20.2	16.1	11.4	17.3	11.2
NRA nonagric.	6.1	7.4	7.4	5.5	4.1	3.8	3.7	3.3	2.1	1.5	1.3
RRA	6.0	2.9	3.3	1.8	3.4	9.7	15.8	12.4	9.1	15.5	9.7
ANZ											
NRA agric.	5.5	6.6	8.3	7.9	7.3	10.6	8.7	4.3	2.9	1.0	0.6
NRA nonagric.	20.0	21.5	24.0	19.7	14.3	13.5	10.3	6.4	3.4	2.4	2.4
RRA	-12.1	-12.2	-12.6	-9.9	-6.1	-2.6	-1.5	-2.0	-0.5	-1.4	-1.8
Developing countries[b]											
NRA agric.	na	-24.0	-27.3	-31.9	-25.5	-21.0	-15.6	-3.9	4.0	7.4	na

(continued)

Table 2.3 (continued)

	1955–59	1960–64	1965–69	1970–74	1975–79	1980–84	1985–89	1990–94	1995–99	2000–04	2005–07
NRA nonagric.	na	58.3	60.0	45.8	37.3	34.6	27.0	16.7	9.8	6.3	na
RRA	na	−52.0	−54.5	−53.3	−45.8	−41.3	−33.6	−17.6	−5.3	1.1	na
High-income countries											
NRA agric.	23.0	30.9	36.8	26.5	34.7	43.0	55.5	48.2	36.6	33.9	18.3
NRA nonagric.	7.5	8.5	7.7	5.4	3.6	3.4	3.2	2.5	1.7	1.3	−0.7
RRA	14.3	20.6	27.1	19.9	30.1	38.3	50.6	44.6	34.3	32.1	19.2
World[b]											
NRA agric.	na	5.6	7.6	0.8	2.6	5.7	18.7	19.7	18.4	18.6	na
NRA nonagric.	na	19.0	20.5	16.1	13.7	10.0	9.8	7.6	6.0	4.0	na
RRA	na	−11.3	−10.7	−13.2	−9.8	−3.6	8.1	11.3	11.8	14.0	na

[a] The RRA is defined as $100*[(100+NRAag^t)/(100+NRAnonag^t)-1]$, where $NRAag^t$ and $NRAnonag^t$ are the percentage NRAs for the tradables parts of the agricultural and nonagricultural sectors, respectively.

[b] Estimates for the RRA for China pre-1981 and India pre-1965 are based on the assumption that the agricultural NRAs in those years were the same as the average NRA estimates for those countries for 1981–84 and 1965–69, respectively, and that the value of production in those missing years is that which gives the same average share of value of production in total world production in 1981–84 and 1965–69, respectively.

Developing and world country aggregates are computed accordingly.

Source: Authors' derivation, using data in Anderson and Valenzuela (2008).

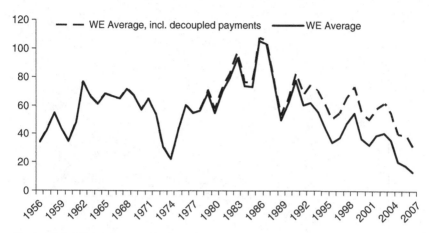

Figure 2.1. NRAs to agriculture without and with decoupled payments, Western Europe, 1956 to 2007 (percent).
Source: Anderson and Valenzuela (2008) as reported in Josling (2009), which draws heavily on OECD (2008) for calculations from 1979.

decline in manufacturing protection has accentuated the improvement in farm incentives prior to the 1990s.

Western Europe is the only significant region where the agricultural sector trend RRAs have declined as incomes have grown, and only since the late 1980s. That does not take account of the fact that there has been much reinstrumentation of support for farmers in Western Europe over the past two decades. When payments decoupled from farm production are included in the NRA, there was very little decline in the trend level of overall farmer assistance between 1986 and 2004. The drop since then (Figure 2.1) is not due to any policy change in Europe but simply a rise in international food prices that has not been passed on to farmers there – and which will have since bounced back with the decline in those food prices from the second half of 2008.

Using the full dataset of countries and years, the positive relationship between RRA and real national GDP per capita is very clear from Figure 2.2, with developing countries having the archetypical antiagricultural bias (RRA<0) and high-income countries having the proagricultural bias described in Anderson (1995). The negative relationship between agricultural comparative advantage and NRA or RRA is not quite as strong, but it is certainly visible, as in Figure 2.3 for RRAs. The individual country average agricultural NRA and RRA, shown for 2000–04 in Figure 2.4, lends further visual support to these tendencies. They suggest strongly

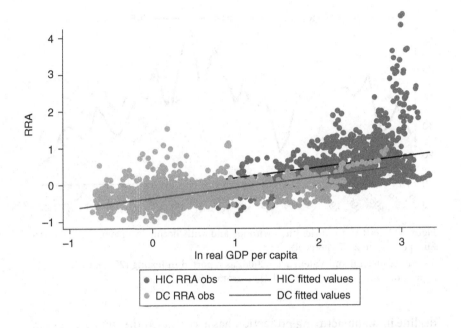

	Coefficient	Standard error	R^2
DCs	0.26	0.02	0.15
HICs	0.25	0.02	0.17

Figure 2.2. Relationships between real GDP per capita and RRA, all 75 focus countries, 1955 to 2007 (RRA is in percent/100).
Source: Authors' derivation with country fixed effects, using data in Anderson and Valenzuela (2008).

that the world's agricultural production is far from optimally distributed around the globe, or even within each continent. That is, the world's farm resources are being squandered by this wide dispersion of NRAs and RRAs.

Together, these data suggest at least six stylized facts:

- **Fact 1**: National nominal and relative rates of assistance to agriculture tend to be higher, the higher the country's income per capita.
- **Fact 2**: National nominal and relative rates of assistance to agriculture tend to be higher the weaker the country's agricultural comparative advantage.
- **Fact 3**: As a corollary to Facts 1 and 2, national nominal and relative rates of assistance to agriculture tend to rise over time as the country's

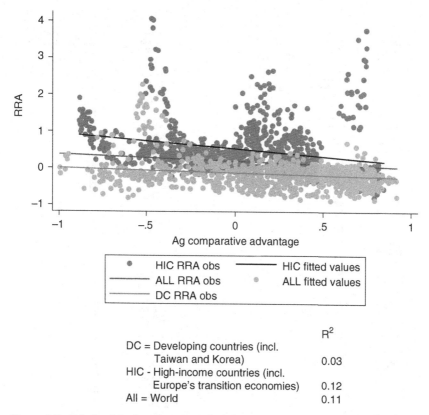

Figure 2.3. Relationships between agricultural comparative advantage[a] and RRA, all 75 focus countries, 1955 to 2007 (RRA is in percent/100).

[a] Net exports divided by the sum of exports and imports of agricultural products.

Source: Authors' derivation with country fixed effects, using data in Anderson and Valenzuela (2008).

per capita income rises, and more so the more that growth is accompanied by a decline in agricultural comparative advantage.

- **Fact 4:** While there is a wide range in the trend levels of agricultural sector NRAs and RRAs and in their rates of change in both high-income and developing countries, over most of the past half century, the policy regime on average in developing countries has had an anti-agricultural bias and in high-income countries it has had a proagricultural bias.
- **Fact 5:** The only significant region where the agricultural sector trend RRAs have declined as incomes have grown is Western Europe since the late 1980s, but the decline in the trend level of overall farmer

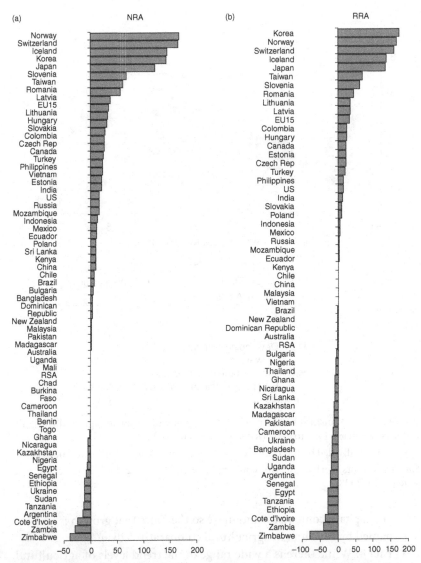

Figure 2.4. Cross-country dispersion of NRA (all agriculture products, including non-product-specific support) and RRA, 2000 to 2004 (percent).
Source: Authors' derivation, using data in Anderson and Valenzuela (2008).

assistance has declined little when payments decoupled from farm production are included.

• **Fact 6:** The only other countries where the agricultural sector trend NRA has declined as incomes have grown are Australia and New

Zealand since the 1970s, but there it was tolerated by farmers because it was accompanied by even larger reductions in manufacturing protection, such that the RRA rose for farmers there (not unlike in many developing countries).

Wide Dispersion of Product NRAs

The regional average NRAs just discussed hide a great deal of diversity across products and countries, including within each region. This can be seen clearly from national Box plots shown in Figure A.4 in the Appendix to this volume (Anderson and Croser 2010). One other way of summarizing the within-country NRA diversity across products is to calculate the standard deviation around the mean NRA for all covered farm products each year. Even when that is averaged over 5-year periods and for whole geographic regions, the diversity is still evident (Table 2.4). What is also evident from that table is that the average of those standard deviations for all seventy-five focus countries is hardly any lower in the second half of the period than it is in the first half. This has important welfare implications, because the cost of government policy distortions to incentives in terms of resource misallocation tend to be greater the greater the degree of substitution in production (Lloyd 1974). In the case of agriculture that involves the use of farm land that is sector-specific but transferable among farm activities, the greater the variation of NRAs across industries within the sector, the higher will be the welfare cost of those market interventions.

That wide range of product NRAs carries over globally, too. The Box plots for the regions are shown in Figure A.3 in the Appendix to this volume (Anderson and Croser 2010), and a summary for the world is provided in Figure 2.5 for a dozen key products. Each of those figures reveals the range within which 95 percent of the NRAs fall over the sample time period (the long bar), with the shaded area showing where 50 percent of the NRAs fall, and the vertical line within that shows the median NRA for the sample for each product.

When developing and high-income countries are considered separately, it is revealed that the rice pudding ingredients of sugar, rice, and milk are the most protected in both sets of countries in 2000–04 (Figure 2.6). Cotton, on the other hand, is protected in high-income countries but taxed in developing countries, while prices of inputs into livestock feedmix (maize, soybean) and of intensive livestock products (pork, poultry) are distorted relatively little in both sets of countries.

Table 2.4. Dispersion of NRAs across covered agricultural products,[a] focus regions, 1965 to 2007 (percent)

	1965–69	1970–74	1975–79	1980–84	1985–89	1990–94	1995–99	2000–04	2005–07
Africa	31	30	37	36	36	31	25	25	na
Asia	56	42	49	53	66	56	57	64	na
Latin America	49	44	52	52	44	42	32	40	na
Europe and Central Asia	34	33	41	26	39	56	39	45	44
Western Europe	119	85	112	98	122	86	69	74	64
United States and Canada	29	15	31	62	71	39	31	37	28
Australia and New Zealand	40	45	26	17	20	14	12	7	5
Japan	69	82	156	143	175	162	136	143	116
All focus countries (wted. average)	54	45	55	51	59	53	43	48	na
Product coverage[b]	68	70	71	73	73	72	71	68	70

[a] Dispersion for each region is a simple average of the country-level annual standard deviations around a weighted mean of NRAs per country across covered products each year.

[b] Share of gross value of total agricultural production at undistorted prices accounted for by covered products.

Source: Authors' derivation, using data in Anderson and Valenzuela (2008).

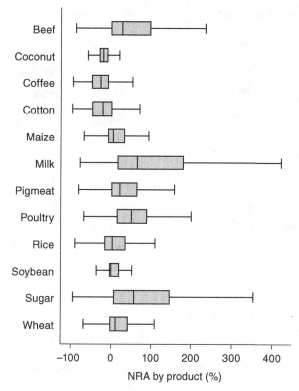

Figure 2.5. Distribution[a] of output-based global average NRA, 12 key products, 1955 to 2007 (percent).

[a] The long bar shows the range within which 95 percent of the NRAs fall: 50 percent fall in the shaded area, and the vertical line within the shaded area is the median NRA for the sample period.

Source: Authors' derivation using data in Anderson and Valenzuela (2008).

These data suggest another three stylized facts:

- **Fact 7**: Within the agricultural sector of each country, whether developed or developing, there is a wide range of product NRAs.
- **Fact 8**: Despite the fall in average agricultural NRAs, the across-product standard deviation of NRAs around the national average each year is no less in the present decade than it was in the three previous decades for both developed and developing countries.
- **Fact 9**: Some product NRAs are positive and high in almost all countries (sugar, rice, and milk), others are positive and high in developed economies but highly negative in developing countries (most noticeably cotton), and yet others are relatively low in all countries (feedgrains, soybean, pork, and poultry).

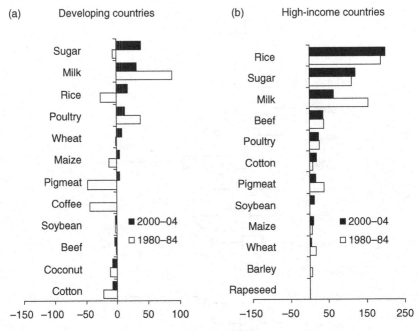

Figure 2.6. NRA, key covered products, high-income and developing countries, 1980 to 1984 and 2000 to 2004 (percent).

Source: Authors' derivation, using data in Anderson and Valenzuela (2008).

Antitrade Bias in NRAs

The most robust NRA estimates are for the covered farm products for which direct price comparisons have been made. Those products have been categorized each year as either exportable, import-competing, or nontradable. Figure 2.7 summarizes those NRAs and reveals a marked difference in the levels of support to import-competing versus exportable farm products. Exportables in high-income countries received relatively little support other than during the export subsidy "war" of the mid-1980s, while in developing countries they were increasingly taxed from the late 1950s until the 1980s and then that taxation was gradually phased out (although some taxes remained in 2000–04, for example in Argentina). Importables, by contrast, have been assisted throughout the past five decades in both developed and developing countries on average (even though some import subsidization of staple foods occurred from time to time in low-income countries), and the long-run fitted trend line has almost the same slope for both sets of countries, albeit with a lower intercept for developing countries.

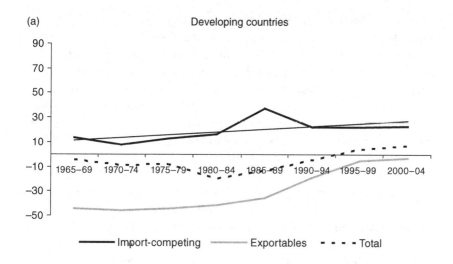

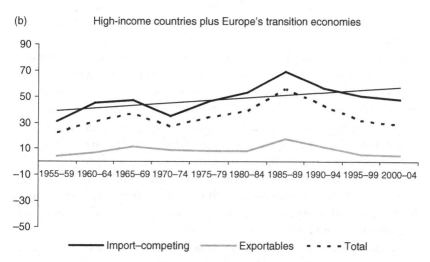

Figure 2.7. NRA for exportable, import-competing and all covered agricultural products,[a] high-income and developing countries, 1955 to 2004 (percent).

[a] Covered products only. The total also includes nontradables.

Source: Authors' derivation, using data in Anderson and Valenzuela (2008).

Part of the antitrade bias in developing countries was the result of government intervention in the domestic market for foreign currency. The most common arrangement was a dual exchange rate, whereby exporters had to sell part or all of their foreign currency to the government at a low

price. This effectively taxed and thus discouraged production of exportables. At the same time, it created an artificial shortage of foreign currency so that potential importers bid up its purchase price, which had the
same effect as an import tax and thus encouraged import-competing production. The size of these effective, if implicit, trade taxes depends on the
extent to which the government purchase price is misaligned with what
would be the free-market equilibrium price of foreign currency, the price
elasticities of demand for and supply of foreign currency, and the retention
rate. In some countries, there were more complex multiple exchange rates,
whereby traders of some products were subject to more favorable treatment
than others. In estimating NRAs in developing countries, participants in
the Agricultural Distortions research project endeavored to include the
effects of these implicit trade taxes and to show how much impact they had
on the NRAs and RRA (see Anderson et al. 2008, which draws on Dervis,
de Melo and Robinson 1981). The practice was rife in newly independent
developing countries in the 1960s and 1970s, but was gradually phased out
over the 1980s and early 1990s as part of overall macroeconomic policy
reform initiatives.

The net effect of all the explicit and implicit trade taxes and subsidies,
together with domestic taxes and subsidies on tradable farm products, is
that the NRA for exportable farm products is typically well below the NRA
for importables, so that the TBI, as defined in the methodology section
above, is negative. Table 2.5 shows that the antiagricultural trade bias has
declined over time for the developing country group, but mainly because
of the decline in agricultural export taxation and in spite of growth in agricultural import protection. For the high-income group, the agricultural
trade bias index has shown little trend over time. That is mainly because
the rise and then decline in agricultural export subsidies has been matched
by a similar trajectory for import protection.

The two subsectors to which that index's NRAs refer (exportable and
import-competing farm products, respectively) are not equal contributors to overall farm production, however, so the TBI when weighted across
numerous products/countries is not an ideal indicator. A superior one is
the trade reduction index discussed in the methodology section above. The
trade reduction index (and, incidentally, the welfare reduction index) associated with NRAs and CTEs for covered agricultural products have fallen
substantially since the latter 1980s for both high-income and developing
country groups and hence globally (Figure 2.8). That fall in the TRI has
been more because of the fall in national mean NRAs than in their variance, however.

Table 2.5. NRAs[a] for agricultural exportables, import-competing products, and the trade bias index,[b] focus regions, 1955 to 2007 (percent)

	1955–59	1960–64	1965–69	1970–74	1975–79	1980–84	1985–89	1990–94	1995–99	2000–04	2005–07
Africa											
NRA agric. exportables	na	-30.1	-38.4	-42.6	-42.6	-35.0	-36.7	-35.8	-26.1	-24.6	na
NRA agric. imp-comp	na	18.6	11.8	1.9	14.5	13.2	58.3	5.2	9.8	1.6	na
Trade Bias Index	na	-0.41	-0.45	-0.44	-0.50	-0.43	-0.60	-0.39	-0.33	-0.26	na
Latin America											
NRA agric. exportables	na	-20.4	-12.8	-27.0	-25.2	-27.1	-25.0	-10.5	-3.5	-4.6	na
NRA agric. imp-comp	na	26.3	8.7	-2.8	1.1	13.6	5.1	19.4	12.5	20.6	na
Trade Bias Index	na	-0.37	-0.20	-0.25	-0.26	-0.36	-0.29	-0.25	-0.14	-0.21	na
South Asia[c]											
NRA agric. exportables	na	-37.5	-37.2	-30.0	-36.1	-27.9	-20.6	-15.8	-12.0	-6.2	na
NRA agric. imp-comp	na	39.2	41.2	39.4	45.1	37.9	63.3	25.1	14.5	26.5	na
Trade Bias Index	na	-0.55	-0.56	-0.50	-0.56	-0.48	-0.51	-0.33	-0.23	-0.26	na
China and Southeast Asia[c]											
NRA agric. exportables	na	-55.5	-55.1	-51.8	-50.1	-50.0	-41.0	-20.8	-2.2	0.1	na
NRA agric. imp-comp	na	-10.3	-8.9	-9.4	-2.6	0.5	15.1	3.3	13.3	12.3	na
Trade Bias Index	na	-0.50	-0.51	-0.47	-0.49	-0.50	-0.49	-0.23	-0.14	-0.11	na
Japan, Korea and Taiwan											
NRA agric. exp	-18.1	5.7	4.3	15.4	10.3	25.1	48.9	57.1	57.0	70.3	na
NRA agric. imp-comp	35.6	43.3	52.8	54.1	76.6	83.7	124.9	127.4	127.0	134.6	122.6
Trade Bias Index	-0.40	-0.26	-0.32	-0.25	-0.38	-0.32	-0.34	-0.31	-0.31	-0.27	na

(continued)

Table 2.5 (continued)

	1955–59	1960–64	1965–69	1970–74	1975–79	1980–84	1985–89	1990–94	1995–99	2000–04	2005–07
European transition econs.											
NRA agric. exportables	na	na	na	na	na	na	na	-3.2	-1.0	-1.0	15.2
NRA agric. imp-comp	na	na	na	na	na	na	na	32.5	35.4	35.7	32.3
Trade Bias Index	na	na	na	na	na	na	na	-0.27	-0.27	-0.27	-0.13
Western Europe											
NRA agric. exp	9.3	17.4	31.7	22.5	33.3	31.1	50.1	38.0	15.0	8.1	1.7
NRA agric. imp-comp	59.4	77.2	82.9	55.7	61.7	79.5	87.6	67.2	52.8	50.5	28.9
Trade Bias Index	-0.31	-0.34	-0.28	-0.21	-0.18	-0.27	-0.20	-0.17	-0.25	-0.28	-0.21
North America											
NRA agric. exportables	2.7	2.8	6.1	5.1	2.9	5.4	10.5	6.0	5.4	7.6	4.1
NRA agric. imp-comp	8.6	9.3	8.8	6.7	10.5	19.7	23.6	18.6	11.3	16.8	11.0
Trade Bias Index	-0.05	-0.06	-0.02	-0.01	-0.07	-0.11	-0.10	-0.10	-0.05	-0.08	-0.06
ANZ											
NRA agric. exportables	3.8	4.7	6.6	5.8	5.5	7.6	6.5	3.6	2.2	0.2	0.2
NRA agric. imp-comp	7.9	8.3	9.3	11.7	8.7	8.4	6.5	3.8	2.0	2.0	1.5
Trade Bias Index	-0.04	-0.03	-0.02	-0.05	-0.03	-0.01	0.00	0.00	0.00	-0.02	-0.01
Developing countries[c]											
NRA agric. exportables	na	-46.5	-44.6	-45.4	-43.9	-41.4	-35.8	-18.7	-5.5	-3.0	na
NRA agric. imp-comp	na	12.7	13.5	7.8	12.8	16.5	37.7	22.6	22.0	23.0	na
Trade Bias Index	na	-0.53	-0.51	-0.49	-0.50	-0.50	-0.53	-0.34	-0.23	-0.21	na

	1955–59	1960–64	1965–69	1970–74	1975–79	1980–84	1985–89	1990–94	1995–99	2000–04	2005–07
High-income countries											
NRA agric. exportables	4.2	7.4	13.5	10.3	11.3	12.1	22.3	15.9	8.1	6.9	2.9
NRA agric. imp-comp	31.2	45.9	50.2	36.5	47.4	58.1	71.4	62.4	53.9	50.7	30.8
Trade Bias Index	-0.21	-0.26	-0.24	-0.19	-0.24	-0.29	-0.29	-0.29	-0.30	-0.29	-0.21
World [c]											
NRA agric. exportables	na	-23	-20	-23	-25	-24	-17	-1	-1	0	na
NRA agric. imp-comp	na	35	37	27	34	38	57	43	38	36	na
Trade Bias Index	na	-0.43	-0.42	-0.39	-0.44	-0.45	-0.47	-0.35	-0.28	-0.26	na

[a] NRAs for noncovered products are included here.

[b] Trade Bias Index, TBI = $(1+NRAag_x/100)/(1+NRAag_m/100) - 1$, where $NRAag_x$ and $NRAag_m$ are the weighted average percentage NRAs for the exportable and import-competing parts of the agricultural sector, with weights based on production valued at undistorted prices. TBIs shown here are calculated using the regional five-year averages of $NRAag_x$ and $NRAag_m$.

[c] Estimates for China pre-1981 and India pre-1965 are based on the assumption that the nominal rate of assistance to agriculture in those years was the same as the average NRA estimates for those countries for 1981–84 and 1965–69, respectively, and that the gross value of production in those missing years is that which gives the same average share of value of production in total world production in 1981–84 and 1965–69, respectively. The developing country and world averages are computed accordingly.

Source: Authors' derivation, using data in Anderson and Valenzuela (2008).

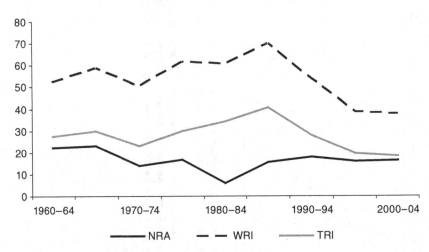

Figure 2.8. Global NRA and Trade and Welfare Reduction Indexes for covered tradable farm products, 1960 to 2004 (percent).
Source: Authors' calculations based on NRAs and CTEs in Anderson and Valenzuela (2008).

These features of government intervention suggest another five stylized facts:

- **Fact 10**: With respect to individual farm products, the NRA tends to be lower the stronger the country's comparative advantage in that product.
- **Fact 11**: As a corollary to Fact 10, the agricultural policy regime of each country tends to have an antitrade bias.
- **Fact 12**: The antiagricultural trade bias has declined over time for the developing country group, but mainly because of the decline in agricultural export taxation and in spite of growth in agricultural import protection, whereas for the high-income group, the antiagricultural trade bias has shown little trend over time, mainly because the rise and then decline in agricultural export subsidies has been matched by a similar trajectory for import protection.
- **Fact 13**: The trade reduction (and the welfare reduction) indexes associated with NRAs and CTEs for covered agricultural products have fallen substantially since the latter 1980s for both high-income and developing country groups and hence globally, but more because of the fall in national mean NRAs than in their variance.
- **Fact 14**: Up to the 1980s, and in some cases early 1990s, it was not uncommon for government interventions in the market for foreign

exchange in developing countries to add to the overall antitrade bias in policy regimes, but those interventions had all but disappeared by the mid-1990s as part of overall macroeconomic policy reform initiatives.

Volatility of NRAs

If a country would be close to self-sufficient in a product under free markets, but there is a significant transport cost associated with importing or exporting it, then there would be no trade in this product except in years when the international price was relatively high or low. In the absense of government intervention, the NRA would be zero regardless of whether trade took place, but without trade the domestic price could be anywhere within the range of the fob export price and the cif import price, depending on domestic market conditions each year. If import and export taxes or quantitative restrictions applied, they would make trade even less likely and they would widen the range of variation in the domestic price of this mostly nontraded good. In that case, the interventions would cause the estimated NRA to switch from negative to zero to positive and back to zero as and when the international price gyrated well above and below trend.

A much more common reason for NRAs to vary from year to year, though, is because the government deliberately seeks to reduce fluctuations in domestic food prices and in the quantities available for consumption. One way for a country to achieve that objective is by varying the restrictions on its international trade in food according to seasonal conditions domestically and changes in food prices internationally. Effectively, this involves exporting domestic instability and not importing instability from abroad.

To distinguish between these two sources of volatility in the NRA for a product whose national self sufficiency is always close to zero, one can compare the movements in domestic versus border prices. As an illustration, Figure 2.9 does that for rice in India: Clearly in that case, the government has been able to maintain an almost constant real domestic rice price for decades despite huge fluctuations in the international price of rice. Indeed, that has been the practice of most governments in South and Southeast Asia, where rice is the predominant food staple. As a result, since Asia produces and consumes four-fifths of the world's rice (compared with about one-third of the world's wheat and maize), this market-insulating behavior of Asian policy makers means that very little rice production has

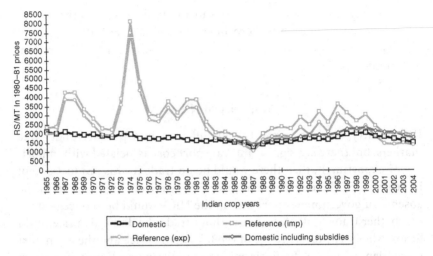

Figure 2.9. Real domestic producer and international reference prices for rice, India, 1965 to 2004 (Rs/tonne in 1981 prices).
Source: Pursell, Gulati and Gupta (2009).

been traded internationally: less than 7 percent in 2000–04,[15] compared with 14 and 24 percent for maize and wheat. This insulating behavior of governments[16] also means international prices are much more volatile for rice than for those other grains.

To get a sense of how much this practice varies across products and whether it has changed much since policy reforms began around the mid-1980s, Table 2.6 reports the average across focus countries of the percentage point deviation each year of national NRAs for twelve key farm products around their trend value for the subperiods before and from 1985. For most products, this indicator is lower in the latter period, the exceptions being rice, wheat, and (at least in developing countries) soybean. Rice had one of the smaller average deviations in the earlier period, but by the latter period, rice shared with sugar and milk the honor of the largest deviations.

That nominal rates of protection tend to be above trend in years of low international prices and conversely in years when international prices are high is clear from Table 2.7, which shows the extent of the negative

---

[15] This was up from the pre-1990s half-decade global shares, which are all less than 4.5 percent (Anderson and Valenzuela 2008).

[16] This beggar-thy-neighbor dimension of each country's policy is not restricted to developing countries. In high-income countries, however, the motivation for intervention is more commonly concern for instability in producer prices and farm incomes rather than in instability of prices and availability of staples for urban consumers.

Table 2.6. *Deviation of national NRA around its trend value,[a] 12 key covered farm products,[b] developing, high-income and all focus countries, 1965 to 1984 and 1985 to 2004 (NRA percentage points)*

	Developing countries		High-income countries		All focus countries	
	1965–1984	1985–2004	1965–1984	1985–2004	1965–1984	1985–2004
Grains, oils, sugar						
Rice	32	64	66	229	37	103
Wheat	33	47	80	91	56	65
Maize	36	33	53	58	43	41
Soybean	46	117	75	61	56	94
Sugar	53	66	179	173	132	116
Tropical cash crops						
Cotton	38	33	42	28	35	32
Coconut	22	20	na	na	22	20
Coffee	41	27	na	na	41	27
Livestock products						
Milk	76	69	239	190	200	137
Beef	45	52	128	127	101	93
Pigmeat	81	60	92	77	90	62
Poultry	109	74	164	197	145	134

[a] Deviation is computed as the absolute value of (residual – trend NRA) where trend NRA in each of the two subperiods is obtained by regressing NRA on time.
[b] Unweighted average of national deviations.
Source: Authors' derivation, using data in Anderson and Valenzuela (2008).

correlation between the NRAs for various products and their international price. That coefficient globally and in high-income countries is negative for all but beef, and even in the various developing country regions it is negative in all but one-quarter of the cases. For almost all of those twelve products, the regional correlation is highest for the South Asian region. Among the developing countries, it is again rice, sugar, and milk that have the highest correlation coefficients.

One other way of capturing this phenomenon is to estimate the elasticity of transmission of the international product price to the domestic market. Following Tyers and Anderson (1992, pp. 65–75), we use a geometric lag formulation to estimate elasticities for each product for all focus countries

Table 2.7. *Coefficient of correlation between regional NRA and international price, 12 key covered farm products,[a] various regions, 1965 to 2007*

	Africa	South Asia	South East Asia and China	Latin America	High–income countries	All focus countries[b]
Grains, oils, sugar						
Rice	–0.19	–0.58	–0.51	–0.52	–0.10	–0.16 (0.99)
Wheat	0.01	–0.81	0.09	–0.12	–0.28	–0.41 (0.85)
Maize	–0.20	–0.70	–0.55	–0.04	–0.29	–0.57 (0.71)
Soybean	–0.15	–0.42	0.16	–0.27	–0.07	–0.18 (0.30)
Sugar	–0.57	–0.74	–0.57	–0.40	–0.69	–0.70 (0.99)
Tropical cash crops						
Cotton	0.28	–0.33	–0.16	–0.29	–0.74	–0.57 (0.96)
Coconut	na	–0.16	–0.14	na	na	–0.12 (0.99)
Coffee	–0.35	na	0.02	–0.30	na	–0.28 (0.99)
Livestock products						
Milk	0.19	–0.57	–0.70	0.33	–0.10	–0.31 (0.98)
Beef	0.20	na	0.05	0.55	0.29	0.32 (0.97)
Pigmeat	na	na	–0.53	–0.47	–0.60	–0.76 (0.98)
Poultry	0.59	na	–0.52	–0.78	–0.22	–0.34 (0.87)

[a] Computed using the weighted average regional NRAs and a common international reference price for each product, from World Bank (2008).

[b] Numbers in parentheses are the coefficient of correlation between the unweighted average regional NRAs and CTEs for individual covered products. For all covered products, the coefficient is 0.93.

Source: Authors' derivation, using data in Anderson and Valenzuela (2008).

for the period 1985 to 2007. The average of estimates for the short run elasticity ranged from a low of 0.3 for sugar and milk to 0.5 for rice, wheat, and pigmeat, 0.6 for cotton, cocoa, maize, and poultry, and 0.7 for beef, soybean, and coffee. The unweighted average across all of those twelve key products is 0.54, suggesting that within the first year, little more than half the movement in international prices is transmitted domestically. Even the long-run elasticity appears well short of unity after full adjustment: The average of the elasticities for those twelve products across the focus countries is just 0.69.

These data provide two more stylized facts about government distortions to agricultural incentives:

- **Fact 15:** Around the long-run trend for each country, there is much fluctuation from year to year in individual product NRAs, and while this tendency has diminished since the mid-1980s for most key products, it has increased for rice and wheat.
- **Fact 16:** Product NRAs tend to be negatively correlated with movements in international prices of the products in question (most so in developing countries for rice, sugar, and milk), and on average, barely half of the change in an international price is transmitted to domestic markets within the first year and only two-thirds in the long run.

Dominance of Trade Measures in Farm Policy Instrument Choice

Since the mid-1980s, when the GATT's Uruguay Round got underway, it has been common in trade negotiations to focus on three sets of agricultural policy instruments that distort production and trade: import restrictions, export subsidies, and domestic producer subsidies. When the Doha round of negotiations was launched a decade ago, much of the focus of attention by developing countries was on farm subsidies by high-income countries, until it was shown that import restrictions were far more important to theirs – and global – economic welfare. According to the GTAP global economywide model and protection database, 93 percent of the global welfare cost of government interventions in agricultural markets as of 2001 was due to market access restrictions, and only 5 percent to domestic support and 2 percent to export subsidies (Anderson, Martin and Valenzuela 2006).

However, that GTAP protection database does not include all the apparent export taxes, import subsidies, and domestic producer taxes in developing countries identified in the World Bank's new Database of Agricultural Distortions. Yet even when the fuller set of policy instruments from the new database is included, and even when the relatively new decoupled payments to farm households are counted, it is still the case that trade measures at the border (export and import taxes or subsidies and their equivalent from quantitative trade restrictions and multiple exchange rates) are the dominant forms of intervention. Table 2.8 shows the various contributions of different policy measures to the overall estimated NRAs as of 1981–84 and 2000–04. In both periods, trade measures accounted for around three-fifths of the total NRA for both developing and high-income countries.[17]

Trade measures are responsible for an even larger share – almost 90 percent – of the distortion to consumer prices of food, since direct domestic consumer subsidies (or taxes), as distinct from the indirect ones provided by border measures, are relatively rare (Table 2.9).

The dominance of trade measures in both consumer tax equivalents (CTEs) and NRAs for agricultural products means we should expect those two indicators to be highly correlated. And indeed that is the case: For all focus countries, covered products, and available years in the panel set, the coefficient of correlation between NRAs and CTEs is 0.93 (see numbers in parentheses in the last column of Table 2.7).

Subsidies to farm inputs (and support for public agricultural research, not included in the NRA calculations) have been common but have added little to overall farmer assistance in high-income countries, and have done very little to offset the effective taxation of farmers in developing countries. The most notable exception is India, where large subsidies to fertilizer, water, and power for irrigation add several percentage points to India's agricultural NRA. The bottom row of Table 2.8 reports expenditure on public agricultural research and development expressed as a percentage of gross agricultural production valued at undistorted prices. Despite the

---

[17] If one assumes that the price elasticities of supply and demand for farm products are equal, and that there are no costs of collecting taxes and dispersing them as subsidies, then the trade-reducing effects of trade measures would be twice as high as for an equally high NRA provided by production subsidies – and an even bigger multiple of the effects of so-called decoupled payments, depending on the extent to which the latter are in practice truly decoupled from production decisions. Furthermore, the welfare-reducing effects of trade measures are in proportion to the square of the trade tax-cum-subsidy. Thus border measures would be responsible for much more than three-fifths of the global welfare cost of distortions to agricultural prices, and possibly not much below the more limited but widely quoted estimate for 2001 of 93 percent by Anderson, Martin and Valenzuela (2006).

Table 2.8. *Contributions to total agricultural NRA from different policy instruments,[a] by region, 1981 to 1984 and 2000 to 2004 (percent)[b]*

Border measures	1981–84			2000–04		
	All developing countries	High–income countries	All focus countries	All developing countries	High–income countries	All focus countries
Import tax equivalent	6	34	18	8	24	14
Export subsidies	1	2	2	1	1	2
Export tax equivalent	–20	0	–13	–3	0	–2
Import subsidy equivalent	–2	0	–2	–1	0	–1
ALL BORDER MEASURES	–15	36	5	5	25	13
Domestic measures						
Production subsidies	1	2	1	1	1	1
Production taxes	–5	0	–3	–1	0	–1
Net subsidies to farm inputs	1	3	2	2	2	2
Non-product-specific assistance (except to inputs)	1	1	1	2	5	3
ALL DOMESTIC PRODUCTION SUPPORTS	–2	6	1	4	8	5
Decoupled payments to farm households	0	6	2	0	11	4
NRA (including decoupled payments)	–17	48	8	9	44	22
Gross subsidy equivalent, in real 2000 US$ billion	*–113*	*223*	*99*	*58*	*173*	*250*
Agric R&D as % of undistorted gross value of prod'n	*0.9*	*3.4*	*1.6*	*1.0*	*1.5*	*1.1*

[a] In the absence of data, we assume the share of input tax/subsidy, domestic production tax/subsidy, and border tax/subsidies for noncovered farm products is the same as that for covered farm products. The first period begins in 1981 because that was the first year for which estimates for China are available.

[b] All table entries have been generated by dividing the Gross Subsidy Equivalent of all (including decoupled) measures by the total agricultural sector's gross production valued at undistorted prices.

Source: Authors' derivation, using distortion data in Anderson and Valenzuela (2008) and agricultural research expenditure data from the CGIAR's Agricultural Science and Technology Indicators website at http://www.asti.cgiar.org (accessed October 2008).

Table 2.9. *Contributions to CTE on covered agricultural products from different policy instruments, by region, 1981 to 1984ᵃ and 2000 to 2004 (percent)*

	1981–84			2000–04		
	All developing countries	High-income countries	All focus countries	All developing countries	High-income countries	All focus countries
Border measures						
Import tax equivalent	10	46	24	10	32	19
Export subsidies	1	2	1	1	1	2
Export tax equivalent	-22	0	-13	-2	0	-2
Import subsidy equivalent	-3	0	-2	-1	0	-1
ALL BORDER MEASURES	-14	48	10	8	33	18
Domestic measures						
Consumption subsidies	-1	0	-1	-1	-6	-3
Consumption taxes	0	0	0	1	0	1
ALL DOMESTIC CONSUMPTION MEASURES	-1	0	-1	0	-6	-2
TOTAL CTE (covered farm products only)	-15	48	9	8	27	16
Consumer tax equivalent, in real 2000 US$ billion	-67	146	73	34	79	125

ᵃ This period begins in 1981 because that was the first year for which estimates for China are available.

Source: Authors' derivation, using distortion data in Anderson and Valenzuela (2008).

estimated high social rates of return at the margin to such public investment (Pardey et al. 2007), developing countries invest only 1.0 percent of the value of their farm output on agricultural research, and much less if China is not included. It is one-third less than the historically low intensity of agricultural R&D in high-income countries in 2000–04.

Three more stylized facts about government distortions to agricultural incentives thus can be listed:

- **Fact 17:** Even when decoupled payments are added to total support payments, trade policy instruments (export and import taxes, subsidies or quantitative restrictions plus dual exchange rates) account for no less than three-fifths of the enhanced estimates of agricultural NRAs, and hence for an even larger share of their global welfare cost (since trade measures also tax consumers, and welfare costs are proportional to the square of a trade tax), with domestic subsidies to or taxes on farm output making only minor contributions.
- **Fact 18:** Direct subsidies to (or taxes on) food consumption have been very minor, hence consumer tax equivalents (CTEs) tend to be highly correlated with NRAs for agricultural products.
- **Fact 19:** Subsidies to farm inputs, and support for public agricultural research, have been common but have added little to overall farmer assistance in high-income countries, and have done very little to offset the effective taxation of farmers in developing countries as reflected in their RRAs.

Contribution to Rising RRA of Reforms in Nonfarm Sectors

Trade policies have contributed even more to agricultural distortions than indicated in the NRA and CTE estimates in Tables 2.8 and 2.9, because they are also responsible for all of the estimated distortions to the NRA facing producers of nonfarm tradable goods. Most of the country case studies contributing to the World Bank's Agricultural Distortions database were able to include only tariffs (in addition to exchange rate distortions) in their estimates of nonagricultural NRAs. They therefore understate those NRAs, especially in earlier decades when nontariff barriers to imports of manufactures were rife. Hence they also understate the contribution of the decline in those rates to the rise in the RRA. Notwithstanding those biases, that latter contribution is still estimated to have been very substantial. To see this, we report in Table 2.10 what the RRA would have been in different regions in 2000–04 had the NRA for nonagricultural tradable

Table 2.10. *Contribution to change in RRA since 1984 of NRA for nonfarm tradables, by region (percent)*

	Estimated RRA	Estimated RRA	Counterfactual RRA[a]	Proportion of RRA change since 1984 due to change in NRA nonagric.
	1960–84	2000–04	2000–04	
Africa	−25.0	−18.0	−17.4	−0.08
Latin America	−30.6	−0.5	−15.0	0.48
South Asia[b]	−47.1	3.4	−42.8	0.91
Southeast Asia + China[b]	−56.7	1.5	−20.9	0.38
Japan, Korea, Taiwan	40.7	136.7	124.3	0.13
Western Europe	46.2	34.9	29.8	−0.46
North America	3.5	15.5	10.5	0.41
Australia/New Zealand	−10.6	−1.4	−15.8	1.57
All developing countries (incl. Korea and Taiwan)[b]	−47.3	3.1	−22.5	0.51
All high-income countries	22.4	32.1	25.7	0.66

[a] The counterfactual RRA is the RRA computed using the 2000–04 NRA for agriculture and the 1960–84 NRA for nonagriculture.

[b] Regional aggregate includes back casting, which means estimates for China pre-1981 and India pre-1965 are based on the assumption that the nominal rate of assistance to agriculture in those years was the same as the average NRA estimates for those countries for 1981–89 and 1965–74, respectively, and that the gross value of production in those missing years is that which gives the same average share of value of production in total world production in 1981–89 and 1965–74, respectively.

Source: Authors' derivation, using distortion data in Anderson and Valenzuela (2008).

goods not changed from its (relatively high) level during the pre-reform period of 1960–84. The final column of that table indicates that slightly over half of the rise in the RRA for developing countries since the mid-1980s, and two-thirds of the RRA rise for high-income countries, is due to falls in protection to producers of nonfarm tradable goods. This suggests much of the reduction in relative prices faced by farmers over the past two decades can be attributed to general trade liberalization rather than to specific farm policy reform.

Our final stylized fact is thus:

- **Fact 20:** The fall in assistance to producers of nonfarm tradable goods has contributed to more than half the rise since the mid-1980s in the RRA for developing countries, and as much as two-thirds of the RRA rise for high-income countries.

WHAT STILL NEEDS EXPLAINING

The above stylized facts confirm some things that were well established and understood two decades ago and highlight that much variation in NRAs and RRAs across countries and products and time still remains and thus requires explanation.

The most robust facts have to do with the correlation between assistance to farmers and both per capita income and agricultural comparative advantage. Reasons for expecting those facts have been spelt out in such writings and Anderson, Hayami and Others (1986), Krueger (1992), Anderson (1995) and de Gorter and Swinnen (2002). To see how much they can account for the variation across countries and time in national NRAs and RRAs that is captured in the new agricultural distortions panel database, Tables 2.11 and 2.12 report the simplest of OLS regressions using the full panel of data for all focus countries from 1955 to 2007. The log of real GDP per capita on its own accounts for nearly 40 percent of the national average NRA variation. Figure 2.2 suggests a quadratic relationship, and indeed when the square of that income variable is included the adjusted R^2 rises to 0.44. If the log of arable land per capita is added, to represent the factor endowment ratio affecting agricultural comparative advantage, the adjusted R^2 increases further to 0.55.[18] In each of those regressions, all variables are significant at the 1 percent level and with the expected sign.[19] When we switch the variable being explained from NRA to RRA, the adjusted R^2 is a few points higher in each case and is 0.59 in the case of the final regression (Table 2.12). That is, these two exogenous variables

[18] Logs of these variables are used to reduce the influence of outliers.
[19] So too is a variable representing comparative advantage in nonfarm primary products (net exports as a proportion of the sum of gross exports and gross imports of such products), although it has little impact on the R^2 and slightly reduces the adjusted R^2 so we have not included that regression in the table.

Table 2.11. *Regression results to account for variations in national average agricultural NRAs, all focus countries, 1955 to 2007 (using ordinary least squares regression)*

Log(real GDP per capita)	0.207*** (0.00535)	−0.943*** (0.0614)	−0.943*** (0.0558)	−0.989*** (0.0682)
Log(real GDP per capita) squared		0.0741*** (0.00395)	0.0743*** (0.00359)	0.0765*** (0.00432)
Log(Arable land per capita)			−0.204*** (0.00851)	−0.211*** (0.00931)
TSI,[a] nonfarm primary products				0.0508*** (0.0165)
Constant	−1.356*** (0.0422)	2.875*** (0.229)	2.593*** (0.208)	2.805*** (0.260)
Observations	2584	2584	2551	2095
Adjusted R^2	0.37	0.44	0.55	0.54

Standard errors in parentheses *** $p<0.01$, ** $p<0.05$, * $p<0.10$
[a] Trade Specialization Index = net exports divided by exports plus imports of nonfarm primary products.
Source: Authors' derivation, using distortion data in Anderson and Valenzuela (2008).

alone – per capita income and a factor endowment indicator of agricultural comparative advantage – explain a little more than half of the variation in the full panel's NRAs and RRAs.

When those panel data are separated by region, however, there is a considerable range in the extent to which those two variables account for the variation across countries. In the case of RRAs, Table 2.12 shows that the adjusted R^2 is a high 0.72 for Asia, a moderate 0.33 and 0.42 for Latin America and high-income countries, respectively, but just 0.07 for Africa. Clearly there is a great deal more heterogeneity among countries to be explained outside of Asia, and especially in Africa.

Incidentally, we used the NRA counterparts to the RRA regressions in Table 2.12 to predict the NRAs in nonfocus countries in each developing country region, so as to explore the representativeness of the sample of focus developing countries (which account for 91 percent of agricultural output of all developing countries, as compared with virtually 100 percent for high-income countries). Those predictions, shown in Table 2.13, suggest three things. One is that the impact on the aggregate average NRA for developing countries of omitting those nonfocus countries is very minor, changing it in 2000–04 only from 9 to 8 percent (and hence affecting the

Table 2.12. *Regression results to account for variations in national average RRAs, focus countries by region, 1955 to 2007 (using ordinary least squares regression)*

	Asia	Africa	Latin America	High–income countries	All focus countries
Log (Real GDP per capita)	−1.847*** (0.160)	−0.481*** (0.185)	−1.634*** (0.371)	−1.871* (1.103)	−0.713*** (0.0657)
Log (Real GDP per cap.) squared	0.157*** (0.0114)	0.0448*** (0.0143)	0.112*** (0.0241)	0.122** (0.0580)	0.0627*** (0.00418)
Log(Arable land per capita)	−0.100*** (0.0236)	−0.0170 (0.0172)	−0.215*** (0.0180)	−0.309*** (0.0179)	−0.228*** (0.00933)
Constant	4.894*** (0.558)	0.948 (0.597)	5.463*** (1.407)	6.897 (5.245)	1.382*** (0.250)
Observations	405	619	295	872	2336
Adjusted R–squared	0.72	0.07	0.33	0.42	0.59

Standard errors in parentheses *** $p<0.01$, ** $p<0.05$, * $p<0.10$

Source: Authors' derivation, using distortion data in Anderson and Valenzuela (2008).

estimated global NRA by only half of one percentage point). The second thing to note is that the predicted NRA for the developing countries of the Middle East and North Africa (excluding Egypt) is slightly above the estimated NRA for focus developing countries, because those MENA countries have relatively high per capita incomes and low agricultural comparative advantages – a finding that is consistent with the fact that this relatively hot and dry region has been protective of its mostly import-competing agricultural industries. And thirdly, for the other developing country regions, the missing developing countries have an average predicted NRA that is well below that estimated for the region's focus developing countries in 2000–04. This reflects the fact that the nonfocus countries of each region are poorer and/or more agrarian than the focus countries of the region. The differences are greatest for Africa and Asia, in each case averaging around 25 percentage points. For Africa, the predicted NRA for the two dozen plus nonfocus countries is –32 percent. (If new empirical estimates were to confirm that prediction, it would suggest the antiagricultural policy bias of the past is still a major problem for that region.)

Also well known two decades ago was that NRAs vary greatly across the product range, both within country groups and globally, and tend to be

Table 2.13. *Impact of including predicted nonfocus country NRAs[a] on the aggregate developing country NRA estimate for 2000 to 2004[b] (percent)*

	Share of focus countries in regional agricultural output[b]	Share of region in global agricultural output[b]	Predicted nonfocus developing countries' NRA[a]	Focus developing countries' estimated NRA	All developing countries' NRA[e]
	(1)	(2)	(3)	(4)	(5)
SSAfrica + Egypt[c]	92	6	−32	−7	−9
Asia	98	37	−14	12	11
Latin America	80	10	−7	5	3
M. East & N. Africa[d]	0	3	11	na	11
All developing countries (incl. Turkey)	91	55	−1	9	8

[a] Predictions are generated using the NRA counterparts to the RRA regressions in Table 2.12. The aggregate developing country NRA is a weighted average, with weights based on shares in column 2 times 100 minus the shares in column 1.

[b] Weighted averages, using farm production valued at undistorted prices as weights.

[c] The sub-Saharan African prediction is based on regression results for all focus African countries except South Africa and Egypt.

[d] The focus countries used for predicting the NRA for the developing countries of the MENA region (excluding Egypt) comprises all developing countries, including Turkey. The MENA countries for which pertinent data are available are Algeria, Iran, Iraq, Jordan, Lebanon, Libya, Morocco, Oman, Syria, Tunisia, and Yemen.

[e] Weighted average of columns 3 and 4, with weights based on shares in column 1.

Source: Authors' derivation, using distortion data in Anderson and Valenzuela (2008).

higher for import-competing producers than for exporters of the product in question. The former point is illustrated in Figure 2.6 above for the most important traded farm products, and the antitrade bias of farm policies is clear from Table 2.5. When the global NRAs for each of ten key traded products are regressed on the log of real GDP per capita, log of arable land per capita, and a dummy for to distinguish exportable from import-competing products, the adjusted R^2 is above 0.32 for beef, milk, rice, and wheat, and between 0.28 and 0.31 for pigmeat, poultry, soybean, and sugar (and 0.23 for cotton and 0.20 for maize – see Table 2.14). The income

Table 2.14. *Regression results to account for variations in product NRAs across all focus countries, 12 key covered products, 1955 to 2007 (using ordinary least squares regression)*

	Log(Real GDP per capita)	Log(Real GDP per capita) sq.	Log(Arable land per capita)	Exportable dummy[a]	Constant	No. of obs.[a]	Adjusted R^2
Rice	-2.014*** (0.154)	0.156*** (0.0100)	-0.392*** (0.0222)	-0.727*** (0.0453)	5.946*** (0.570)	1281	0.50
Wheat	-0.895*** (0.117)	0.0689*** (0.00735)	-0.162*** (0.0161)	-0.397*** (0.0369)	2.730*** (0.458)	1661	0.33
Maize	-0.419*** (0.0943)	0.0325*** (0.00606)	-0.166*** (0.0146)	-0.194*** (0.0294)	1.261*** (0.356)	1525	0.20
Soybean	0.959*** (0.344)	-0.0425** (0.0212)	-0.548*** (0.0368)	-0.127 (0.0892)	-5.239*** (1.365)	703	0.31
Sugar	-0.925*** (0.193)	0.0781*** (0.0123)	-0.239*** (0.0277)	-0.450*** (0.0601)	2.833*** (0.727)	1648	0.31
Cotton	-0.358*** (0.0925)	0.0314*** (0.00625)	0.00620 (0.0164)	-0.276*** (0.0442)	0.997*** (0.325)	883	0.23
Milk	-0.879*** (0.301)	0.0844*** (0.0184)	-0.356*** (0.0322)	-0.401*** (0.0847)	1.962 (1.203)	1389	0.32
Beef	-0.763*** (0.205)	0.0667*** (0.0122)	-0.280*** (0.0194)	-0.317*** (0.0467)	1.771** (0.849)	1426	0.43
Pigmeat	1.406*** (0.211)	-0.0716*** (0.0125)	-0.313*** (0.0186)	0.190*** (0.0445)	-6.754*** (0.885)	1213	0.28
Poultry	-1.693*** (0.351)	0.118*** (0.0209)	-0.485*** (0.0301)	-0.307*** (0.0795)	5.785*** (1.460)	1304	0.29

[a] Observations are included only in years when the product is tradable. The constant coefficient refers to importables, whereas for exportables, the coefficient on the exportables dummy needs to be added to that coefficient for the constant.

Source: Authors' derivation, using distortion data in Anderson and Valenzuela (2008).

coefficients are all highly significant with the expected signs, as are the coefficients for land endowment, except for cotton. The coefficients on the dummy variable used to distinguish exportable from import-competing products are significant at the 1 percent level for all but soybean, and have the expected sign in all cases except pigmeat. This table of results suggests that another area where further political economy analysis would be helpful is at the commodity level. In addition to seeking to explain the differences in R^2 values in that table, a more specific question is why some farm industries are more protected than others in both rich and poor countries (e.g., sugar, dairy), more taxed than others in poor countries (e.g., perennial tropical crops), and taxed in poor countries but subsidized in rich countries (even though they may be exported by the latter, as with cotton in the United States).

The tables and figures presented earlier provide but a beginning to the questions that might be posed following further scrutiny of the panel data. We conclude this section by simply listing some of the other questions that political economists might address, a few of which are taken up in the chapters that follow in this volume:

- What are the political economy forces behind the trend declines in positive agricultural NRAs in some high-income countries, and how do they differ from those in countries where agricultural NRAs remain or continue to grow?
- What are the political economy forces behind the more reforming developing countries that have reduced/eliminated their antiagricultural policy bias, and how do they differ from those in less successful countries where negative distortions to agricultural incentives remain?
- In particular, what explains the differing pace and timing of the reforms in the various reforming countries?
- What explains the exceptional developing country policy reversals in which the antiagricultural bias has worsened (such as in Zimbabwe from the mid-1990s and the reversion back to agricultural export taxation in Argentina after 2001)?
- What explains the choices of (typically n^{th} best) policy instruments, including exchange rates and the simultaneous use of measures that help and hurt farmers, and the differences across countries and changes over time in their relative contributions to the aggregate NRA?

- In particular, why have countries tended to have an antitrade bias in their distortions pattern within the agricultural sector?[20] What explains the exceptions such as export or import subsidies?
- What explains the evolution of policy instrument choice over time, including toward more decoupled forms of domestic support in some but not all high-income countries (e.g., single farm payments) and yet a continuing reluctance to end inefficient farm programs such as by providing one-off lump-sum buyouts?
- Why have governments used trade policy instruments when trying to reduce year-to-year fluctuations around trend levels of domestic prices for producers or consumers of some (but not all) farm products, rather than more efficient instruments?
- Why have societies tended to underinvest in what appear to be high-payoff public investments such as in agricultural research, rural infrastructure, and basic rural education and health, and instead spent scarce public funds on distortionary subsidies (e.g., credit, fertilizer) or charged inadequately for some other items (e.g., water, power, environmental damage), all of which tend to add to inequality by assisting large farmers more than small farmers?
- What influence have international institutional influences such as loan conditionality, GATT rounds, regional integration agreements, WTO accession, and nonreciprocal trade agreements (e.g., for former colonies and Least Developed Countries), and market forces such as the globalization of supermarkets and other firms along the value chain, had on the extent, pattern, and evolution of distortions to agricultural incentives, relative to domestic political forces, especially in bringing about reform during the past two decades in contrast to the earlier decades of worsening distortions analyzed by Krueger, Schiff and Valdes (and others) in the 1980s?

WILL MORE DEVELOPING COUNTRIES INCREASE ASSISTANCE TO FARMERS?

The first wave of densely populated industrializers (Britain, other Western Europe, then Japan, and then Korea and Taiwan) chose to slow the growth

---

[20] Theorists who have addressed this question in general provide some testable hypotheses that might also apply within the agricultural sector. See, for example, Long and Vousden (1991), McMillan (2001), and Limão and Panagariya (2007).

of food import dependence by raising their NRA for import-competing agriculture even as they were bringing down their NRA for nonfarm tradables, such that their RRA became increasingly above the neutral zero level. Only in the past decade or two has the world seen a second example of declining RRAs (the first one being in the mid-19th century in Europe), as the European Union (EU) began to reinstrument its assistance by moving toward decoupled payments. The reason for that exception has to do with the EU's unique institutional provision of supra-national support via its Common Agricultural Policy (CAP). As explained by Josling (2009), the decline in price supports in the EU is occurring largely because the budgetary cost of continuing past levels of support would have escalated following the EU membership expansion eastwards, with little if any of those extra payments going to the traditional lobbyists for the CAP.

This almost complete absence of examples of reforms aimed at reducing relative assistance to farmers is not inconsistent with the fact that the GATT and now WTO members have found it extremely difficult to conclude multilateral agreements to reduce support for agriculture. It begs a key question: Will more developing countries follow the example of earlier industrializers? The past close association of RRAs with rising per capita income and falling agricultural comparative advantage (see Figures 2.2 and 2.3) suggests that, in the absense of any new shocks to the political equilibria, one should expect this to continue in the decades ahead.

From a global viewpoint, the most important developing countries to watch are the largest and fastest growing, namely China and India, both of which also happen to be relatively densely populated and hence vulnerable to declines in their agricultural comparative advantages as they become more industrialized. When their RRA trends are mapped against per capita income for the past three-plus decades as in Figure 2.10, it is clear that to date China and India have been on the same trajectory as richer Northeast Asian economies.

One reason one might expect different government behavior now is because the earlier industrializers were not bound under GATT to keep down their agricultural protection. At the time of China's accession to WTO in December 2001, its NRA was 7.3 percent for just import-competing agriculture (Huang et al. 2009). Its average bound import tariff commitment was about twice that (16 percent in 2005), but what matters most is China's out-of-quota bindings on the items whose imports are restricted by tariff rate quotas. The latter tariff bindings as of 2005 were 65 percent for grains, 50 percent for sugar, and 40 percent for cotton (WTO, ITC and UNCTAD 2007, p. 60). China also has bindings on farm product-specific

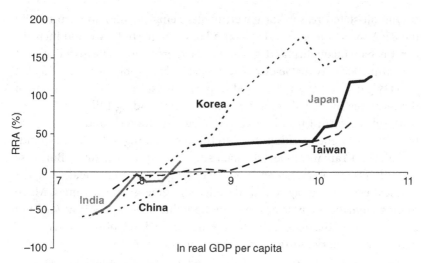

Figure 2.10. RRAs and log of real per capita GDP, China, India, and Northeast Asian focus economies, 1955[a] to 2005 (percent).

[a] From only 1965 for India and 1981 for China.

Source: Authors' derivation based on RRAs in Anderson and Valenzuela (2008).

domestic supports of 8.5 percent, and can provide another 8.5 percent as non-product specific assistance if it so wishes – a total of 17 percent NRA from domestic support measures alone, in addition to what is available through out-of-quota tariff protection. Clearly the legal commitments China made on acceding to WTO are a long way from current levels of domestic and border support for its farmers, and so are unlikely to constrain the government very much in the next decade or so[21]; and the legal constraints on Asia's developing countries that joined the WTO earlier (except for Korea) are even less constraining. For India, Pakistan, and Bangladesh, for example, their estimated NRAs for agricultural importables in 2000–04 are 34, 4, and 6 percent, respectively, whereas the average bound tariffs on their agricultural imports are 114, 96, and 189 percent, respectively (WTO, ITC and UNCTAD 2007). Also, like other developing countries, they have high bindings on product-specific domestic supports of 10 percent and another 10 percent for non-product-specific assistance, a total of 20 more percentage points of NRA that legally could come from domestic support measures – compared with currently 10 percent in India and less than 3 percent in the rest of South Asia (Anderson and Martin 2009, Chapter 1).

---

[21] For more on this point, see Anderson, Martin and Valenzuela (2009).

One oft-stated reason for governments being inclined to keep raising the RRA over time is that they fear a laissez faire strategy could increase rural-urban inequality and poverty and thereby generate social unrest (Hayami 2007). Available evidence suggests that problems of rural-urban poverty gaps have been alleviated in parts of Asia and Africa by some of the more mobile members of farm households finding full- or part-time work off the farm (including abroad as guest workers) and repatriating part of their higher earnings back to those remaining in farm households (Otsuka and Yamano 2006, Otsuka, Estudillo and Sawada 2009). But these are only fragmentary elements of the developments that are altering the political economy of agricultural policies in emerging economies. Much more systematic analysis of the evolving political economy is needed not only to address the question as to whether more developing countries will become more agricultural protectionist in the absence of external influences, but also to suggest politically feasible ways of countering that tendency of the past.

References

Anderson, J.E. and J.P. Neary (2005), *Measuring the Restrictiveness of International Trade Policy*, Cambridge MA: MIT Press.

Anderson, K. (1995), "Lobbying Incentives and the Pattern of Protection in Rich and Poor Countries," *Economic Development and Cultural Change* 43(2): 401–23, January.

Anderson, K. (ed.) (2009), *Distortions to Agricultural Incentives: A Global Perspective, 1955–2007*, London: Palgrave Macmillan and Washington DC: World Bank.

Anderson, K. (2010), "Krueger/Schiff/Valdés Revisited: Agricultural Price and Trade Policy Reform in Developing Countries Since the 1980s," *Applied Economic Perspectives and Policy* 32(2): 195–231, Summer.

Anderson, K. and J. Croser (2009), *National and Global Agricultural Trade and Welfare Reduction Indexes, 1955 to 2007*, Supplementary database at http://www.worldbank.org/agdistortions

(2010), "Coverage and Distribution of Assistance Across Countries and Products, 1955–2007," Appendix in this volume.

Anderson, K., Y. Hayami and Others (1986), *The Political Economy of Agricultural Protection: East Asia in International Perspective*, London: Allen and Unwin.

Anderson, K., M. Kurzweil, W. Martin, D. Sandri and E. Valenzuela (2008), "Measuring Distortions to Agricultural Incentives, Revisited," *World Trade Review* 7(4): 1–30.

Anderson, K., P.J. Lloyd, and D. MacLaren (2007), "Distortions to Agricultural Incentives in Australia Since World War II," *Economic Record* 83(263): 461–82.

Anderson, K. and W. Martin (eds.) (2009), *Distortions to Agricultural Incentives in Asia*, Washington DC: World Bank.

Anderson, K., W. Martin and E. Valenzuela (2006), "The Relative Importance of Global Agricultural Subsidies and Market Access," *World Trade Review* 5(3): 357–76.

(2009), "Long Run Implications of WTO Accession for Agriculture in China", Ch. 7 in I. Sheldon (ed.), *China's Agricultural Trade: Issues and Prospects*, St. Paul MN: International Agricultural Trade Research Consortium. http://iatrc.software. umn.edu/publications/proceedingsissues/proceedings_2007Jul-Beijing.html

Anderson, K. and W. Masters (eds.) (2009), *Distortions to Agricultural Incentives in Africa*, Washington DC: World Bank.

Anderson, K. and J. Swinnen (eds.) (2008), *Distortions to Agricultural Incentives in Europe's Transition Economies*, Washington DC: World Bank.

Anderson, K. and A. Valdés (eds.) (2008), *Distortions to Agricultural Incentives in Latin America*, Washington DC: World Bank.

Anderson, K. and E. Valenzuela (2008), *Global Estimates of Distortions to Agricultural Incentives, 1955 to 2007*, core database at http://www.worldbank.org/ agdistortions

Anderson, K. and L.A. Winters (2009), "International Trade and Migration Barriers," Ch. 8 in B. Lomborg (ed.), *Global Crises, Global Solutions* (2nd edition), Cambridge and New York: Cambridge University Press.

Bates, R.H. (1981), *Markets and States in Tropical Africa: The Political Basis of Agricultural Policies*, Berkeley: University of California Press.

de Gorter, H. and J.F.M. Swinnen (2002), "Political Economy of Agricultural Policies", pp. 2073–2123 in B. Gardner and G. Rausser (eds.), *The Handbook of Agricultural Economics, Volume 2*, Amsterdam: Elsevier.

Dervis, K., J. de Melo and S. Robinson (1981), "A General Equilibrium Analysis of Foreign Exchange Shortages in a Developing Country," *Economic Journal* 91: 891–906.

FAO (2007), FAOSTAT, available at http://www.fao.org (accessed June 2009).

Haberler, G. (1958), *Trends in International Trade: A Report by a Panel of Experts*, Geneva: General Agreement on Tariffs and Trade, October.

Hayami, Y. (2007), "An Emerging Agricultural Problem in High-Performing Asian Economies," Policy Research Working Paper 4312, World Bank, Washington DC.

Huang, J., S. Rozelle, W. Martin and Y. Liu (2009), "Distortions to Agricultural Incentives in China", Ch. 3 in K. Anderson and W. Martin (eds.), *Distortions to Agricultural Incentives in Asia*, Washington DC: World Bank.

Johnson, D.G. (1973), *World Agriculture in Disarray*, London: St Martin's Press (revised in 1991).

Josling, T. (2009), 'Western Europe', Ch. 5 in Anderson, K. (ed.) *Distortions to Agricultural Incentives: A Global Perspective, 1955–2007*, London: Palgrave Macmillan and Washington DC: World Bank.

Krueger, A.O. (1992), *The Political Economy of Agricultural Pricing Policy, Volume 5: A Synthesis of the Political Economy in Developing Countries*, Baltimore: Johns Hopkins University Press for the World Bank.

Krueger, A.O., M. Schiff and A. Valdés (1988), "Agricultural Incentives in Developing Countries: Measuring the Effect of Sectoral and Economy-wide Policies," *World Bank Economic Review* 2(3): 255–72, September.

(1991), *The Political Economy of Agricultural Pricing Policy, Volume 1: Latin America, Volume 2: Asia, and Volume 3: Africa and the Mediterranean*, Baltimore: Johns Hopkins University Press for the World Bank.

Lerner, A. (1936), "The Symmetry Between Import and Export Taxes," *Economica* 3(11): 306–13, August.

Limão, N. and A. Panagariya (2007), "Inequality and Endogenous Trade Policy Outcomes," *Journal of International Economics* 72(2): 292–309, July.

Lloyd, P.J. (1974), "A More General Theory of Price Distortions in an Open Economy," *Journal of International Economics* 4(4): 365–86, November.

Lloyd, P.J., J.L. Croser and K. Anderson (2010), "Global Distortions to Agricultural Markets: New Indicators of Trade and Welfare Impacts, 1960 to 2007," *Review of Development Economics* 14(2): 141–60, May.

Long, N.V. and N. Vousden (1991), "Protectionist Responses and Declining Industries," *Journal of International Economics* 30(1&2): 87–103, February.

McMillan, M. (2001), "Why Kill the Golden Goose? A Political-Economy Model of Export Taxation," *Review of Economics and Statistics* 83(1): 170–84, February.

OECD (2008), *Producer and Consumer Support Estimates* (online database accessed at http://www.oecd.org for 1986–2007 estimates; and OECD files for estimates using an earlier methodology for 1979–85).

(2009), *Agricultural Policies in Emerging Economies: Monitoring and Evaluation 2009*, Paris: Organization for Economic Co-operation and Development, March.

Orden, D., F. Cheng, H. Nguyen, U. Grote, M. Thomas, K. Mullen and D. Sun (2007), *Agricultural Producer Support Estimates for Developing Countries: Measurement Issues and Evidence from India, Indonesia, China and Vietnam*, IFPRI Research Report 152, Washington DC: International Food Policy Research Institute.

Otsuka, K., J.P. Estudillo and Y. Sawada (eds.) (2009), *Rural Poverty and Income Dynamics in Asia and Africa*, London and New York: Routledge.

Otsuka, K. and T. Yamano (2006), "Introduction to the Special Issue on the Role of Nonfarm Income in Poverty Reduction: Evidence from Asia and East Africa," *Agricultural Economics* 35 (supplement): 373–97, November.

Pardey, P.G., J. Alston, J. James, P. Glewwe, E. Binenbaum, T. Hurley and S. Wood (2007), *Science, Technology and Skills*, InSTePP Report, International Science & Technology Practice & Policy Center, University of Minnesota, October. (Prepared as a background paper for the World Bank's *World Development Report 2008*.)

Pursell, G., A. Gulati, and K. Gupta (2009), "India," Ch. 10 in K. Anderson and W. Martin (eds.), *Distortions to Agricultural Incentives in Asia*, Washington DC: World Bank.

Sandri, D., E. Valenzuela and K. Anderson (2007), "Economic and Trade Indicators, 1960 to 2004," Agricultural Distortions Working Paper 02, World Bank, Washington DC. Posted at http://www.worldbank.org/agdistortions

Tyers, R. and K. Anderson (1992), *Disarray in World Food Markets: A Quantitative Assessment*, Cambridge and New York: Cambridge University Press.

Valdés, A. (1996), "Surveillance of Agricultural Price and Trade Policy in Latin America During Major Policy Reforms," World Bank Discussion Paper No. 349, Washington DC, November.

Valdés, A. (ed.) (2000), 'Agricultural Support Policies in Transition Economies', World Bank Technical Paper No. 470, Washington DC, May.

World Bank (2007), *World Development Indicators*, Washington DC: World Bank.

(2008), *Commodity Price Data*, Washington DC: World Bank.

WTO, ITC and UNCTAD (2007), *World Tariff Profiles 2006*, Geneva: World Trade Organization.

PART TWO

CONCEPTUAL FRAMEWORKS AND
HISTORICAL ORIGINS

THREE

Political Economy of Agricultural Distortions

The Literature to Date

Johan F. M. Swinnen[1]

The 1980s and the first half of the 1990s were a very active period in the field of political economy of agricultural protection and distortions. The research was triggered by a combination of factors. First and foremost, there was the puzzling question: Why was agriculture supported in rich countries and taxed in poor countries? Second, emerging general theories of "new political economy" were coming out from the University of Chicago with the important contributions of Stigler (1971), Peltzman (1976) and Becker (1983), from the public choice school by Buchanan and Tullock (1962), and from the influential work by Downs (1957) and Olson (1965). A third factor was the arrival of new data, in particular the developing country dataset assembled as part of the World Bank study organized by Krueger, Schiff and Valdés (1988, 1991) and the high-income dataset compiled by Anderson, Hayami and Others (1986). The combination of an intriguing question, a rich set of new general theories to apply, and fascinating data induced a rich and vast literature on the political economy of agricultural distortions in the 1980s and the first part of the 1990s, with important contributions by, among others, Kym Anderson, Robert Bates, Harry de Gorter, Bruce Gardner, Yujiro Hayami, and Gordon Rausser. In our chapter for the *Handbook of Agricultural Economics*, Harry de Gorter and I reviewed most of this empirical and theoretical literature on the political economy of agricultural economics (de Gorter and Swinnen 2002).

Research interest in the political economy of agricultural policies was waning in the second half of the 1990s and has been less intensive in the

[1] The author is grateful to Xiang Tao for research assistance, to Harry de Gorter, Alessandro Olper, and Gordon Rausser for many discussions and insights on this issue, and to Kym Anderson for collaboration and encouragement on this project.

past decade – although some important contributions have been made, as explained below.

Some of the conditions that sparked an intense interest in the political economy of agricultural policies in the 1980s are present again at this moment. First, there are new and innovative datasets available, the most important being the global dataset compiled by the World Bank's agricultural distortions project (Anderson and Valenzuela 2008). This new data set provides a much wider and longer series of data on agricultural distortions than has ever been available. In addition, there are much better series of data available on some (potential) explanatory variables from a variety of sources. This holds in particular for institutional and political variables, where data series have been created or improved, especially by the Database of Political Institutions (DPI) project under the auspices of the World Bank (see Beck et al. (2001), since updated).

Second, there have been important new developments in political economy in other parts of the economics profession. This includes extensions of the Grossman and Helpman (1994, 1995, 2001, 2002) model in the field of the political economy of trade policies, by Acemoglu, Johnson and Robinson (2001) and colleagues on the interactions between institutions and policy making, by Baron and Ferejohn (1989) and colleagues on decision-making rules and the role of agenda setting; by North, Wallis and Weingast (2009) and colleagues on limited access orders, by Roland (2000) and colleagues on the political economy of transition, by Shleifer (1997) and colleagues on the role of bureaucracies and corruption in policy making, and by Persson and Tabellini (2000, 2003) on the "political economics" of fiscal policy and macroeconomic policy and on the role of constitutions. There are a number of books and survey papers that provide good overviews of these recent developments. They include Roland (2000), Grossman and Helpman (2001, 2002), Persson and Tabellini (2000, 2003), Gawande and Krishna (2003), Acemoglu and Robinson (2006), Weingast and Wittman (2006), Dewan and Shepsle (2008a,b) and Rausser, Swinnen and Zusman (2010). See also the next chapter in this volume (Rausser and Roland 2010). While the present chapter cannot review this entire literature, it focuses on a selection of these developments, theoretical and empirical, which appear particularly relevant for the study of the political economy of agricultural distortions.

The third reason for the return to analyzing reasons for agricultural distortions is that there are new questions to be addressed. One is how important institutional and political reforms in the 1980s and the 1990s have affected agricultural distortions. In particular, how have they been affected by changes in international organizations and international trade agreements, including the Uruguay Round Agreement on Agriculture, the establishment of the WTO, EU enlargement, and preferential trading agreements such as NAFTA?

This chapter begins with a brief summary of insights from the earlier literature and then reviews new insights of the general political economy literature, focusing particularly on those parts that are most relevant for understanding the determinants of (changes in) agricultural distortions.[2] The last section of the chapter draws specific implications for empirical analyses of the political economy of agricultural distortions.

A BRIEF SUMMARY OF THE LITERATURE TO THE MID-1990s[3]

Empirical evidence on agricultural protection/taxation that emerged from numerous studies in the 1980s and the 1990s can be summarized by three patterns: the "development pattern," the "antitrade pattern," and the "anti-comparative advantage pattern" (or "relative income pattern").[4]

The "development pattern" refers both to observations on the positive correlation between agricultural protection and average country incomes across countries and on the historically observed shift from taxation to protection of agricultural producers that countries make as they develop economically.

The "antitrade pattern" refers to the observation that import-competing sectors (products) tend to be more assisted (or taxed less) than sectors producing exportable products.

The "anti-comparative advantage pattern" [or "relative income pattern"] refers to the observation that protection is lower (or taxation higher) for products with a comparative advantage and that protection increases when farm incomes (or incomes in particular farm industries) fall relative to those in the rest of the economy. The latter may occur for any of several reasons, such as the world market terms of trade shifting against

---

[2] Important new contributions on the issue of instrument choice in agricultural policy are not reviewed here, but can be found in de Gorter (2008).

[3] See de Gorter and Swinnen (2002) for a more extensive summary and review of that literature.

[4] See Anderson, Hayami and Others (1986), Honma and Hayami (1986) and Lindert (1991) for countries of North America and East Asia; Bates (1989) and Krueger, Schiff and Valdés (1988, 1991) for developing countries; Tracy (1989) and Swinnen, Banerjee and de Gorter (2001) for the specific evolution of farm protection in Western European countries; and Gardner (1987) for a perspective on the United States.

the commodity, or exchange rate fluctuations, or because of technological innovations that reduce incomes from producing a specific commodity.[5]

Political Economy Explanations

These global patterns of agricultural distortions cannot be explained by economic arguments, but are consistent with predictions from political economy theories. While a large variety of arguments and variables have been included in the models, and with the risk of oversimplifying the insights from the literature, the political economy explanations forwarded in the 1980s and the 1990s focused importantly on (economic) structural factors. In particular, several studies have explained how changes in structural conditions in an economy have an impact on the costs of distribution and distortions associated with protection, the intensity of political activities, and the ability to organize politically and influence the government.[6]

As average incomes increase in an economy, changes in the structure of the economy affect the distribution and the size of political costs and benefits of agricultural protection and thus the governments' political incentives in decision making. For example, the share of food in consumer expenditures falls as a share of total expenditure, reducing the opposition to agricultural protection of not only consumers but also capital owners in other sectors, who oppose the (wage) inflation pressures that come from increased food costs with agricultural protection.

Another factor that coincides with economic growth is a declining share of agriculture in employment. With a declining number of farmers (in relative terms), the per-unit costs of increasing farm incomes through protection decrease for the rest of society.

Further, typically incomes in the rest of the economy grow faster than in agriculture in the course of a country's economic development. This creates political incentives, both on the demand side (farmers) and on the supply side (politicians), to exchange government transfer for political support. When incomes from farming decline relative to opportunities in other sectors, farmers look for nonmarket sources of income such as government support, either because returns to investment in lobbying

---

[5] Technological innovation effects can come both from within agriculture or from without. For example, several studies have shown that innovations in agricultural research in the presence of inelastic demand for food may lead to a sufficient decline in farm prices as to the make farmers worse off.

[6] See, for example, Anderson (1995), Bates and Rogerson (1980) and Swinnen (1994) for theoretical analyses of the impact of these structural variables on agricultural policy.

activities are larger than in market activities, or because willingness to vote for and support politicians is strong. For similar reasons, governments are more likely to support sectors with a comparative disadvantage than sectors with a comparative advantage.[7] These explanations are consistent with observations of agricultural protection being countercyclical to market conditions.

Political economy theories predict that exports will be subsidized less (or taxed more) than imports because of differences in demand and supply elasticities. The distortions (deadweight costs) and transfer costs of policy intervention typically increase with the commodity's trade balance, that is, when net exports increase. Another factor is the differential effect on government border tax revenues. Therefore, protection of the sector in many countries is found to increase with decreases in their agricultural trade surplus.

With a declining share of agriculture in employment, studies drawing on Olson's (1965) logic of collection action argument have hypothesized that this makes political organization of farmers less costly and therefore is likely to increase effective lobbying of farmers.

Empirical Studies

The vast majority of empirical studies on agricultural protection were cross-sectional studies or those using panel data with relatively short time periods. While they yielded important insights, the observed trend relationships mask strong occasional fluctuations in protection levels, generally coinciding with periods of general macroeconomic depression and severe food shortages. Such fluctuations demonstrate how sensitive and responsive agricultural protection (income transfers) can be to the external changes. Fluctuations in support to agriculture are clearly visible in the few historical studies using time-series data and econometric analyses, such as Gardner (1987). However, these historical studies focus on a single country, making it difficult to generalize.

Implications

An important, and obvious, contribution of the new World Bank dataset by Anderson and Valenzuela (2008) is to provide a much larger dataset of

---

[7] The relative income hypothesis in agricultural policy is developed formally in de Gorter and Tsur (1991) and Swinnen and de Gorter (1993). Related, more general theories are provided by Hillman (1982, 1989) and Krueger (1974). An earlier approach, although differently formulated, is Corden's (1974) conservative social welfare function.

pooled time-series and cross-section data for testing the relative importance of these various theories. Another potential advantage/contribution
is that the more extensive dataset will contribute better insights by distinguishing between the "observational equivalence" of competing explanations. This was constrained in previous studies by data limitations. For
example, the negative relationship between the share of farmers in the
economy and agricultural protection is explained both by the increased
effectiveness of political organization argument and by the reduced cost of
redistribution argument.

RECENT DEVELOPMENTS IN THE LITERATURE

Interest in the field of political economy of agricultural distortions was
waning in the second part of the 1990s, once the above arguments became
more established and the puzzling question of why agriculture was subsidized in rich countries and taxed in poor countries apparently received an
answer. However, since then, important developments have occurred in
the general political economy literature, including important new insights
on the political economy of agricultural policies. The most pertinent of
those new developments and insights are reviewed in what follows. The
discussion is organized under several headings, and in each I start with
some general developments and end with a discussion of implications for
studies on agricultural policies.

Trade Theory: Growth of the Grossman-Helpman Model

The widespread presence of trade distortions – despite centuries of economists' advise in favor of free trade – have puzzled economists for a long
time and have contributed to a vast literature on the political economy of
trade (see Rodrik [1995] for an extensive survey). This literature is closely
related to studies on the political economy of agricultural policies and has
served as a source of inspiration since many distortions in agricultural
markets are trade distortions.

The literature on the political economy of trade policy was transformed
by the "Protection for Sale" paper of Grossman and Helpman (1994). The
fact that the Grossman-Helpman (GH) model has become the standard
model in this field is remarkable, given the fact that the predictions of
the original model were inconsistent with some of the basic empirically
observed relationships on trade distortions, including basic patterns of
agricultural distortions as summarized above. For example, the GH model
does not predict that protection is countercyclical to market incomes.

Neither does it predict that sectors in (relative) economic decline will be protected.

Surveys of the political economy of trade literature indicate two useful characteristics of the GH model. According to Rodrik (1995), the main attraction of the GH model is that it provides clear-cut micro foundations for lobbying and its effects in a tractable and fairly general setting. According to Gawande and Krishna (2003), another major advantage of the GH model is for empirical applications: It allows one to go beyond structural econometric models and to relate empirical specifications more closely with theoretical models. The rest of this section focuses on the theoretical developments and the empirical issues are discussed in the next section.

Instead of dismissing the model because of its obvious inconsistencies with the real world, various authors have used the basic structure of the GH model and have modified it to make its theoretical predictions more consistent with reality.

For example, Baldwin and Robert-Nicoud (2007) have expanded the GH model to explain the support that goes to declining industries. They do this by incorporating an asymmetry in the ability of interest groups to appropriate the benefits of lobbying. In an expanding industry, policy-created rents attract new entry that erodes those rents, whereas in declining industries, this is not the case. Since sunk market-entry costs create quasi-rents, profits in declining industries can be raised without attracting entry (as long as the level of quasi-rents is not raised above a normal rate of return on the sunk capital). The result is that losers lobby harder, and government policy reflects this.

Cadot, de Melo and Olarreaga (2004) adjust the GH model to make it more consistent with empirical observations by introducing factor-market rivalry and input-output linkages. These extensions of the model give rise to counter lobbying, which yields results that protection escalates with the degree of processing and that rich countries protect agriculture more than industry whereas poor countries do the reverse.

The importance of downstream linkages is also emphasized by Francois, Nelson and Pelkmans-Balaoing (2008). They use a computable general equilibrium (CGE) analysis that partly draws on the GH model to show the importance of the strength of downstream linkages for political weights and its effect on redistributive policy.

Implications

These results are more in line with empirical observations and provide interesting hypotheses for further testing. In particular, the relationship between farms and agribusiness and food companies (or between raw materials and processed farm products) is sometimes mentioned but seldom tested in studies. The World Bank's agricultural distortions database (Anderson and Valenzuela 2008), and in particular its incorporation into the GTAP datasets (Valenzuela and Anderson 2008), provides an important opportunity to test this relationship, because in the past, it was often not possible to separate primary and processed farm products. There is a complex interaction between them. For example, while farmers may be many and dispersed, often food processing and agribusiness companies are few and concentrated, and hence it is easier for them than for farmers to organize. They are also typically more capital intensive than farms, and their shares of employment and GDP decline much slower with economic development than those of primary agriculture (Figure 3.1). This implies that their predicted structural relationships would differ.

Empirical Analyses: Testing the Grossman-Helpman Model

The empirical literature on the political economy of trade policy has focused strongly on testing the implications of the factor-endowments

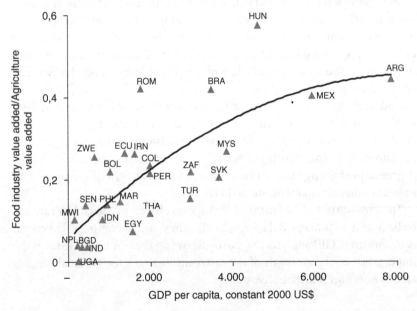

Figure 3.1. Relative importance of food industry and agriculture with development. *Source*: World Bank (2008).

and sector-specific models (Mayda and Rodrik 2005). The early empirical work, at least until the late 1980s, mostly involved the estimation of correlations between trade policies and various political economy factors that had been conjectured to be relevant in determining trade policy (Gawande and Krishna 2003). More recently, developments in the theoretical literature were accompanied by new empirical studies, for two reasons. First, the growth in importance of the GH model in the theoretical literature induced a response by empirical analysts trying to test its predictions. Second, as mentioned already, one of the major advantages of the GH model in empirical work is that it allows one to go beyond the structural econometric models, which characterized much empirical work in the 1980s, and to relate the empirical specifications more closely to the theoretical models.

However, there are several problems with empirical analyses based on the GH model. First, the estimated importance of lobbying is very small. For example, studies by Goldberg and Maggi (1999) and Gawande and Bandyopadhyay (2000) estimate that the weight associated with lobbying is very low and the weight for national welfare in the politicians' objective function is much higher than expected. This surprising empirical result has induced several researchers to search for adjustments of the empirical specifications to reduce the estimates of the domestic welfare weight in the political objective function. For example, alternative assumptions have been made by Lopez and Matschke (2006) and Lopez (2008) on the import demand functions, by Mitra, Thomakos and Ulubasoglu (2006) on the political organization schemes, by Gawande and Li (2004) on the effectiveness of lobby contributions, by Facchini, Van Biesebrouck and Willmann (2006) on rent capturing, and by Francois, Nelson and Pelkmans-Balaoing (2008), who use a CGE approach, to assess the weights indirectly.

Second, to estimate the GH model empirically requires data on lobbying. This makes estimating the model interesting for the United States, where data on lobbying through political action committees (PAC) are available (Bombardini 2005). However, this is typically not the case in other countries, which makes such estimations more problematic. There are a few studies that have tried to estimate the GH model for other countries. They include Gawande, Singuinetti and Bohara (2005) on Mercosur; Mitra, Thomakos and Ulubasoglu (2006) on Turkey; and Belloc and Guerrieri (2008) on the EU. However, where data on actual lobbying are not available, lobby activities are proxied by other indicators in these studies. Typically these proxies are quite ad hoc. For example, the Gawande, Singuinetti and Bohara (2005) study on Mercosur takes industries whose imports surpass the sample mean as actively lobbying for protection. Mitra (1999) makes lobby formation endogenous in the GH framework but as a discrete (0–1) process, hence not accounting for heterogeneity within a sector. Bombardini (2005) extends this and shows (theoretically and empirically) how US firms of different sizes have different incentives to participate in lobbying.

Implications

While there appears considerable enthusiasm in this literature as to the benefits of the GH model for more careful econometric work, these benefits appear limited for broad application to agricultural policy. Actual data on lobbying are typically not available outside the United States. Not surprisingly, the only GH applications in agriculture, as far as I know, are to U.S. agricultural policies by Gawande and Hoekman (2006) and to protection of US food industries by Lopez (2008). In other countries, the need to use proxies means that the studies have to rely on indicators used already in earlier structural models – or worse! In fact, the two general applications of the GH model to the EU, by Belloc and Guerrieri (2008) and Francois, Nelson and Pelkmans-Balaoing (2008), both assume ex ante that agriculture enjoys a "privileged position for historical reasons" and give agriculture an ad hoc dummy with a high value for lobbying – hence not reflecting careful analysis or progress on this issue.

The Role of Ideology and Political Institutions

While the importance of political systems for policy (and thus agricultural policy distortions) has long been emphasized, for example in the seminal work by Buchanan and Tullock (1962), the past decade and a half has witnessed a growing set of studies analyzing the roles of political regimes and ideology on policy making.

Persson and Tabellini (2000, 2003) have made important recent contributions, both theoretically and empirically, in analyzing the relationship between electoral systems and economic policy. To relate some of these insights to agricultural policy making, consider the political regime (or the "constitutional choice" in the framework of, e.g., Aghion, Alesina and Trebbi 2004) as providing the degree of "insulation" for policy makers. As such, the political regime determines to what extent the government, once appointed, can rule without ex post control, what type of majorities it needs to ensure to pass legislation, whether groups have veto power, and so on. A crucial factor is (information on) the nature of the politicians who will form the government (that is, the ruler's preferences): Will they implement policies that are good or bad for social welfare if given authority to rule without control? Another factor is how different mechanisms translate voter preferences into controls on government, majority formations, and hence, policies. These issues not only relate to the differential effects of democracy and autocratic regimes (Acemoglu and Robinson 2006, North, Wallis and Weingast 2009), but also those between different electoral systems, such as proportional versus majoritarian systems (Rogowski and Kayser 2002, Roelfsema 2004), and the autonomy given to bureaucrats and implementing institutions (Prendergast 2007).

To illustrate the importance of these issues for agricultural policy, I draw on a recent application of these issues to decision making on agricultural policy in the European Union. Pokrivcak, Crombez and Swinnen (2006) show how agricultural policy reforms there are determined by a complex interaction of majority voting rules, changes in the external environment, and the preferences of the European Commission (the agenda setting bureaucracy in Brussels). The authors show that reforms are not possible unless external changes are sufficiently large and the influence of the bureaucracy depends on voting rules (an example of the more general principle on insulation discussed above).

In terms of empirical predictions, it is intuitive that a greater insulation of decision-makers implies that they can follow their private preferences to a greater extent. However, this in itself has little predictive power, since there is no direct relationship to be expected between the preferences of rulers and the nature of the political regime on issues such as protectionism (O'Rourke and Taylor 2007). Intuitively one would expect that there may be more variation in policy choices under dictatorial regimes than under democracy, ceteris paribus, if dictatorial leaders are less constrained in setting policies. This is consistent with Olper's (2007) finding that his regression model works better in democracies than in dictatorships as the government response to pressure from interest groups is stronger in democracies. This may also be the reason why early studies with simple relations between agricultural policy and political regimes in cross-section studies find limited impact (Beghin and Kherallah 1994).

An interesting approach to deal with some of these issues is by Dutt and Mitra (2005), who focus on the impact of ideology but interact the ideology variable with an indicator of the structure of the economy (meaning its relative resource endowment) and an indicator for political liberties, to measure the conditional impact of ideology. Interestingly, they find that a more left-wing government (that is, one that attaches higher weight on the welfare of workers/labor) is more protectionist in the case of capital-abundant countries but less protectionist in the case of capital-scare countries. They find nuanced evidence of the impact of political institutions. They interpret their results as follows: Dictators who have consolidated their power may not face any electoral threats and may have fewer incentives to formulate trade policies according to their ideological affinities. However, if they do decide to favor their core constituent groups, they face less constraints in implementing redistributive trade policies.

An application of this model to agricultural policy is not straightforward, as increasing food costs through agricultural protection hurts both workers and industrial capital. Hence rulers who support "labor" and "capital" would both oppose agricultural protection – as they did in reality (see Chapter 6 in this volume by Swinnen [2009] on the history of agricultural protection in Europe). In this sense, distinguishing between right-wing versus left-wing rulers may not yield robust or useful results. For example, right-wing dictators may be more inclined to support agriculture if agriculture is dominated by large-scale farms and estates, typical supporters of right-wing rules; and not if agriculture is dominated by small farms and peasants, a potential revolutionary group. Left-wing regimes may do the opposite.

The first studies (and the only one so far) that have tried to econometrically estimate these effects on agricultural policies, while taking into account some of these interaction effects with political regimes and structural conditions, are by Olper (2001, 2007). He finds indeed that, on average, right-wing governments are more protectionist than left-wing governments in agriculture; but that left-wing governments may support agriculture in more unequal societies. This is consistent with studies by Bates (1983), who argues that socialist governments in Africa tend to impose lower commodity prices on farmers, and by Swinnen (2009) who finds that right-wing governments in Europe (such as those dominated by Catholic parties and conservative parties, including the Nazi party in Germany) tend to support farm interests and increase protection.

Implications
Integrating measures of political regimes and ideology into econometric models is essential, in particular since indicator data on these variables are now available for a wide group of countries. Hence, in combination with the new World Bank agricultural distortions database (Anderson and Valenzuela 2008), this presents an excellent opportunity for further tests

of the ideology and political regime effects. In addition, the combination of cross-section and time-series data should allow a more careful estimate of the effect of political regime changes. However, it appears important to test sufficiently complex interactions between ideology, economic structure, and protection to understand better how this web of interactions affects agricultural distortions. In this respect, further improvements can be made.

First, interaction effects as used in the studies listed earlier in the Chapter may require further refinement. Consider, for example, agricultural policies of extreme left-wing regimes. Communist dictators such as Stalin in Russia, Mao in China, and Hoxha in Albania heavily taxed agriculture; yet farmers were subsidized under Brezhnev in the Soviet Union and in most East European Communist countries in the 1970s and 1980s.

Second, the political institution variables used can be improved. Thies and Porsche (2007) provide an interesting extension with a much larger set of political variables than that used in other studies.

Third, cross-section studies have their limitations. Long-run time-series studies allow us to measure the impact of shifts from one system to the next and to measure changes in political institutions more carefully. For example, Swinnen, Banerjee and de Gorter (2001) find that some of the changes in voting rules in Belgium had effects on agricultural protection, while others had no effect. In particular, those changes in electoral rules that disproportionately benefited people involved in agriculture (e.g., by extending voting rights to small farmers and tenants in the early 20th century) induced an increase in agricultural protection, while electoral changes (such as extending voting rights to women) did not affect agricultural protection as they increased voting rights both of those in favor and of those against protection.

The Role of Inequality

A series of recent studies have emphasized the importance of inequality, both on political institutions (Acemoglu and Robinson 2006) and on government policies, including trade policy (Dutt and Mitra 2002) and agricultural policy (Olper 2007). Moreover, Dutt and Mitra (2002) find that a rise in asset inequality is likely to have different effects in a labor-abundant than in a capital-abundant economy – and these findings appear robust in both cross-section and time-series regressions. Olper (2007) finds that agricultural protection is negatively related to inequality. This is counter to the traditional Olson-type arguments that large farmers are better at overcoming collective action problems. In contrast, La Ferrara (2002) argues the opposite, that is, that inequality may cause collective action problems that could explain why protection is negatively correlated with inequality. There is also historical evidence on this in Europe: Strong inequality in England, Germany, and France weakened the pro-tariff demands of large grain farmers at the end of the 19th century, as they were opposed by small farmers who were often livestock producers. In France, large and small farms were even organized in different unions and associated with different political parties. However, Olper (2007) finds that the inequality effect is conditional on the ideology of the ruling government. Left-wing governments, while on average supporting agriculture less, tend to support farmers more in unequal societies.

A longer time perspective on the impact of inequality is offered in papers by Acemoglu and Robinson (2000, 2001, 2006). They theoretically and empirically demonstrate the dynamic interactions of initial structural conditions of a country, its constitutional design, the nature of the government, and the redistributive policies implemented by the government. In societies with highly unequal distributions of assets (such as land), societies tend to be politically unstable, moving back and forward between (left-wing) revolutionary efforts of the poor trying to redistribute wealth through revolutions and land reforms and (right-wing) dictatorships trying to protect the concentrated resources of the rich. In more equal societies, redistribution can occur within a more stable democratic setting. Hence, these studies indicate that inequality not only affects redistribution directly, but also indirectly via the political system. As far as I know, nobody has tested these complex interactions of institution and redistribution on agricultural policy.

Implications
These new insights are important for the studies on agricultural policies for several reasons. First, many earlier studies on the political economy of agriculture have not included inequality, or change in inequality, as an explanatory variable, or not focused on it as a major variable. Second, the studies confirm that impacts of variables may well be conditional on the structure of the economy, a finding consistent with that of other studies such as by Swinnen et al. (2000), who show that the impact of economic development on some agricultural policies is conditional on the level of development. Third, when studying agricultural distortions in the global framework provided by the Anderson and Valenzuela (2008) dataset where poor countries are included, it appears to be important to look at

inequality in various assets, including land. This is done by both O'Rourke and Taylor (2007) and Olper (2007).

International Agreements

An interesting issue that has received considerable attention over the past decade is the impact of international organizations and international trade agreements on trade distortions. Examples of these developments over the past decade include the effects of the Uruguay Round Agreement on Agriculture (URAA), the establishment of the WTO, NAFTA, and EU enlargement. Bagwell and Staiger (2002) have derived predictions on the impact of international agreements. Dutt and Mitra (2007) derive the empirical hypothesis from these models that countries with a comparative advantage in agriculture who join the GATT/WTO will exhibit a larger fall in agricultural protection levels.

While there is an extensive discussion on the impact of the URAA on agricultural protection, there is little econometric work on this issue. Most experts seem to agree that while the URAA may have constrained the growth of agricultural protection, it has done little to reduce it, at least in the countries that were GATT members during the negotiations (see various chapters in Anania et al. 2004).

However, there are at least four problems with identifying the impact of the GATT/WTO on agricultural policy in econometric analyses. Examples from Europe illustrate their empirical relevance. First, the impact of the GATT/WTO on agricultural distortions should not be expected to be identical across countries, because they start from different positions. For example, among the transition countries, the impact of the GATT/WTO on their agricultural policies differs strongly depending on whether they were part of the GATT before 1995 or not (Anderson and Swinnen 2008). Second, the GATT/WTO impact may have been more important for the instruments than for the level of support. For example, GATT/WTO accession triggered an important change in the instrument choice in the EU over the past decades, but much less on the level of protection. Third, the impact may be strong but indirect, or due to an interaction with other changes. For example, while the URAA per se did not require (much) policy reform in the EU, the interaction of GATT/WTO constraints and (the anticipation of) EU enlargement triggered important agricultural policy changes at the end of the 1990s (under the Agenda 2000 reforms). Fourth, the impact may be anticipated and thus occur prior to the agreement. For example, it is generally agreed that the 2003 CAP Reform was influenced by the anticipation of Doha round agreements and the ongoing WTO discussions.

External Changes, Crises, and Discontinuous Policy Change

A review of the most dramatic changes in agricultural policy distortions that have occurred in the past decades reveals that these have been triggered by "external changes." For example, it is well known that budgetary problems played an important role in stimulating agricultural policy liberalization in Sweden and New Zealand in the 1980s. Similarly, regime changes in China, in Eastern Europe, and in the former Soviet Union triggered important changes in agricultural policies.

Furthermore, in many cases, external change by itself was not enough, but it took a "crisis" to trigger (major) policy reforms. Crises may be needed to overcome the inherent status quo in the political-institutional equilibrium that exists in a society, to break the power of interest groups that are entrenched in the institutions as they exist in a society (Rausser, Swinnen and Zusman 2010).

Moreover, there is increasing evidence that dramatic policy reversals require the combination of a change in political regimes and a crisis. This was the case in China in the mid-1970s where the combination of widespread hunger in the countryside and the death of Mao allowed major reforms to occur (Swinnen and Rozelle 2006). It was also the case in Europe at the end of the 19th and in the early 20th century when the combination of enhanced political rights and a dramatic rural crisis caused major changes in agricultural policies, including land reforms (Swinnen 2002).

Implications

The periods and policies captured by the World Bank distortion database are subject to such crises. Political, institutional, and economic crises occurred in recent decades in China (following the hunger in the 1960s and the death of Mao in the 1970s), sub-Saharan Africa (with their structural adjustment programs in the 1980s), Latin America (debt crises in the 1980s), and Asia and Russia (debt crises in the 1990s).

A first implication is the importance of the choice of which "crisis" and which "external change" to include as explanatory variables. Authors pursuing single country or regional econometrics may be well aware of key external factors that need to be incorporated. However, it is much harder to select such variables for studies using the entire (global) dataset, although the analytical narratives in the volumes of case studies from the World Bank's project make that much easier than in the past.[8]

Second, the crises may cause "large" and discontinuous changes in policy, which may have important implications for econometric specifications. From a dynamic perspective, one could think of the pre- and post-crisis periods. During the pre-crisis period, there may be "undershooting" of policy adjustments since institutional constraints prevent adjustment of policies to pressures for change. Conversely, during the post-crisis period, there may be "overshooting" of policy adjustments.

However, notice that such discontinuous policy effects can also occur without institutional changes and be triggered by just external changes, such as market developments, with a fixed institutional framework. These effects are shown by Pokrivcak, Crombez and Swinnen (2006) for EU decision making. External changes will only trigger changes in agricultural policy if they are beyond a certain threshold level. This threshold is itself depending on the decision-making rules (voting majority in the EU framework). This implies that changes in the external environment may not lead to policy adjustments for a certain period (when the changes are below the threshold level) and when they do occur, they may induce large shifts in policy. Hence these effects are not linear.

Third, what if (some) agricultural policies are elements in broader reform packages and are used to get other (possibly more important) reforms approved? For example, what if agricultural protection is part of a "social contract" to invest strongly in innovation and R&D throughout the economy, stimulating productivity growth and restructuring? In such a setting, agricultural protection is used to cushion the blows for the least mobile, as has been suggested by Rausser (1982) and de Gorter, Nielson and Rausser 1992), and for which there is empirical evidence (e.g., Swinnen, Banerjee and de Gorter 2001). The compensation package may even be within the agricultural sector: What if subsidies in some sectors are part of a broader set of reforms, such as so-called package deals in CAP decision making in the EU?

Notice also that the sign of the effects will differ between the first group of changes and the second. Agricultural policy reform as part of a broader reform package could work in favor of a reduction of distortions (e.g., a "change in paradigm" such as in Eastern Europe or China) or counter to a

---

[8] See the global overview by Anderson (2009) but also the more detailed country case studies of European transition economies in Anderson and Swinnen (2008), of Latin America in Anderson and Valdés (2008), of Asia in Anderson and Martin (2009), and of Africa in Anderson and Masters (2009).

reduction of distortions (if part of a [compensation] package deal). There is even a broader problem here. Not including the right estimation framework is not just causing bias in the estimation model (allocating explanatory power to variables that are not influential in reality, or vice versa) but also in one of normative interpretations of the results.

Agents in the Models

Which are the crucial "agents" to include in the models? Many (agricultural) political econometric models effectively focus on producers (farmers), consumers, and taxpayers. Some recent models have tried to include preferences of politicians by including an "ideology" variable. However, this may need to be improved in order to correctly measure influences.

The food industry and agribusiness are seldom included.[9] However, it is clear that all over the world these companies play an important role in agricultural policy negotiations and debates, and that their interests are often aligned with those of the farmers, but not always. In other cases, there is very little relationship with farmers (think of the banana regime in the EU). Moreover, these organizations differ strongly from the farms when considering their capital/labor ratio and the votes they can muster and their ability to organize. In addition, as Figure 3.1 illustrates, there is a very different relationship with economic development of the food industry and agribusiness. The data in the Anderson and Valenzuela (2008) dataset allow one to account for tariff escalation and to measure differences between farms and food processing industry and thus to measure the role of vertical differentiation within the commodity chain (see also Cadot, de Melo and Olarreaga [2004] for theoretical arguments). However, to capture this, it is important to include the right explanatory variables in the econometric specification.

The role of other organizations (such as the bureaucracy, as with the EU Commission) is mostly not captured, although they may play an important role (Prendergast 2007). For example, many involved in the reforms of the EU's Common Agricultural Policy in the past decade point at the very important role that (then) Commissioner Franz Fischler played in pushing through the 2003 CAP reforms. It has been argued that the reforms would have never occurred without his leadership.

An important issue that has received little attention in the literature is the role of political or bureaucratic entrepreneurship. While there is a

---

[9] Exceptions are studies such as that of Lopez (2008), who focuses explicitly on the U.S. food industry.

growing literature in economics and econometrics on the role of entrepreneurship, this is not the case in formal political economic studies. The role of individuals may be acknowledged and emphasized by political scientists in analytical narratives of policy reforms, but this is typically not the case for more quantitative approaches. There is some relationship to the preferences of politicians in models that capture ideology, but this measures preferences and not entrepreneurship.

However, political entrepreneurs may also play a role in organizing interest groups and making their preferences more influential. For example, politicians played a key role in organizing farmers in rural Europe in the late nineteenth and early twentieth centuries, as they tried to set up farm organizations that were closely associated with certain parties. Examples are the Catholic Party in Belgium, the Nazi Party in Germany in the 1930s, and two different (opposing) parties in France: Small farmers lined up with the Republican Party, and larger farmers with the Catholic Church and conservative politicians. More recently, some (politically savvy) African leaders have been using rural interests to ensure their political survival, such as in Ethiopia and Zimbabwe.

CONCLUSION

This chapter summarizes important recent developments in the literature and identifies key implications for study of the political economy of agricultural distortions using the new agricultural distortions database. This review also identifies some remaining challenges. These challenges suggest that "narrative interpretations" and detailed knowledge of the countries and the policies remain important, first in combination with econometric models to get a complementary set of insights, second as preconditions for the specifications of the models, and third for the correct interpretations of the results.

References

Acemoglu, D., S. Johnson and J.A. Robinson (2001), "The Colonial Origins of Comparative Development: An Empirical Investigation," *American Economic Review* 91(5): 1369–1401.

Acemoglu, D. and J.A. Robinson (2000), "Why Did the West Extend the Franchise? Growth, Inequality and Democracy in Historical Perspective," *Quarterly Journal of Economics* 65: 1167–99.

(2001), "A Theory of Political Transitions," *American Economic Review* 91: 938–63.

(2006), *Economic Origins of Dictatorship and Democracy*, Cambridge and New York: Cambridge University Press.

Aghion, P., A. Alesina and F. Trebbi (2004), "Endogenous Political Institutions," *Quarterly Journal of Economics* 119(2): 565–612.

Anania, G., M.E. Bohman, C.A. Carter and A.F. McCalla (eds.) (2004), *Agricultural Policy Reform and the WTO: Where Are We Heading?* London: Edward Elgar.

Anderson, K. (1995), "Lobbying Incentives and the Pattern of Protection in Rich and Poor Countries," *Economic Development and Cultural Change* 43(2): 401–23.

Anderson, K. (ed.), (2009), *Distortions to Agricultural Incentives: A Global Perspective, 1955-2007*, London: Palgrave Macmillan and Washington DC: World Bank.

Anderson, K., Y. Hayami and Others (1986), *The Political Economy of Agricultural Protection: East Asia in International Perspective*, London and Boston: Allen and Unwin.

Anderson, K., P.J. Lloyd and D. MacLaren (2007),"Distortions to Agricultural Incentives in Australia Since World War II," *The Economic Record* 83(263): 461–82.

Anderson, K., and W. Martin (eds.) (2009), *Distortions to Agricultural Incentives in Asia*, Washington, DC: World Bank.

Anderson, K., and W. Masters (eds.) (2009), *Distortions to Agricultural Incentives in Africa*, Washington, DC: World Bank.

Anderson, K., and J.F.M. Swinnen (eds.) (2008), *Distortions to Agricultural Incentives in Europe's Transition Economies*, Washington, DC: World Bank.

Anderson, K., and A. Valdés (eds.) (2008), *Distortions to Agricultural Incentives in Latin America*, Washington, DC: World Bank.

Anderson, K. and E. Valenzuela (2008), *Global Estimates of Distortions to Agricultural Incentives, 1955 to 2007*, database available at http://www.worldbank.org/agdistortions

Bagwell, K. and R.W. Staiger (2002), *The Economics of the World Trading System*, Cambridge MA: MIT Press.

Baldwin, R. and F. Robert-Nicoud (2007), "Entry and Asymmetric Lobbying: Why Governments Picks Losers," *Journal of the European Economic Association* 5(5): 1064–93.

Baron, D.P. and J.A. Ferejohn (1989), "Bargaining in Legislatures," *American Political Science Review* 83 (4): 1181–1206.

Bates, R.H. (1983), "Patterns of Market Intervention in Agrarian Africa," *Food Policy* 8(4): 297–304.

(1989), *Beyond the Miracle of the Market: The Political Economy of Agrarian Development in Rural Kenya*, Cambridge and New York: Cambridge University Press.

Bates, R.H. and W.P. Rogerson (1980), "Agriculture in Development: A Coalition Analysis," *Public Choice* 35: 513–27.

Beck, T., G. Clarke, A. Groff, P. Keefer and P. Walsh (2001), "New Tools in Comparative Political Economy: The Database of Political Institutions," *World Bank Economic Review* 15(1): 165–76.

Becker, G. (1983), "A Theory of Competition Among Pressure Groups for Political Influence," *Quarterly Journal of Economics* 98: 371–400, August.

Beghin, J.C. and M. Kherallah (1994), "Political Institutions and International Patterns of Agricultural Protection," *Review of Economics and Statistics* 76(3): 482–9.

Belloc, M. and P. Guerrieri (2008), "Special Interest Groups and Trade Policy in the EU," *Open Economies Review* 19(4): 457–78.

Bombardini, M. (2005), "Firm Heterogeneity and Lobby Participation," mimeo, University of British Columbia, Vancouver.

Buchanan, J.M. and G. Tullock (1962), *The Calculus of Consent*, Ann Arbor: University of Michigan Press.

Cadot, O., J. de Melo and M. Olarreaga (2004), "Lobbying, Counter-lobbying, and the Structure of Tariff Protection in Poor and Rich Countries," *World Bank Economic Review* 18(3): 345–66.

Corden, W.M. (1974), *Trade Policy and Economic Welfare*, Oxford: Clarendon Press.

De Gorter, H. (2008), "Agricultural Instrument Choice", Agricultural Distortions Working Paper 75, World Bank, Washington DC, available at http://www.worldbank.org/agdistortions

De Gorter, H., D.J. Nielson and G.C. Rausser (1992), "Productive and Predatory Public Policies: Research Expenditures and Producer Subsidies in Agriculture," *American Journal of Agricultural Economics* 74(1): 27–37.

De Gorter, H. and J.F.M. Swinnen (2002), "Political Economy of Agricultural Policies," pp. 2073–123 in B. Gardner and G. Rausser (eds.), *Handbook of Agricultural Economics, Volume 2*, Amsterdam: Elsevier Science.

De Gorter, H. and Y. Tsur (1991), "Explaining Price Policy Bias in Agriculture: The Calculus of Support-Maximizing Politicians", *American Journal of Agricultural Economics* 73(4): 1244–54.

Dewan, T. and K. Shepsle (2008a), "Recent Economic Perspectives on Political Economy: Part I," *British Journal of Political Science* 38(2): 363–82.

(2008b), "Recent Economic Perspectives on Political Economy: Part II," *British Journal of Political Science* 38(3): 543–64.

Downs, A. (1957), *An Economic Theory of Democracy*, New York: Harper and Row.

Dutt, P. and D. Mitra (2002), "Endogenous Trade Policy Through Majority Voting: An Empirical Investigation," *Journal of International Economics* 58(1): 107–33.

(2005), "Political Ideology and Endogenous Trade Policy: An Empirical Investigation," *Review of Economics and Statistics* 87(1): 59–72.

(2007), "Political Economy of Agricultural Protection: A Framework," Paper presented at the World Bank workshop on the political economy of agricultural distortions, Portland, OR.

(2009), "Impacts of Ideology, Inequality, Lobbying, and Public Finance," Ch. 11 in this volume.

Facchini, G., J. Van Biesebrouck and G. Willmann (2006), "Protection for Sale with Imperfect Rent Capturing," *Canadian Journal of Economics* 39: 845–73.

Francois, J.F., D. Nelson and A. Pelkmans-Balaoing (2008), "Endogenous Protection in General Equilibrium: Estimating Political Weights in the EU," CEPR Discussion Paper 6979, London, October.

Gardner, B.L. (1987), "Causes of U.S. Farm Commodity Programs," *Journal of Political Economy* 95(2): 290–310.

Gawande, K. and U. Bandyopadhyay (2000), "Is Protection for Sale? Evidence on the Grossman-Helpman Theory of Endogenous Protection," *Review of Economics and Statistics* 82(1): 139–52.

Gawande, K. and B. Hoekman (2006), "Lobbying and Agricultural Trade Policy in the United States," *International Organization* 60: 527–61.

Gawande, K. and P. Krishna (2003), "The Political Economy of Trade Policy: Empirical Approaches," pp. 213–50 in E.K. Choi and J. Harrigan (eds.), *Handbook of International Trade*, Oxford: Blackwell Publishing.

Gawande, K. and H. Li (2004), "The Case of the Missing Contributions," Working Paper, Texas A&M University, College Station TX.

Gawande, K., P. Sanguinetti and A.K. Bohara (2005), "Exclusions for Sale: Evidence on the Grossman-Helpman Model of Free Trade Agreements," NAFTA-MERCOSUR Working Paper No. 4, University of New Mexico.

Goldberg, P. and G. Maggi (1999), "Protection for Sale: An Empirical Investigation," *American Economic Review* 89(5): 1135–55.

Grossman, G.M. and E. Helpman (1994), "Protection for Sale," *American Economic Review* 84(4): 833–50.

(1995), "Trade Wars and Trade Talks," *Journal of Political Economy* 103(4): 675–708.

(2001), *Special Interest Politics*, Cambridge MA: MIT Press.

(2002), *Interest Groups and Trade Policy*, Princeton NJ: Princeton University Press.

Hillman, A.L. (1982), "Declining Industries and Political-Support Protectionist Motives," *American Economic Review* 72(5): 1180–7.

(1989), *The Political Economy of Protection*, London: Taylor and Francis.

Honma, M. and Y. Hayami (1986), "The Determinants of Agricultural Protection Levels: An Econometric Analysis," Ch. 4 in K. Anderson, Y. Hayami and Others, *The Political Economy of Agricultural Protection: East Asia in International Perspective*, London: Allen and Unwin.

Kaufmann, D., A. Kraay and M. Mastruzzi (2003), "Governance Matters III: Governance Indicators for 1996–2002", Policy Research Working Paper No. 3106, World Bank, Washington DC.

Krueger, A.O. (1974), "The Political Economy of the Rent-seeking Society," *American Economic Review* 64(3): 291–303.

Krueger, A.O., M. Schiff, and A. Valdés (1988), "Agricultural Incentives in Developing Countries: Measuring the Effect of Sectoral and Economywide Policies," *World Bank Economic Review* 2(3): 255–72.

Krueger, A.O., M. Schiff and A. Valdés (1991), *The Political Economy of Agricultural Pricing Policy*, London: Johns Hopkins University Press for the World Bank.

La Ferrara, E. (2002), "Inequality and Group Participation: Theory and Evidence from Rural Tanzania," *Journal of Public Economics* 85(2): 235–73.

Lindert, P.H. (1991), "Historical Patterns of Agricultural Policy," in C. Timmer (ed.), *Agriculture and the State: Growth, Employment, and Poverty*, Ithaca NY: Cornell University Press.

Lopez, R.A. (2008), "Does 'Protection for Sale' Apply to the US Food Industries?" *Journal of Agricultural Economics* 9(1): 25–40.

Lopez, R.A. and X. Matschke (2006), "Food Protection for Sale," *Review of International Economics* 14(3): 380–91, August.

Mayda, A.M. and D. Rodrik (2005), "Why Are Some People (And Countries) More Protectionist Than Others?" *European Economic Review* 49(6): 1393–1430.

Mitra, D. (1999), "Endogenous Lobby Formation and Endogenous Protection: A Long-run Model of Trade Policy Determination", *American Economic Review* 89(5): 1116–34.

Mitra, D., D.D. Thomakos and M. Ulubasoglu (2006), "Can We Obtain Realistic Parameter Estimates for the 'Protection for Sale' Model?" *Canadian Journal of Economics* 39(1): 187–210.

North, D.C., J.J. Wallis and B.R. Weingast (2009), *Violence and Social Orders: A Conceptual Framework for Interpreting Recorded Human History*, Cambridge and New York: Cambridge University Press.

Olper, A. (2001), "Determinants of Agricultural Protection: The Role of Democracy and Institutional Setting," *Journal of Agricultural Economics* 52(2): 75–92.

(2007), "Land Inequality, Government Ideology and Agricultural Protection," *Food Policy* 32(1): 67–83.

Olson, M. (1965), *The Logic of Collective Action*, New Haven: Yale University Press.

O'Rourke, K. and J. Taylor (2007), "Democracy and Protection", in *The New Comparative Economic History: Essays in Honor of Jeffrey G. Williamson*, edited by T. Hatton, K.H. O'Rourke and A.M. Taylor, Cambridge MA: MIT Press.

Peltzman, S. (1976), "Towards a More General Theory of Regulation," *Journal of Law and Economics* 19: 211–40, August.

Persson, T. and G.E. Tabellini (2000), *Political Economics: Explaining Economic Policy*, Cambridge MA: MIT Press.

(2003), *The Economic Effects of Constitutions: What Do the Data Say?* Cambridge MA: MIT Press.

Pokrivcak, J., C. Crombez, and J.F.M. Swinnen (2006), "The Status Quo Bias and Reform of the Common Agricultural Policy: Impact of Voting Rules, the European Commission, and External Changes," *European Review of Agricultural Economics* 33(4): 562–90.

Prendergast, C. (2007), "The Motivation and Bias of Bureaucrats", *American Economic Review* 97(1): 180–96.

Rausser, G.C. (1982), "Political Economic Markets: PERTs and PESTs in Food and Agriculture", *American Journal of Agricultural Economics* 64(5): 821–33.

Rausser, G.C. and G. Roland (2010), "Special Interests Versus the Public Interest in Policy Determination", Ch. 3 in Anderson, K. (ed.), *Distortions to Agricultural Incentives: A Global Perspective, 1955–2007*, London: Palgrave Macmillan and Washington DC: World Bank.

Rausser, G.C., J.F.M. Swinnen and P. Zusman (2010), *Political Power and Endogenous Policy Formation*, Cambridge and New York: Cambridge University Press (forthcoming).

Rodrik, D. (1995), "Political Economy of Trade Policy," pp. 1457–94 in G.M. Grossman and K. Rogoff (eds.), *Handbook of International Economics*, Vol, 3, Amsterdam: North-Holland.

Roelfsema, H. (2004), "Political Institutions and Trade Protection," Tjalling C. Koopmans Research Institute Working Paper No. 04–06. Universiteit Utrecht, Utrecht.

Rogowski, R. and M.A. Kayser (2002), "Majoritarian Electoral Systems and Consumer Power: Price-Level Evidence from the OECD Countries," *American Journal of Political Science* 46(3): 526–39.

Roland, G. (2000), *Transition and Economics: Politics, Markets and Firms*, Cambridge MA: MIT Press.

Shleifer, A. (1997), "Government in Transition," *European Economic Review* 41(3–5): 385–410.

Stigler, G.S. (1971), "The Theory of Economic Regulation," *Bell Journal of Economics and Management Science* 2: 137–46, Spring.

Swinnen, J.F.M. (1994), "A Positive Theory of Agricultural Protection," *American Journal of Agricultural Economics* 76(1): 1–14.

(2002), "Political Reforms, Rural Crises, and Land Tenure in Western Europe," *Food Policy* 27(4): 371–94.

(2009), "Agricultural Protection Growth in Europe, 1870–1969", Ch. 6 in Anderson, K. (ed.), *Distortions to Agricultural Incentives: A Global Perspective, 1955–2007*, London: Palgrave Macmillan and Washington DC: World Bank.

Swinnen, J.F.M., A.N Banerjee and H. de Gorter (2001), "Economic Development, Institutional Change, and the Political Economy of Agricultural Protection: An Econometric Study of Belgium Since the 19th Century," *Agricultural Economics* 26(1): 25–43.

Swinnen, J.F.M., H. de Gorter, G.C. Rausser, and A. Banerjee (2000), "The Political Economy of Public Research Investment and Commodity Policies in Agriculture: An Empirical Study," *Agricultural Economics* 22: 111–22

Swinnen, J.F.M. and H. de Gorter (1993), "Why Small Groups and Low Income Sectors Obtain Subsidies: The 'Altruistic' Side of a 'Self-Interested' Government," *Economics and Politics* 5(3): 285–96.

Swinnen, J.F.M. and S. Rozelle (2006), *From Marx and Mao to the Market: The Economics and Politics of Agricultural Transition*, London and New York: Oxford University Press.

Thies, C.G. and S. Porche (2007), "The Political Economy of Agricultural Protection," *Journal of Politics* 69(1): 116–27.

Tracy, M. (1989), *Government and Agriculture in Western Europe 1880–1988*, 3rd ed., New York: Harvester Wheatsheaf.

Valenzuela, E. and K. Anderson (2008), "Alternative Agricultural Price Distortions for CGE Analysis of Developing Countries, 2004 and 1980–84," GTAP Research Memorandum No. 13, December. Available at http://www.gtap.agecon.purdue.edu/resources

Weingast, B.R. and D. Wittman (eds.) (2006), *The Oxford Handbook of Political Economy*, London and New York: Oxford University Press.

World Bank (2008), *World Development Report 2008*, Washington DC: World Bank.

FOUR

Special Interests versus the Public Interest in Policy Determination

Gordon C. Rausser and Gérard Roland[1]

In any public policy-making process, political and economic forces are at play in resolving the strategic interactions among the public and special interests. A schematic representation of the policy-making process reflecting these forces is represented in Figure 4.1. Historically, the right-hand box has been the domain of political science, whereas the left-hand box has been the domain of economics. At the top of the right box, particular governance structures set the constitutional design establishing voting rules, the rule of law, property rights, laws governing exchange, and more generally the rules by which rules are made. Governance structures also determine the nature and scope of the political feedback mechanisms from groups affected by public policies. In its most expansive representation, any causal analysis of constitutional rules investigates the implications of alternative legal, regulatory, and institutional frameworks, as well as various degrees of political, civil, and economic freedoms. In other words, governance structures set the boundaries for the political-economic link. Over the course of the last few decades, economists have begun to make significant theoretical and empirical advancements in analyzing the link between governance structures, political economics, and the selection of actual policies.

Political-economic analysis seeks to explain the selection and implementation of public policies. This link in the policy-making process endogenizes the instrument settings as a function of governmental bureaucracy and the actions of stakeholders. Interest groups, as agents representing stakeholders, are the units of analysis. In these links of the policy-making process, interest groups compete by spending time, energy, and money on

[1] The authors are grateful to Johan F.M Swinnen, Harry de Gorter, and Bruce Gardner for helpful discussions and insights.

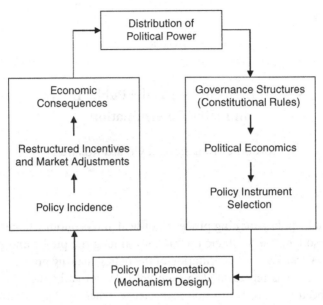

Figure 4.1. The policy-making process and economic consequences.
Source: Rausser, Swinnen and Zusman (2010).

the production of pressure to influence both the design and the tactical implementation of policies.

The box at the bottom of Figure 4.1 recognizes that the implementation of public policies can lead to both intended and unintended consequences. For this link, the potential strategic conduct of both public and private sector agents and their representatives becomes critical. Modern economics has used the concepts of asymmetric information, incentive compatibility, participation constraints, and credible commitments to isolate the incentives embodied in specific policy regimes. Unintended consequences often result from hidden actions or hidden information. Hidden actions are typically characterized as moral hazard problems, whereas hidden information is generally divided into adverse selection or signaling problems.

Once policies are designed and/or implemented, the process of incidence begins with the assessment of winners and losers. Some groups or segments of the market may bear costs associated with public policies, whereas other groups may reap gains. The actual incidence of any designed and implemented public policy depends on individual agent incentives and ultimately on the market structure. The economic consequences are generally measured both in terms of economic growth or the size of the economic pie and its distribution among various interests. These economic consequences in turn lead to a distribution of political power, represented in the top box of Figure 4.1.

Much of the academic literature compartmentalizes the links depicted in Figure 4.1. This compartmentalization has allowed at least four analytical dimensions of public policy to be distinguished in accordance with their imposed assumptions or maintained hypotheses (Rausser and Goodhue 2002). Until the last few decades, the vast majority of public policy analysis has focused on an incidence analytical dimension represented in the left box of Figure 4.1. For this dimension, the impact of existing policies and/or the consequences of alternative policy instruments are evaluated. The second analytical dimension generally takes place at the policy implementation link of Figure 4.1. For this dimension, the perfect implementation assumption is relaxed, allowing the application of mechanism design concepts while still maintaining no feedback effects from interest group or coalition formation, and a given governance structure. Modern political economy is a third analytical dimension that comes in many shapes and forms. All of these formulations, however, relax the assumption of no feedback effects from interest group or coalition formation, but typically impose a given governance structure. A fourth analytical dimension that has gained recent favor focuses on governance structures that delineate the boundaries on the negotiations and bargaining that takes place among stakeholders and governmental agents. In its most general form, this analytical dimension relaxes the assumptions of perfect implementation, no feedback effects among interest group or coalition formation, as well as given governance structures. As reflected in Figure 4.1, this dimension is capable of analyzing how the distribution of political power leads to alternative governance structures.

In the context of this general framework, the purpose of this chapter is to isolate three principal policy instruments: redistributive instruments, national public good expenditures, and local public good expenditures. Not until the recent work in general economics has there been drawn a sharp distinction between national public good and local public good expenditures. In much of the work on agricultural distortions, only a general distinction between national public good policies (particularly agricultural research and development) and redistributive policies have been examined, including the joint determination hypothesis (Rausser 1982, 1992). In accordance with North's seminal work (1981), we treat as synonymous public good policies as productive or PERT (political-economic research transactions) policies. To be consistent with recent economic literature, PERT interventions are national public policies that are intended to correct for institutional and market failures by reducing transaction costs of the private economic system. In contrast, both local public policies and redistributive policies can be treated as synonymous with predatory policies or PEST (political-economic seeking transfers) policies. With these policies come deadweight losses and wasteful political-economic activities resulting from rent seeking of interest groups or policy-making authorities.

For the three generic groups of policies – national productive policies, local productive/redistributive policies, and pure redistributive or predatory policies – our purpose is to isolate the potential causal influence of political institutional structures, the assigned authority for governmental decision making, the role of market structure and other socioeconomic characteristics, and finally the effect of sector mobility and asset diversification. In the next section, we investigate recent political governance structures and their potential implications for agricultural distortions. The focus is on the role of democratic mechanisms that have distinguished presidential from parliamentary regimes. We also investigate the potential explanatory role of electoral rules that have been theoretically examined in a number of recent publications.[2]

As revealed in the recent theoretical literature, the critical role of the separation of powers under different political systems has implications for the specification of the assigned authorities for actual settings on the policy instruments. Accordingly, in the third section of this chapter, we specify polycentric configurations comprised of policy-making centers and the influence and pressure that is brought to bear on the policy-making process by organized interest groups. This framework recognizes that most policies that are implemented are determined by a combination of national and local decisions, for example, state, county, province, individual communities (Cremer and Palfrey 2000). The objective functions of the various governmental policy-making centers and the organized interest groups determine what is relevant from a particular country's market structure.

In the fourth section, we turn to the empirical analysis for each of the three types of policy instruments. We suggest reduced form of econometric specifications, paying particular attention to the various explanatory variables that are suggested by our review of the recent theoretical literature.

---

[2] In the recent debate within Congress on the 2008 farm legislation in the United States, coalitions were formed that are largely reflective of electoral rules. House Speaker Nancy Pelosi has supported the continued heavy subsidization of US agriculture as a means for protecting newly elected Democrats from conservative Midwest farming districts.

For the dependent variables, decomposing nominal rates of assistance into their various sources (such as taxes or subsidies on imports, exports, domestic output or intermediate inputs) results in time-series data for the redistributive policy instruments, but expenditures on national and local public goods will require additional data sources. For the explanatory variable, emphasis is placed on two potential variables, sector mobility and asset diversification, which are often swept under the rug in recent theoretical formulations of political economy (Grossman and Helpman 1994, 1995, 2001).

POLITICAL INSTITUTIONAL STRUCTURES: IMPLICATIONS FOR AGRICULTURAL DISTORTIONS

On an economywide basis in democratic societies, the traditional framework for evaluating political economy issues is the median voter model. It has been the workhorse model for most work in political economy in the last few decades. The median voter model predicts that policy in a democracy with competitive elections will cater to the preferences of the median voter. Competitive forces in a two-party system will lead to convergence of electoral platforms toward the preferences of the median voter.

Economists have always known the technical problems associated with the median voter model. It is restricted to one policy dimension, to two competing parties, and it assumes perfect knowledge about voter preferences and politicians who only care about being elected and have no intrinsic preferences for policy. Apart from its technical weaknesses, the empirical predictions of the median voter model have also often been at odds with reality. Its main prediction, namely that more income inequality will lead to more redistribution, has been contradicted by recent economic trends that have seen strong increases in inequality but few increases in redistribution. On the contrary, many countries such as the United States, the United Kingdom, and others have had reductions in redistribution associated to increases in inequality.

Closer to our concerns, the median voter model does not fit nicely in the political economy of agricultural policy. The fact that support for agriculture is universal in the more affluent countries can only be made consistent with the median voter model if we believe that the median voter is a farmer. In most advanced economies, it is difficult to argue that there are many farmer incomes at the median income level. If we cannot make sense of the observed political support for agriculture using the electoral channel, then we should conclude that the only channel through which agricultural interests get expressed is through lobbying and political pressure. Such an argument might be more convincing for generic trade policy but seems less convincing for agricultural policy, since agricultural and rural votes are generally courted during campaigns. As a result, we must develop models other than the standard median voter formulation that might account for observed patterns of agricultural distortions.

There has been much progress already in the theory of political economy away from the traditional median voter model (Persson and Tabellini 2000). This progress has generated many new insights. Some of these new results are very promising and make it possible to construct more plausible electoral channels for the political economy of agricultural distortions. The newer class of theories tends to incorporate more institutional details than the standard median voter model. These institutional features include the comparison of electoral rules, different rules for choosing and ousting the executive, as well as different rules for designing and making legislative decisions. Moreover, the newer theories have lifted the unsatisfactory restriction of a one-dimensional policy space. Different classes of models such as the probabilistic voting models (Lindbeck and Weibull 1987) or partisan and citizen-candidate models (Alesina 1988, Osborne and Slivinski 1996, Besley and Coate 1998) can tackle multi-dimensional policy spaces in a rather standard fashion. The resulting formulations make it possible to analyze and test predictions relative to the composition of public expenditures as well as the policy mix of PERTs and PESTs in various countries. In particular, it makes it possible to generate predictions relative to the importance of special interest politics and expenditures and policies targeted to narrow interest groups (PESTs) versus general interest politics (PERTs) whose public goods benefiting large groups of the population. While this literature is still in its infancy, interesting results have been generated for at least two major categories, namely the comparative politics of democratic regimes and the comparative politics of electoral rules. Consider each in turn.

The Comparative Politics of Democratic Regimes

A major distinction in political science is between democracies and non-democracies. This is, of course, a difference of first order. There are, however, also differences between democracies themselves. The literature has distinguished two main types of democratic regimes: presidential and parliamentary regimes. These two regimes differ in the relations between the executive and legislative branch of government.

In a parliamentary democracy, the executive is chosen (or supported) by a majority in parliament. The government is formed after parliamentary elections, usually by the party perceived to have won the elections or the party that has received the most votes. If the winning party has the majority of elected representatives in parliament, then the government is formed by that party alone. Otherwise, a coalition government is formed with one or several other parties with which a coalition agreement is forged. The government is thus formed directly as a result of the outcome of parliamentary elections.

At least equally important is the fact that the executive can be brought down at any time by the parliament via a vote of confidence. A legislative bill can generally always be associated with a vote of confidence in the government. Different parliamentary democracies have different vote of confidence rules, but they all share the feature that a majority of representatives in parliament has the power to bring down the executive by a vote of no confidence. Votes of confidence are usually more threatening when they come from inside the government coalition. Members of the coalition need not fear a confidence vote initiated by the opposition, since the opposition usually only commands a minority of votes. However, it has happened repeatedly that a party belonging to the coalition brings up a vote of confidence in order to make the government fall.

In a presidential democracy, the executive is elected independently of the legislative branch of government, usually by popular vote, and cannot be brought down by the legislature except in extraordinary circumstances such as an impeachment procedure. Impeachment procedures are exceptional and justified by exceptional circumstances, certainly not by political disagreement as is the case with a vote of confidence. The source of power of the executive thus lies with the electorate and is independent of the majority coalition in the legislative branch of government.

These institutional differences between presidential and parliamentary democracies have implications that affect decision making and the policy mix. First of all, presidential systems have more *separation of powers* between the executive and legislative branch of government, since the source of power of the executive is independent of the legislative branch and cannot be voted down by the legislature as is the case in parliamentary democracies. This stronger separation of power between both branches of government implies potentially more conflicts between the executive and the legislative branch of government. Second, parliamentary systems have more *legislative cohesion*. This means that there is stronger voting discipline. Not only do elected representatives from the same party generally vote the same way, but members from the governing coalition also do so. This is closely related to the fact that a vote of confidence can be associated with a legislative bill. Indeed, since members of the governing coalition have majority support in the legislature, they also carry a lot of agenda-setting powers, since only the coalition parties can make legislative proposals that have a material probability of being accepted. The possibility to associate a vote of confidence to a bill acts as a credible threat to discipline members of the coalition. A coalition member who would want to deviate from the majority and vote against a coalition proposal would be deterred from doing so if the other members threaten to stage a vote of confidence. This would lead to a fall of the government and a possible change of coalition, representing a loss of precious agenda-setting powers for the incumbent coalition.

Persson, Roland and Tabellini (2000) have examined theoretically and empirically the implications of these policy differences on the policy mix within the framework of an accountability model, that is, a model where voters can vote retrospectively to punish elected representatives who have not brought them an endogenously determined utility level, in terms of the policy mix. The main results are that presidential systems have a smaller size of government and a composition of government expenditures that is less tilted toward national public goods and more toward local public goods and smaller rents to politicians. These results are derived from the two institutional features defined above.

The *separation of powers* under a presidential system creates checks and balances between the executive and the legislative branch of government. These checks and balances make it possible to exploit the conflict of interest between both branches of government (Madison, Federalist Paper No. 10). If the executive branch controls the agenda-setting power over the size of the budget but the legislative branch controls the agenda-setting power over composition of expenditures, and the approval of both is needed in each case, the separation of powers allows the exploitation of the conflict between both in the interest of voters.

The executive branch has no interest in proposing a large budget size, since the composition of expenditures will favor the constituencies who control the legislature. On the contrary, in order to be re-elected by its own constituency, the president's interest is to propose a low budget. Separation of powers thus makes it possible to obtain a smaller size of government. It is a device to prevent collusion against voters. This is not the case in a parliamentary democracy. Since the executive emanates from the majority in the legislature, the same party or parties control both the legislature and the executive branch of government. There are thus less checks and balances between both branches of government. There is thus no internal institutional mechanism to limit the size of government. The only force present is the reelection motive. The majority in parliament must satisfy the demands of their voters. This can help limit taxation but only to a limited degree. Indeed, it is always possible to "tax the minority" in order to please the majority constituencies. The smaller size of government may serve to support or detract from economic growth. However, separation of powers will lead to fewer rents for politicians, as the conflict of interest between them will prevent collusion to capture rents. This is not the case in a parliamentary regime.

The *legislative cohesion*, on the other hand, makes it possible to service in a stable way the broad constituencies representing the majority in place. This feature of parliamentary democracy makes it possible to provide general public goods to a majority. Indeed, as the costs are internalized broadly within the government coalition, providing these public goods is politically advantageous to the incumbent majority. In contrast, the absence of legislative cohesion in a presidential system leads to a failure to provide as large an amount of public goods as in a parliamentary democracy. The reason is that within a presidential system, the lack of legislative cohesion leads to ad hoc coalitions, on a case-by-case basis. Representatives of the same party also vote less often with their party, especially if they feel they need to do so to protect their constituencies' interests.

Since the politician who controls the agenda can build coalitions on an ad hoc basis, he or she can exploit the desire of other representatives to be part of the coalition. Indeed, the latter will compete to be part of a majority on a given bill and will bid down their demands, giving de facto the bargaining power to the agenda-setter. The latter will trade off her own constituencies' narrow interests against personal rents in order to be reelected. As a result, in a presidential system, there is underprovision of national public goods, and politicians focus more on "pork," that is, on local public goods for their own narrow constituency. Presidential systems will thus, in contrast with parliamentary systems, have a composition of public expenditures that is more focused toward local public goods and less toward national public goods. Of course, this is directly related to the differences in legislative cohesion in the two systems, which is derived from the institution of the vote of confidence in a parliamentary democracy.

These results have a flavor of reality if one compares the parliamentary democracies of Europe with the presidential system in the United States. The United States has a smaller size of government but it also lags in the provision of some general public goods such as health and education. The predictions of the model have also been borne out in empirical work by Persson and Tabellini (2003). One should, however, keep in mind that not all presidential systems have a strong separation of powers between the executive and the legislative branch of government. In strong presidential systems like in Russia and Eastern Europe, but also in various Latin American countries, the elected legislature has much less powers than the U.S. Congress, and there is strong concentration of powers in the hands of the president.

What are the implications of the comparative politics of democratic regimes for the political economy of agricultural distortions? If these distortions take mainly the form of local public goods, or redistributive policy instruments, via special subsidies to agriculture for example, then we should observe relatively more distortions in presidential systems than in parliamentary systems for developed countries and vice versa for developing countries whose rural population represents a large proportion of the total population. This prediction has not yet been tested. The theory also predicts that the public good component of support to agriculture (PERTs) is likely to be stronger in parliamentary systems.

The Comparative Politics of Electoral Rules

Electoral rules are also thought to have an important impact on policy. This is because they affect the rules of democratic selection of representatives, and this may affect the actions taken by the latter when in power in order to be reelected. In principal, one should distinguish between electoral rules in parliamentary democracies and in presidential democracies, but this has not been seriously examined in the literature. In some cases this should not matter, but in others it might. In assessing the differences between electoral rules, we briefly outline the applicability of the results in both types of democratic regimes.

The two main polar electoral rules are the *majoritarian* electoral rule and the *proportional* electoral rule. There are other electoral rules and variants of both majoritarian and proportional, but they are the most common and are also polar opposites.

Under the proportional electoral rule, the representation of a party in terms of seat share in the legislature is proportional to the vote share of that party. Exact proportionality can never be obtained because representatives, contrary to vote shares, come in discrete numbers, and there are various methods to convert vote shares into seats. Nevertheless, seat shares are approximately equal to vote shares. Countries with proportional electoral rule have generally large district magnitudes, potentially covering the whole country, as is the case in the Netherlands or in Israel.

Large district magnitudes are consistent with the proportional rules since the larger the number of seats that need to be allocated, the closer vote shares and seat shares will be. To give an example, say that one party has 65 percent of the votes and the other has 35 percent of the votes: If a district has only two seats, it will, even under proportional rule, generally allocate the two seats to the winning party, whereas if the district has 200 seats then the first party will have 130 seats and the other 70 seats. In the latter case, the seat shares will be exactly equal to the vote shares, but not in the former case. Therefore, researchers tend to use a higher district magnitude (larger number of seats competing in an electoral district) as an indication of a higher proportionality of seat shares to vote shares.

Under the majoritarian electoral rule, the winner of an election is the candidate with the plurality of votes, that is, having more votes than all other candidates. Majoritarian electoral rule is therefore usually associated with single-member districts. Majoritarian electoral rule may deviate significantly from proportionality. Suppose that one party gets 55 percent in all districts and the other gets 45 percent in all districts. According to the majoritarian electoral rule, the first party should have 100 percent of the seats and the second 0 percent. Researchers usually interpret a smaller district size as closer to majoritarian. Note first that a single-member district is majoritarian by definition. Since there is only one seat, it must go to the winner. However, in the example above with two seats, one senses that it is closer to majoritarian than to proportional.

To summarize, under proportional electoral rule, seat shares are proportional to vote shares and under the majoritarian electoral rule, the party who gains the most votes in a district wins the seat. The larger the district magnitude, the more proportional the electoral rule and the smaller the district magnitude, the closer it is to the majoritarian rule.

Differences in electoral rules are also found to influence policy making, and a literature has developed in recent years to explore these distinctions. Lizzeri and Persico (2001) and Persson and Tabellini (1999) have examined the effect of electoral rules on policy in the framework of a two-party competition with a multi-dimensional policy space. Both have models that deviate from the standard median voter model in the sense that they are able to deal with multiple policy dimensions. The former use a methodology advanced by Myerson (1993), inspired by the colonel Blotto games, where candidates choose platforms in the form of mixed strategies. The latter use the probabilistic voting model. In both papers, the main difference between the two electoral rules lies in district magnitude. There is assumed to be only one district under proportional rule and a large number of single-member districts under majoritarian rule. The main result from the two papers is that the majoritarian rule favors local public good provision over national public good provision, whereas under the proportional rule, it is the opposite.

In both cases the intuition for the result is the same. Under the majoritarian rule, in order to get a majority of seats in the legislature or in order to win the presidency (the logic is thus valid for both presidential and parliamentary democracy), a party needs to target the pivotal voter in the pivotal district, whereas under the proportional rule, they target the pivotal voter in the country. Indeed, under the proportional rule, to get a majority, one needs to get the vote of the median voter in the country, whereas under the majoritarian rule, there is a "median" district that will give a majority to one of the two parties. In that district, there is a pivotal voter, the median in that district, who will decide which party gets the seat in the district. Therefore, proposing local public goods targeted to the pivotal voter in the pivotal district is electorally "cheaper" than proposing national public goods.

A corollary is that voters in the pivotal districts need not pay taxes for public goods in other districts. On the contrary, tax revenues from other districts can be used to finance local public goods in the pivotal district. They thus get more "value for money." Under proportional electoral rule, it is the opposite. Since national public goods have many externalities, they may deliver more utility per voter per unit of tax revenue. In other words, they are assumed to be more efficient relative to local public goods. Nevertheless, majoritarian systems are biased toward local public goods because of the electoral incentives associated to the majoritarian rule.

These results have clear implications for the political economy of agricultural distortions. In developed countries, if we assume that these distortions take mainly the form of local public goods or redistributive policy instruments, then one should observe, everything else being equal, relatively more distortions under the majoritarian electoral rule than under the proportional electoral rule. One is more likely to find agricultural voters as pivotal voters under the majoritarian rule rather than under the proportional system. Indeed, it is less likely to find a farmer whose income is median in a developed country. However, it is much more plausible that a farmer may be median in a rural district if that district is pivotal for the elections.

Persson, Roland and Tabellini (2007) model the effect of electoral rules within a parliamentary democracy. The model goes further than the rest of the literature on electoral rules by incorporating not only different electoral rules but also their effect on party formation and government formation. It can indeed be argued that it is not very satisfactory to analyze electoral rules within the framework of a two-party system. Countries with proportional electoral rules typically have more than two parties represented in parliament, and countries with majoritarian rule are not necessarily all countries with two-party systems.

Once we allow for more than two parties in a formal model, then we must model the interaction between the electoral process and legislative bargaining. Indeed, the election outcome or future election outcomes affect the choice of coalition partners, which will in turn affect policy making. Moreover, the electoral rule also affects incentives of parties to merge. The majoritarian rule gives an incentive to parties to merge, so as to win a maximum number of districts given the "winner take all" nature of the electoral rule. In other words, the merger of two parties may be able to achieve a number of seats that is much superior to the sum of the seats they would achieve as separate parties. Under the proportional system, this incentive is by definition absent. If two parties merge, they would get the sum of seat shares that the two separate parties would have.

Under majoritarian electoral rule, the stronger incentive of parties to merge will lead more often to a two-party system and therefore less often to coalition governments. Under proportional rule, since there are fewer incentives to merge, there will be more parties represented in parliament and thus coalition governments will be more frequent. Under a coalition government, government expenditures will tend to be larger since parties in the coalition cater more to their own constituency and do not internalize the interests of the other party (-ies) in the coalition. This is related to the "common pool" problem. Therefore, one should see a larger number of parties, more coalition governments, and higher government expenditures under proportional electoral rule compared to the majoritarian electoral rule. This is also verified empirically.

The implications of this last model are less obvious in terms of the political economy of agricultural distortions, since there are no specific predictions in the model as to the type or composition of public expenditures. However, one could argue that a higher party fragmentation under the proportional electoral rule might lead to a higher frequency of parties in government representing rural interests. This implication runs counter to that of previous models discussed earlier in this Chapter.

GOVERNMENT DECISION-MAKING STRUCTURE

Another crucial component of the policy-making process depicted in Figure 4.1 is the assignment of authority to select and actually implement policies. Regardless of the political institutional structure, how political-economic coalitions are formed, whether temporary or "permanent," is critical. Here, we follow the work of Rausser, Swinnen and Zusman (2010) and adopt the Nash-Harsanyi bargaining game, where both the first-stage disagreement payoffs and the second-stage cooperative solution are endogenously determined. For this framework, the election outcomes affect the choice of coalition partners.

In the simple version of the model, the objective function for the policy-making center can be represented by what's defined as the extended objective function:

$$U_0 = U_0(x)$$
$$= u_0(x_0) + \sum_{i=1}^{n} s_i(x_i, \delta_i) \tag{1}$$

where $u_0(x_0) = \bar{u}(y(x_0), x_0)$, $\bar{u}_0 : \mathfrak{R}^G \times X_0 \to \mathfrak{R}$, $y(x_0)$ is the G-vector of endogenous variables whose values are determined by the policy vector x_0, δ_i is a strategy indicator variable indicating whether a "reward" or "penalty" strategy has been adopted in the strategic interaction by the corresponding organized interest group, and $s_i(\cdot)$ represents the strength or influence of interest group i. The index $i = 0$ is reserved for the policy-making center, and $i = 1, 2, \ldots, n$ for the n organized interest groups. That is,

$$U_i = U_i(x)$$
$$= u_i(x_0) - c_i(\delta_i) \qquad i = 1, 2, \ldots, n \tag{2}$$

where $u_i(x_0) = \bar{u}_i(y(x_0), x_0)$; $\bar{u}_i : \mathfrak{R}^G \times X_0 \to \mathfrak{R}$ and c_i represents the cost to interest group i of exercising strength or influence.

From the basic specification (1) and (2) and the two-stage Nash-Harsanyi bargaining and coalition formation process, Rausser, Swinnen and Zusman (2010) derive a governing criterion function (sometimes referred to in the literature as a policy or political preference function) that isolates the distribution of political power across various coalitions.

This basic structure for the governing criterion function can incorporate several levels of government, from the local to the national. The number of echelons in this hierarchy and the degree of interdependence among levels are determined by numerous factors, such as the geographic extent of the country, its population size and geographic dispersion, the development of infrastructure, the available organizational technology, the prevailing political culture, and the country's history.

In addition to vertical differentiation, there also exists a horizontal differentiation, which becomes more pronounced at the governmental hierarchy's upper levels. Particularly with respect to agricultural distortions, two dimensions of governmental horizontal differentiation are important: first, differentiation by the governmental branch (legislative, executive, judicial); and second, the functional differentiation by fields of activity or economic industry (e.g., agriculture, trade). In some countries, policy-making authority is concentrated, whereas in other countries it is distributed across the entire governmental structure. The distribution determines the configuration of policy-making centers relative to particular policies. To be specific, consider a group configuration comprising g interested policy-making centers and n organized interest groups. Let $j = 1, 2, ..., g$ index the policy-making centers and $i = 1, 2, ..., n$ index the organized interest groups. Also, let $x_0 = (x_0{}^1, x_0{}^2, ..., x_0{}^g)$ be the vector of policy instruments controlled by the various policy-making centers. Under this specification, the extended objective functions of the policy-making centers are

$$U_j = u_j(x_0) + \sum_{i=1}^{n} s_{ij}(c_i^j, \delta_i^j) + \sum_{k \neq j} S_{kj}(c_k^j, \delta_k^j) - \sum_{k \neq j} c_j^k \quad j, k = 1, 2, ..., g \quad (3)$$

where $u_j(x0)$ is the policy objective function of center j reflecting the center's decision agents' preferences over the entire policy space, X_0, $s_{ij}(c_i^j, \delta_i^j)$ is the strength of power of the ith interest group over the jth center, $S_{kj}(c_k^j, \delta_k^j)$ is center k's strength of power over center j; c_i^j, c_k^j, and c_j^k are, respectively, the costs of power of the ith interest group over the jth center, and the kth center over the jth center, and the jth center over the kth center. Note that δ_i^j and δ_j^j are strategy indicator variables determining whether a "reward" or "penalty" strategy has been adopted in the strategic interaction between the corresponding organized groups.

Since reciprocal power relationships prevail among all organized groups, the equilibrium solution of the political economy is a solution to the corresponding $(g + n)$-person bargaining game. For a case where all disagreement payoffs are treated as given, Rausser, Swinnen and Zusman (2010) show that the political-economic equilibrium is obtained by maximizing the following policy governance function with respect to $x_0 \in X_0$:

$$W(x_0) = \sum_{i=1}^{n} B_i u_i(x_0) + \sum_{j=1}^{g} B_j u_j(x_0) \tag{4}$$

where

$$B_i = \frac{1}{\overline{U}_i - t_i^0} > 0 \text{ and } B_j = \frac{1}{\overline{U}_j - t_j^0} > 0 \text{ for all } i \text{ and } j \tag{5}$$

where t_i^0 and t_j^0 are the specified disagreement outcomes or in general the noncooperative solutions to the bargaining game.

EMPIRICAL ANALYSIS

An operational empirical analysis cannot be implemented without specifying the feasible set that constrains the optimization of the governing criterion or policy governance function, namely equation (4). Each of the relevant objective functions specified in this equation are interpreted in much of the literature as performance variables (endogenous variables) that are determined in part by the policy instruments. The actual constraint structure that the maximization of (4) is subject to depends on the underlying market structure, socioeconomic conditions, factor mobility, asset diversification, electoral rules, and the democratic or nondemocratic regimes discussed in the previous section.

For equality constraint structures, the mapping from the policy instruments to the performance or endogenous variables is straightforward. Under these circumstances, the empirical analysis can focus on estimating the "political weights" or distribution of political power parameters in equations (4) and (5). Moreover, policy reaction functions can be empirically estimated by deriving the choice equations. Obviously, the former is a revealed preference analysis, while the latter is a typical direct analysis of the actual policy choices that are implemented. Although consistency (see the validation tests in Chapter 17 of Rausser, Swinnen and Zusman 2010) can be investigated by providing both analyses, in this section we consider only the reduced form specifications for the policy reaction functions (Rausser and Goodhue 2002), referred to as the *minimal political-economy theory reduced form*.[3]

---

[3] Due to space limitations, we cannot review the empirical insights presented in Rausser (2007) relating to interest group size, relevant demand, and supply elasticities, size of deadweight losses, etc.

Endogenous Variables

For the redistributive policy instruments, two readily available alternative datasets exist. The first is for the aggregate agricultural nominal rates of assistance (NRAs) of each country covered over the period 1955 through 2007 (Anderson and Valenzuela 2008). This same source has also decomposed the aggregate NRAs into their various sources such as taxes or subsidies on imports, exports, domestic output or intermediate inputs (depending on whether the product is classified as an import-competing or exportable good, or if it is a nontradable). The NRAs show in most instances that the dominant portion of the NRA is the rate of assistance to output conferred by the border market price support, but border measures are also the most common forms of tax on exportables that should be explained. Regardless, this basic dataset allows a number of potential redistributive policy instruments to be evaluated.

As previously noted, in the empirical literature a distinction has not been drawn between local versus national public goods. For the case of national public goods, the principal measure has been total expenditures on agricultural research and development. Here, the ISNAR agricultural research expenditures by country and year are available. These data have been used in a number of empirical studies that appear in the literature (e.g., Lee and Rausser 1992, Swinnen, de Gorter and Banerjee 2000).

For local public goods, a readily available data source does not exist. As a result, piecing together the relevant time series data across countries will require a number of sources. One source is the rural public expenditure data reported by FAO that has recently been used by Allcott, Lederman and Lopez (2006). This data source would have to be augmented by the recent surge in agrienvironmental expenditures, particularly by the developed countries in the dataset. Still another source is the categories of expenditures reported by Anderson and Valenzuela (2008), particularly non-product-specific subsidies net of abnormal taxes for primary agriculture, and agricultural research and extension.

Explanatory Variables

In addition to the explored explanatory variables identified in Anderson (1995) and de Gorter and Swinnen (2002), a number of unexplored or weakly explored subsets of explanatory variables should be considered. Many of these variables are summarized and maintained by the World Bank. However, one of the principal problems is that many of these data sources do not stretch over the full time period that is covered by the redistributive policy instruments in Anderson and Valenzuela (2008). Nevertheless, the critical political-economic regimes outlined above can be captured through discrete regimes: dictatorial, parliamentary-democratic, and presidential-democratic. Similarly, discrete regimes can be used to distinguish at least two electoral rules: majoritarian and proportional.

For the governance structures, including branches of government, role of bureaucracy, interest group access, and admissible coalitions, we are guided by the discussion in the previous section of this paper. Once again, discrete regimes will be critical in allowing us to distinguish across countries with regard to their propensity to pursue redistribution or provide local or national public good expenditures. Also note that here, the various data sources on temporal consistency and credible commitment indicators should be assessed. Unfortunately, few of these indicator variables stretch back as far as even 1980. Finally, there is no need to restrict our investigation to internal polycentric governance structures. For many countries, external institutions such as GATT/WTO accession and World Bank and IMF conditionality effectiveness may prove to be significant explanatory variables.

Another potential subset of explanatory variables, largely unexplored, is sector mobility and asset diversification. As demonstrated in Rausser, Swinnen and Zusman (2010), when sector mobility or asset diversification are complete, a convergence takes place between "the special interest" and "the public interest." For those countries with constitutional principles and institutional structures that promote resource mobility or asset diversification, a political-economic interest group structure will emerge that has little if any incentive to acquire and exercise political power. In essence, in the limit there is no incentive for various private sector interests, or for that matter for policy-making centers, to engage in the implementation of redistributive policies. One of the few empirical studies that focus on one dimension of farmer mobility was the seminal analysis of Gardner (1987). In his analysis, Gardner specified two geographic mobility variables, both of which were statistically significant in explaining the degree of distortions across commodities in the United States. More generally, with respect to all countries, potential data sources are available relating to *sources for mobility* and *sources for asset diversification*. For the former, various human capital measures of potential mobility stretch back as far as 1960, while for the latter, outputs by Deininger and Squire (1996, 1998) and their colleagues can be employed to initiate an investigation of asset diversification on the three groups of proposed endogenous variables.

CONCLUSION

Our purpose in this chapter has been to shine the spotlight on recent theoretical developments in political economy and what role they might play in explaining and reforming individual country and global distortions in food and agricultural markets. We have isolated a number of potential explanatory variables that may allow us to explain and distinguish between predatory or redistributive policies that result in market distortions, local public goods that serve the interest of political well-positioned geographic regions of a particular country, and national public goods that promote economic growth and generally serve the "public interest."

The remarkable dataset on agricultural distortions compiled by the World Bank (Anderson and Valenzuela 2008) provides a watershed opportunity for describing patterns across time and countries that might potentially isolate the critical forces that explain the magnitude of redistribution and governmental support for both national and local public goods. To be sure, a number of challenges remain. These challenges include *inter alia* completing the time series for both agricultural public research and development expenditures and local public good expenditures across the time frame for which the net effects of redistributive instruments have been captured by the first stage of the World Bank analysis. The next major challenge is completing the statistical analysis, wisely separating the sample data, which allows exploratory investigations (some would characterize as data mining) to be concluded before proposing the analysis that will allow testable hypotheses to be evaluated and assessed. A third challenge is to capture the dynamic implications of both "policy traps" and crisis shocks resulting from external changes that motivate new political-economic equilibriums. In characterizing the patterns that emerge across time and countries, our emphasis should be on discontinuous jumps in the degree of redistribution or the investment in public good policies, both local and national. Finally, in the empirical sketch outlined in the previous section, capturing regime changes in the reduced form specifications may well allow insights to emerge on sustainable policy reform.

References

Alesina, A. (1988), "Credibility and Policy Convergence in a Two-Party System with Rational Voters," *American Economic Review* 78(4): 796–805.

Allcott, H., D. Lederman and R. Lopez (2006), "Political Institutions, Inequality, and Agricultural Growth: The Public Expenditure Connection," World Bank Policy Research Working Paper 3902, April.

Anderson, K. (1995), "Lobbying Incentives and the Pattern of Protection in Rich and Poor Countries," *Economic Development and Cultural Change* 43(2): 401–23.

Anderson, K. and E. Valenzuela (2008), "Global Estimates of Distortions to Agricultural Incentives, 1955 to 2007," core database at http://www.worldbank.org/agdisrtortions

Besley, T. and S. Coate (1998), "Sources of Inefficiency in a Representative Democracy: A Dynamic Analysis," *American Economic Review* 88(1): 139–56.

Cremer, J. and T.R. Palfrey (2000), "Federal Mandates by Popular Demand," *Journal of Political Economy* 108: 905–27.

De Gorter, H. and J.F.M. Swinnen (2002), "Political Economy of Agricultural Policy", Ch. 36 in B.L. Gardner and G.C. Rausser (eds.), *Handbook of Agricultural Economics, Volume 2*, Amsterdam: North-Holland.

Deininger, K. and L. Squire (1996), "Measuring Inequality: A New Data-Base," *World Bank Economic Review* 10(3): 565–9.

   (1998), "New Ways of Looking at Old Issues: Inequality and Growth," *Journal of Development Economics* 57: 249–87.

Gardner, B.L. (1987), "Causes of US Farm Commodity Programs", *Journal of Political Economy* 95(2): 290–310.

Grossman, G.M. and E. Helpman (1994), "Protection for Sale," *American Economic Review* 84: 833–50.

   (1995), "Trade Wars and Trade Talks," *Journal of Political Economy* 103: 675–708.

   (2001), *Special Interest Politics*, Cambridge MA: MIT Press.

Lee, D.R. and G.C. Rausser (1992), "The Structure of Research and Transfer Policies in International Agriculture: Evidence and Implications," Occasional Paper, International Association of Agricultural Economists.

Lindbeck, A. and J.W. Weibull (1987), "Balanced-budget Redistribution as the Outcome of Political Competition," *Public Choice* 52: 273–97.

Lizzeri, A. and N. Persico (2001), "The Provision of Public Goods under Alternative Electoral Incentives," *American Economic Review* 91(1): 225–39.

Madison, J. (1898), *Federalist Paper No. 10*. In E. H. Scott (ed.) *The Federalist and Other Constitutional Papers*, Chicago: Scott, Forsman.

Myerson, R.B. (1993), "Incentives to Cultivate Favored Minorities under Alternative Electoral Systems," *American Political Science Review* 87(4): 856–69.

North, D.C. (1981), *Structure and Change in Economic History*, New York: Norton.

Osborne, M.J. and A. Slivinski (1996), "A Model of Political Competition with Citizen-Candidates," *Quarterly Journal of Economics* 111: 65–96.

Persson, T. and G. Tabellini (1999), "The Size and Scope of Government: Comparative Politics with Rational Politicians," *European Economic Review* 43 (4–6): 699–735.

   (2000), *Political Economics: Explaining Economic Policy*, Cambridge MA: MIT Press.

   (2003), *The Economic Effects of Constitutions: What Do the Data Say?*, Cambridge MA: MIT Press.

Persson, T., G. Roland, and G. Tabellini (2000), "Comparative Politics and Public Finance," *Journal of Political Economy* 108: 1121–61.

Persson, T., G. Roland and G. Tabellini (2007), "Electoral Rules and Government Spending in Parliamentary Democracies," *Quarterly Journal of Political Science* 2: 155–88.

Rausser, G.C. (1982), "Political Economic Markets: PERTs and PESTs in Food and Agriculture," *American Journal of Agricultural Economics* 64: 821–33.

(1992), "Predatory Versus Productive Government: The Case of U.S. Agricultural Policies," *Journal of Economic Perspectives* 6(3): 133–57.

(2007), "Second Stage: Political Economy Analysis of Distortion Patterns," Presentation at the World Bank's *Political Economy of Distortions to Agricultural Incentives* conference, Portland OR, July 2007.

Rausser, G.C. and R. Goodhue (2002), "Public Policy: Its Many Analytical Dimensions," in B.L. Gardner and G.C. Rausser (eds.), *Handbook of Agricultural Economics, Volume 2*, Amsterdam: North-Holland.

Rausser, G.C., J.F.M. Swinnen and P. Zusman (2010), *Political Power and Endogenous Policy Formation*, Cambridge and New York: Cambridge University Press (forthcoming).

Swinnen, J.F.M., H. de Gorter, and A. Banerjee (2000), "Political Economy of Public Research Investment and Commodity Policies in Agriculture: an Empirical Study," *Agricultural Economics* 22(2): 111–22.

FIVE

Anglo-French Trade, 1689-1899

Agricultural Trade Policies, Alcohol
Taxes, and War

John V. C. Nye

Britain – contrary to received wisdom – was not a free trader for most
of the 1800s and, despite the repeal of the Corn Laws, continued to have
higher tariffs than the French until the last few decades of the 19th century.
Moreover, British tariffs tended to be reformed by first lowering or abolish-
ing duties on items in which Britain had enjoyed a comparative advantage
or which were usually not significant for their trade. The few tariffs that
remained – particularly on items such as wine and spirits – were among
the most protective of all tariffs and were mostly the same sorts of tariffs
decried by Adam Smith in the *Wealth of Nations*. These, in fact, went back
to the earliest period of British mercantilism in the 17th century, when war
and politics totally distorted trade relations between Britain and France
for the next 200 years.

Although later authors have tended to dismiss these high tariffs as being
"merely" for revenue, their high level, the selective nature of the duties, the
difficulty of separating out revenue from protection, and the seriousness
with which British rivals such as France treated changes in these tariffs
shows how misleading has been the simplistic story of free-trade Britain
that we have inherited.

The argument is this: An English state eager to reduce its trade deficit
with France in the late 17th century found that opportunity as a result of
the wars that ran from 1689–1713. War with Louis XIV's France provided
the excuse that protectionists had sought to cut off virtually all commerce
with the French. This was especially important for the trade in wine and
spirits, one of the largest components of the 17th-century English trade
deficit. Prohibition and protection led to the creation of powerful interests at home and abroad (notably the brewing industry in London and the
English-dominated wine industry in Portugal) that benefited from the
absence of competing French imports. These groups successfully lobbied

to impose new and nearly prohibitive tariffs on French goods – notably on wine and spirits – when trade with France resumed after the war. Protection of domestic interests in turn allowed the state to raise domestic excises in a credible fashion, therefore leading to a dramatic increase in government revenues without the need to increase taxes on landed property. The state ensured compliance not simply through the threat of lower tariffs on foreign substitutes, but also through the encouragement of oligopoly in the production and sale of beer. Both entry into wholesale brewing and retail distribution were more tightly regulated and restricted throughout the 18th century, making for a concentrated domestic interest that could work in concert with Parliament.

The net result was an expansive British state with revenues collected through the newly created central tax administration, and a cooperative brewing industry that found it easy to shift much of the burden of this taxation onto consumers, who had little say in the matter. The growth of British revenues in the 18th century was so dramatic that it made possible Britain's rise to prominence as a world power (Brewer 1988).

In addition, the protective tariffs had long-term consequences for the pattern of British domestic consumption, perhaps even altering or at least shaping the fundamentals of British "taste." Deforming the centuries-old wine trade with France meant that wine was kept out of the British Isles during the century and a half that included the Industrial Revolution and the rise of mass consumption. It ensured that beer would be the dominant component of the ordinary Briton's drinking habits, and it restricted the consumption of fine Bordeaux and Port to the upper classes.

But this also had long-term effects on the structure of British tariffs. As early as 1789 – owing to the Eden Treaty – there were early attempts to reform the trade arrangements, but these were interrupted by the French Revolution.

By the 19th century, the leaders of the political class were increasingly favorable to liberal policy, though there was still much political opposition to the notion of free trade. It is, therefore, striking that when the momentous series of reforms in Parliament leading to the removal of the Corn Laws passed in the 1840s, reform of the tariff on wine, spirits, and related products were not changed at all.[1] Yet these self-evidently protectionist tariffs antedated the Corn Laws that are often seen as the epitome of British mercantilism, and were even explicitly noted in Smith's *Wealth of Nations*

---

[1] It should be noted that the sugar tariff was significant in this regard, because the conversion of sugar into alcohol was a significant component of the spirits industry.

(Nye 2007). Nonetheless, lowering or reforming the tariffs on wine, rum, sugar, coffee, tea, and so on now threatened British revenues. It did so both directly through the reduction of duties and more indirectly through the likely need to pare domestic excises to avoid complaints from local producers of competing products that even the most ardent free traders did not see fit to challenge these duties after Britain has supposedly moved to free trade in the 1840s. The net result was that Britain was not a truly free-trade nation until very late in the 19th century.

The simplest way to appreciate the seriousness of the issue is by examining average tariffs for Britain and France in the 19th century. This basic measure – the sum of duties divided by the value of all imports – is the most common approximation used to indicate the extent to which a nation is or is not a free trader.

Figure 5.1 shows average tariff rates for Britain and France throughout the 19th century. What is most surprising is that – contrary to conventional wisdom – British tariffs were higher than in France for most of that century. The two curves do not cross until the mid-1870s, and the degree to which French tariffs were higher than in Britain in the last few decades of the 19th century was not nearly as pronounced as the reverse comparison for the early 1800s. This is especially striking because conventional

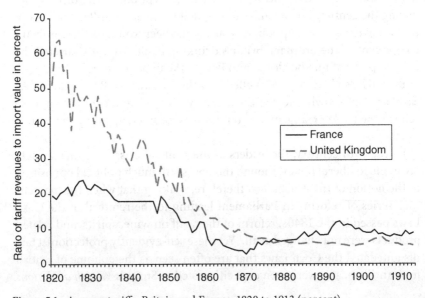

Figure 5.1. Average tariffs, Britain and France, 1820 to 1913 (percent).
Source: United Kingdom data from Imlah (1958), French data from Levy-Leboyer and Bourguignon (1985).

historical narrative has tended to treat Britain as having become a free trader after the repeal of the Corn Laws in the 1840s, while France is said to have remained stubbornly opposed to free trade at least until the 1860s (Kindleberger 1964).

Part of this was rhetorical: The British claimed to have moved to free trade and the French nearly the reverse. But part of it has to do with the peculiar nature of British tariffs. For the most part they were concentrated in comestibles, beverages, and nonindustrial goods such as liquor, coffee, tea, sugar, and wine. In contrast, the French had a larger number of tariffs and even had prohibitions on a number of items, including some textiles and various manufactures, prior to the 1860s.

But what was significant is that the British tariffs were so much more binding. They imposed very high rates on items that were a large component of consumption of foreign products. More importantly, these were items in which Britain did not have a comparative advantage. Hence the establishment of high and even prohibitive (sometimes reaching several hundred percent) duties on items that Britain did not specialize in producing corresponded to the classic Ricardian case of distortions from free trade.

Many scholars have tended to view these tariffs as mere fiscal impositions that were in no way protective of domestic industry (e.g., Irwin 1993, Tena 2006). But these claims tend to limit considerations of trade distortions to the narrow policy of mere producer protection (as opposed to all distortions in both consumption and production introduced by duties). They also take us too far into questions of the intended purpose of duties as being relevant to the question of who was and was not a free trader. In the British case, this was especially inappropriate because many of the so-called revenue tariffs of the 19th century were so clearly put into place in an earlier period as part of protectionist policies targeted quite specifically at Britain's rivals, notably the French. Moreover, the view that all the tariffs were offset by equivalent excises on domestic beverages has been shown to be false (Nye 1993). Above all, even a uniform excise on domestic and foreign beverages would have a protectionist effect to the extent that the taxes are imposed solely on the class of goods in which Britain did not have a comparative advantage.[2]

---

[2] Consider the difference between raising revenue by taxing all textiles versus taxing all alcohol. Both could have been designed not to favor local versus imported products, but the choice of which class of goods to tax has implications for the trade balance. The only neutral tax would be a uniform excise on all goods and services.

The tariffs on wine and spirits went back to the period 1689–1713, when England ceased all commerce with France as a result of the Nine Years' War and the War of Spanish Succession. This cessation of trade was especially significant because France was England's largest trading partner in the 17th century and the largest source of imports. Stopping trade with France turned England's large merchandise trade deficit into a surplus for several years. And a very large portion of Anglo-French trade – at least 20 percent – was wine. The cessation of imports from France led to a surge in imports from Spain and, more significantly, Portugal. As Portugal was not noted for its capacity to produce wine and spirits prior to this period, the heavy shift in production directed almost exclusively toward the English market was quite significant (Nye 2007). Portugal was an ally, even something of a dependency of England, and Englishmen dominated the Portuguese wine and spirits trade as growers, producers, merchants, and shippers. When the fabled Methuen Treaty of 1704 was signed, England was granted the right to sell textiles freely to the Portuguese in exchange for a promise that Portuguese wine would enter England (and later Britain) at a duty level never to exceed two-thirds of duties imposed on other nations (Nye 2007). Since Portugal was not particularly successful at selling wine to other nations, this arrangement was a clear distortion aimed at creating a supplier of alcoholic beverages that would be favorable to England. Indeed, as Portugal had enjoyed only the most minimal success in exporting wine and spirits prior to the quarter century of war with the French, the Methuen Treaty virtually created the overseas wine market for Portugal.

As has been detailed elsewhere, the end of war with France did not lead to free trade with France but rather a highly limited trade based on elevated volume tariffs that were designed specifically to exclude the bulk of French products from the British market. Supplementary tariffs on items that passed through French ports, or were delivered by French ships, or duty reductions on colonial products increased the favoritism against France and in favor of British domestics and allies. Moreover, the fact that – alone among all the British tariffs – the wine and spirits duties were set by volume rather than ad valorem meant that cheaper products were entirely excluded from Britain, while small quantities of higher-end alcohol, such as the best claret from Bordeaux, would continue to make their way to Albion (Nye 2007).

This was also significant because the other group that benefited tremendously from protection was local brewers and distillers. Beer had emerged as the most important, mass-produced beverage during the years of the

Anglo-French wars at the end of the 17th century. Technical improvements leading to economies of scale in brewing, coupled with the growth of London as the major British urban center, promoted beer as the common beverage and also encouraged the transformation of the industry from small-scale home production to concentrated large-scale industry. This tendency was further enhanced by laws designed to limit entry into the brewing industry and to lessen concentration in the retail trade as well (Mathias 1959, Nye 2007). Thus, the brewing industry was well placed to benefit from protection afforded by wine tariffs, but also to bargain directly with the government as a powerful special interest that could (and did) argue for continued protection throughout the 18th century. Attempts to invade the oligopoly tended to fail as late as the early 19th century (Nye 2007).

This also provided the state with a reliable means of imposing a credible tax on domestic consumption of beer and spirits. Whereas previous attempts (in the 17th century) to raise the excise on beer only raised revenues by a modest amount (due to the varieties of evasion that were practiced), the 18th century saw the successful imposition of a variety of excises that were effectively enforced and paid to the government.

Figure 5.2 shows the steep rise in income earned by the British state throughout the 18th century, of which the largest share was due to earnings

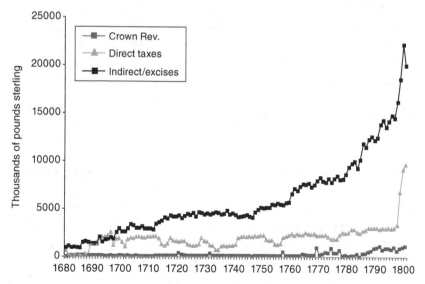

Figure 5.2. Net public revenue, Britain, 1688 to 1800.
Source: O'Brien and Hunt (1993).

Table 5.1. *Major taxes, Britain, 1788 to 1792*

Tax item	Tax revenue	Type of tax		Share of total taxes (percent)
	(£'000)			
1 Direct taxes				
Land, windows, etc.	3388	Direct		21.2
2 Food				
Tea	583	Customs	3.6	
Salt	999	Customs	6.3	
Sugar	425	Excise	2.7	
			subtotal	12.6
3 Heat, Light, Fuel	969	Cust & Exc		6.1
4 Construction material	648	Cust & Exc		4.1
5 Clothing, footwear	1010	Cust & Exc		6.3
6 Soap and Starch	501	Excise		3.1
7 Alcohol and tobacco				
Beer	1968	Excise	12.3	
Malt	1838	Excise	11.5	
Hops	121	Excise	0.8	
Wine	739	Customs	4.6	
Foreign Spirits	990	Customs	6.2	
Domestic Spirits	654	Excise	4.1	
Tobacco	607	Customs	3.8	
			subtotal	43.3
8 Commercial Services				
Newspapers, etc.	533	Stamp		3.3
Overall total	£15,973			100.0

Source: O'Brien (1988, p. 11).

from customs and excises. Table 5.1 indicates that during 1788–92, some 40 percent of the major British taxes were due to alcoholic beverages or inputs to brewing and distilling. The striking feature is the stability of the share of revenues from property and land; it remained fairly constant throughout the 18th century. At a time when Britain managed a dramatic increase in the size of state and built up its military to become the dominant power in world affairs, this shift in the relative source of the tax burden was quite remarkable. Moreover, there has been no rigorous analysis of why only Britain and none of the other major powers were able to accomplish this.

North and Weingast (1989) famously point to the role of the Glorious Revolution in making state borrowing and taxation more credible but give no reasons why the government was able to collect more revenue. A focus on the struggle over wine tariffs and brewing excises makes clear that this shift in interest group politics led to a configuration of interests in which taxes could be imposed and credibly collected from the parties most likely to attempt evasion (Nye 2007).

This also meant that when the time came to reform the British tariff system in the 19th century, the importance of the tariffs for revenue – not primarily for the direct revenue they generated but for their ability to collect revenue from producers of domestic substitutes – served as a drag on legislators' capacity to implement reforms that substantially altered duties on these new luxuries. Indeed, even the repeal of the Corn Laws, which were a much later set of agricultural tariffs than the various duties on alcohol and luxuries, proved so politically difficult that the proponents of the legislation were forced out of power as a result in the 1840s (Schonhardt-Bailey 2006).

In addition, the way in which the tariffs were imposed drastically reshaped the consumption patterns of the British citizenry. Fixed volume duties had the effect of excluding all trade in the lowest-quality wines and of tilting the import mix of the remaining products toward wine that was high in alcoholic content or to very high-quality products. For the most part, the Portuguese wines benefited from the double effect of their higher alcoholic content and, of course, from the lower level of the duty itself. Spanish products did not have quite the same preference as that of wines from Portugal, but they still benefited from the shift toward more alcoholic products. For the most part, an overwhelming share of the market left to the French was at the highest end.

Detailed records of what types of wines were being imported and in what quantities are not available but, as Nye (2007) has demonstrated, one can infer the extent of the quality shift simply by examining the ratio of wines imported in the barrel versus those in the bottle. Given high transportation costs and the possibilities of breakage, only the best wines tended to be shipped directly in bottles. Hence, it was typical for the ratio (by volume) of barrel to bottled wines from France to reside in the range of 15 to 1 up to 25 to 1. In contrast, the ratio for Britain tended to be on the order of 3 gallons of barrel wine for every gallon imported in bottles (Nye 2007). Hence, the perception of wine as primarily being a luxury product in Britain had less to do with any essential qualities of the wine itself or any peculiarities of British culture. Rather, a policy designed to exclude cheap wine and promote beer shaped what we think of as the canonical British penchant for beer, whiskey, gin, and rum for the masses and claret, sherry, and port for the elites.

A DIGRESSION ON EFFECTIVE PROTECTION

It is common to speak of protection as being the opposite of free trade. But this depends on how narrowly one defines protection. In theory, what one would like to do is to have a benchmark of pure free trade and observe how far a country deviates from that benchmark. The problem is that there has been no generally accepted measure that does this for the diverse mix of policies that countries have implemented to distort their trade. The beginnings of a theoretically rigorous basis for measuring trade distortions probably stem from the work of Anderson and Neary (1996) in which they propose a trade restrictiveness index (TRI) that is equivalent to whatever uniform tariff rate would produce the same economic welfare effect as the mix of actual tariffs, quotas, and other trade restrictions in place.

It has been commonplace in the applied trade policy literature to rely very heavily on measures of effective protection – that is, on the extent to which a given tariff protects the competing domestic industry taking into account taxes and restrictions on that industry's inputs as well as outputs. This, however, is a conceptual error. For one thing, it limits attention to only some of the many distortions introduced by tariffs. For example, a focus on effective protection tends to ignore the overall effect of tariffs on welfare when there are no clear domestic substitutes. And yet the baseline Ricardian case taught in every course in trade is one in which the importing and exporting nation each specializes in producing one importable and one exportable, so that any tariff would lead to distortions from the ideal benchmark. Thus, no "effective" protection is achieved, yet tariffs in both nations would clearly be distortionary deviations from the free trade ideal. Indeed, in this most basic case, a distortionary import tariff is identical to a revenue tariff on consumption of the importable. Nonetheless, a measure of effective protection at distorted prices would be zero in that instance, since there would be no domestic industry to protect. Indeed, in most cases, the presence of a protected domestic industry benefitting from tariffs would probably be indicative of a smaller overall distortion than the case where the domestic industry is only a weak substitute or is nonexistent (since there is less surplus loss from limiting trade when local goods are closer equivalents to foreign imports). Most important of all is that there are rarely tariffs that are purely for revenue or purely for protection.

High tariffs for revenue induce the production and use of goods that are weak substitutes. Tariffs that are designed to be protective may nonetheless raise substantial sums for the treasury.

This is especially relevant for the case of Britain and France in the mid-19th century. One of the justifications for British tariffs is that many were merely revenue tariffs or, as in the case of wine versus beer, tariffs were offset by domestic excises. But as Nye (1993) notes, British excises were, in fact, far below the tariff levels on French wine, especially when taking into account the distortions that led to the lowest-quality wine (the ones most likely to compete with beer) being totally excluded from the market in the first place by the high level of fixed, volumetric excises.

More importantly, a more rigorous investigation of the effect of tariff distortions using a computable general equilibrium framework (that improves on Anderson and Neary [1996]) makes possible a precise calculation of the extent of distortions introduced by tariffs in Britain versus France. The calculations demonstrate that the overall welfare distortions of British tariffs in the period prior to the 1860 Treaty were substantially greater than they were for France (see Dakhlia and Nye [2004], and also see the appendix in Nye [2007]). Welfare losses as a percentage of GDP were approximately three times larger for British tariffs than for French trade barriers, based on a simulation where both countries eliminated all tariffs completely.

Most important of all, we have already seen that the entire history of tariffs on imported alcohol was deeply protective by design, and that this protection was tied into the state's capacity to extract revenue from the protected industry.

Given the high levels of duties and regulations, it is also quite likely that the generally weak substitution effects between all imported beverages (including tea and coffee) and on items that were inputs into the production of spirits (such as sugar) were more important than one would expect from a cursory examination of direct substitutes. That we have done little to examine the equally complicated links between other production categories and the variety of duties and regulations surrounding imports and exports suggests that a superficial treatment of tariffs that seeks to disaggregate "good" from "bad" or liberal from illiberal duties is likely to mislead.

The significance of the wine tariffs can be seen by comparing the ex post ad valorem rates of protection on wine (using total wine import duties divided by wine import value) with the excise on beer. Using average tariff rates on wines and comparing them with the ad valorem rates on domestic

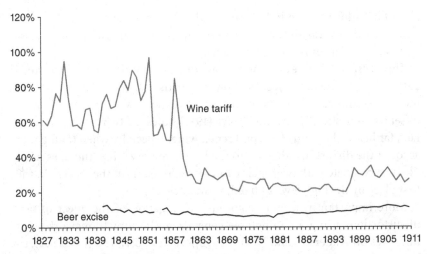

Figure 5.3. Beer excise ratio and wine tariff protection, Britain, 1827 to 1913.
Source: Tena (2006).

beer shows that the wine rates were several times higher than the rates on beer until the 1860 Treaty of Commerce. For the rest of the century, the average wine tariffs were approximately two to three times the rate charged on beer (Figure 5.3). However, even these differences understate the differences between the wine tariffs and the beer excises, because the wine tariffs were not imposed ad valorem. The tendency to levy them first by volume and then (after 1860) by alcoholic content would mean that the cheapest and lowest alcoholic beverages would be most highly discriminated against. Those drinks, of course, would have been the ones most likely to be competitive with beer, even though the 1860 reform partially redressed the discrimination between French wine and Portuguese products. Domestic beer, however, remained somewhat protected from foreign competition throughout the 19th century. In addition, high tariffs on weak substitute beverages such as coffee or tea also added a layer of protection.

Most important of all, the mere fact of high taxes on the entire class of beverages, both nonalcoholic and alcoholic, would have distorted British production and consumption to favor those industries (manufactures) in which Britain enjoyed a strong comparative advantage.

THE LATE NINETEENTH CENTURY

It was only after the passage of the 1860 Anglo-French Treaty of Commerce that Britain and France began to conform to the more common narrative about British free trade. In particular, the removal of French prohibitions on British goods in exchange for a lowered tariff on French wine led to steadily lower average British tariffs so that, by the late 1870s, British tariffs were clearly below those of France.

Some of the theories that derived from the conventional view of unilateral British free trade policy need to be reconsidered in the light of this revised history. For example, a classic claim by Kindleberger (1964) is that free trade was a public good and that individual nations had incentives to free-ride on other free traders by raising tariffs strategically. Depending on the game being played, this might not have been economically rational (if a nation has no market power in world trade, any tariff is suboptimal), but there may have been political reasons for nations to engage in strategic tariffs even if it were economically rational to stick to unilateral free trade. As a consequence, Kindleberger hypothesizes that what is needed is a free trade leader that benefits differentially from open trade and that is willing to hold fast to free trade in the midst of free-riding by minor powers. This thesis has been elaborated in the political science literature under the heading of hegemonic stability (see also Gilpin 1987 and Keohane 1984).

If we do not start from the assumption that Britain uniquely and unilaterally moved to free trade, the theory of hegemonic stability is discredited. Instead, we see that bilateral agreements stemming from negotiations between the leading trading powers played the pivotal role in promoting Europe-wide freer trade. Thus, even someone who insists that Britain was the sole free trader prior to the 1860 Treaty of Commerce would be hard-pressed to show that this led to a copycat effect. There was no movement to free trade self-evidently triggered by British moves. Parallel or similar moves in France and the Zollverein states either preceded or were independent of the British changes.

The really important and critical event was the signing of the 1860 Anglo-French Treaty of Commerce. Of great significance was the use of Most Favored Nation clauses in the trade treaty that allowed Britain and France to expand the sphere of open trade by concluding equivalent agreements with other European powers. Anxious not to be left out of the trading bloc resulting from the two leading powers in Europe ending centuries of trade war, virtually all of Europe was quickly drawn into the fold. The result was the period of perhaps the freest intra-European trade ever seen before or since (Nye 2007, Pahre 1998).

This also changes the conventional narrative about the British influence on European trade. If the new view is taken into account, not only was Britain not the unilateral free trader, but British exhortations to move to freer trade did little to change the pattern of European commerce. If anything, it was the bilateral agreement with France that was the strategic lynchpin of European liberalization. Since bilateral agreements were viewed then and now as undesirable compromises away from a purist liberalization strategy, it is ironic that the 1860 and the subsequent treaties signed throughout Europe were the proximate cause of the continental expansion of commerce in the late 1800s.

If Britain did not succeed in igniting free trade by repealing the Corn Laws at the beginning of the 19th century, did she at least preserve free trade by her principled adherence to low tariffs at the end of the century? As we will see, British exceptionalism did not allow Britain to serve as a successful free-trade hegemon, and most leading nations moved to partially protectionist policies by the end of the 1800s.

The period of political enthusiasm for nearly free trade following the 1860 Treaty was to be short-lived, at least in its purest form. Within a decade of the Anglo-French agreement, changes in the world market for primary goods, particularly in agriculture, led to reversals in policy, such as the core supporters of the European agreements – notably France and Germany – reinstating targeted protective tariffs.

The crucial factor seems to have been the increasing importance of grain from both Russia and the New World in raising supply and lowering world prices, partially as a result of openness, but primarily resulting from the drastic lowering of transportation and transactions costs throughout the 19th century. Land rents fell, and incomes to the owners of agricultural land declined relative to labor wages (Findlay and O'Rourke 2007). Thus, the Germans implemented both agricultural and industrial tariffs in 1879 in an alliance that – in principle – turned back on the liberal principles of the 1860s and 1870s. The French began to return to agricultural and industrial tariffs as agricultural imports grew.

The most damaging argument against the Kindleberger thesis of a free-trade hegemon is that British adherence to genuinely liberal trade policy at the end of the century does not seem to have prevented the major European powers from abandoning earlier agreements. However, there might be some merit in the leadership argument, at least if one wanted to weaken the case to claim that British free trade served to moderate the protectionist upsurge that was seen in the late 1800s. It is worth noting that these changes, drastic as they were, still kept overall average tariff levels in the last decades of the 19th century below their levels in the decades immediately following the end of the Napoleonic wars. For example, German average tariffs from 1880–1913 were 8.6 percent below the average rate of

10.4 percent for the period from 1834–65, and only slightly above the 8.4 percent average rate for the period from 1834–1913 (Dedinger 2006). In France, average tariffs for 1880–1900 were around 7.9 percent compared with 12.5 percent for 1840–60.[3] Whether the abandonment of free trade, in principle, and its replacement by an only moderately protectionist regime was partly due to a British influence or was completely dependent on domestic considerations is an issue that scholars will have to take up in future work. What is clear is that any consideration of the role of British leadership in the promotion of freer trade in this period needs to be reconsidered, and a fuller account must be given of the interplay between domestic and foreign policy considerations. Furthermore, it is clear that an economically robust treatment of agricultural distortions will have to take fiscal considerations into account where there is a strong tax-collecting reason for import tariffs. This is almost certainly the case for nations where excises and customs are of comparable or greater importance for revenue than income and property taxes, as was the case in Britain prior to the 20th century.

References

Anderson, J.E. and J.P. Neary (1996), "A New Approach to Evaluating Trade Policy," *Review of Economic Studies* 63: 107–25.

Brewer, J. (1988), *The Sinews of Power*, Cambridge MA: Harvard University Press.

Dakhlia, S. and J.V.C. Nye (2004), "Tax Britannica: Nineteenth-Century Tariffs and British National Income," *Public Choice* 121(3–4): 309–33.

Dedinger, B. (2006), "From Virtual Free-Trade to Virtual Protectionism: Or, Did Protectionism Have Any Part in Germany's Rise to Commercial Power 1850–1913?", in J. P. Dormois and P. Lains (eds.), *Classical Trade Protectionism 1815–1914*, London and New York: Routledge.

Findlay, R. and K. O'Rourke (2007), *Power and Plenty: Trade, War, and the World Economy in the Second Millennium*, Princeton NJ: Princeton University Press.

Gilpin, R. (1987), *The Political Economy of International Relations*, Princeton NJ: Princeton University Press.

Imlah, A. (1958), *Economic Elements of the Pax Britannica*, New York: Russell and Russell.

---

[3] Averages calculated from Levy-Leboyer and Bourguignon (1985). Tena (2006) has advanced arguments that would indicate that tariff averages for France should be much higher than the official statistics suggest, especially for the periods before 1860 and after 1880, but only as a result of his excluding items that were "fiscal products." I have argued (Nye 1991 and 1993) that such exclusion is arbitrary and inappropriately conflates the intent of tariffs with their overall effects. In any case, the symmetry of the adjustments make clear that, even in this extreme case, one should not see the late 19th century as unusually protectionist in France.

Irwin, D.A. (1993), "Free Trade and Protection in Nineteenth-Century Britain and France Revisited: A Comment on Nye", *Journal of Economic History* 51(1): 146–52.

Keohane, R. (1984), *After Hegemony: Cooperation and Discord in the World Political Economy*, Princeton NJ: Princeton University Press.

Kindleberger, C.P. (1964), *Economic Growth in France and Britain: 1851–1950*, Cambridge MA: Harvard University Press.

Levy-Leboyer, M. and F. Bourguignon (1985), *L'Économie française au XIXe siècle*, Paris: Economica.

Mathias, P. (1959), *The Brewing Industry in England: 1700–1830*, Cambridge: Cambridge University Press.

North, D.C. and B.R. Weingast (1989), "Consitutions and Commitment: The Evolution of Institutions Governing Public Choice in Seventeenth-Century England," *Journal of Economic History* 49(4): 803–32.

Nye, J.V.C. (1991), "The Myth of Free Trade Britain and Fortress France: Tariffs and Trade in the Nineteenth Century", *Journal of Economic History* 51(1): 23–46, March.

(1993), "Reply to Irwin on Free Trade", *Journal of Economic History* 53(1): 153–8, March.

(2007), *War, Wine, and Taxes: The Political Economy of Anglo-French Trade 1689–1900*, Princeton NJ: Princeton University Press.

O'Brien, P.K. (1988), "The Political Economy of British Taxation, 1660–1815," *Economic History Review* 41(1): 1–32.

O'Brien, P.K. and P.A. Hunt (1993), "Data Prepared on English Revenues, 1485–1815," European State Finance Database, available at www.le.ac.uk/hi/bon/ESFDB/frameset.html (files used: \obrien\engd002.ssd).

Pahre, R. (1998), "Reactions and Reciprocity: Tariffs and Trade Liberalization from 1815 to 1914," *Journal of Conflict Resolution* 42(4): 467–92.

Schonhardt-Bailey, C. (2006), *From the Corn Laws to Free Trade: Interests, Ideas, and Institutions in Historical Perspective*, Cambridge MA: MIT Press.

Tena, A. (2006), "Assessing the Protectionist Intensity of Tariffs in Nineteenth-Century European Trade Policy", in J.P. Dormois and P. Lains (eds.), *Classical Trade Protectionism 1815–1914*, London and New York: Routledge.

SIX

Agricultural Protection Growth in Europe, 1870–1969

Johan F. M. Swinnen[1]

Over the past decades, European countries spent more than 50 billion euros annually on subsidizing their farmers and protecting them against imports from other countries. This is not only the case in countries belonging to the European Union (EU), but also in countries such as Iceland, Norway, and Switzerland that have highly protected agricultural sectors. The most important form of government intervention in European agricultural markets is undoubtedly the Common Agricultural Policy (CAP) of the EU. While the EU has since reformed the CAP, the introduction of the CAP between 1962 and 1967 created a highly protectionist and distortive system of government intervention in agricultural markets across a large part of the continent.

How things changed in a century: 100 years earlier, Europe was characterized by free trade in agricultural and food products. The abolishment of the Corn Laws in 1846 signaled the end (or rather the beginning of the end – see Nye 2010) of farm import protection in England; and the English-French trade agreement of 1860 was the start of a series of trade agreements across Europe, effectively removing most trade constraints in agricultural markets.

These contrasting observations beg several questions: How and when did this change in policy occur? Why did it occur? Which events triggered these dramatic changes in policy preferences in Europe over the course of a century, and what were the fundamental causes that made them possible? These are the questions that this chapter tries to answer.

[1] The author is grateful to Kym Anderson and Will Martin for encouragement and guidance, and to Liesbeth Colen, Anja Crommelynck, Isabelle Lindemans, Joris Stiers, Gunilde Simeons, and Els Compernolle for assistance with the data analysis.

The focus of this paper is on the century between 1870 and 1969, by which time the Common Agricultural Policy (CAP) of the European Union (EU) had been implemented.[2]

A BRIEF HISTORY OF AGRICULTURAL POLICIES IN EUROPE

At the start of the 19th century, there was substantial government intervention in agricultural markets in Europe. Several countries, including France, Belgium, and the United Kingdom, had import tariffs for several commodities. Probably the most well-known form of protection was the Corn Laws in the United Kingdom. The Corn Laws were introduced centuries earlier to regulate grain prices and still imposed import tariffs on grains in the early 19th century.

The Liberalizations of the 19th Century

Most of the 19th century, from the late 1820s to the late 1870s, was characterized by a move toward free trade. In the United Kingdom, reforms in 1828 and 1842 first relaxed the import regulations of the Corn Laws, which were finally abolished in 1846. Around the same time, import tariffs on live animals, meat, potatoes, and vegetables were abolished. In the Netherlands, the government reduced import tariffs under the Grain Laws in the mid-1840s and abolished all import tariffs in the 1870s (Bieleman 1992, Sneller 1943). Similarly, in Prussia, import tariffs were reduced after the Napoleonic wars in the early 19th century. These reductions in tariffs were extended to other parts of Germany with the establishment of the Zollverein, and in 1853, the tariffs on grain were abolished.

A series of trade agreements contributed to the spread of free trade throughout Europe (Kindleberger 1975, Tracy 1989). The first was the English-French trade agreement in 1860 which was followed by several other trade agreements between European countries, including the 1862 French-German trade agreement, reducing tariffs also on manufacturing goods. The French-German Peace Treaty of 1871 renewed trade relations

---

[2] For historical political economy analyses of earlier periods, see Schonhardt-Bailey (1998) and Nye (2007); for more recent periods see, among others, Grant (1997), Josling (2009), Moyer and Josling (2002), Olper (1998), Pokrivcak, Crombez and Swinnen (2006) and Swinnen (2008); and for other regions, see Anderson, Hayami and Others (1986), Gardner (1987) and Lindert (1991). For more details and background on the arguments in this paper, see Swinnen (2009).

indefinitely and established the principle of the "most favored nation" on a reciprocal basis. German agriculture was strongly in favor of free trade. The large Junker estates in Prussia benefited from grain exports and feared that import tariffs on industrial goods would increase their costs or could lead to reprisal grain tariffs (Tracy 1989).

While the move toward free trade is associated with the intellectual contributions of Adam Smith and his colleagues, it comes as no surprise that liberalization of imports comes in a period of relative prosperity for farmers. The 1840s through most of the 1870s were generally a period of relatively high farm incomes and productivity growth. In England, it is referred to as the period of "high farming." It was also a period of relatively high grain prices, partly due to the Crimean War that reduced exports from Russia and the Black Sea region.

The Agricultural Crisis of 1880–1895

The period between 1880 and 1895 is marked by a sharp reduction in grain prices due to a dramatic increase in imports from Canada, the United States, Argentina, and Russia (Kindleberger 1951, O'Rourke 1997). There are two reasons for this. First, there was a major expansion of agricultural production, especially in the United States, where land was abundant and cheap. Second, technological innovations dramatically decreased production costs, through agricultural machinery that allowed for the exploitation of vast areas, as well as transport prices, as the steam engine allowed much cheaper transport via trains and the steamboat. A decade later, the dispersion of new freezing technology also allowed long-distance transport of frozen meat.

As a consequence of these changes, imports in Western Europe surged and wheat prices fell by almost half in real terms over the period 1880–95. The decline in wheat prices was particularly intense during the periods 1881–86 and 1891–94. With wheat being an important part of the agricultural sector, and because of the spillover effects on other (especially arable) commodity markets, incomes of crop farmers decreased significantly throughout Europe.

The impact on livestock (meat) markets was quite different. Initially, there was no surge of imports in livestock or meat, and livestock farmers benefitted from declining grain prices as their feed costs fell. Only a decade after the surge in grain imports, when freezing technology spread in meat processing and trading, did meat imports from overseas grew and prices started falling also in the livestock sector. However, the induced price declines appeared later and were not as severe.

Table 6.1. *Average NRAs for key commodities,[a] selected Western European
countries, 1870 to 1969 (percent)*

	Belgium	Netherlands	France	United Kingdom	Germany	Finland
1870–79	.	.	.	.	.	.
1880–89	.	.	.	.	−4	.
1890–99	−2	.	.	.	16	.
1900–09	−3	.	16	6	22	.
1910–19	−1	13	24	1	.	.
1920–29	8	34	32	6	39	.
1930–39	35	61	98	45	115	87
1940–49	19	−36	41	28	21	40
1950–59	18	−8	33	12	77	97
1960–69	89	.	.	18	149	164

[a] Commodity coverage: Belgium: wheat, barley, butter, beef, sugar; Netherlands: wheat, barley, butter; France: wheat, barley, butter, pork, sugar; United Kingdom: wheat, barley, butter; Germany: wheat, barley, beef, sugar; Finland: wheat, barley, milk, sugar.
Source: Swinnen (2009).

The dramatic changes in the agricultural markets induced strong pressure from farmers on governments to intervene. The reactions of European governments to these changes and pressures were mixed. It is impossible to summarize in this chapter all the details of the policy proposals, debates, and decisions, but we can distinguish different patterns in government reactions.

The average nominal rates of assistance (NRAs), as summarized in Table 6.1 and Figure 6.1, show that NRAs remained close to zero in the United Kingdom and Belgium, whereas they increased in France and Germany after 1880. These variations in NRAs reflect real differences in policy choices: the United Kingdom and Belgium (as well as other countries such as the Netherlands and Finland) did not impose import tariffs, whereas the French and German (as well as the Swedish) governments protected their farmers by increasing import restrictions.

First, the governments in Belgium and the United Kingdom refused to increase import tariffs in grains. Both countries were already quite industrialized by the time of the agricultural crisis. In both countries, a coalition of industrial capital owners and workers opposed protection to arable farmers. Workers and industry opposed tariffs because they benefited from low food prices (and thus low wages) with cheap grain imports. While UK

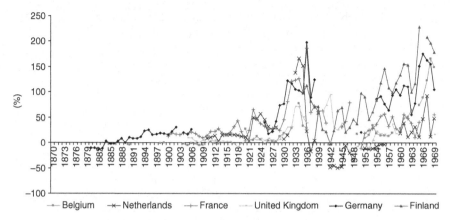

Figure 6.1. Average NRAs for key commodities,[a] selected Western European countries, 1870 to 1969 (percent).

[a] Commodity coverage: Belgium: wheat, barley, butter, beef, sugar; Netherlands: wheat, barley, butter; France: wheat, barley, butter, pork, sugar; United Kingdom: wheat, barley, butter; Germany: wheat, barley, beef, sugar; Finland: wheat, barley, milk, sugar.

Source: Swinnen (2009).

landlords had always been very powerful (e.g., through the representation system in parliament), their influence was waning and they were now confronted with a strong opposition of labor and industrial capital, who had gained increasing political power.

In addition, the "agricultural sector" was not united in its support for import tariffs. This was particularly pronounced in the United Kingdom, where there were very heterogeneous interests within agriculture. The main people hurt by the low grain prices were large landlords, mostly located in the southern regions of England. However, many of the other actors in agriculture actually favored low grain prices. This was the case for livestock farmers, mostly located in the northern part of the country, who benefited through low feed prices. Moreover, livestock had become more important. At the time of the crisis, grains only accounted for 12 percent of agricultural output, while meat (42 percent) and milk (21 percent) were much more important. In fact, the divergent interests of the farms caused a split among farm organizations.

Furthermore, the English landlords were not even supported in their demand for protection by those who worked on their farms. Farm workers were paid in wages. They were generally very poor and they benefited more from low prices of staple food (grains) than they lost from the negative pressure on their wages, which by then were strongly influenced by industrial wages. A budget survey from 1874 showed that farm workers

Table 6.2. *Import tariffs in Prussia, the Zollverein, and*
Germany, 1857 to 1914 (percent)

	Wheat	Rye	Barley	Oat
1857–64	5	1	2	2
1865–79	0	0	0	0
1880–85	10	10	5	10
1885–87	30	30	15	15
1887–91	50	50	23	40
1892–1902	35	35	20	28
1902–14	75	70	70	70

Source: Henning (1978).

spent 90 percent of their income on grains and potatoes; meat and milk
were unknown luxuries. Their welfare actually increased during the agricultural crisis (Burnett 1969). While farm workers' interests had little
influence during most of the 19th century, this changed with the political
reforms of 1885, which gave them equal voting rights and thus substantial
political representation in parliament.

Second, in contrast to the free trade position of the United Kingdom
and Belgium, the governments of France and Germany introduced import
tariffs to protect their grain farms (Table 6.2). Both countries were characterized by a large agricultural population, a less industrialized economy,
and a more important crop sector. For example, in France, crops made up
more than 70 percent of total agriculture during all of the 19th century,
and still accounted for 60 percent by 1950 (Table 6.3).

In France, the government initially opposed import tariffs, but when
grain prices kept falling, the government gave in to strong pressure from
the French grain farms, and import tariffs were introduced in the 1880s
(Agulhon and Desert 1976). In Germany, the introduction of grain tariffs
signaled a major reversal of policy, not just of the government but even
more of the main farmer organization (Schonhardt-Bailey 1998). Until the
1870s, the large grain farmers of Prussia had been the main proponents of
the German free trade regime to protect their export position. However,
as grain started arriving on the world market and even inside Germany at
prices below Prussian farmers' costs, they changed position. During the
1880s, there was considerable debate among farmers as to what position to
take, but when prices kept falling they ultimately shifted to a protectionist

Table 6.3. *Shares of crops and livestock in total value of agricultural output,*
United Kingdom, France, and Germany, 1815 to 1974 (percent)

	United Kingdom		France		Germany	
	Crops	Livestock	Crops	Livestock	Grains	Beef, Pork
1815–24	.	.	76	24		
1865–74	45	55	76	24	.	.
1885–94	38	62	71	29	37	22
1925–34	30	70	65	35	41	38
1950–54	.	.	59	41	30	43
1965–74	.	.	.	.	27	54

Sources: Fletcher (1973), Toutain (1961), German national statistics.

stance. Since German industry had already been demanding trade protection, import tariffs were introduced across the entire economy and gradually increased in Germany (Table 6.2).

Third, *all* governments introduced some protection in the livestock sector, sometimes as import tariffs but mostly in the form of nontariff barriers such as animal disease controls. As livestock prices also started falling in the 1890s, there was additional pressure on the government to intervene, now also from livestock producers. This occurred despite the fact that the price decline in livestock was considerably less than in grains: in the United Kingdom, prices fell between the 1870s and the 1890s on average by more than 40 percent for crops but only by around 25 percent for livestock products (Tracy 1989).

France and Germany early on raised import tariffs on livestock products. Also, Belgium introduced small import tariffs on livestock and meat and on butter and margarine in 1895. In addition, a series of payments were made from the budget to the animal disease prevention program.

With the implementation of import tariffs on livestock, border controls increased and with that the use of health arguments as protectionist instruments. Such hidden protectionism through sanitary regulations increased in the 1890s. In Germany, a law restricted the import of live animals by 1880, ostensibly for sanitary reasons. By 1889, the government had all but closed the border to imports of live animals, and meat imports were restricted as well. Also, in the other countries, borders were closed regularly to prevent the "import of infections." In 1892, the French government imposed a ban on imports of cattle and the United Kingdom introduced the "Animal Disease Act", which prohibited the import of live animals under the guise of safety rules (while allowing frozen meat imports). The impact on consumers was mixed: The Act mainly hurt richer consumers since poor consumers could continue to benefit from cheap frozen meat imports.

Fourth, there were substantial investments by governments, in particular those in Belgium, the Netherlands, and Finland – who did not introduce (or limited) import tariffs – to initiate a variety of programs to support the restructuring of the agricultural sector from grains to livestock production. The governments of these countries considered modernization and restructuring of agriculture by stimulating livestock production as the only realistic development strategy in the face of cheap grain imports, which made competition in grains more difficult but also made feed costs cheaper for the livestock sector. A series of government initiatives were taken to stimulate and help farmers shift to livestock production: in research and extension; the subsidization of activities that provided incentives for improved quality of livestock breeding; and compensation of farmers for the slaughter of infected animals. Furthermore, some governments stimulated the creation of dairy marketing and processing cooperatives.

More generally, European governments increased investments in public goods such as agricultural research, extension, and education, to increase agricultural productivity. Policies to reduce fraud and to improve rural transport also were introduced. Ministries of Agriculture and agricultural schools and universities were established then too.

The Pre-World War I Period

By 1900, the crisis subsided. Prices started increasing because production costs increased in grain-exporting countries and because industrial growth increased demand for food, in particular for livestock and horticultural products. The demand for protection by farmers declined with an improvement in their incomes. In a review of the political debates on agricultural policy in Belgium, Van Molle (1989) concludes that, in strong contrast to the long and ardent debates in the 1880s and 1890s, there was no substantial debate on agricultural protection in most of the period between the turn of the century and World War I. The members of parliament representing farm interest voiced little interest or did not sponsor new farm laws for the next two decades, until the end of the 1920s. This suggests that the agricultural crisis, which had been the driving force behind agricultural protection, was over.

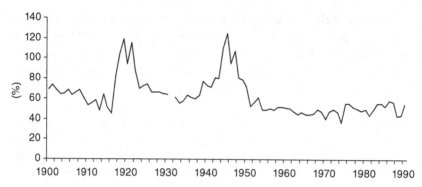

Figure 6.2. Household incomes in agriculture as a percentage of incomes in industry, Finland, 1900 to 1990 (percent).

Source: Crommelynck, Kola and Swinnen (2001).

World War I

The war brought destruction and disruptions of the food production and distribution systems. International trade broke down, with warships controlling the sea and blockades being set up. During and immediately after the war, food markets were strongly regulated. Food was generally scarce and expensive, and government regulations were introduced to secure sufficient food for consumers under war conditions. Maximum prices, compulsory deliveries, and export restrictions were introduced. However, where governments imposed maximum prices and mandatory deliveries on farmers, a black market emerged, yielding high prices. Hence, despite the war-related problems, the war years typically yielded high prices for farmers and, in comparison with the rest of the economy, farmers did generally better. Figure 6.2 uses annual data from 1900 to 1990 from Finland to illustrate that the only two periods when farm incomes substantially increased compared to incomes in the rest of the economy were during the two World Wars, and the years immediately after. The situation was similar in the other European countries.

The Interwar Period

In general, agricultural and food policy between the wars was characterized by a shift from consumer protection to producer protection. Immediately after the war, food was still expensive and governments continued to apply strict regulations to food consumption and production. Most prices were fixed, with maximum grain prices set below international prices.

Production was claimed and imports and exports were strongly regulated. Given the high prices, important investments took place immediately after the war. More land was brought into production, yields rose, and the number of the livestock was increased. At the same time, land prices and rents increased both due to increasing product prices and the large war savings of farmers.

However, with removal of war regulations in the early 1920s, prices came down. This price decline was further reinforced in the second half of the 1920s as the investments by farmers started resulting in substantially increased productivity and supplies. At the same time, demand fell with the general economic crisis of the late 1920s and early 1930s (1929 was the great stock market crash on Wall Street, symbolizing the start of the Great Depression). As a result, farm prices fell substantially in the late 1920s and early 1930s.

Again, there was strong pressure on governments to intervene and support farmers. At the same time, governments faced strong pressures from industry and workers to keep basic food prices low in the midst of the Depression. There were again different reactions from governments, with some more inclined to protect agriculture than others. Overall, there was a greater willingness by governments to protect farmers than in the 1880s, and import constraints were introduced in many countries, particularly in the early 1930s.

Tariff protection to livestock products emerged soon after prices started declining, but it took more discussion and a stronger decrease in prices before protection to grains was granted. Among the grains, protection for feedgrains (barley, oats) was easier to obtain than protection for wheat and rye. Another difference was that when the government decided to support bread grain production, this was primarily done by a system of production subsidization rather than import tariffs, as it has a differential impact on consumer prices.

Governments increased protection to livestock, a sector in which they had already invested in the preceding decades, and whose products were less crucial for the poorest workers. Substantial increases in import protection emerged in the 1930s for animal products. For example, NRAs for butter increased from close to zero in the 1920s to around 40 percent in the 1930s.

There was much more opposition from industry and workers to raising tariffs for (bread) grains. For example, a 1935 proposal by the Belgian government, under pressure from farmers, to increase grain import tariffs caused a general strike that resulted in the fall of the government, after which the tariff proposal was abolished. Overall, the NRAs for wheat actually fell significantly in the early 1930s. Because of strong opposition from industry and workers, support to grain farmers occurred to an important extent through measures other than import tariffs.

One policy measure used in several European countries was the compulsory use of domestic grain by millers. Millers were obliged by the government to use a minimum percentage of domestic grain in their flour. Another measure was government payments to grain producers, such as deficiency payments in the United Kingdom and per hectare subsidies in Belgium – measures that did not increase grain prices.

Governments also intervened in other ways to assist farmers, in particular with measures that did not affect consumers. During the 'good years' of the 1920s, farmers rented more land and signed contracts with high land rents – which they were unable to pay as agricultural prices fell. Both in the Netherlands and Belgium, the government intervened to assist tenants.

World War II

By the end of the 1930s, prices rose again as war preparations began. Many protectionist measures were sustained until 1939, but others were relaxed from the mid-1930s as farm profits started recovering (Tracy 1989). During World War II, food production and consumption were strongly regulated. As in World War I, food prices were high on the black market, and farmers' incomes soared, certainly compared with incomes in the rest of the economy.

The Post-World War II Period

The developments after World War II were similar to those after World War I. During the war, food production and consumption were strongly regulated. Immediately after the war, the existing regulatory system was sustained in most European countries and used to ensure a sufficient and "affordable" food supply. Maximum prices were imposed and harvests and stocks claimed by the government. In the next years, the strongly regulated agricultural markets were slowly liberated.

Agricultural prices started declining again from the late 1940s onward. As a result, farmers' incomes started falling, unlike incomes outside the agricultural sector. Economic growth was strong in the rest of the economy, so the income gap between farmers and people working in other sectors increased strongly in favor of nonfarm households. There were two reasons for the income gap. The first was the strong growth in the industrial and service sectors of the economy. The second was the introduction of labor-saving technologies in agriculture. Because demand for food had become more inelastic, there was downward pressure on agricultural incomes.

From the 1950s on, "income parity" became a central issue in agricultural policy debates. In speeches of politicians, in political discussions, and in the agricultural press, the relative income situation of farmers was at the top of the agenda. In response, European governments introduced a series of measures to support farm incomes. Such measures as minimum prices, target prices, and import quotas were introduced. The regulatory system installed during the war was now used to support farm incomes by intervening in markets in favor of farmers. From the NRA indicators in Figure 6.1, it is clear that this led to important increases in agricultural protection throughout Europe.

An argument often invoked to support these measures, especially in continental Europe, was the importance of food security (often interpreted as food self-sufficiency). On a continent twice devastated in a fifty-year period and twice facing food shortages during war times, the argument of sufficient food through local production touched a nerve. Politicians who had to address the nation's basic concerns, and consumers who faced hunger and food shortages during times when food imports and long-distance food supplies were interrupted, were sympathetic to the call for supports for local food production.

European Integration

The period 1945–1970 was a period of intense discussion and negotiation over international economic integration. The first European integration treaty was the Benelux customs treaty, signed by Belgium, Luxembourg, and the Netherlands in 1944 but only implemented several years later. Fear that highly competitive Dutch agriculture would overtake the Belgian market resulted in political opposition to the extension of the treaty to the agricultural sector. In 1947, a protocol was agreed upon that included minimum import prices for agricultural products. The farmers' opposition to the removal of this protocol was so strong that the 1958 Benelux Economic Union Treaty was not enacted until two years later. By then, the Rome Treaty had been signed for the creation of the European Economic Community by the six original members (France, Germany, Italy, Belgium, Luxembourg, and the Netherlands). With unfavorable relative income evolutions for farmers in European countries, and a variety of government support measures in the various countries, protectionist policies were ultimately sustained under the Common Agricultural Policy (CAP) – see Josling (2009) for details – leading to high farm support and large distortions in agricultural markets. The specifics of the CAP were decided at the Stresa Conference in 1958 and implemented in 1968.

CAUSES OF THE GROWTH IN AGRICULTURAL PROTECTION IN EUROPE

Numerous influences impacted on the growth in support for farm incomes, so the discussion below is divided into several parts.

Market Fluctuations, Income Gaps, and the Demand for Protection

It is clear from the previous section that agricultural protection in Europe did not increase monotonically over time. Instead, there were very important fluctuations over time. Over the 1870–1969 century, there were three periods when European farmers intensely demanded protection from international competition. Those were the end of the 19th century (1880–1895), during the two world wars (and especially the period 1928–1935), and the post-1950 period. These were periods either when world market prices were depressed and imports were increasing strongly, putting pressure on domestic farms, or when the gap between incomes from farming and those in the rest of the economy grew rapidly. In other periods, there was less or no demand for protection. In some periods, consumers demanded governments to protect them from increasing food prices. This happened in particular during and just after the two wars when food was scarce and food prices very high.

The empirical observations summarized in the previous section indicate the importance of agricultural market conditions and the income gap between agriculture and the rest of the economy as influencing the demand for agricultural protection. If income from market activities are low, either absolutely or compared to the rest of society, farmers demand government support to increase their incomes. These observations are consistent with studies that have shown the relative income of farmers to be an important factor in agricultural protection (e.g., de Gorter and Tsur 1991, Gardner 1987, Swinnen and de Gorter 1993).

However, while farmers' demands for protection were intense during three periods in the century we analyze (the end of the 19th century, the interwar years, and the post-1950 period), government responses to these demands for protection by farmers were markedly different. Governments mostly resisted protectionist demands at the end of the 19th century, except in France and Germany. European governments were more likely to provide protection in the 1930s, and substantially more so from 1950 onward. Hence, in the course of economic development, governments responded more favorably to farmers' demands to provide protection.

The increased willingness of governments to provide protection over time is due to fundamental changes in the economic and political structure of society.[3]

The Cost of Food, Industrial Development, and Opposition to Protection

In the course of economic development, the importance of expenditures on food, and in particular on staple foods, declined (Table 6.4). This reduced opposition to import protection by the coalition of workers and of industrial interests. This opposition coalition was so strong at the end of the 19th century, and for some basic food commodities it still was in the 1930s, that they were able to block substantive import tariffs for agriculture, and in particularly for (bread)grain farms. The opposition was strongest in the most industrialized countries, such as the United Kingdom, Belgium, and the Netherlands. There, the share of employment in agriculture was lowest and both capital investment and employment in industry were largest. In France and Germany, where tariffs were introduced, the economic importance of agriculture was comparatively large (and that of industry still small) at the end of the 19th century.

The combination of different industrial development and different farm structures (see below) may explain to some extent the differences in government policies in the early 20th century between the United Kingdom on the one hand and France and Germany on the other. In all three countries, large grain farms were important and relatively well organized. However, in the United Kingdom, they were unsuccessful in obtaining protection against imports as the opposition from industry, workers, and the rest of agriculture was stronger. In Germany and France, they were able to obtain support. The latter countries had a manufacturing sector that was under pressure from imports from more advanced industrial nations, such as the United Kingdom. Both in Germany and France, the manufacturing industry wanted import protection (particularly the textile and iron

---

[3] See Anderson (1995) and Swinnen (1994) for theoretical arguments on this issue.

Table 6.4. *Share of food in overall consumption expenditure, selected Western European countries, 1870 to 1969 (percent)*

	Belgium	Netherlands	France	United Kingdom	Germany	Finland	Sweden
1870–79	62	62	57	.	40	.	.
1880–89	62	.	55	43	40	.	.
1890–99	61	.	50	.	40	.	.
1900–09	63	61	47	34	40	.	.
1910–19	63	.	46	36	40	.	.
1920–29	65	.	.	34	38	.	.
1930–39	56	49	.	30	41	42	.
1940–49	50	.	.	29	40	44	37
1950–59	49	.	40	31	33	38	35
1960–69	39	.	.	.	31	30	34

Source: Swinnen (2001).

industries in France). In Germany, the main opponents of import tariffs were the Prussian grain-exporting farms, but this changed when cheap grain swamped the European markets in the second half of the 1870s. With French and German farmers now switching sides in favor of protection, an anti-free trade coalition of industry and agriculture emerged in both countries – in contrast to the United Kingdom and Belgium, for example, where industry wanted export opportunities and cheap food. This caused the introduction of substantial general import tariffs, not just on agricultural products but also on industrial products, in 1879 in Germany and in 1892 in France.

Interestingly, this alliance was only temporary. By the 1890s, German industry was in a much stronger competitive position and started becoming worried about the negative effects of high food costs and high wages. In addition, it was being harmed by tariffs that the United States had imposed in reaction to the German agricultural tariffs. However, by the 1890s, industrial interests had changed. Industry, and industrial workers, wanted cheaper food and access to international export opportunities. This effectively lead to a reversal of German trade policies: Despite strong opposition from farming interests, especially the Prussian landlords, a series of new trade agreements in the 1890s lowered agricultural tariffs and brought benefits for manufacturing. New trade agreements with Romania and Russia, through the most favored nation principle, also reduced tariffs on grains from the United States and other grain exporters (Tracy 1989).

Feudalism and Farm Structures

Differences in farm structure may affect the political equilibrium in several ways. First, in general, livestock farms opposed grain import tariffs. In countries where livestock farming was well established, livestock producers organized to lobby against import tariffs for grains rather than form a coalition with grain farmers. This was particularly important in the period before World War II.

Second, in feudal systems (as in the United Kingdom), the role and divergent interests of farm workers are important. In low-income societies (such as the United Kingdom still was at the end of the 19th century), farm workers opposed import tariffs on staple foods because they lost more as consumers than they gained through increased wages.

Third, in feudal systems, small farms and tenants are more concerned with their tenure rights than with import tariffs and they see landlords, not cheap imports, as their main problem. Their political struggle focuses on improving tenure conditions by opposing landlords, rather than forming a coalition with them to increase farm prices (Swinnen 2002).

The Organization of Farmers and Agricultural Crises

The impact of political organization on agricultural protection is difficult to assess. A simple comparison between 1860 and 1960 would suggest that agricultural protection had increased with the political organization of farms, which grew importantly at the end of the 19th and in the beginning of the 20th century (Swinnen 2009). However, such a comparison would ignore important periods in the course of this century when farms were well organized and when protection was not given to agriculture.

My hypothesis is that the relationship is more complex: Farmers will get protection when three conditions are fulfilled: (a) they have substantive political influence, either through votes in parliament of through extra-parliamentary political organizations; (b) there is an (economic) crisis that triggers strong political action by farmers to influence governments; and (c) the opposition to protection is sufficiently low, either because support to agriculture has relatively little effect on consumers and the rest of the economy, or because the rest of the economy has relatively little political influence.

To illustrate the logic behind this, it is important to keep in mind that landlords and large farmers were the most powerful and politically well organized groups in many societies in the 18th and most of the 19th century, when protection was low or declining. Moreover, protection did not increase (or only mildly) despite the fact that many new farm organizations emerged and existing farm organizations (as well as a network of rural organizations linked to farming) grew in importance during the crisis at the end of the 19th century and in the first decades of the 20th century. In addition, during the same period, voting rights were extended to small farmers and farm workers in most European countries (Swinnen 2002).

These political institutional factors did enhance the political organization and the influence of agricultural interests when the next crisis emerged, which was in the late 1920s and 1930s. Governments increased support to farmers but the support remains limited because opposition from industry and workers was still strong. Food still accounted for a major part of worker expenditures; moreover, the general economy was hit by the economic crisis of the late 1920s and early 1930s, making cheap food an important concern. As a result, there was some increase in agricultural import tariffs, but less on food staples such as bread grains or potatoes where support was more likely given under the form of direct payments.

After World War I, all factors in favor of more protection and more support to agriculture came together. Farm incomes fell increasingly behind incomes in the rest of the economy, increasing demands for agricultural support. Importantly, after World War II, opposition of industry and workers in the rest of the economy fell strongly. With strong growth in the rest of the economy, the share of food in total consumer expenditures and its impact on wages declined strongly and with this so did opposition to protection from workers and industry. Well established farm organizations then contributed to translating these changed circumstances into changes in the political equilibrium, resulting in a shift towards more agricultural protection.

Government Administration and Agribusiness Organizations

The administrative organizations set up during the world wars to regulate food distribution and prices were used after the wars to regulate agricultural and food markets to support farmers. This appears to be especially important after World War II. The widespread networks of farm and agribusiness organizations, often cooperatives, also allowed the organization of more intervention in markets. At the same time, these organizations became important interest groups themselves, with, for example, dairy and sugar processing companies actively lobbying for government support and import protection for their sectors.

The Wars

Wars appear to have played an important role as well. First, "war memories" make support of domestically produced food an important concern and more easily acceptable for consumers, and an important political argument for politicians. After suffering from food shortages and high food prices in both world wars, especially in continental Europe, food self-sufficiency was an important factor in the policy debates. The emergence of the Cold War in the 1950s and 1960s reinforced these arguments. In some countries, these arguments resonate with earlier concerns. In Finland, for example, food shortages following its separation from Russia and the disruption of trade ties in the early 20th century made food self-sufficiency an important political objective during the first half of the 20th century, and that was reinforced by the experience during the wars.

Imperial Germany in the early 20th century sought rearmament and made food self-sufficiency an important consideration. During the Weimar republic, the Nazi's nationalistic (emphasizing the importance of domestic production) and right-wing ideology found a close ally (and many votes) in the conservative rural population and among Prussian landlords. The farm organizations reorganized in a Nazi-dominated Green front. After World War II, when Germany had lost most of its grain production areas, it became preoccupied with stimulating domestic food production through high prices on the smaller western and southern farms.

Political Change: the Growth of Democracy

What is the impact of growing democracy on agricultural support? In an econometric study using long run data from Belgium, Swinnen, Banerjee and de Gorter (2001) assess the impact of various economic and political variables. They find that, of the four voting reforms since the mid-19th century, each time extending votes to other social groups, the only vote reform that had an impact on agricultural protection was when in 1919 the extension of voting rights included farm workers and small farmers. This "pro-agricultural bias" in voting reform has a significant positive effect on protection levels in their study, but none of the other reforms have.

Such subtle impacts of democratization on agricultural protection seem consistent with the evidence that we have reviewed here: Extending voting rights "from the rich to the poor" (as is the standard evolution) shifts parliamentary power from the landlords and industrial capital (the rich) to industrial and farm workers and small farmers (the poor). Hence it is not immediately clear why this would lead to an increase in agricultural protection. In fact, in the UK, the opposite seems to have been the result: Almost all the poor, even the farm workers and small livestock farms, benefited from cheap grains and therefore opposed the import protection which landlords and grain farmers demanded. As and when electoral reforms gave these groups voting rights, the political opposition against grain import tariffs in the nineteenth and early twentieth centuries was reinforced.

Democratization and the growth of farm associations enhanced the political influence of small farmers, tenants, and farm workers. This enhanced political influence seems to have been more important in affecting the distribution of rents within the agricultural sector rather than average protection for agriculture as a whole. Tenure rights of tenants were enhanced through a variety of laws in many continental European countries, as well as increases in land taxes and inheritance taxes contributing to the break up of large estates and the growth of (smaller) operator-owned farms in the United Kingdom (Swinnen 2002).

CONCLUSION

Important changes took place in agricultural policies in Europe in the nineteenth and twentieth centuries. In the 1860s, free trade spread across the continent. A century later, in the 1960s, European integration coincided with an agreement for heavy government intervention in agricultural markets and strong protection against imports. The growth of agricultural protection was not linear, but rather there were substantial fluctuations over those ten decades. Factors that appear to have played an important role in causing the increase in agricultural protection in Europe are the decline of income from markets for farmers, in particular in comparison with incomes from the rest of the economy, the reduced share of consumer expenditures for food, the farm structure, the political organization of farmers and the growth in government administrative capacity for regulating markets, the food shortages during the world wars, and democratization.

However, the impact of each of these factors is complex and almost always interrelated with other factors. Periods of substantial increases in agricultural protection were characterized by three conditions. First, farmers had substantive political influence, either through votes in parliament or through extra-parliamentary political organizations. Second, a crisis in agriculture or growing income gap with the rest of the economy triggered strong political action by farmers to influence governments. Third, the opposition to protection was sufficiently low, either because support to agriculture had relatively little effect on consumers and the rest of the economy or because the rest of the economy had relatively little political influence. The combination of these three factors was needed to induce major increases in protection. Such combinations were present to some extent in the 1930s, but especially in the 1950s, when protection grew strongly.

References

Agulhon, M. and G. Desert (1976), "L'essor de la paysannerie 1789–1852", pp. 19–58 in G. Duby (ed.), *Histoire de la France rurale*: 3, Paris: Editions du Seuil.

Anderson, K. (1995), "Lobbying Incentives and the Pattern of Protection in Rich and Poor Countries," *Economic Development and Cultural Change* 43(2): 401–23.

Anderson, K., Y. Hayami and Others (1986), *The Political Economy of Agricultural Protection: East Asia in International Perspective*, Boston and London: Allen and Unwin.

Bieleman, J. (1992), *Geschiedenis van de landbouw in Nederland 1500–1950 (Dutch agricultural history 1500–1950)*, Amsterdam: Boom Meppel.

Burnett, J. (1969), *A History of the Cost of Living*, Harmondsworth: Penguin Books.

Crommelynck, A., J. Kola and J.F.M. Swinnen (2001), "The Political Economy of Agricultural Policy in Finland 1900–1990", Working Paper No. 98, LICOS, K.U.Leuven.

De Gorter, H. and Y. Tsur (1991), "Explaining Price Policy Bias in Agriculture: The Calculus of Support Maximizing Politicians," *American Journal of Agricultural Economics* 73(4): 1244–54.

Fletcher, T.W. (1973), "The Great Depression of English Agriculture, 1873–1896," pp. 30–55 in P.J. Perry (ed.), *British Agriculture, 1875–1914*, University Paperbacks, Debates in Economic History, London: Methuen & Co. Ltd.

Gardner, B.L. (1987), "Causes of US Farm Commodity Programs," *Journal of Political Economy* 95(2): 290–310.

Grant, W. (1997), *The Common Agricultural Policy*, Basingstoke: Palgrave Macmillan.

Henning, F.W. (1978), *Landwirtschaft und ländliche Gesellschaft in Deutschland, vol. 2, 1750–1976*, Bonn: Paderborn.

Josling, T. (2009), "Western Europe," Ch. 3 in K. Anderson (ed.), *Distortions to Agricultural Incentives: A Global Perspective, 1955–2007*, London: Palgrave Macmillan and Washington DC: World Bank.

Kindleberger, C.P. (1951), "Group Behavior and International Trade," *Journal of Political Economy* 59(1): 30–47.

(1975), "The Rise of Free Trade in Western Europe, 1820–1875," *Journal of Economic History* 35(1): 20–55, March.

Lindert, P.H., 1991, "Historical Patterns of Agricultural Policy," pp. 29–83 in C.P. Timmer (ed.), *Agriculture and the State*, Ithaca, NY: Cornell University Press.

Moyer, W. and T. Josling (2002), *Agricultural Policy Reform: Politics and Process in the EU and US in the 1990s*, Aldershot: Ashgate.

Nye, J.V.C. (2007), *Wine, War and Taxes: The Political Economy of Anglo-French Trade, 1689–1900*, Princeton NJ: Princeton University Press.

(2010), "Anglo-French Trade, 1689–1899: Agricultural Trade Policies, Alcohol Taxes and War," Ch. 5 in this volume.

Olper, A. (1998), "Political economy determinants of agricultural protection in EU member states: an empirical investigation," *European Review of Agricultural Economics* 24: 463–87.

O'Rourke, K. (1997), "The European Grain Invasion, 1870–1913," *Journal of Economic History* 57(4): 775–801, December.

Pokrivcak, J., C. Crombez and J.F.M. Swinnen (2006), " The Status Quo Bias and Reform of the Common Agricultural Policy: Impact of Voting Rules, the European Commission, and External Changes," *European Review of Agricultural Economics* 33(4): 562–90.

Schonhardt-Bailey, C. (1998), "Parties and Interests in the 'Marriage of Iron and Rye," *British Journal of Political Science* 28: 291–330.

Sneller, Z.W. (ed.) (1943), *Geschiedenis van den Nederlandschen landbouw 1795–1940 (History of Dutch agriculture 1795–1940)*, Groningen: Universitaire Pers.

Swinnen, J.F.M. (1994), "A Positive Theory of Agricultural Protection," *American Journal of Agricultural Economics* 76(1): 1–14.

(2001), *Agricultural Protection in Europe: a Historical Database*, LICOS: K.U.Leuven.

(2002), "Political Reforms, Rural Crises, and Land Tenure in Western Europe," *Food Policy* 27(4): 371–94.

(2008), *The Perfect Storm: The Political Economy of the Fischler Reforms of the Common Agricultural Policy*, Brussels: Centre for European Policy Studies.

(2009), "The Growth of Agricultural Protection in Europe in the 19th and 20th Centuries," *The World Economy, Global Trade Policy 2009*, Oxford: Blackwell.

Swinnen, J.F.M., A.N. Banerjee and H. de Gorter (2001), "Economic Development, Institutional Change, and the Political Economy of Agricultural Protection: An Econometric Study of Belgium Since the 19th Century," *Agricultural Economics* 26(1): 25–43.

Swinnen J.F.M. and H. de Gorter (1993), "Why Small Groups and Low Income Sectors Obtain Subsidies: The 'Altruistic' Side of a 'Self-Interested' Government," *Economics and Politics* 4: 285–93.

Toutain, J.-C. (1961), "La croissance du produit de l'agriculture entre 1700–1958," *Cahiers de l'I.S.E.A.* 115: 1–287.

Tracy, M. (1989), *Government and Agriculture in Western Europe 1880–1988*, London: Granada.

Van Molle, L. (1989), *Katholieken en Landbouw. Landbouwpolitiek in Belgie 1984–1914*, Leuven: Universitaire Pers Leuven.

SEVEN

Determinants of United States Farm Policies

David Orden, David Blandford, and Timothy Josling

This chapter focuses on the political economy of U.S. farm policy since the Uruguay Round trade negotiations concluded in 1994 and established the World Trade Organization (WTO). The significance of this point of reference is that it introduced a new element into the consideration of farm programs by setting out, in the Agreement on Agriculture (URAA), a multilateral framework for government policies in the areas of domestic support, market access, and export competition. Though few would have expected the United States to make substantial commitments with an immediate impact on its domestic programs, changes might have been anticipated over time in the formulation of U.S. farm policy as a result of its incorporation into an international treaty. Yet the broad thrust of agricultural policies in the United States since the URAA has exhibited a remarkable consistency with earlier decades. Old instruments have been adapted and new ones developed, but the policy mix serves essentially the same purposes, and benefits the same groups, as in the mid-1980s. This resilience of U.S. policy in the context of a potentially increasingly assertive set of multilateral trade rules is a core theme of the chapter.

As an exporter of its primary agricultural products, the United States has maintained a relatively open market. Tariffs on agricultural imports are generally low and have been stable, with limited cuts to bound rates to meet Uruguay Round commitments (Blandford, Laborde and Martin 2008). The policy story is more fluid in the domestic support arena where there have been substantial changes in policy instruments during the four-teen-year period since the URAA came into effect. Annual acreage idling, a cornerstone of farm programs since the 1950s, was abandoned in 1996 and was not resurrected during the subsequent period of low commodity prices. Deficiency payments that had been tied to prices and the production of specific crops were also replaced in 1996 by fixed direct payments that were largely decoupled from production decisions. Public stockholding and the use of export subsidies to dispose of government-held surpluses have almost disappeared, and binding production quotas for peanuts and the entire tobacco price-support program have been eliminated.

There have also been steps back toward subsidies tied to prices or production. Deficiency payments linked to market prices (but less closely than before to planted acreage) were reintroduced in 2002. Biofuel mandates and subsidies have emerged as an influential aspect of U.S. policy under the security responses to the September 11, 2001 terrorist attacks and higher oil prices beginning in 2003. With agriculture's new battle cry of providing "food, fiber and fuel", the demand-augmenting and price-stimulating effects of biofuel policies have turned upside down the debate about U.S. subsidies depressing world market prices. When agricultural commodity prices rose sharply in the first half of 2008, this even revived pressure not felt since the 1970s on a policy of idling millions of acres of land for supply-control and environmental purposes under the long-term Conservation Reserve Program (CRP).

What explains U.S. farm policy innovations and do they display over time any systematic movement toward less distortion of agricultural incentives? What dictates the levels of observed relative protection and the instruments used for support? We assess the driving factors behind three farm bills: two enacted under relatively high international commodity prices, in 1996 and 2008, and one enacted under low prices, in 2002. With agriculture a small but relatively prosperous and concentrated sector of the national economy, it is plausible to maintain that U.S. farm policy outcomes are an equilibrium result of interest group lobbying. In this context, we examine the influence on policy instrument choices of commodity price movements, the interests among agricultural groups, and log rolling to attain majority congressional coalitions. We place these considerations in the broader context of party control of Congress, macroeconomic circumstances, and the concurrent state of WTO negotiations and dispute resolution.

The continued ability of the powerful farm lobby in the United States to elicit support in the political arena is evident from this analysis. Under the 2008 farm bill, farmers retained a stream of direct payments through to 2012 despite back-to-back years of record farm incomes from strong commodity markets. Direct payments are perhaps the least trade-distorting among support policy instruments, and the international disciplines on farm subsidies leave the determination of their level to domestic debate. But this is not all the farm lobby retained in 2008. Price-support and countercyclical income support programs were extended, and the new farm bill included an Average Crop Revenue Election (ACRE) program under which payments could ratchet up substantially in an era of high prices. Agriculture also has strengthened political clout to influence agricultural prices through energy policy. Thus, the farm sector is well positioned to be supported in the event of a wide range of contingencies. This is a sobering result for those examining farm policies internationally and hoping to find evidence that a wealthy country such as the United States, with its significant agricultural comparative advantage, has reached the point where subsidies that distort agricultural incentives would subside.

OUTCOMES OF THE THREE POST-URUGUAY ROUND FARM BILLS

The twentieth-century transformation of American agriculture and the circumstances and associated outcomes of farm policy are well described by Gardner (2009). World agricultural markets became depressed in the 1920s, but this did not evoke substantive intervention until wider economic collapse and Democratic election victories in the 1930s brought a fundamental policy change that altered the government's role in the economy. Once farm programs were established, powerful constituencies formed to defend them, and they secured high wartime price supports in the 1940s. In the 1950s, post-war policy was dominated by supply-control measures designed to keep up farm commodity prices in the face of downward pressure from rapid increases in productivity. By the 1960s, payments made directly by the government emerged as an instrument to compensate farmers for the relaxation of intervention to control supply. A commodity market boom in the early 1970s briefly eliminated government interventions altogether in several markets, but farm support programs proved impossible to terminate in the inflationary era that followed. In the 1980s, a farm crisis arose, in part from inflation miscalculations, and commodity prices and land values fell under a regime of tight monetary policy and U.S. dollar appreciation. Supply controls were restored, implemented through annual and long-term acreage idling, and record payments were made to compensate farmers for lower prices. The URAA subsequently brought modest commitments to reduce border protection and to cap export subsidies and trade-distorting domestic support for agriculture. Yet the commitments made at the end of the Uruguay Round did little to force fundamental reform in the United States.

Market-Oriented Reforms in 1996

Reforms adopted in the 1996 Federal Agriculture Improvement and Reform (FAIR) Act included an unexpected decoupling of payments on eligible base acres from market prices and planting decisions, an end to annual supply-control acreage reduction programs (ARPs), and capping of price-support loan rates at low levels (Orden, Paarlberg and Roe 1999). Two key factors stimulated these reforms. The first was the capture of control of Congress in November 1994 by the Republican Party for the first time in forty years. The Republican-controlled 104th Congress was more inclined than earlier Democratic congresses towards unencumbered agricultural production. Consistent with the economic deregulation being promoted under their party's ideological orientation, the Republican agricultural leadership set as a key objective the elimination of ARPs, which their farm constituents found onerous and their agribusiness constituents had always opposed.

The second key factor that drove the FAIR Act reforms was a sharp rise in commodity prices in late 1995. Decoupling of payments from prices and production was not considered seriously by Congress when it rewrote farm policy in 1990 and remained off the table when the 1995 farm bill debate began. Early efforts by the Republican agricultural leadership to sell the radical idea of fully decoupled payments were unsuccessful. But by November, market prices were well above the target prices that triggered subsidy payments under the 1990 farm bill. This turned a previously unacceptable option into a plausible choice.

Beyond the agricultural producer groups, a broader coalition has historically been formed to move farm program legislation through Congress. Commodity-based agricultural issues are salient only to a small fraction of the members of Congress, well short of a minimum winning floor coalition. To be enacted, farm bills must be acceptable to a mix of other constituencies. The various environmental and recreational benefits associated with idling land under the CRP, and several related wetland, grassland, and other programs, had attracted a strong constituency among conservationists and sportsmen, as well as among the landowners and farmers who receive nearly $2 billion annually in land retirement payments. The CRP was retained in the FAIR Act, idling over 30 million acres under long-term contracts. The Republican congressional leadership then appealed for support for the new farm bill to the conservative Congress and made enough concessions to other interests (among them agribusiness, food consumers, and advocates for the rural and urban poor) to secure its passage with the new planting flexibility and lucrative commodity title.

Other factors were at play in determining the outcome of the FAIR Act, though they did not have a dominant role. The URAA itself had a minimal impact on U.S. farm policy in 1996. The international agreement required few policy changes and no support level reductions beyond those already undertaken in the 1985 and 1990 farm bills. In WTO terms, the policy shift in the FAIR Act was from one nonlimited category of farm support to another – from the blue box, which exempted U.S. (and European) deficiency payments made on partial base acreage and tied to ARP authority, to the WTO green box that included fixed direct payments deemed not to be trade distorting (Josling, Tangermann and Warley 1996).

Nor was federal budget discipline a major factor in shaping key reforms in the FAIR Act. Instead, it was the arcane budget rules used by Congress rather than the deficit that were influential for the reforms adopted. If there had not been a pay-as-you-go rule (which put a high budget cost on ARP elimination assuming traditional deficiency payments), and if there had not been an outdated Congressional Budget Office (CBO) baseline budget projection (making it possible to capture higher spending with decoupled payments once market prices started to rise), the move toward decoupling in 1995 would have been less compelling.

Several features of the 1995–96 farm bill debate also suggest that new ideas reflecting an ideological shift about the role of government in agricultural policy were not being embraced. The support programs for dairy, sugar, and peanuts were renewed and the permanent farm programs from the 1940s were left in place as an incentive for Congress to enact future replacement legislation. As long as the farm lobby remained powerful, and the agricultural committees in Congress retained control of the policy process, there were ready venues under the FAIR Act either for traditional program defense or for the design of new support policies.

Re-Institutionalized Support in 2002

Both short-term and structural factors were cited in 1995–96 as evidence that agricultural prices would remain high through the decade, but these projections proved erroneous. As prices fell sharply from forecast levels, continuation of the traditional deficiency payment programs would have increased fiscal outlays by 1997 had it not been for the FAIR Act decoupling. Falling prices also would have undermined arguments to abandon ARPs. The most important reforms in the FAIR Act simply would not have been enacted had the 1996 farm bill been delayed.

Party-based farm policy differences were also evident as Congress weighed its options in response to falling market prices. Congressional Democrats called for a virtual rewriting of farm policy in 1998 to restore the traditional safety net. An election year bidding war ensued between Democrats and Republicans over granting new benefits to farmers. With Republicans still in the majority, the key structural reforms of the FAIR Act were retained: Planting flexibility continued, ARPs were not reimposed, loan rates were not raised, and the "emergency" payments that were appropriated remained nominally decoupled from market prices. But the budget discipline of fixed payments touted by Republican leaders as a virtue under the FAIR Act collapsed by 1998 as nearly $7 billion of aid was granted and similar additional aid was appropriated annually as prices remained low over the next three years.

In these circumstances, the farm lobby promoted a new farm bill a year before the FAIR Act was scheduled to expire. It secured congressional commitments for $73 billion in additional spending over ten years, increasing by three-fourths the FAIR Act baseline of projected commodity spending (Orden 2002, Moyer and Josling 2003). The Farm Security and Rural Investment (FSRI) Act, signed into law in May 2002, continued direct payments and extended them to soybeans and other oilseeds. The emergency payments that Congress had authorized annually were turned into new mandatory countercyclical payments (CCPs) tied to market prices and historical, but not current, production. In addition, loan rates were raised slightly and new price supports were added for several minor commodities. Farmers retained planting flexibility with the new CCPs, although the decoupling of support from production decisions was partly undermining by a one-time option to update the acreage bases determining their direct payments and the base acreage, and fixed yields determining their countercyclical payments. Thus, the bill offered substantial new support guarantees and familiar policy instruments to farm constituents. Most of the newly available money (nearly $50 billion) went to anticipated commodity support.

The mix of conservation and environmental programs included in the FSRI Act highlights the discretion involved in U.S. programs toward long-term acreage idling. The authority for the CRP was increased from 36.4 million acres to 39.2 million acres, but most new environmental expenditures went to measures to assist livestock operations (expanding an existing Environmental Quality Incentives Program [EQIP] program) and for conservation measures on land that remained in production (a new Conservation Security Program [CSP]). Long-term land idling historically has been enacted as a supply-control and conservation measure during times of low prices (the 1930s, the 1960s, and again in 1985) and has expired when market demand strengthened (during World War II and in the 1970s). The expenditure on the CRP falls in the WTO green box and competitors in world markets naturally do not complain about the reduction of U.S. production it causes. The CRP had occasionally been criticized for unnecessarily restricting output and keeping world prices higher than otherwise, but this was not a policy issue with the low market prices in 2002.

Passage of the 2002 FSRI Act was met with derision by domestic and international critics of U.S. policy. In reply, the House Agriculture Committee offered a strident defense of the farm bill. A document posted on the Committee's web page asserted that "Critics of U.S. farm policy would cede our food production to unstable places like the Third World," then asked "but in these times does any American want to depend on the Third World for a safe and abundant supply of food and fiber?" Such sharply worded views of the 2002 farm bill are indicative of the conflict that festers over U.S. agricultural support programs. Yet severe critics of the 2002 FSRI Act and its staunch defenders both overstated their case. The 2002 U.S. farm bill took few constructive unilateral steps toward reduction of subsidies. But nor did it expand the least desirable subsidy policies, as is sometimes implied.

The 2002 FSRI Act included only modest individual payment limitations and a weak income-based eligibility cap, with producers having average adjusted gross income of more than $2.5 million ineligible for payments unless at least three-fourths of their income came from farming. Imposing limits on the level of payments to individual beneficiaries is controversial in U.S. farm policy, and such measures have a critical regional and commodity dimension because per-acre payments are higher for cotton and rice than for other crops.

Low prices from 1997 onward provided the main political dynamic underlying passage of the 2002 FSRI Act. With low prices, the effort to turn the emergency payments legislated annually from 1998 to 2001 into permanent support entitlements was endorsed by farm groups and marshalled aggressively by the House Agriculture Committee, still under Republican control but chaired by a dissenting southern opponent of decoupling. Under Democratic leadership, the Senate sought to go further to reverse the FAIR Act policies. Farm groups sought additional support but nearly unanimously favored continuing the planting flexibility provided by the FAIR Act. With substantial new money to allocate, the agriculture committees had a relatively easy task to orchestrate support for a new bill.

During early deliberations on the farm bill in 2001, the administration had argued for fiscal restraint, but its voice was muted. The administration had made implicit commitments to future agricultural spending during its push to secure votes for broad ten-year legislation to lower taxes. The president also sought backing from agriculture for new international trade negotiating authority. This further weakened the administration's resolve to limit farm spending, even if higher spending posed a threat to progress in future trade negotiations. Advocates of fiscal discipline hoped the tax cuts and a weakening economy would result in reassessment of the large budget allocated to agricultural subsidies, but that failed to happen after the September 11 terrorist attacks that occurred in New York and Virginia. The House floor debate on the farm bill was scheduled to begin September 12. It was put off just 21 days, and the House passed its version of an expensive new farm bill with strong bipartisan backing.

The U.S. commitments under the URAA also proved too lax to limit farm spending levels effectively as prices fell after 1997. The annual total U.S. Aggregate Measurement of Support (Current Total AMS) for subsidies tied to production was well below its WTO cap of $19.1 billion when the FAIR Act was passed (Josling 2007). When support provided to farmers began to rise automatically, and Congress added emergency subsidies as market prices fell, the United States avoided exceeding the WTO discipline by reporting the supplemental payments as non-product-specific support, which remained well below the *de minimis* limit of 5 percent of the total value of agricultural production. The WTO negotiations on agriculture launched in 2000 were incorporated into the full Doha Development Agenda (Doha Round) in 2001. But Congress largely ignored the WTO in drafting the FSRI Act.

Reforms to the main U.S. support programs initiated in 1996 partially decoupled subsidies from production but did not succeed in reducing support levels. A more radical reform option that is sometimes suggested is a compensated end to a support program through a buyout. A buyout of peanut production quota rights was included in the FSRI Act, but the bill also included new direct and countercyclical payments to peanut producers. In 2004, a tobacco buyout ended domestic production quotas and completely eliminated the price-support program. Adoption of the peanut quota and tobacco program buyouts drew substantial support among producers of these crops because their benefits were declining as quota acreages and prices fell. The losses of quota revenue were most severe for tobacco, and the tobacco buyout was the most complete.

Payments associated with the peanut and tobacco buyouts were quite generous. For peanuts, a lump-sum quota buyout payment of $0.55 per pound was equivalent to the average of annual past quota rental payments, discounted at a 5 percent rate, for a period of twenty-four years (Womak 2003, Orden 2007). Payments to quota owners were equivalent to discounted average rental payments for 15–20 years for flue-cured and burley tobacco, with additional buyout payments made to the tobacco producers (Brown, Rucker and Thurman 2007).

While the peanut and tobacco buyouts were costly, they have ended government interventions in these markets dating back to the 1930s. In contrast, there has been little reform for sugar, where the cost of U.S. protection and support is borne by consumers rather than taxpayers. Domestic sugar producers have not seen their benefits erode dramatically so there has been little impetus to seek a buyout. Instead, the FSRI Act strengthened the sugar support program by requiring that it operate at no net cost to the government and by stipulating that restrictive domestic marketing allotments could only be imposed to sustain the supported price when low-tariff imports were below 1.32 million metric tons. Under these conditions, the sugar program had to be administered with tight import restraints, which set the farm bill firmly counter to sugar trade liberalization.

Continued Support under the 2008 Farm Bill

There was a high level of interest in a new farm bill by 2006, with an array of listening sessions and hearings held by the administration, Congress, and farm organizations. Coalitions of groups arguing for reform were active and gained some traction in 2007, with widespread criticisms of farm policy appearing in major urban newspapers (Arha et al. 2007). However, the broader political agenda for both parties was keeping the support of voters and special interests in the swing states of the Midwest, and reform of farm programs carried political risks.

As the legislation made its way through Congress, the strategy of farm groups was to keep the structure and budget allocated to the commodity programs intact while seeking additional funding for nutrition and conservation as well as for specialty crops and other new farm sector constituents, to build a coalition for congressional voting majorities. With both houses of Congress under Democratic majorities after the elections in November 2006, the prospect of increased funding for food stamps and other food assistance to the poor was as important as the future of commodity programs. If this additional funding was forthcoming, then the farm coalition would have been successful in expanding the scope of the farm bill without any sacrifice from commodity support. The safety net would be preserved. By 2006, commodity prices had strengthened from the low levels of the early 2000s, and they were projected to remain high enough to reduce price-linked payments sharply (see Table 7.1). A new farm bill was anticipated in 2007 but the debate spilled over into 2008, forcing Congress to pass five short-term extensions of the FSRI Act.

Whereas the Democratic administration in 1995–96 and Republican administration in 2001–02 had been relatively passive in formulating farm bill proposals, throughout initial discussions of the 2007 bill, the Secretary of Agriculture called for policies that were "equitable, predictable and beyond challenge." In January 2007, despite the loss of control of Congress to the Democrats, the administration released a detailed proposal to meet its criteria through a set of incremental reforms along the decoupling path (USDA 2007).

Several of the administration's key recommendations related primarily to domestic aspects of farm policy. The administration endorsed direct payments but proposed that over ten years, nearly $8 billion be shifted from commodity support to conservation programs through changes in policy design. Part of the claimed savings came from converting countercyclical payments from a price basis to a nationally calculated revenue basis. This was asserted to lower expenditures by taking advantage of the natural price-quantity hedge (when output is low, prices are higher, and vice versa), which partly stabilizes revenue. The administration also proposed a strict means test, with a $200,000 adjusted gross income limit for support eligibility. In aggregate, the administration's proposal held spending for agricultural commodity programs within the level projected under a continuation of the FSRI Act. Spending was expected to be much lower than during 2002–2007 because of the projected higher prices. In short, under the administration's proposal, there was to be a squeeze-down of traditional commodity subsidies, with countercyclical payments and loan rate-based price support falling sharply.

Additional administration proposals related to improving U.S. compliance with WTO rules. For cotton, lower loan rates were recommended, compensated by higher direct payments. This potentially addressed the call for particularly strong reforms under the special cotton initiative within the WTO negotiations. The administration recommended that cultivation of fruits and vegetables be permitted on base acres. This would address the issue of whether U.S. direct payments could be counted in the WTO green box raised by the Brazilian challenge to the cotton program

Table 7.1. *Costs of major farm subsidies, United States, 1996 to 2012 (US$ billion)*

Year	Commodity program payments				Other subsidies	
	Direct[a] payment (fixed)	Price-Linked Payment		Conservation[d]	Ad hoc and disaster[e]	Crop and revenue insurance[f]
		Countercyclical[b]	Price support[c]			
Actual						
1996	5.19	0.00	0.00	2.01	0.16	0.64
1997	6.29	0.00	0.58	1.96	0.16	0.12
1998	5.66	2.81	4.11	1.95	2.32	0.75
1999	5.47	5.47	9.71	1.76	2.34	1.51
2000	5.07	5.46	9.04	1.79	3.67	1.39
2001	4.10	4.63	8.43	1.91	1.43	1.77
2002	5.30	1.80	3.52	2.51	3.58	2.89
2003	5.27	0.54	1.14	2.45	1.74	1.86
2004	5.26	4.29	5.55	3.04	2.10	1.12
2005	5.22	4.75	6.62	3.40	0.30	0.76
2006	5.58	3.16	1.40	3.43	0.27	1.60
Estimated/Projected						
2007	5.44	1.03	0.91	3.46	0.06	0.87

172

Year	Commodity program payments			Other subsidies		
	Direct[a] payment (fixed)	Price-Linked Payment		Conservation[d]	Ad hoc and disaster[e]	Crop and revenue insurance[f]
		Countercyclical[b]	Price support[c]			
2008	5.36	0.35	0.03	3.75	0.76	5.04
2009	4.56	0.10	0.08	4.19	0.76	4.39
2010	4.53	0.23	0.11	4.41	0.76	4.38
2011	4.53	0.40	0.11	4.52	0.76	4.39
2012	4.56	0.54	0.09	4.82	0.76	4.42

[a] Includes production flexibility contract and direct and peanut, excludes peanut and tobacco buyout payments.

[b] 1996–2005 includes crop market loss assistance payments and countercyclical payments, excludes dairy market loss payments.

[c] Includes four loan-rate-related programs (loan deficiency payments, marketing loan gains/payments, certificate exchange gains, and commodity loan forfeit); 1996–2005 also includes dairy market loss payments, oilseed payments, cotton user marketing payments, and miscellaneous smaller payments; 2007–2012 includes only dairy market loss payments (from CBO score of FCE Act).

[d] 1996–2005 includes resource retirement and environmental payments notified in the green box; 2006–2012 includes all CCC conservation programs (interpolated for 2006).

[e] Includes disaster relief reported in the green box, emergency payments reported in Total AMS (before de minimis) and various disaster assistance programs reported as non-product-specific de minimis support; 2006 estimate from USDA, 2007 from CBO; 2008–2012 equal division of FCE new mandatory permanent disaster relief projected outlays.

[f] Net indemnities calculated as indemnities minus premiums paid by producers.

Sources: U.S. notifications to the WTO for all columns through 2005; Blandford-Josling WTO notifications simulator for Commodity Programs 2006–2012; and Congressional Budget Office (2008b) for Conservation and Crop and Revenue Insurance 2006–2012.

(see discussion below). Greater flexibility in U.S. food aid programs was recommended, which would provide reform that the EU was demanding in the Doha Round and defuse objections that U.S. food aid programs were implicitly subsidizing exports.

The House of Representatives acted next on new farm legislation. By July 2007, it had rejected most of the administration's reform recommendations and drawn objections from the administration through proposals for tax increases and the use of timing and other gimmicks to mask spending increases. The House bill retained the direct, countercyclical, and loan-rate tiers of existing support, assuring farmers the traditional programs would be in place in the event prices fell to lower levels than being projected. The loan rate for sugar was increased and the dairy support program modified to establish price supports directly for processed products rather than fluid milk, potentially reducing substantially the dairy support that would be reported in WTO notifications while having no real market effects. The House bill offered new demand-augmenting support for fruits and vegetables but did not allow production of these crops on base acres, which was opposed by domestic growers.[1] Overall, the House bill partly mitigated the squeeze-out of farm sector spending that higher prices were creating, but did not avoid the substantial reduction anticipated for commodity support.

The Senate did not complete a farm bill until December 2007, as various groups squabbled over specific programs and how to fund them under the limited CBO budget baseline. The Senate bill also retained the three-tiered support structure as an assurance to farmers in the event of lower prices. It added an optional crop revenue program in place of the existing loan rates and countercyclical payments. The Senate proposal differed substantially from the revenue-based program suggested by the administration because it linked the new revenue guarantees to a moving average of actual market prices and crop yields rather than to fixed target prices and fixed base-acreage production levels. The Senate revenue insurance program was estimated to provide similar benefits to the existing programs for corn, wheat, and soybeans when prices were relatively low, but higher benefits if prices remained high (Zulaf 2007). This was another step toward avoiding

---

[1] Domestic growers of fruit and vegetables were concerned about expanded supplies and lower prices and objected to having to compete with farmers receiving subsidies on base acres. The domestic growers' objections parallel the challenges being raised within the WTO to the notification of direct payments in the green box as allegedly decoupled. In the WTO challenge, however, the objection is to the adverse effect on prices of the subsidized crops from planting restrictions that limit movement into fruits and vegetables.

a squeeze-out of commodity support. Even so, at anticipated prices, the Senate bill was expected to lead to a decline in projected commodity program spending.

It took another six months for Congress to finalize the Food, Conservation and Energy (FCE) Act of 2008. Calls intensified for farm program reform and reduced commodity expenditures as prices of crude oil and agricultural commodities shot upward early in the year. Congress faced both continued internal disunity about specific provisions of the legislation and its funding, and the threat of a veto by the administration. The veto threat required Congress to either reach a compromise acceptable to the administration or pass a bill with veto-proof majorities. The administration reiterated its earlier proposals and criticized the congressional bills for failing to enact reforms and disguising higher levels of likely expenditures. When the administration showed little inclination to negotiate, Congress passed a bill with enough support to be enacted into law over a presidential veto that the administration made almost no effort to sustain.

ASSESSMENT OF THE 2008 FCE ACT

In aggregate terms, the FCE Act distributes expected mandatory expenditures for fiscal years 2008–2012 in a similar way to levels anticipated under extension of the FSRI Act, as shown in Table 7.2. An increase of total expected outlays of $5 billion and significant shifts in spending among categories at the margin reflect the effort to attract a broad coalition of congressional backers through increased expenditures for nutrition, conservation, energy, and a host of other programs targeted at specific constituencies. For the out-years 2013–17 (not shown in the table), there is a further substantial increase in anticipated nutrition expenditures, and the FCE Act only remained within the CBO ten-year baseline budget projection by including nearly $10 billion of new revenues.

The projected commodity program spending of $41.6 billion under the FCE Act, which reflects $1.1 billion of estimated five-year savings simply from postponed timing of anticipated payments for 2012, is comprised mostly of direct payments that traditional subsidy recipients defended against reductions. In contrast, commodity support had been $59.3 billion during the previous five fiscal years and had been projected to be $78 billion during those years when the 2002 farm bill was written (Chite 2007). Authority for the CRP was reduced to 32 million acres by the FCE Act, but expected expenditures for conservation programs increased by $2.7 billion to $24.1 billion, reaching almost 60 percent of the projected commodity

Table 7.2. *Aggregate projected outlays under the 2008 FCE Act, United States,*
2008 to 2012 (US$ billion, fiscal years)

Category	CBO projected baseline under 2002 FSRI	Proposed adjustments (House; Senate versions of the new farm bill)	Final FCE Act
Commodity support	43.3	−1.0; −3.5	41.6
Conservation	21.4	2.8; 4.4	24.1
Crop insurance	25.7	−4.0; −3.7	21.8
Energy	0.0	2.4; 1.0	0.6
Nutrition	186.0	4.2; 5.3	188.9
Other	7.9	1.5; 2.0	12.0
Total	284.0	5.9; 5.5	289.0

Source: Congressional Budget Office (2008a), Chite (2007), and Johnson (2008).

support compared to just one-quarter during the previous five years. In this sense, in the event of projected high prices, a substantial relative shift toward conservation will take place in farm program outlays. But farmers remain well protected if prices turn out lower than projected – through retention, and even a marginal strengthening, of the loan-rate and countercyclical tiers of commodity support. The FCE Act included only a small pilot program to allow production on base acreage of certain fruits and vegetables (for processing on 60,000 acres in seven Midwestern states), with any such acreage planted ineligible for support payments during that year. The FCE Act also extended support through dairy market loss payments, and it created new payments to processors of domestic or imported cotton to replace the "Step 2" payments to processors of domestic cotton that had been ruled in violation of WTO rules in the case brought by Brazil (WTO 2005). Various other titles of the farm bill expanded and added programs for biofuels, horticultural crops, and disaster assistance.

The FAIR and FSRI acts demonstrate the responsiveness of U.S. farm policy to proximate market circumstances, as well as movement toward somewhat less market intervention. Throughout the 2007–08 debate, most farm groups remained wary of any changes to existing programs, despite the rising prices for oil and farm commodities in 2006–07 and the boom that caused commodities to hit record price levels early in 2008. Nor was there much of a budgetary incentive to change policy instruments.

Relatively high prices were built into the 2007 CBO baseline budget projection. Therefore, there was little opportunity, unlike in 1995–96, to capture projected expenditures that would not materialize because of high prices. New instruments could deliver higher spending in the FCE Act only if their fiscal cost was approved by the Congress or misjudged in budget analysis, while holding on to the existing loan rate and countercyclical programs bore little political cost to the farm lobby.

One of the proximate causes of the 2007–08 boom in commodity markets was the U.S. ethanol fuel tax credit and ethanol use mandates designed to promote corn-based fuel production. These are highly product-specific policy instruments and were reinforced by a high import duty. Initiated in 1978, the tax credit, together with other federal and state incentives, had only induced a modest level of ethanol output (less than two billion gallons in 2005) until oil prices rose and new blending mandates were enacted. The federal ethanol tax credit of $0.51 per gallon added more than $1.50 to the break-even price that could be paid for corn converted into ethanol (Tyner 2007). The subsidy exceeded $3 billion by 2007, and the Energy Policy Act of 2005 mandated that production reach 7.5 billion gallons by 2012. As oil prices rose and armed conflicts dragged on in Iraq and Afghanistan, both political parties called for increased energy security for the United States. The Energy Independence and Security (EIS) Act of December 2007 expanded the mandate for ethanol production to 36 billion gallons by 2022, of which 15 billion gallons were to come from corn-based production. Model-based estimates of the effect on corn market prices ranged from an increase of 25 percent ($0.74 per bushel) in 2006 due to the tax credit assuming the mandate was not binding (de Gorter and Just 2007) to 12–14 percent (by then also around $0.70) in 2008–09 (Babcock 2008) or averaged for 2011–17 (FAPRI 2008) due to the mandates, tax credits, and import duties. With record oil prices stimulating ethanol production in the first half of 2008, the new farm bill reduced the ethanol tax credit to $0.46 per gallon but extended the ethanol import duty through 2012.

With increasing farm commodity prices in 2008, direct payments came under intense scrutiny in the domestic policy debate. Decoupling is encouraged by WTO rules as a way of providing an attractive non-trade-distorting support option. But with the direct payments making up so large a share of the commodity support anticipated under the FCE Act, proponents of alternative spending eyed a reduction in direct payments to fund other priorities. The direct payments were retained only after a rancorous domestic confrontation, particularly in terms of income eligibility limits for recipients. Payment eligibility criteria were tightened modestly (to caps on nonfarm income of $500,000 for all three commodity support programs and farm income of $750,000 for direct payments only). Payments were also reduced by 2 percent by limiting the base acreage on which they were made from 85 percent to 83.3 percent through 2011, then restoring the initial level in 2012 to retain a larger budget baseline for future payment projections.

In one respect the sharp rise in prices in 2008 shifted policy toward a new instrument, as occurred in 1995–96. In this case, however, the shift was toward a program more closely tied to market prices. The FCE adopted a modified version of the optional Senate revenue guarantee as an optional new Average Crop Revenue Election (ACRE) program, which is likely to be considered product-specific trade-distorting support in the WTO. Starting with the 2009 crop, farmers electing ACRE for all covered commodities for the duration of the FCE Act incur a 20 percent cut in direct payments and a 30 percent cut in their loan rates. In exchange, if crop revenue for the state (yield per planted acre times the national price) is below a guaranteed level, and enrolled producers incur a loss of revenue for the crop on their farm, then they are assured of payments of up to 25 percent of the revenue guarantee. The guarantee is 90 percent of the revenue derived from the two-year national average of lagged prices times the five-year Olympic average of state average yields (Committee on Agriculture 2008). This guarantee covers 83.3 percent of the acreage planted (or considered to be planted) by a farmer to the covered commodities; thus it is based on current production. Once the initial guarantee is established for a farmer entering the program, it cannot vary by more than 10 percent from the previous year's guarantee, moderating any sharp revenue downturn.

In assessing the cost of the farm bill, the CBO concluded that only a relatively small fraction of farmers would enroll in the ACRE program and that its cost would be modest. But with prices at historically high levels in the first half of 2008, the administration argued that initiating ACRE on the basis of the moving average of prices prevailing in 2007–08 ran the risk of inducing subsidy payments at much higher price levels than under the target prices of the countercyclical payments program. As an example, the administration assumed that 90 percent of farmers opted for the ACRE program and found that payments for corn alone would be nearly $4 billion in 2009 at prices as high as $4.00 per bushel, compared to no CCP payments at prices above the corn target of $2.63 per bushel (USDA 2008b). Although the ACRE payments decline once prices stabilize, this example illustrates that ACRE ratchets up the price level at which subsidy payments would occur during a transition period from higher to lower prices. The

ACRE program opened the most substantial opportunity within the FCE Act to avoid a squeeze-down of subsidy payments due to high prices, as acknowledged by its proponents (Brasher 2008). Subsequently, Blandford and Josling (2008) concluded that ACRE program payments would in some years exceed commodity-specific caps under negotiation in the Doha Round if prices of corn, wheat, and soybeans during 2007–12 followed a pattern similar to the 1970s, 1980s, or 1990s.

Other than the ACRE program, which provides an optional new revenue guarantee, the traditional crop and revenue insurance programs had expanded at increased government costs in the early 2000s. The FCE Act stipulated that total premiums be adjusted slightly to equal total indemnities payments over time (resulting in an expected loss ratio equal to one) and reduced the administrative costs of delivering crop and revenue insurance programs by lowering payments made to the insurance agents. Larger claimed savings (almost $2.8 billion of the savings shown in Table 7.2) were again achieved simply by postponing the timing of some payments.

Congress had also appropriated annual disaster relief to agriculture that averaged about $2.5 billion annually during 2000–05. The FCE Act created mandatory funding for five disaster relief programs by amending the Trade Act of 1974 to establish a mandatory program (of nearly $4 billion over five years) financed from import duties. Again this was a step toward avoiding a squeeze-down of support to agriculture by ensuring at least partial availability of funds for disaster relief without requiring annual congressional appropriations.

Slight increases in loan rates and target prices contained in the FCE Act strengthen policy instruments coupled to production. This will prove innocuous (with the exception of raising the sugar loan rate) if prices remain well above loan-rate levels as projected.[2] However, these parameter adjustments are another signal of the strength of the farm lobby. With the Democrats in control of Congress, the effort to increase rather than lower price support parameters is not surprising. The argument made (and which will be extended if farm price and income circumstances deteriorate from their high levels since 2008) is that higher energy prices and related production costs render inadequate the safety net that was good enough, indeed lauded by many farm groups, from 2002 to 2006. Traditional price

---

[2] The loan rate for raw cane sugar rises from $0.18 per pound to $0.1875 by 2012. The Secretary of Agriculture is required to set domestic marketing allotments at no less that 85 percent of estimated quantities for domestic human consumption and to purchase sugar to produce biofuels if necessary to avoid forfeitures of sugar to the CCC, thus insulating domestic producers from pressure of increased imports under trade agreements.

and income support levels that were raised only slightly in 2008 could be increased further in the future.

Despite all of these considerations, the high world prices that in early 2008 were straining the global food system and prompting defensive policy reactions among exporters and importers worldwide had only modest effects on the commodity support provisions of the U.S. farm bill. There was no significant shift toward decoupled policy instruments, as had occurred when prices rose sharply in 1995–96, nor calls for an end to the permanent support legislation, as had been articulated in the earlier debate. Still, the farm lobby did not avoid, at least for the time being, a projected squeeze-down of anticipated subsidy payments under the price-linked support programs. Passing a bill proved difficult with high prices prevailing, as it had with high prices in 1995–96. In the end, the veto-proof majorities assembled in Congress demonstrated the ability of the farm lobby to secure a continuation of support programs that largely serve the same purposes and benefit the same interest groups as did earlier legislation.

POSSIBLE WTO DISCIPLINES

Steps to align U.S. policies with WTO disciplines underlay the "beyond challenge" objective articulated by the Secretary of Agriculture in the 2007–08 farm bill debate. This goal was advanced also by the Agricultural Task Force of the Chicago Council on Global Affairs (2006). Task force co-chairman Robert Thompson argued that the required adjustments were not as severe as some farm groups anticipated (even under early 2000s market price levels). Moreover, farm groups could be reminded of some tangible benefits from the WTO. Even without a Doha agreement, there were gains from China's accession, the potential accession of Russia, and from a number of dispute settlement rulings in favor of the United States.

Despite these arguments, the historical record demonstrates very little preemptive movement of U.S. policy to be consistent with WTO disciplines. Under low prices, the 2002 FSRI Act simply included a clause authorizing the Secretary of Agriculture to make adjustments to payments if necessary to maintain U.S. compliance. Whether this authority would be adequate to make significant changes to farm policy to comply with WTO payment limits has never been tested. The challenge launched by Brazil in 2003 against the U.S. cotton program under the WTO dispute settlement process led to slight changes in policy. The United States eliminated the "Step 2" payments made to processors of domestic cotton and modified or eliminated some export credit guarantee programs prohibited by the WTO, but it did not change the basic cotton support programs found to cause serious prejudice to Brazil's interests. There has been little appetite in Congress for making explicit changes designed to reposition U.S. programs so that conflict with WTO agreements is minimized. In the 2008 FCE Act, only a few modest steps were taken: The dairy support program was redefined to reduce notified support with no real effects on dairy markets as described above, the payments compliance adjustment authority was extended, and authority was repealed for the GSM-103 export credit program, for the 1-percent fee cap on the GSM-102 program and for the inactive Export Enhancement Program (EEP).

Dispute cases brought by Canada and Brazil in 2007 raise the broad question of whether the United States violated its Total AMS commitment under the URAA during certain years (WTO 2007 a, b). A primary issue is whether fixed direct payments to farmers have been correctly notified as meeting the criteria of the green box or should be included in the AMS because they are paid for base acreage on which production of fruit and vegetables is prohibited. A second issue is whether U.S. countercyclical payments under the 2002 farm bill (and the prior crop market loss assistance payments) should be classified as non-product-specific (NPS) AMS, as notified by the United States. Some consider that they should be considered product-specific payments, because they are inherently linked to specific commodity prices and because they also rest on the fruit and vegetable production exclusion. The outcomes of these dispute settlement cases will have implications both for the United States and for other countries in terms of the manner in which certain policies are notified, whether domestic support is judged consistent with WTO obligations, and which policy reforms might be undertaken in the future.[3]

New Doha Round commitments might also constrain U.S. farm programs in terms of instrument choices or subsidy levels. In a series of papers, Blandford and coauthors have examined this possibility. Taking into account the provisions of the 2008 FCE Act (excluding possible ACRE payments), USDA's January 2008 projections of prices through 2014 (USDA 2008a,b), and the most ambitious modalities included in the May 2008 draft negotiating document from the WTO, Blandford, Laborde and Martin (2008) conclude that, if relatively high prices continued, the United States would be able to adapt to the new WTO constraints with little change in its policies, with the possible exception

---

[3] Were direct and countercyclical payments and their antecedents included in product-specific support notified in the U.S. Current Total AMS, the United States would have exceeded its commitment in 1999, 2000, 2001, 2004, and 2005.

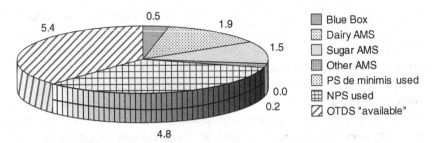

Figure 7.1. Projected composition of notified support and "available" OTDS support (excluding ACRE payments), United States, 2014 (US$ billion).
Source: Blandford and Orden (2008).

of binding commodity-specific constraints for cotton and sugar. The strengthened disciplines would squeeze-down the leeway the United States would have for providing support reported to the WTO as trade-distorting but would still provide substantial flexibility. This outcome is illustrated in Figure 7.1. It shows projected blue box, dairy and sugar AMS, and product-specific and non-product-specific *de minimis* expenditures projected for 2014 based on the updated projections for production and prices and the proposed modalities (WTO 2008) at the time of the suspension of Doha Round negotiations in July (Blandford and Orden 2008). The sum is compared to the potential limit of $14.5 billion under a WTO constraint on Overall Trade Distorting Support (OTDS) by showing a projected residual category of unused spending within the constraint. Projected blue box expenditures (countercyclical payments) are only $0.5 billion, well under the modalities cap of $4.8 billion. Likewise, Total AMS (excluding *de minimis*) is projected at $3.4 billion, well under the proposed cap of $7.6 billion. Product-specific *de minimis* is negligible and non-product-specific *de minimis* is projected at $4.8 billion, largely due to subsidized crop and revenue insurance. These projections and caps leave room for various additional OTDS expenditures of $5.4 billion. The latitude available partly reflects the redesign of the dairy support program in the FCE Act, which reduced the dairy AMS that might be reported by as much as $3.6 billion.

The apparent ease of complying with new WTO constraints under relatively high commodity prices made it possible for the Bush administration to pursue a Doha Round agreement in mid-2008. Yet past experience with farm support legislation shows that any required adjustments would not be easy to make politically. The stringent proposed modalities for cotton could pose a challenge, particularly in terms of meeting blue box commitments.

Moreover, the proposed large reductions in the allowed OTDS and Total AMS constrain the contingent room for maneuver for support that is most closely linked to prices. The optimistic price environment of USDA's 2008 projections was for higher prices than in the early 2000s but not at the very high levels seen in the first half of 2008. This scenario may not materialize through 2014. In that case, unless price-linked support programs were modified or some other alternative to current support policies were adopted, the limit on the Total AMS and additional product-specific AMS caps could be exceeded. This would be even more likely if many farmers were to opt for the ACRE program.

There is also the increasingly germane issue of how ethanol subsidies will be notified in the future. Some ethanol production subsidies were notified by the United States in 2007 for the period 2002–05, and these will increase under the FCE Act. More significantly, the forgone revenue from the federal ethanol tax credit to blenders and additional state tax provisions could reach $7–8 billion or more on corn-based ethanol. If these amounts were to be counted, the level of the annual Total AMS would be substantially higher.[4]

FUTURE PROSPECTS

What emerges from our analysis of post-Uruguay Round U.S. farm policy is the continued persistent ability of a powerful farm lobby to extract support

---

[4] The federal ethanol fuel blenders' tax credit is currently notified to the WTO by the United States as an industrial subsidy. However, ethanol itself is considered an agricultural product. Because ethanol policies affect corn prices, they could also be judged to be a "measure directed at processors" that provides "benefit to the producers of the basic agricultural product" and thus subject to inclusion in the AMS under Annex 3, number 7 "to the extent that such measures benefit producers of the basic agricultural product." This would correspond to the way the United States formerly notified Step 2 processor payments for cotton. It will be interesting to observe how the United States decides to report the new subsidies to processors of both domestic and imported cotton created in the FCE Act, to see whether an analogy between cotton processor subsidies and ethanol processor tax credits can continue to be drawn. Of course, if ethanol policies are justified on environmental grounds or as related to national security, they could be exempted from the AMS subsidy disciplines, provided they meet the relevant criteria of the green box or GATT articles. The use of mandates versus tax credits raises an issue of which policy is judged a "measure" subject to possible disciplines. As shown by de Gorter and Just (2007), when there is no binding mandate, the tax credit adds substantially to the level of production of ethanol, its price, and the price and output of corn. When there is a binding mandate, the effects of the tax preference are minimal. Since a binding blending or consumption mandate affects ethanol and corn production and prices, it would be the policy instrument to which WTO agricultural disciplines might apply.

in the political arena. Yet there have been some substantial changes in policy. A review of the three post-Uruguay Round farm bills suggests tentative answers to questions that arise about whether the skilful use of political support will continue to preserve the main farm programs; whether high prices, if they persist, will change the nature of support; or whether trade agreements will impose changes on the United States despite the apparent unwillingness of Congress to be constrained by the international rules regarding the domestic farm policies it enacts.

Both the FAIR Act in 1996 and the FCE Act in 2008 were framed under favorable market prices. In a number of respects, ending farm subsidies should have been easier in 2008 than in 1996. Supply-control annual acreage set asides and high-price supports had waned as an intervention strategy. Farmers had benefited from planting flexibility through enhanced ability to shift acreage among crops in response to market opportunities. Buyouts of restrictive production quotas had occurred for two specialty crops. Net farm income was at record levels. Yet with the possibly significant exception of the ACRE program, which reverts to coupling potential payments to market prices and planting decisions, the structure of farm support policies was essentially unchanged by Congress in the 2008 farm bill.

The absence of reform to existing commodity programs in 2008 compared to 1996 rests in part on party political differences. Instead of the overarching call for deregulation and scaling back of social welfare programs by the 1995–96 House Republican majority, the Democrats in 2008 were championing new government help for constituents in financial trouble and the inclusion of more funds for food stamps and other nutrition programs as the economy slowed and inflation picked up. In that political environment, certainly among Democrats and even among many Republicans in Congress, there were few calls for eliminating the farm safety net.

There was also less need for changes in farm policy in 2008 than in 1996 because the increased flexibility achieved through the earlier reforms had been retained for large segments of agriculture. There was little opportunity for budget "capture" compared to 1996 and little political cost to the farm lobby of retaining the existing support structure. More radical buyouts that had occurred for peanuts and tobacco were hardly illustrative of broader reform options, as these policy outcomes had a narrow sectoral basis among the specialty crops. The rapidly declining rents from peanut and tobacco quotas had made them conducive to buyouts, but this had less relevance for the main commodity programs.

There was also a difference in macroeconomic circumstances between 1996 and 2008. The short-lived farm commodity boom in 1995–96 occurred during a time when the U.S. dollar had been quite stable for the preceding eight years. Oil prices were also stable in this period, and there was little concern at the time about either excessive inflation or an economic downturn and recession. The circumstances were quite different during the later period of high prices. The terrorist attacks in September 2001 created both security fears and economic uncertainty. In such an environment, and with low farm commodity prices after 1997, the farm lobby had little trouble securing renewed support in 2002. The macroeconomic uncertainty in 2008 had its origins partly in these earlier events. With the substantial depreciation of the dollar that ensued after 2001 and oil prices starting to rise in 2003, concerns arose about the possibility of a repeat of the stagflation of the 1970s. This gave the farm commodity boom in 2007 and 2008 a precarious dimension – a premonition of the financial crisis and global recession that ensued later in 2008. The farm lobby could not forecast this new crisis at the time it marshalled votes for the 2008 FCE Act. But it knew from past experience that retaining price-linked support programs, even with few anticipated payouts, provided a structure of support whose nominal parameters could be ratcheted up if the sector were to fall on hard times through rising costs or declining revenues.

Despite the ability of the farm lobby to retain its support programs through 2012, there are several uncertainties about the alignments that have allowed U.S. farm subsidies to endure. The nutrition title has come to dominate total expenditures in farm bills, and is projected to increase its share further. Likewise, at least when prices are relatively high, conservation spending becomes a substantial part of total expenditures on the production side of agriculture. Further realignment could occur if future democratic majorities put together the coalitions needed for congressional passage of farm bills. Nutrition and conservation interests might at some stage decide that their interests could be better served outside the context of the farm bill. At a minimum, the traditional farm lobby could find itself no longer the dominant partner in the broader coalition that has secured the enactment of farm bills, but instead in a supporting position within a coalition dominated by other interests. Yet there are few hints of any related decline in the influence of the farm lobby in the protracted debate over the 2008 FCE Act.

That fixed direct payments became a critical focus of domestic controversy in a high-price environment is also indicative that there may be a limit to the power of the farm lobby, though again that limit proved largely ineffective in 2008. The international disciplines that allow unrestricted decoupled payments in the WTO green box provide room for this domestic debate, but acrimony over the direct payments in the United States makes them unattractive to farm groups and their representatives who seek to minimize controversy over the support provided. This outcome may make direct payments less useful than intended for fostering international coordination to reduce trade-distorting subsidies.

We have argued that WTO disciplines have had little influence on post-Uruguay Round U.S. farm policy decisions. Under high prices, the United States will likely be able to stay within the tighter limits on support if there is eventually a Doha Round agreement. These considerations do not diminish the value of potential new subsidy constraints through the WTO. However, the latitude allowed by the Doha Round disciplines proposed in 2008 illustrates the substantial distance still to be crossed to achieve a more liberalized rules-based global trade system for agriculture. Some combination of lower world prices, adverse WTO dispute settlement rulings on the notification of support in the green box, a reclassification of ethanol subsidies from industrial to agricultural, and a Doha Round agreement that reduced the Total AMS ceiling and bound the OTDS for the first time could lead to WTO domestic support compliance problems for the United States. In that case, the next farm bill could be framed under a very different set of circumstances.

The deepening entrenchment of the domestic ethanol sector during the oil-price boom that peaked in mid-2008 both demonstrates the continued political strength of the agricultural lobby and constitutes a substantial new intervention coupled to production. In addition, the restrictive land-use policy was never completely abandoned – the CRP has always been a supply-reducing as well as a conservation policy instrument. If biofuel demand persists under ethanol mandates and subsidies, conservation spending may decline as farmers voluntarily abandon the CRP. This would shift the political balance within farm bill deliberations back toward the commodity lobby, but it could also provoke a break in the political alliance that forged the 2008 farm bill.[5]

---

[5] With sharply rising prices in the first half of 2008, the Secretary of Agriculture used his authority to allow haying and grazing on some CRP land, which was opposed by the National Wildlife Federation and other environmentalists who sought a court injunction to overturn the decision. He also considered but decided against authorizing an early release of CRP acreage without payment penalties. There are CRP contracts for over 5 million acres scheduled to expire during 2008 or 2009 that had not been renewed by July 2008 and could be returned to production (Harris et al. 2008). Subsequently, as commodity prices fell, there was less political pressure on the CRP.

A Doha Round that agreed on a reduction in allowed OTDS, tighter Total AMS commitment, and product-specific AMS and blue box limits would be a valuable check in the event that traditional U.S. programs are ratcheted up or agricultural prices return to the downward trend that has characterized most of the past half century. In such circumstances, an option for U.S. policymakers would be to expand green box support for farmers under the environmental category, disaster relief, or direct payments that are modified if necessary to meet any WTO challenges. If U.S. policy inches toward recoupled instruments with greater emphasis on energy crops, disaster assistance, crop and revenue insurance, and environmental programs on working lands, scrutiny for consistency with the green box will be an essential bulwark against new forms of production- and trade-distorting programs. But as policy stood in mid-2008, it is unlikely that the WTO will affect ethanol tax credits and mandates or long-term land idling under the CRP. These instruments, largely outside WTO disciplines, work to drive agricultural prices up and arguably have become, along with other environmental payments and crop and revenue insurance subsidies, the most important elements of U.S. farm policy. The boom-related optimism in the agricultural sector arose in 2008 in part because demand augmentation through "food, fiber and fuel" reinforced environmentally rationalized supply control as a mechanism for keeping farm commodity prices higher than otherwise. The WTO has little ability to limit these distortions.

In his review of United States and Canadian agricultural policies, Gardner (2009) offered his views on the prospects for future reforms that would lessen market distortions. He concluded that the best prospects for reform pressure would arise from the WTO Doha Round negotiations, from a combination of environmental/taxpayer interests that would shift agricultural support spending toward public-good provision, or from the resurrection of a general predisposition to economic liberalism. Our assessment of the three post-Uruguay Round farm bills implies each of these pressures is a weak reed upon which to rest prospects for reform.

Were the reform pressures nonetheless to progress in a substantial way, Gardner argued that there could be a politically salient case for one-time buyout payments. He noted that the direct payments in the 1996 farm bill were a step in that direction, but the buyout did not subsequently materialize, as we have described. A broad buyout of the main commodity programs received slight attention in the 2007–08 farm bill debate (Stokes 2007, James and Griswold 2007). However, any such proposals were summarily rejected in Congress, and the buyout idea remained far from the center of the farm bill debate. One conclusion that may be drawn from the experience of the U.S. farm policies since 1995 is that a rather generous buyout would be needed to convince the recipients of farm program benefits to relinquish their entitlements. Yet despite Gardner's hope, based on our assessment of the three farm bills since the advent of the WTO, we do not see this happening in the foreseeable future.

References

Anderson K. (ed.) (2009), *Distortions to Agricultural Incentives: A Global Perspective, 1955–2007*, London: Palgrave Macmillan and Washington DC: World Bank.

Arha, K., T. Josling, D.A. Sumner and B.H. Thompson (eds.) (2007), *U.S. Agricultural Policy and the 2007 Farm Bill*, California: Woods Institute for the Environment, Stanford University, Stanford CA.

Babcock, B. (2008), "Statement Before the U.S. Senate Committee on Homeland Security and Government Affairs," Presented at the Hearing on Fuel Subsidies and Impact on Food Prices, Washington DC, May 7.

Blandford, D., D. Laborde and W. Martin (2008), "Implications for the United States of the May 2008 Draft Agricultural Modalities," Paper published jointly by the International Centre for Trade and Sustainable Development, the International Food and Agricultural Trade Policy Council and the International Food Policy Research Institute, Washington DC. Available online at http://www.ifpri.org/pubs/cp/ictsd_WTOpapers.asp

Blandford, D. and T. Josling (2008), "The WTO July 10th Agricultural Modalities Proposals and their Impact on Domestic Support in the EU and the US," Paper prepared for the World Bank, Washington DC, July 15.

Blandford, D. and D. Orden (2008), "United States: Shadow WTO Agricultural Domestic Support Notifications," Discussion Paper 821, International Food Policy Research Institute, Washington DC.

Brasher, P. (2008), "Farm Bill's Potential Cost 'Off the Charts'," *Des Moines Register*, May 16.

Brown, A.B., R. Rucker and W. Thurman (2007), "The End of the Federal Tobacco Program: Economic Impacts of the Deregulation of U.S. Tobacco Production," *Review of Agricultural Economics* 29(4): 635–55.

Chicago Council on Global Affairs (C. Bertini, A. Schumacher Jr. and R.L. Thompson, Agriculture Task Force co-chairs) (2006), *Modernizing America's Food and Farm Policy: Vision for a New Direction*, Chicago IL: Chicago Council on Global Affairs.

Chite, R. (2007), "Farm Bill Budget and Costs: 2002 vs. 2007," RS22694, Congressional Research Service, Washington DC, November 7.

Committee on Agriculture (2008), *Joint Explanatory Statement of the Committee of Conference, Food, Conservation, and Energy Act of 2008 (H.R. 2419)*, U.S. House of Representatives, Washington DC. Available online at http://agriculture.house.gov/inside/2007FarmBill.html

Congressional Budget Office (2008a), "Estimated Effects on Spending and Revenue of the Conference Agreement for H.R. 2419, the Food, Conservation and Energy Act of 2008," Washington DC.

(2008b), "CBO March 2008 Baseline for CCC and FCIC," prepared by Dave Hull, Jim Langley and Greg Hitz, Washington DC, 20 February.

de Gorter, H. and D.R. Just (2007), "The Law of Unintended Consequences: How the U.S. Biofuel Tax Credit with a Mandate Subsidizes Oil Consumption and Has No Impact on Ethanol Consumption," Working Paper # 2007–20, Department of Applied Economics and Management, Cornell University, Ithaca NY. Available online at http://papers.ssrn.com/sol3/papers.cfm?abstract_id=1024525

FAPRI (2008), "Biofuels: Impact of Selected Farm Bill Provisions and other Biofuel Policy Options," FAPRI-MU Report #06–08, University of Missouri, Columbia MU, June.

Gardner, B. (2009), "United States and Canada", Ch. 4 in K. Anderson (ed.), *Distortions to Agricultural Incentives: A Global Perspective, 1955–2007,* London: Palgrave Macmillan and Washington DC: World Bank.

Harris, W., B. Lubben, J. Novak and L. Sanders (2008), "The Food, Conservation and Energy Act of 2008: Summary and Possible Consequences," DAERS-WP-1-72008, Prepared for the Extension National Farm Bill Train the Trainer Conference, Kansas City, Missouri, July 8–9.

James, S. and D. Griswold (2007), "Freeing the Farm: A Farm Bill for All Americans," Washington DC: Cato Institute.

Johnson, R. (2008), "Farm Bill Legislative Action in the 110th Congress," RL33934, Congressional Research Service, Washington DC, June 19.

Josling, T. (2007), "The Impact of the WTO and Bilateral Trade Agreements on U.S. Farm Policy," in B. Gardner and D.A. Sumner (eds.), *Agricultural Policy for the 2007 Farm Bill and Beyond,* Washington DC: American Enterprise Institute.

Josling, T., S. Tangermann and T.K. Warley (1996), *Agriculture in the GATT,* London and New York: Macmillan Press.

Moyer, H.W. and T. Josling (2003), *Agricultural Policy Reform: Politics and Process in the EU and US in the 1990s,* Burlington VT: Ashgate Press.

Orden, D. (2002), "Reform's Stunted Crop," *Regulation* 25(1): 26–32, Spring.

(2007), "Feasibility of U.S. Farm Program Buyouts: Is It a Possibility for U.S. Sugar," pp. 147–162 in K.M. Huff, K.D. Meilke, R.D. Knutson, R.F. Ochoa and J. Rude (eds.), *Achieving NAFTA Plus,* College Station TX: Texas A&M University/ University of Guelph/Inter-American Institute for Cooperation on Agriculture-Mexico.

Orden, D., R. Paarlberg and T. Roe (1999), *Policy Reform in American Agriculture: Analysis and Prognosis,* Chicago: University of Chicago Press.

Stokes, B. (2007), "Ending Farm Subsidies," *National Journal,* February 24.

Tyner, W. (2007), "U.S. Ethanol Policy: Possibilities for the Future," Bioenergy, Purdue Extension ID-342-W, West Lafayette ID, January.

USDA (2007), *America's Farm Bill: 2007 Farm Bill Proposals,* Washington DC: U.S. Department of Agriculture.

(2008a), *USDA Agricultural Projections to 2017,* Office of the Chief Economist, World Agricultural Outlook Board, Long-term Projections Report OCE-2008-1, Washington DC: U.S. Department of Agriculture.

(2008b), *Charts Showing Budget Exposure from the ACRE Revenue Support*, Office of the Chief Economist, Washington DC: U.S. Department of Agriculture.

Womach, J. (2003), "Comparing Quota Buyout Payments for Peanuts and Tobacco," Congressional Research Service Report RS 1642, Washington DC, October.

WTO (2005), *United States – Subsidies on Upland Cotton*, Reports of the Appellate Body, WT/DS265/AB/R, WT/DS266/AB/R, and WT/DS267/AB/R, Geneva: World Trade Organization.

(2007a), *United States – Domestic Support and Export Credit Guarantees for Agricultural Products, Request for the Establishment of a Panel by Brazil*, WT/DS365/13, Geneva: World Trade Organization.

(2007b), *United States – Subsidies and Other Domestic Support for Corn and Other Agricultural Products, Request for the Establishment of a Panel by Canada*, WT/DS357/12, Geneva: World Trade Organization.

(2008), *Revised Draft Modalities for Agriculture*, TN/AG/W/4/Rev. 3, July 10, Geneva: World Trade Organization.

Zulaf, C. (2007), "Analysis of Alternative Farm Bill Support Programs for Corn, Soybeans and Wheat," AEDE-RP0095–07, Ohio State University, Columbus.

EIGHT

Agricultural Distortions in the Transition Economies of Asia and Europe

Scott Rozelle and Johan F. M. Swinnen

Until in the late 1970s, a large share of the globe – from the center of Europe to the southeast reaches of Asia – was under Communist rule. The lives of more than 1.5 billion people were directly controlled by Communist leaders. Under this rule, agricultural incentives were massively distorted. The leaders of the Soviet Bloc and China were committed to Socialist ideology and designed their economies to be insulated from the world and its markets.

Since then, there have been dramatic changes in these countries. Yet there are large differences between these transition countries in the extent and the nature of their remaining price distortions. In 1978, China embarked on its economic reform path by introducing the household responsibility system (HRS) in agriculture. A few years later, Vietnam followed. Both countries reduced price distortions and reallocated key land rights from collective farms to rural households. In the initial years, however, market forces played little role and only became important later on. Other communist regimes did not follow this path in the 1980s. Only a series of timid reforms were tried out in the former Soviet Union during the 1970s and 1980s. However, in the 1990s, many nations of Central and Eastern Europe (CEE) and the former Soviet Union (FSU) implemented a series of bold policy reforms that often went far beyond the reforms that had been implemented in China and Vietnam.

While the record on what happened and the effects of those reforms are now fairly well understood (Macours and Swinnen 2002, Roland 2000, Rozelle and Swinnen 2004), it is less clear why the decisions were made in the ways that they were. If price changes, rights reforms, and market emergence led to growth, why did leaders in many transition nations not choose to follow such a comprehensive prescription? More explicitly, why was it that leaders in China decided to implement their reforms gradually, whereas those in CEE did so all at once? Why was it that leaders in CEE undertook a broad spectrum of reforms, whereas those in many nations of the FSU did not? Even more fundamentally, why is it that the policies were implemented by the leaders of some Communist regimes, whereas in others it took a major regime shift for policies to gain momentum? More generally, there is much less of an understanding of why decisions were made in the way that they were.

The goal of this Chapter is to explore these questions. The Chapter draws partly on our previous work on the political economy of the general reforms from a Communist system to a market-based system (Swinnen and Rozelle 2006) and partly on our contributions to a World Bank research project (Huang et al. 2009 on China, Anderson and Swinnen 2008, and in particular Ciaian and Swinnen 2008 on CEE and FSU). In what follows, we also generate a set of additional new arguments.

A SUMMARY OF CHANGES IN DISTORTIONS TO AGRICULTURAL INCENTIVES

There have been dramatic changes in the agricultural and food policies in almost all transition countries since the 1980s, albeit with important differences among nations.

In the FSU, agriculture was subsidized under the Communist regime. After the fall of the Berlin Wall in 1989 and the disintegration of the Soviet Union in 1991, many of the region's trade and price distortions were removed. Price, exchange rates, and trade policies were all liberalized, subsidies were cut, hard budget constraints were introduced, property rights were privatized, and production decisions were shifted to companies and households.[1] As a result, on average, support to agriculture fell to low levels in the early 1990s (see Figure 8.1) – as it did also for industrial production.

---

[1] While most of the FSU and CEE followed more of a Big Bang approach, there were important variations within the region. In Europe, the Central European countries moved first and most rapidly towards market-based systems. The reforms in the Balkan countries, such as Romania and Bulgaria, were more half-hearted and involved many inconsistencies during most of the 1990s, with government interventions continuing to distort incentives. In the large FSU countries (Russia, Kazakhstan, and Ukraine), governments continued important controls of the agricultural economy through a variety of interventions such as regional trade controls, input supply controls, and the continuation of soft budget constraints. The slowest reform progress was in Belarus and in some of the Central Asian countries. While the Kyrgyz Republic relatively quickly liberalized, the other Central Asian countries have restricted reforms and liberalization. In particular, major controls remain in place in such countries as Uzbekistan and Turkmenistan today.

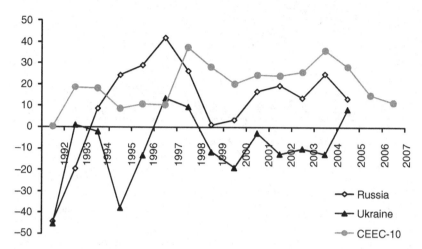

Figure 8.1. Nominal rates of assistance to agriculture, European transition economies,[a] 1992 to 2005 (percent).

[a] CEEC-10 refers to the eight Central and Eastern European countries that joined the European Union in May 2004 plus Bulgaria and Romania (who joined in January 2007).

Source: Anderson and Swinnen (2009).

Between 1992 and 1996, direct assistance to agriculture averaged just 8 percent in the CEE countries, while in Russia and Ukraine the averages were below zero.

In the mid-1990s, support to agriculture increased again in some of the ECA countries. In the CEE region, this was driven by the introduction of new support policies. In Russia, by contrast, it reflected primarily exchange rate developments in the presence of institutional mechanisms which constrained the pass-through of border prices to farm-gate prices. Between 2000 and 2004, average rates of assistance to agriculture were around 20 percent in CEE countries, about one-third of the level in the EU15. In Russia the average support level was positive, but only around 10 percent, while it appears to have been close to zero in Kazakhstan and Ukraine and probably negative in the rest of Central Asia.

China's reform differed fundamentally in its pace. Certainly China's first move was bold – it decollectivized agricultural production and replaced it with a system of household-based farming (Lin 1992) – but in the initial years after reform, it made no move to continue to radically change its economy (Sicular 1995). There were more favorable agricultural prices in the early reform days, but these prices were administratively raised by officials in the planning bureau, who retained control over the economy. It

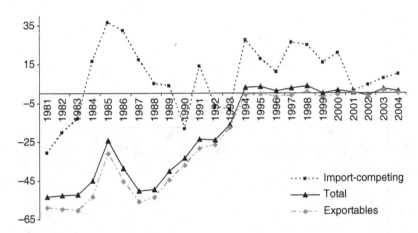

Figure 8.2. Nominal rates of assistance to import-competing and exporting subsectors of agriculture, China, 1981 to 2004 (percent).
Source: Huang et al. (2009).

was not until property rights had been fully reformed in the mid-1980s that the leadership decided to begin to move to marketing and other reforms. Vietnam closely followed China in the pace of its reform. McMillan and Naughton (1992) describe this process as one that is gradual and deliberate but unplanned.

The pace of liberalization and the rate of elimination of the distortions in agriculture are linked. With the gradual dismantling of China's state-run agricultural marketing, the level of distortion also gradual diminished. The reforms increasingly allowed farmers to sell their output to private traders (Park et al. 2002). Entry by nonstate entities and individuals was allowed. Ultimately, competition forced the entire state-owned marketing system to be disbanded. It took 20 years, but China's planned agricultural marketing system of the early 1980s had been replaced by a system of competitive markets by 2000. Although a large share of the distortions had been eliminated by the mid- to late 1990s (by the time market liberalization was complete), it took tariff reductions and trade liberalization to finish the process (Huang et al. 2009). Pingali and Xuan (1992) describe largely the same strategy in Vietnam.

Despite this gradual approach – unlike the Big Bang in CEE and FSU – the impact on distortions has been very important. Huang et al. (2009) show that in China between the mid-1980s and 2000, the Nominal Rate of Assistance (NRA) to agriculture fell (in absolute value terms) from -50 to nearly zero (Figure 8.2). The shift from high distortions in Vietnam

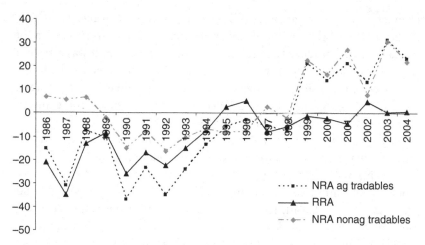

Figure 8.3. Nominal rates of assistance to agricultural and nonagricultural tradable sectors,[a] Vietnam, 1986 to 2004 (percent).

[a] The Relative Rate of Assistance (RRA) is defined as $100*[(100 + NRAag^t)/(100 + NRAnonag^t)-1]$, where $NRAag^t$ and $NRAnonag^t$ are the percentage NRAs for the tradables parts of the agricultural and nonagricultural sectors, respectively.

Source: Athukorala, Huong and Thanh (2009).

followed the same path as that in China (Figure 8.3). Although highly negative in the early 1990s, by 2000, the rate of assistance to producers of farmers relative to that for producers of nonagricultural tradables in Vietnam was around zero.

POLITICAL ECONOMY 1: REGIME CHANGE
AND DISTORTION REDUCTIONS

As explained earlier in this Chapter, dramatic reductions in distortions occurred throughout the former Communist countries of Asia and Europe. Although the nature of the changes differed among countries (reduction of farmer taxation in East Asia and reduction of farmer subsidization in East Europe and the FSU), changes in political regimes played an important role in triggering these changes in all countries.

From Mao to Deng in China

The reductions in distortions were part of the transition from Socialism to Reform in China. This economic transition followed the political transition from Mao Zedong to Deng Xiaoping. China before 1980 was fully a product of Mao. The influence of his politics was inescapable. Mao's fear of the outside world, his commitment to Socialism, and his skepticism of markets helped produce the pre-reform economic system. It was a system that was fundamentally closed to trade, run without markets, and administered by a controlled pricing system that discriminated against agriculture. It was a system that also failed to raise per capita income and to produce rises in total factor productivity.

While there was no dramatic overthrow of the Communist Party or outward change in the political system after Mao's death, the shift from Mao to his successor, Deng Xiaoping, nonetheless signaled the start of a new age. Committed in part by a self-learned belief in incentives and pragmatism, and also attracted by the rapid growth that was transforming most of the rest of East Asia outside its borders, Deng's policy approach could not have been more different than if there had been a revolution. Deng believed in an Open Door. Deng believed in technology wherever it came from – from foreign direct investment or an investment into domestic science and engineering. Deng wanted to incentivize the economy. It is no wonder that the beginning of the Reform Era is so clearly marked by a rise of Deng in the wake of Mao's death.

However, while Deng's fundamental ideology was radically new, China did not experience a sudden revolution, for several reasons. First, Deng assumed power from within the system. The Communist Party was in control both before and after Deng's accession to the position of supreme leader. Moreover, while Deng had a number of bold ideas, he also was essentially committed to the same system that had been built during the previous three decades. Even if he wanted to move more rapidly (which is not at all clear), Yang (1996) describes how there were many factions that were embedded deep in the system that were fundamentally reluctant to change. All of this guaranteed that change would move – at most – gradually.

From Stalin to Brezhnev in the Soviet Union

Interestingly, the distortions under Mao in China resembled much more the distortions under Stalin in the Soviet Union than the distortions in the Soviet Union in the 1970s. As with Mao, Stalin's desire to modernize fast and his commitment to heavy industry – and his distrust of farmers – led to his policy to use his centrally controlled economic system to tax the countryside to finance industrial development. This system, as in Mao's

China, reduced incentives for farms to invest and produce and left agriculture stagnant.

Soviet agricultural policy changed after World War II. When Khrushchev took over as Soviet leader following Stalin's death, he initially continued Stalin's agricultural policies. However, gradually he introduced important changes. He reduced taxes on agriculture and started to provide substantial assistance from the state, both in terms of investment support and in terms of higher prices for its products. This pro-agricultural policy was continued and reinforced under Brezhnev's Soviet leadership in the 1960s and 1970s.

The Fall of the Berlin Wall and the Collapse of Communism in East Europe and FSU

While the Soviet Union reduced taxation of agriculture through its pricing policy after World War II, what was different from China is that the Soviet leadership never let go of its centrally imposed collective and state farm system – which was a dramatic reform in China under the Communist regime at the end of the 1970s. It took a much more dramatic political reform (the fall of the Communist regime) in the Soviet Union (and in Eastern Europe) to trigger these fundamental changes, which were then also accompanied by changes in price and subsidy regimes.

The fall of the Berlin Wall in 1989 signaled the beginning of the collapse of the Communist regimes throughout Eastern Europe and the (former) Soviet Union. This in turn caused dramatic changes in the economy: Prices and trade were liberalized, subsidies cut, property rights privatized, and production and trade organizations restructured (Rozelle and Swinnen 2004). As documented in Anderson and Swinnen (2008), this led to a dramatic reduction in distortions to agricultural incentives: Agricultural support fell, on average, to very low levels in many countries of the region.

Importantly, political changes did not occur everywhere in the former Soviet Union. Even now, twenty years after the changes, some of the leaders have not changed. This is the case, for example, in countries such as Belarus, Turkmenistan, and Uzbekistan. In other countries, such as Russia, political freedoms have been reduced again. The relationship between political reforms and agricultural reforms is illustrated in Figure 8.4. This relationship is consistent with the idea that the lack of political reform (particularly in the least-reformed countries) has constrained the progress of economic reforms – and on reducing distortions in agriculture – in these countries.

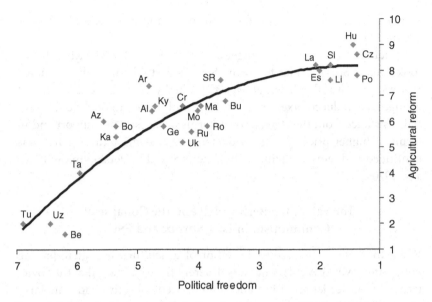

Figure 8.4. Correlation between agricultural reforms and political reforms in Europe's transition economies.
Source: Swinnen and Heinegg (2002).

Why was Reform Possible with the Communist Party in China and not in the FSU?

The previous discussion raises the interesting question why radical reforms of the agricultural economic system was possible in China but not in the Soviet Union under the Communist regime. In Swinnen and Rozelle (2006), we argue that radical reforms under the Communist regimes could only occur when there was simultaneously strong grassroots support for the reforms and support at the top of the Communist Party. If support from both above and below is not there, it is likely that the policy efforts will succumb to inertia, foot dragging, and resistance from those that are not in favor of reform. For example, reform failed in China in the 1960s because there was no support by the top leadership for radical decollectivization demanded by households at the grassroots level (Lardy 1983). Reform failed in Russia in the 1970s because there was neither grassroots nor leadership support for radical changes (Brada and Wadekin 1988). Agricultural reform failed in the 1980s in Russia because the reform proposals from the top of the Communist leadership under Gorbachev were not supported at the farm level (Gray 1990). Only in China at the end of the 1970s and the early 1980s was there a confluence of interests in favor of radical reforms at the top and at the grassroots, from both farm households and local officials.

Paradoxically and ironically, the radical, though partial, economic reforms in the Chinese countryside did much to reinforce the Communist Party's hold on power (Oi 1989). The opposite was true in the Soviet Union, where the lack of significant reforms ultimately contributed to the fall of the Communist leadership.

The radical reform actions in China, which looked like moves away from Socialism, probably did more to consolidate the rule of the Communist Party than any other measures taken during this period. Although it is well documented that the decisive changes directly affected the incomes and livelihood of more than 70 percent of the population in the rural areas, the agricultural reform also had a tremendous impact on the urban economy. The rise in food production and increases of food supplies to cities took a lot of pressure off the government. Urban wages, when raised, became real gains to income, since food became relatively cheaper. In addition, the rise of rural incomes created an immediate surge in the demand for nonfood products. Many of the same dynamics occurred in Vietnam (Wurfel 1993, Pingali and Xuan, 1992).

Causes of Differences in Grassroots Support in China and the Soviet Union

Why were the attitudes toward decollectivization of farm workers and local officials in China and the Soviet Union so different? One factor sometimes suggested as an explanation for the difference in farmers' motivation is the historical legacy of Socialism. Rural households in the Soviet Union had been working under the collective system for much longer than in China, and there was no memory of family farming. While this factor no doubt affected the attitudes of rural households, this is unsatisfactory as an explanation because it cannot explain why attitudes in many rural households in East European countries (who had been under Communism as long as China) were equally unenthusiastic about decollectivization.

A more convincing argument is the differences in distortions, which contributed to differences in standard of living offered by pre-reform collective agriculture. In rural China, more than 30 percent of households lived in utmost poverty (Lardy 1983, World Bank 1992). In contrast, farm workers in CEE and FSU benefited from large government subsidies and high wages, and were covered by social welfare benefits. Despite low farm productivity, workers in the Soviet Union's state farms and collectives lived at standards of living far higher than those in China's rural sector. In several countries, rural incomes were actually higher than urban incomes (Ellman 1988). With the reduction of distortions, farm incomes would fall, effort by farm laborers would need to increase, and risks would have been higher. Moreover, with overemployment and soft budget constraints, agricultural reform would trigger layoffs. Not surprisingly, many farm workers in the Soviet Union and CEE resisted agricultural reforms.

Differences in technology and in bureaucratic organization reinforced these differences in attitudes. Farmers in China purchased few of their inputs. Supply channels were simple. They sold relatively little of their output into the market. Almost no farmers interfaced with processors. Most importantly, given the high labor factor share, the potential for effort efficiency-enhanced output would mean significantly higher incomes for farmers. In contrast, farms in the Soviet Union and Eastern Europe were much more integrated into an industrialized production system and a complex network of relations with input suppliers and processors (Johnson and Brooks 1983). Moreover, they were much more capital- and land-intensive. Under these conditions, farms were less likely to get a large boost from incentive improvements, and more likely to face serious disruptions.

The support of officials for reforms in China was sustained by reforms of the bureaucracy and by rural industrialization and fiscal reforms (Qian and Weingast 1997). The fiscal reform policies were shown to be beneficial to local leaders, and they secured support for the overall reform agenda. These changes also stimulated interest of bureaucrats in local economic growth. In the Soviet Union, little change took place in the bureaucracy (Shleifer 1997) and, since the interests of local officials were also here aligned with those of farm managers, the rational response of both was to resist, not support, reform.

Crises, Political Change, and Reforms During Transition

General political and economic crises have continued to play an important role in inducing changes in agricultural distortions. The most obvious example is the fall of the Communist regime and the disintegration of the Soviet Union – and of the central directives coming from Moscow. Also, more recently, there are several examples where more general crises have triggered changes. Most often, policy reforms come only after new elections lead to a change in government, reflecting changed electoral preferences. For example, in Romania and Bulgaria, important progress in market reforms and the removal of distortions only occurred in the late 1990s after electoral change brought reform-minded governments to power. In Ukraine, reform progress was made in the years after the 1999 election in which the large farm lobby fell out with President Kuchma, who consequently introduced a series of important reforms that the farms had successfully opposed previously.

However, democratic political change is not a sufficient condition in itself for better agricultural policies. For example, in both Ukraine and the Kyrgyz Republic, the important political changes (the "Orange Revolution" and the "Tulip Revolution," respectively) in the early 2000s did not contribute to better agricultural policy. In fact, the Ukrainian government seems to have reverted to more-inefficient policies. In the Kyrgyz Republic, change has mostly resulted in more instability while relatively little distortions remain in agriculture.

POLITICAL ECONOMY 2: "BIG BANG" VERSUS GRADUALISM

A fundamental difference between China and many CEE and the FSU states was in the pace of market liberalization. This raises the question: Why did the FSU and CEE not also opt for the gradual process of market liberalization? We believe that there are a number of differences that explain the choices for the alternative approaches.

Once China had successfully implemented property rights reform and restructured its farms (as well as adjusted prices to reduce the implicit tax on farmers), liberalizing markets became less imperative (Rozelle 1996). The early pricing changes (which were not done through markets, but by the planning bureaucracy) and the household responsibility system helped the reformers meet their initial objectives of increased agricultural productivity and higher farm incomes and food output (Sicular 1988, Lin 1992). The agricultural reforms fuelled China's first surge in economic growth and reduced the concerns about national food security. The legitimacy of leaders of being able to run a government that could raise the standard of living of its people was at least temporarily satisfied. A new set of radical reforms might have exposed the leaders to new risks, in particular regarding the impact on the nation's food supply (Putterman 1993). Decollectivization had erased the worst inefficiencies. With the urgency for additional reforms dampened for top leaders (since their goals were met) and for farmers (since their incomes and control over the means of production both had improved), there was less policy pressure from both the top and grassroots.

The situation was very different in the Soviet Union and CEE states in the late 1980s. Communist leaders had failed to substantially reform for decades, not only in agriculture but in the entire economy. Once they lost power, the anticommunist political forces that came to power were determined to get rid of the Communist system and to introduce democracy and a market economy. Reforms were launched despite resistance by farm managers, workers, and local officials (Swinnen 1997). Reformers chose to push through as much of the economic reform agenda as possible at the time that they were (still) in charge – using their "window of opportunity." Hence, for both political and economic reasons, a comprehensive set of radical reforms was pursued. Since the previous reforms had failed to result in efficiency improvements with marginal and slow policy shifts, in the view of the reformers, a more radical and broad-based reform approach was necessary.

These dynamics applied to reform programs across the economy. Within the agri-food system, reforms extended beyond land reforms. The post-communist policy shifts needed to be sufficiently radical to have a significant impact on productivity of the entire food system. This required a broad and encompassing reform strategy that needed to address several key issues. First, the more industrialized nature of the Soviet agricultural production system and the inefficiencies imbedded in the agro-food supply chain required an approach beyond the confines of the farming sector. Organizational inefficiencies in the supply chain would have severely limited the potential impact of farm-level reforms in the Soviet Union. Supply chains inefficiencies were an important cause of low agricultural efficiency (Johnson and Brooks 1983). As a result, solving the problems of Soviet agriculture would require policy reforms beyond the farms.

Second, in terms of administrative feasibility, the more complicated technologies in Soviet agriculture and in CEE meant a more complex set of exchanges between a larger number and greater variety of firms. China's farming sector was largely based on small, mostly subsistence farmers selling grain and oilseed commodities to a trading system that in turn only had to retransfer the stocks to urban sales outlets or, at the most, rudimentary processing firms (such as oil-crushing mills). By contrast, in the Soviet Union and in the CEE, the food economy was dominated by livestock products, dairy, and other products that were part of an agri-industrial complex, including agribusiness, food processing, and retailing companies. To design an optimal sequence of policy in a gradual reform strategy, policy makers would have been required to have access to extensive information on a vast number of processes. This information had not been available for planning, so there is no reason to believe it would have been available for a gradual reform program.

Third, the overall importance of agriculture in the economy (measured as the share of GDP or employment) also was an important feature that helped determine the pace of reform. Unlike in China, where agriculture made up such a huge share of the economy at the outset of reforms, agriculture in the Soviet Union and the CEE was much less important in the economy. Reformers made several decisions that had a major impact on agriculture and on the sequencing of the agricultural reforms as part of a broader reform agenda. Hence, for all of these reasons, the same factors that kept reform from occurring in the Soviet Union and CEE in the prereform era made it imperative that, once the decision to reform was made, the reforms happen all at once.

POLITICAL ECONOMY 3: DOMESTIC PRESSURES AND STRUCTURAL CONDITIONS

Now that the transitions are well advanced, there is more scope for explaining policy evolutions using standard political economy theory. In this section, we consider just domestic forces at work.

Development and Antitrade Patterns

Several political economy-stylized facts that are widely observed in market economies (Anderson, Hayami and Others 1986, Swinnen 1994; de Gorter and Swinnen 2002) are also found in the post-transition CEE and FSU countries. On average, the data indicate that farmer assistance tends to be higher in higher-income countries, and higher for import-competing enterprises than for export-oriented ones. For example, Slovenia, the richest country in the region, has the highest level of agricultural protection. In many CEE and FSU nations, we also observe the same correlations. It is likely that these reflect similar political-economic interactions and mechanisms as in other parts of the world. Anderson and Swinnen (2009) estimate these effects and find that the same correlations apply.

These exact same dynamics have occurred in the case of China (Huang et al. 2009). Whereas China's farmers were taxed heavily in the past, in recent years, they have begun to receive greater assistance from the state. In 2007, for example, farmers received up to US$20 per acre (in RMB equivalents) in production subsidies (Rozelle, Huang and Otsuka 2008).

Table 8.1. *History of taxation and subsidization under Communist regimes in the Soviet Union and China*

Year	GDP/capita[a]	Country	Ag distortions	Ruler
1930	1450	Soviet Union	Tax	Stalin
1940	2150	Soviet Union	Tax	Stalin
1950	2850	Soviet Union	Tax (less)	Kruzhnev
1960	3950	Soviet Union	Subsidy (less)	Brezhnev
1970	5570	Soviet Union	Subsidy	Brezhnev
1980	6420	Soviet Union	Subsidy	Brezhnev
1970	780	China	Tax	Mao
1980	1070	China	Tax	Deng
1990	1860	China	Tax (less)	Jiang
2000	3425	China	Tax (less)	Jiang
2010	?	China	Subsidy?	Hu

[a] GDP per capita is measured in 1990 international Geary-Khamis dollars (for more details see http://unstats.un.org/unsd/methods/icp/ipc7_htm.htm).
Source: Maddison (2003).

While it is unclear if the new subsidies are distorting, there is the tendency in China to begin to support agriculture as the nation's economy grows.

There is an interesting question whether this "development pressure" is also behind the remarkable switch from agricultural taxation to agricultural subsidization in the Soviet Union over the period 1930–70. Table 8.1 presents data on the relationship between income and the shift from taxation to subsidization comparing the shift in the Soviet Union and the current policy developments in China. The data suggest that the change in the Soviet Union occurred when GDP per capita was around US$3,500, which, intriguingly, is roughly the current level of income in China. Hence, these observations are consistent with the interpretation that the pressure to start subsidizing agriculture is real in China and would lead to a net subsidization of agriculture in the future – in the absence of strict constraints, such as WTO may provide.

Concentrated Benefits and Distortions

One of the reasons that protection has not risen more in China as its economy has grown may be related to the observation that protection is greatest when the benefits are most concentrated. Since China has around

200 million farmers, and production of many of its commodities (rice, wheat, maize, soybeans, cotton, fruits, vegetables, and livestock products) is spread out over many provinces, the benefits from protection might be said to be less concentrated than in any other country in the world.

There is an important exception, however. Sugar production in China is highly concentrated. More than 50 percent of its production is in Guangxi province, and most of the rest of China's sugar production is in two other provinces. When looking at protection of different commodities – both assessed rates and those negotiated under the WTO accession agreement – it is clear that sugar is an outlier. Its in-quota tariff is above 25 percent, higher than any other major commodity. Moreover, the execution of sugar border policy is strict in the sense that custom officials have been exceptionally fastidious in collecting all duties.

Also in other transition countries, opportunities for rent seeking from distorted policies inhibit reductions in distortions, as the few who benefit disproportionately from the existing distortions lobby strongly for their continuation. This applies to various policies, such as cotton regulations in Central Asia, grain trade regulations in Bulgaria, Ukraine, and Russia, and water policies in Central Asia. It also applies, however, to several policies in countries in which benefits go to a specific group of farms. For example, the continuation of soft budget constraints in the large FSU countries, and the failure of governments to enforce bankruptcies and enforce strong land rights, all disproportionately benefit large farming companies, whereas smaller family farms are often hurt by these policies.

Exceptionally heavy government intervention is associated with policies that tax agriculture rather than subsidize it. Heavy negative government intervention in the form of depressed incentives tends to be concentrated on commodities that have the potential to provide export tax revenue for the government. This is especially the case in the cotton sectors of Uzbekistan, Turkmenistan, and Tajikistan (Pomfret 2008). There, as in a number of African countries (Baffes 2009), the government controls the cotton chain so as to extract rents, thereby depressing farmers' prices and production incentives.

The grain (and oilseed) export sectors of Ukraine, Bulgaria, and (surplus regions of) Russia are similarly characterized by heavy government regulation and interventions. In traditional grain-exporting countries such as Ukraine and Bulgaria, the grain sector has disproportionate political significance – for historic and psychological reasons. For example, in the mid-1990s in Bulgaria, ministers of agriculture had to resign regularly following reports of grain shortfalls or unregulated exports threatening the local grain supply (Swinnen 1996). In Ukraine, ad hoc grain market interventions continued in recent years (von Cramon–Taubadel et al. 2008).

Causes of Increases in Support During Transition

The increases in agricultural support in Europe's transition economies – in the second half of the 1990s in CEE and more recently in the FSU – are the result of the interaction of domestic political forces with international events. For example, the increase in farmer assistance in CEE countries was likely caused by the "normal" domestic internal pressures, brought to bear in a contestable political environment, which result in rises in agricultural protectionism as per capita income increases and as agricultural comparative advantage declines. In this period, it was a case of reversing somewhat the overshooting in reform during the first few years of transition.

Another factor that is playing a role is the overlay of the EU accession process, which is encouraging CEE governments to target the levels of support expected in the EU by the end of the phase-in period of accession, so as to maximize the transfer of benefits from Brussels. However, it appears that in the years before accession, the EU accession process had more impact on the introduction of new support instruments than on the overall level of support. This is probably because all the cost of that support has to be borne within the national economy prior to EU accession (Swinnen 2002).

In addition, improvements in the government's budgetary situation, which allowed more subsidies to be given to farmers than was possible in the early years of transition, also appear to play a role. While this is common throughout the ECA region, it is particular important in Russia and some of its neighbors, such as Kazakhstan, where recovery from the post-1998 fiscal crisis has been aided by windfall gains from the dramatic rise in the prices of their oil exports. China's nascent use of subsidies coincides with the rebound of fiscal revenues under the control of the central government.

POLITICAL ECONOMY 4: IMPACT OF
INTERNATIONAL AGREEMENTS

In addition to national political forces, there have also been several sets of international pressures influencing policy choices in the transition economies.

Regional Integration Agreements

EU accession, both prospective and then actual, has had obvious and profound influences on policy choices in the CEE region. The eight countries that joined the EU in May 2004 have raised domestic agricultural and food prices up towards EU15 levels. An important part of the EU farm subsidies are in the form of direct payments. EU8 farms receive considerably less of these subsidies than those received by EU15 farmers. The EU8 subsidies will gradually increase, reaching EU15 levels by 2010. Another important difference is that these subsidies in the EU15 will be given earlier than in the EU8 on a per farm (single farm payment) basis, which means they are less coupled with production and therefore less distortive and more efficient.

The EU8 countries have also been induced to undertake major regulatory improvements to stimulate their markets, including private investments in the food chain and public rural infrastructure investments. Their trade policies have likewise changed so as to allow free access for all products from other EU25 member countries and, in most cases, also freer access for nonagricultural products from non-EU countries (the latter because the common external tariff typically was lower than that previously applying in acceding countries).

A further and somewhat erratic influence has been the regional trading arrangements among the ECA countries. These include the Eurasian Economic Community (EAEC), the Central European Free Trade Area (CEFTA), and the Baltic Free Trade Area (BFTA). However, the impact of these agreements on reducing agricultural policy distortions has generally been limited because the agreements include many exceptions for agricultural and food products, and especially for the so-called "sensitive products" that make up a substantial share of production. Moreover, Central Asian countries such as Kazakhstan and the Kyrgyz Republic have been reluctant to join the EAEC, as it would impose Russia's trade and customs preferences on them.

The World Trade Organization

The impact of the WTO is mixed. Some of the transition countries, such as the Czech Republic, Slovakia, Hungary, Poland, Romania, and Slovenia, were members of the GATT and thus have been members of the World Trade Organization (WTO) since its creation in 1995. China, Bulgaria, Estonia, Lithuania, Latvia, the Kyrgyz Republic, Armenia, Georgia, and Albania joined the WTO later. As of 2009, Ukraine, Russia, and Kazakhstan were at different stages in their negotiations for WTO accession.

WTO accession has not strongly disciplined those countries that were the founding members in 1995. For example, the applied tariffs are significantly below bound tariffs in many CEECs. This suggests that these CEECs have not been constrained by the WTO agreements (Bacchetta and Drabek 2002).

For the CEECs that joined early, their commitments were based on the high support levels of the 1980s and therefore caused little constraints on their policies in the 1990s; for the others, the restrictions were more severe. However, for those that had to negotiate their entry in the latter 1990s, the constraints on introducing or maintaining distortions are more serious. Perhaps more than any other acceding country, the accession process has led to a fall in distortions in China (Huang et al. 2009). China's desire to enter the WTO (which probably was motivated by nonagricultural trade issues more than anything – e.g., textiles) led to two phases of adjustments in protection. Huang and Chen (1999) demonstrate that even before China's accession, leaders aggressively reduced protection on a number of commodities (including many importables, such as soybeans and cotton) in anticipation of the negotiations. On accession, protection fell even further. However, according to Huang, Rozelle and Chang (2004), while protection did fall after 2001, the rate of fall was not faster than the reductions that had begun in the early-to mid-1990s in preparation for entry into the WTO. Being a newly acceding country, the constraints imposed on China by international agreements have been real and have led to falling rates of positive protection, especially for a significant number of importable commodities (Huang et al. 2009).

For the CEE countries, the most important WTO impact has been indirect: In anticipation of eastward enlargement, the EU was forced to introduce major changes to its Common Agricultural Policy, which in turn has affected post-accession agricultural distortions in the EU8.

Influence of International Financial Institutions (IFIs)

The role of other international institutions was very important at the start of transition, as it provided policy reform guidance in all these countries. However, in more recent years, this advice has been less effective. For countries joining the EU, policy advice from Brussels was perceived as more relevant than that from Washington, DC (World Bank and IMF) or London (EBRD). This is especially, but not only, the case for the EU accession countries. Also for those countries aspiring to join the EU (such as most of the Balkan countries and even those further east, such as Ukraine) or those seeing the accession countries as models for their own development strategies, policy advice from Brussels is taken seriously. Another reason is that in many of the other ECA countries, their improved fiscal and macro-economic situations have made them less beholden to those international financial institutions requiring reforms as a condition of providing loans or financial assistance.

CONCLUSION

In this Chapter, we provide a series of hypotheses to explain the political economy of the dramatic changes in distortions to agricultural incentives in the transition countries of Asia and Europe. Until the late 1970s, all these countries were under Communist rule, and agricultural incentives were massively distorted. The leaders of the Soviet Bloc and China were committed to Socialist ideology and designed their economies to be insulated from the world and its markets. Since then, there have been dramatic changes in the distortions to agricultural incentives in these countries. Yet there are large differences between the countries in the extent and nature of their remaining distortions.

We have identified four sets of political economy arguments to explain why these changes have occurred and why there are very large differences between the countries in the extent and nature of the remaining distortions. The first set of arguments discusses how the change in political regimes has induced a change in policies. In some cases, particularly in China, this regime change was within the Communist party, while in many other countries, the economic changes only occurred when the Communist regime itself collapsed. We have tried to explain why this was the case.

The second set of arguments is about why some countries have taken a gradual road to market liberalization and others took a "Big Bang" approach. We argue that these differences are related to regime change and whether a broad approach to reforms was needed to introduce irreversible changes to the entire political system.

As in many other countries, structural characteristics of the economy also influenced agricultural policies – and hence distortions – in the transition countries over the past twenty years. In particular, we observe that subsidies to agriculture are positively correlated with economic development and have a negative correlation with exports. These patterns have been observed widely and explained by a variety of political economy models. Finally, we argue that international agreements have influenced agricultural distortions in the transition countries, but that the impact varies importantly across agreements and across countries.

References

Anderson K. (ed.) (2009), *Distortions to Agricultural Incentives: A Global Perspective, 1955–2007*, London: Palgrave Macmillan and Washington DC: World Bank.

Anderson, K., Y. Hayami and Others (1986), *The Political Economy of Agricultural Protection: East Asia in International Perspective*, Boston and London: Allen and Unwin.

Anderson K. and J.F.M. Swinnen (eds.) (2008), *Distortions to Agricultural Incentives in Europe's Transition Economies*, Washington DC: World Bank.

Anderson, K. and J.F.M. Swinnen (2009), "Eastern Europe and Central Asia," Ch. 6 in K. Anderson (ed.), *Distortions to Agricultural Incentives: A Global Perspective, 1955–2007*, London: Palgrave Macmillan and Washington DC: World Bank.

Athukorala, P., P.L. Huong and V.T. Thanh (2009), "Vietnam," Ch. 8 in K. Anderson and W. Martin (eds.), *Distortions to Agricultural Incentives in Asia*, Washington DC: World Bank.

Bacchetta, M. and Z. Drabek (2002), "Effects of WTO Accession on Policy-Making in Sovereign States: Preliminary Lessons from the Recent Experience of Transition Countries," WTO Staff Working Paper DERD-2002–02, Geneva.

Baffes, J. (2009), "Benin, Bukina Faso, Chad, Mali and Togo," Ch. 18 in K. Anderson and W. Masters (eds.), *Distortions to Agricultural Incentives in Africa*, Washington DC: World Bank.

Brada, J.C. and K. Wädekin (eds.) (1988), *Socialist Agriculture in Transition: Organizational Response to Failing Performance*, Boulder: Westview Press.

Ciaian, P. and J.F.M. Swinnen (2008), "Distortions to Agricultural Incentives in New EU Member Countries," pp 53–90 in K. Anderson and J.F.M. Swinnen (eds.), *Distortions to Agricultural Incentives in Europe's Transition Economies*, Washington DC: World Bank.

de Gorter, H. and J.F.M. Swinnen (2002), "Political Economy of Agricultural Policies", pp. 2073–2123 in B.L. Gardner and G.C. Rausser (eds.), *Handbook of Agricultural Economics, Volume 2B: Agricultural and Food Policy*, Amsterdam: Elsevier.

Ellman, M. (1988), "Contract Brigades and Normless Teams in Soviet Agriculture," pp. 23–33 in J.C. Brada and K, Wädekin (eds.), *Socialist Agriculture in Transition: Organizational Response to Failing Performance*, Boulder: Westview Press.

Gray, K.R. (ed.) (1990), *Soviet Agriculture: Comparative Perspectives*, Ames: Iowa State University Press.

Huang, J. and C. Chen (1999), "Effect of Trade Liberalization on Agriculture in China: Institutional and Structural Aspects," CGPRT Working Paper Series, Paper Number 42, United Nations, ESCAP Centre for Research and Development of Coarse Grains, Pulses, Roots and Tuber Crops, Bogor, Indonesia.

Huang, J., Y. Liu, W. Martin and S. Rozelle (2009), "Distortions to Agricultural Incentives in China", Ch. 3 in K. Anderson and W. Martin (eds.) *Distortions to Agricultural Incentives in Asia*, Washington DC: World Bank.

Huang, J., S. Rozelle and M. Chang (2004), "The Nature of Distortions to Agricultural Incentives in China and Implications of WTO Accession," *World Bank Economic Review* 18(1): 59–84.

Johnson, D.G. and K.M. Brooks (eds.) (1983), *Prospects for Soviet Agriculture in the 1980s*, Bloomington: Indiana University Press.

Lardy, N. (1983), *Agriculture in China's Modern Economic Development*, Cambridge and New York: Cambridge University Press.

Lin, J.Y. (1992), "Rural Reforms and Agricultural Growth in China," *American Economic Review* 82(1): 34–51.

McMillan, J. and B. Naughton (1992), "How to Reform a Planned Economy: Lessons from China," *Oxford Review of Economic Policy* 8: 130–43.

Macours, K. and J. Swinnen (2002), "Patterns of Agrarian Transition," *Economic Development and Cultural Change* 50(2): 365–94.

Maddison, A. (2003), *The World Economy: Historical Statistics*, Paris: OECD.

Oi, J. (1989), "Market Reforms and Corruption in Rural China," *Studies in Comparative Communism* 22(2/3): 221–33.

Park, A., H. Jin, S. Rozelle and J. Huang (2002), "Market Emergence and Transition: Transition Costs, Arbitrage, and Autarky in China's Grain Market," *American Journal of Agricultural Economics* 84(1): 67–82.

Pingali, P.L. and V. Xuan (1992), "Vietnam: Decollectivization and Rice Productivity Growth," *Economic Development and Cultural Change* 40(4): 697–718.

Pomfret, R. (2008), "Distortions to Agricultural Incentives in Kazakhstan," pp. 219–64 in K. Anderson and J.F.M. Swinnen (eds.), *Distortions to Agricultural Incentives in Europe's Transition Economies*, Washington DC: World Bank.

Putterman, L. (1993), *Continuity and Change in China's Rural Development*, New York: Oxford University Press.

Qian, Y. and B.R. Weingast (1997), "Federalism as a Commitment to Preserving Market Incentives," *Journal of Economic Perspectives* 11(4): 83–92.

Roland, G. (2000), *Transition and Economics: Politics, Markets, and Firms*, Cambridge MA: MIT Press.

Rozelle, S. (1996), "Gradual Reform and Institutional Development: The Keys to Success of China's Rural Reforms," pp. 197–220 in J. McMillan and B. Naughton (eds.), *Reforming Asian Socialism: The Growth of Market Institutions*, Ann Arbor: University of Michigan Press.

Rozelle, S., J. Huang and K. Otsuka (2008), "Agriculture in China's Development," pp. 467–505 in L. Brandt and T. Rawski (eds.), *China's Great Economic Transformation*, Cambridge and New York: Cambridge University Press

Rozelle, S. and J.F.M. Swinnen (2004), "Success and Failure of Reform: Insights from the Transition of Agriculture," *Journal of Economic Literature* 42(2): 404–56

Shleifer, A. (1997), "Government in Transition," *European Economic Review* 41(3–5): 385–410.

Sicular, T. (1988), "Plan and Market in China's Agricultural Commerce," *Journal of Political Economy* 96 (2): 283–307.

_____ (1995), "Redefining State, Plan, and Market: China's Reforms in Agricultural Commerce," *China Quarterly* 144: 1020–46.

Swinnen, J.F.M. (1994), "A Positive Theory of Agricultural Protection," *American Journal of Agricultural Economics* 76(1): 1–14.

(1996), "Endogenous Price and Trade Policy Developments in Central European Agriculture", *European Review of Agricultural Economics* 23(2): 133–160.

Swinnen, J.F.M. (ed.) (1997), *The Political Economy of Agrarian Reform in Central and Eastern Europe*, Ashgate: Aldershot.

Swinnen, J.F.M. (2002), "Transition and Integration in Europe: Implications for Agricultural and Food Markets, Policy and Trade Agreements," *The World Economy* 25(4): 481–501.

Swinnen, J.F.M. and A. Heinegg (2002), "On the Political Economy of Land Reform in the Former Soviet Union," *Journal of International Development* 14(4): 1019–31.

Swinnen, J.F.M. and S. Rozelle (2006), *From Marx and Mao to the Market*, Oxford: Oxford University Press.

von Cramon-Taubadel, S., O. Nivyevskiy, E.E. von der Malsburg, and V. Movchan (2008), "Ukraine," pp. 175–217 in K. Anderson and J.F.M. Swinnen (eds.), *Distortions to Agricultural Incentives in Europe's Transition Economies*, Washington DC: World Bank.

World Bank (1992), *China: Strategies for Reducing Poverty in the 1990s*, Washington DC: The World Bank.

Wurfel, D. (1993), "Doi Moi in Comparative Perspective," pp. 165–207 in W. Turley and M. Selden (eds.), *Reinventing Vietnamese Socialism: Doi Moi in Comparative Perspective*, Boulder: Westview Press.

Yang, D. (1996), *Calamity and Reform in China: State, Rural Society, and Institutional Change Since the Great Leap Famine*, Stanford: Stanford University Press.

PART THREE

POLITICAL ECONOMETRICS: THE PAST FIFTY YEARS

NINE

Agricultural Price Distortions and Stabilization

William A. Masters and Andres F. Garcia

This chapter describes agricultural policy choices and tests some predictions of major political economy theories, exploiting the new Anderson and Valenzuela (2008) dataset. We start by establishing three broad stylized facts: the development paradox (governments tend to tax agriculture in poorer countries and subsidize it in richer ones), the prevalence of anti-trade bias (governments tend to tax both imports and exports more than nontradables), and the importance of resource abundance (governments tax more and subsidize less where there is more land per capita). We then test a variety of political economy explanations, finding results consistent with hypothesized effects of rural and urban constituents' rational ignorance about small per-person effects, governance institutions' control of rent seeking by political leaders, governments' revenue motive for taxation, and the role of time consistency in policy making.

We find that larger groups obtain more favorable policies, suggesting that positive group size effects outweigh any negative influence from more free-ridership. Some of these results add to the explanatory power of our stylized facts, but others help explain them. A novel result is that demographically driven entry of new farmers is associated with less favorable farm policies, which is consistent with a model in which the arrival of new farmers erodes policy rents and discourages political activity by incumbents. Another new result is that governments achieve very little price stabilization relative to our benchmark estimates of undistorted prices, and governments in the poorest countries have actually destabilized domestic prices over the full span of our data. Price stability is often a stated goal of policy and would be predicted by status quo bias or loss aversion, but the stockholding or fiscal policies used to limit price changes are often unsustainable, and prices tend jump when the intervention ends.

215

The Chapter begins with an outline of the methodology adopted for the study. It then presents evidence for the three stylized facts mentioned above. The third section seeks to explain agricultural policy choices empirically, drawing on six political economy theories. It also tests a new explanation, based on demographic influences on political pressures. The final section of the chapter offers some conclusions.

METHODOLOGY

Following Anderson et al. (2008), our principal measure of agricultural trade policy is a tariff-equivalent "Nominal Rate of Assistance" (NRA), defined as:

$$NRA \equiv \frac{P_d - P_f}{P_f} \qquad (1)$$

where P_d is the observed domestic price in local currency for a given product, country, and year, and P_f is the estimated domestic price that would hold in the absence of commodity-market or exchange-rate intervention. By definition, such an NRA would be zero in a competitive free-trade regime and positive where producers are subsidized by taxpayers or consumers. The NRA is negative where producers are taxed by trade policy, for example through export restrictions or an overvalued exchange rate. In a few cases, we use the absolute value of NRA in order to measure distortions away from competitive markets. Where national-average NRAs are used, they are value-weighted at the undistorted prices.

The NRA results we use are based on the efforts of country specialists to obtain the best possible data and apply appropriate assumptions about international opportunity costs and transaction costs in each market (see Anderson et al. 2008). There is inevitably much measurement error, but by covering a very large fraction of the world's countries and commodities over a very long time period we can detect patterns and trends that might otherwise remain hidden.

The Anderson et al. project is designed mainly to measure policy effects on price levels, but it can also be used to measure policy effects on price variability from year to year by comparing the variability of domestic prices with variability of estimated free-trade prices, both expressed in natural logs. Ratio-detrending is used here to remove the time trend on prices by regressing observed prices $(\ln(P_i)_o)$ on time (t) as in equation (2) below, and using the resulting predicted values $(\ln(P_i)_{\text{Pr}})$ defined in equation (3) to generate detrended prices ($\hat{P}_i$) in equation (4) as the ratio of observed over predicted prices:

$$\ln(P_i)_0 = \alpha + \beta_i \cdot t + \epsilon \tag{2}$$

$$\ln(P_i)_{\mathrm{Pr}} \equiv \alpha + \beta_i \cdot t \tag{3}$$

$$\hat{P}_i = \frac{\ln(P_i)_0}{\ln(P_i)_{\mathrm{Pr}}} \tag{4}$$

To compare the relative variation of domestic and free-trade prices, we use the standard deviation (*sd*) of each price, in a ratio that we call the Stabilization Index (SI):

$$SI \equiv \frac{sd(\hat{P}_f) - sd(\hat{P}_d)}{sd(\hat{P}_f)} \cdot 100 \tag{5}$$

A policy that does not influence proportional price stability at all, such as a strictly ad valorem tax or subsidy, would generate an SI of zero. Policies that stabilize domestic prices, such as a variable tariff that is negatively correlated with the world price, would generate a positive SI. And policies that destabilize domestic prices, such as import quotas that leave domestic prices vulnerable to large local supply or demand shocks, would generate a negative SI. Note that the SI for a particular product in a particular country is calculated over the 1960–2004 period, for which our data are most complete, and refers to the ensemble of all policies over that time period. In this way, we capture not only the impact of a given policy on price stability while that policy is in place, but also the impact on stability of introducing or removing policies. Doing so is very important because many policies achieve short-term stability in unsustainable ways, causing prices to jump when the policy itself is changed.

The NRA and SI estimates allow us to describe key stylized facts about policy choices and then test the degree to which the relationships implied by political economy models actually fit the data. Our tests are all variations on equation (6):

$$Y = \alpha + \beta \cdot X + \gamma \cdot Z + \epsilon \tag{6}$$

where Y represents the policy measures of interest (variously NRA at the country level, NRA at the product level, the absolute value of NRA, or SI), X is a set of regressors that describe stylized facts that could be explained by many different policymaking mechanisms (income, direction of trade, resource abundance, continent dummies), and Z represents regressors that are associated with a specific mechanism hypothesized to cause the policies we observe. Our empirical analysis aims to test the significance of introducing each variable in Z when controlling for X, and to ask whether introducing Z explains the stylized facts (that is, reduces the estimated value of β) or adds to them (that is, raises the equation's estimated R-squared without changing the estimated value of β), or perhaps adds no additional significance at all. Regressors for X and Z are drawn from public data disseminated by the World Bank, FAO, the Penn World Table or others, as detailed in the Annex.

THE STYLIZED FACTS OF AGRICULTURAL POLICY

Our dataset covers an extraordinary diversity of commodities and countries, with huge variation in agricultural policies. In this section, we explore a few key stylized facts to establish the background variation for which we will want to control when testing the predictions of specific theories. A given theory could help explain these patterns or could fit the residual variation they leave unexplained. In either case, controlling for key characteristics of commodities and countries allows us to test each theory's explanatory power in a simple, consistent framework.

The stylized facts we consider include the oldest and most general observations about agricultural policy, linking policy choices to a commodity's direction of trade, a country's real income per capita, and its endowment of farmland per capita. The direction of trade might matter to the extent that agricultural policy is simply trade policy, and so could be linked to a government's more general antitrade bias. A country's real income might matter to the extent that the role of agriculture changes with economic growth, so that it is subject to the development paradox. Finally, land abundance might matter because agriculture is a natural resource-intensive sector and could be subject to a natural resource effect. We address each of these in turn below.

The antitrade bias of governments is a key concern of economists, dating back to Adam Smith and David Ricardo, who first described how restrictions on imports and exports affect incentives for specialization. In this Chapter, we capture antitrade bias of domestic instruments, as well as trade restrictions, by linking measured NRAs to whether a commodity is importable or exportable in a given country and year.

A second stylized fact is the development paradox, in which the governments of poorer countries are typically observed to impose taxes on farm production, whereas governments in richer countries typically subsidize it. The modern literature documenting this tendency begins with Bale and Lutz (1981), and includes notable contributions from Anderson, Hayami and Others (1986), Lindert (1991), and Krueger, Schiff and Valdes (1991), among others. This pattern is paradoxical insofar as farmers are the majority and are poorer than nonfarmers in low-income countries, whereas in high-income countries, farmers are a relatively wealthy minority.

A third kind of pattern involves natural resource effects, whereby countries with a greater resource rent available for extraction from a sector may be tempted to impose a heavier tax burden on it. The political economy of resource taxation is often discussed regarding oil and other mineral resources, as in Auty (2001), while applications to agriculture include McMillan and Masters (2003) and Isham et al. (2005). For our purposes, the resource rent that may be available in agriculture is measured crudely here by arable land area per capita, allowing us to ask whether more land-abundant countries tend to tax the agricultural sector more (or subsidize it less), when controlling for both antitrade bias and the development paradox.

Note that antitrade bias could help account for the development paradox, to the extent that low-income countries tend to be net exporters of farm products whereas richer countries tend to be net importers of them. Both could be driven by changes in the relative administrative cost of taxation, insofar as a country's income growth and capital accumulation allows government to shift taxation from exports and imports (at the expense of farms and farmers) to other things (at the expense of firms and their employees). Thus we need to control for income when testing for antitrade bias and control for antitrade bias when testing for the development paradox, while controlling for both of these when looking at resource effects.

To test the magnitude and significance of these patterns in the NRA data, we use data on the direction of trade from our own database, and data on a country's average income per capita data from the Penn World Table (2007). Income is defined here as real gross domestic product in PPP prices, chain indexed over time in international dollars at year-2000 prices. Finally, data on the agricultural sector's land abundance comes from FAOSTAT (2007) as the per-capita availability of arable land, defined as the area under temporary crops, temporary meadows for mowing or pasture, land under market and kitchen gardens, and land temporarily fallow.

A Graphical View

Our analysis of stylized facts begins with a graphical view of the data, focusing on the development paradox and antitrade bias across countries and regions. One way to test for significant differences in NRAs across the income spectrum is to draw a smoothed nonparametric regression line through the data, which then allows us to compare these relationships across trade sectors. The general tendency of governments in poorer countries to tax their farmers while governments in richer countries tend to subsidize them is illustrated with smoothed lines in Figure 9.1, showing countries' aggregate NRAs relative to their level of real per-capita income in that year. These are weighted averages of the NRAs for all covered products, summing across commodities by their value at undistorted prices, so as to represent the total burden of taxes or subsidies on farm production.

The relationship between taxation/protection and average per-capita income is strong but nonlinear in the log of income, and is different for exportables and importables. Governments in the poorest countries have imposed heavy taxes on all kinds of farmers. Tax rates move rapidly toward

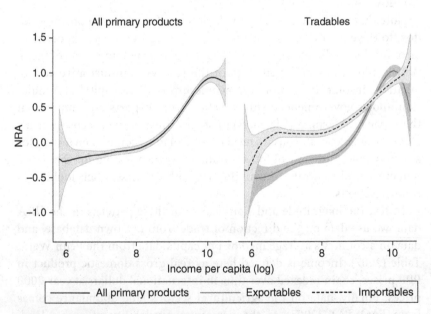

Figure 9.1. National average NRAs and real income per capita[a] (percent/100).
[a] Smoothed line and 95% confidence interval computed with Stata's *lpolyci* using bandwidth 1 and degree 4. Income per capita is expressed in I$ (2000 constant prices).
Source: Authors' derivation based on estimates in Anderson and Valenzuela (2008).

zero as incomes rise then, at income levels of about US $1,000 to $8,000 per year, they stabilize with slight protection of importables and strong taxation of exportables, and as incomes rise above that, all products become heavily protected.

Before we turn to detailed hypothesis tests, we must ask whether the stylized facts in the historical data still apply today. Have liberalizations and other reforms eliminated these relationships? Each country case study provides an analytical history of policy making by successive governments,[1] and it is clear from those studies that national trade policies are not determined in isolation: There are waves of policy change that occur more or less simultaneously across countries, driven by economic conditions and the spread of ideas. These policy trends are often geographically concentrated, perhaps due to common economic circumstances or intellectual conditions.

Figure 9.2 decomposes and summarizes the country NRAs into each region's average for all exportables, importables, and total tax/subsidy burden for all farm production. In each panel of Figure 9.2, the gap between the top and bottom lines measures the region's average degree of antitrade bias: The top line is average NRA on importables, the bottom line is average NRA on exportables, and the gap between them is the degree to which production incentives are distorted toward serving the home market as opposed to international trade. The central line measures the region's average degree of antifarm bias, which includes any policy intervention on nontradable products.

The Africa data in Figure 9.2 reveal a decade-long trend from the early 1960s to the early 1970s toward greater antifarm bias due to less protection on importables and more taxation of exportables. After 1980, this was followed by twenty years of slow reduction in the taxation of exportables, and a rise – and then a fall – in protection on importables, so that antitrade bias actually expanded in the early 1980s and was then reduced substantially after 1990.

The data for other regions in Figure 9.2 show a range of experiences, but all except ECA (Eastern Europe and Central Asia) show a trend toward reduced antitrade bias in the 1990s. In Asia, there were increasingly heavy taxes on farm exports through the 1970s, but reform came earlier and faster than in Africa so that export taxes were largely eliminated by the 1990s.

---

[1] The detailed country case studies are reported in four regional volumes covering Africa (Anderson and Masters 2009), Asia (Anderson and Martin 2009), Latin American (Anderson and Valdés 2008), and Europe's transition economies (Anderson and Swinnen 2008).

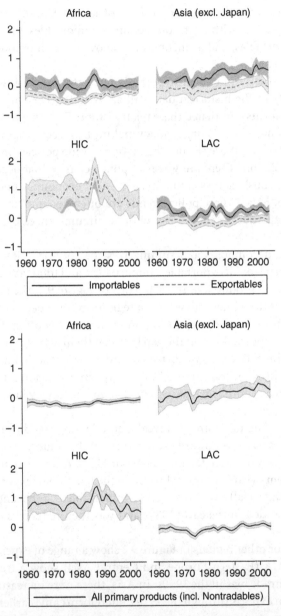

Figure 9.2. National average NRA over time, by trade status and region[a] (percent/100).

[a] LAC – Latin America, HIC – High-income countries. Smoothed line and 95% confidence interval computed with Stata's *lpolyci* using bandwidth 1 and degree 2.

Source: Authors' derivation based on estimates in Table 4: Stylized facts of the covered total NRAs in Anderson and Valenzuela (2008).

Latin America during the 1970s shares some of Africa and Asia's growing antifarm bias and has had an even greater degree of reform toward freer trade (NRAs of zero) in the 1990s. The ECA region, on the other hand, experienced a rapid rise in its NRA levels toward the norms seen in high-income countries, whose NRA levels fluctuate but show little trend from the 1960s to today.

The Stylized Facts: Antitrade Bias, the Development Paradox, and Resource Abundance

Table 9.1 describes the three kinds of stylized facts simultaneously, using a series of OLS regressions to show the correlations between NRAs and each kind of determinant. In each column, we control for the link to income in logarithm form, with log income as the only regressor in columns 1 and 4. The additional regressors in other columns are often significant, but they raise the regression's R^2 relatively little. Income alone explains most of the variance that is explained in any of the regressions shown here, including the variance within countries presented in column 4. Columns 1–4 use over 2,000 observations of national average total NRA for all covered products as the dependent variable, whereas column 5 uses the much larger number of individual commodity-level NRAs.

One of our stylized facts is that governments across the income spectrum tend to tax all kinds of trade, thus introducing an antitrade bias in favor of the home market. From column 5, controlling for income, the average NRA on an importable product is 16.5 percent higher and on an exportable it is 27.6 percent lower than it otherwise might be. Latin America has NRAs that are a further 16 percent lower (column 3) than those of other regions. Relative to Africa, Latin America and the omitted region (Eastern Europe), Asia, and the high-income countries have unusually high NRAs when controlling for their income level.

Trade Policy and Price Stabilization

Trade policy often aims to stabilize domestic prices as well as change their level. As detailed by Timmer (1989) and Dawe (2001), among others, stabilization of agricultural product prices may be especially important for low-income countries, where food prices have a large impact on consumer expenditure and farmgate prices have a large impact on real incomes in rural areas. In practice, however, while stockholding or

Table 9.1. *Initial regression results*

Explanatory variables	Model				
	(1)	(2)	(3)	(4)	(5)
Income (log)	0.3420***	0.3750***	0.2643***	0.2614***	0.2739***
	(0.0121)	(0.0130)	(0.0230)	(0.0226)	(0.0579)
Land per capita		−0.4144***	−0.4362***		
		(0.0264)	(0.0256)		
Africa			0.0651		
			(0.0404)		
Asia			0.1404***		
			(0.0418)		
Latin America			−0.1635***		
			(0.0176)		
High income Countries			0.4311***		
			(0.0340)		
Importable					0.1650*
					(0.0829)
Exportable					−0.2756***
					(0.0849)
Constant	−2.6759***	−2.8159***	−2.0352***	−1.9874***	−2.0042***
	(0.0941)	(0.0965)	(0.2024)	(0.1920)	(0.4174)
R^2	0.28	0.363	0.418	0.827	0.152
No. of obs.	2520	2269	2269	2520	28118

[a] Covered total NRA is the dependent variable for models 1–4, and NRA by commodity for model 5. Model 4 uses country fixed effects. Results are OLS estimates, with robust standard errors (models 1–4), country clustered standard errors (model 5), and significance levels shown at the 99% (***), 95% (**), and 90% (*) levels. The Europe and Central Asia region is the omitted continent variable.
Source: Authors' calculations.

variable-rate subsidies and taxes can achieve stabilization in the short run, such effects may be offset by the jumps in prices that occur when these policies are changed. Empirically, the link between a country's income and the degree to which its trade policies actually stabilize prices is shown in Table 9.2. As it happens, the estimated coefficient on income is positive and the constant is negative: Lower-income countries provide less stability. Less stabilization also occurs in land-abundant countries, and for

Table 9.2. *Stylized facts of the stabilization index*[a]

Explanatory variables	Model					
	(1)	(2)	(3)	(4)	(5)	(6)
Income (log)	5.6507***		7.0059***	7.4730***	9.4113***	8.8422*
	(1.0515)		(2.1454)	(2.5982)	(3.1381)	(4.7925)
Importable		6.5568*	−7.1127	−9.4289*		−10.3265*
		(3.4489)	(4.3119)	(4.8711)		(5.8565)
Exportable		1.5545	−8.4469**	−9.5703**		−11.6999**
		(3.4652)	(3.8169)	(4.1644)		(5.5625)
Land per capita			−9.8402**	−9.4037**		−9.6186**
			(4.1771)	(4.0466)		(4.2018)
Income growth				−444.8959		−547.3185
Variation				(481.5131)		(656.6352)
Exchange rate				2.0297***		1.0391
Variation				(0.6763)		(0.9372)
Africa					8.2332	1.1559
					(7.3334)	(7.5259)
Asia					15.2604**	6.2383
					(7.0633)	(8.3245)
Latin America					−4.4882	−10.931
					(6.3745)	(8.0996)
High income Countries					−3.0503	−1.5757
					(8.5204)	(9.3760)
Constant	−37.7412***	4.6606**	−40.9054**	−44.9126**	−75.4189***	−53.9286
	(8.8035)	(2.1175)	(15.7140)	(20.7327)	(27.7500)	(41.7300)
R^2	0.029	0.005	0.035	0.047	0.032	0.055
No. of obs.	757	766	722	722	771	724
Dropped obs.	20	11	6	6	6	4

[a] Dependent variable for all regressions is the Stabilization Index by country and product. Influential outliers were dropped from the sample based on the Cook's distance criteria [(K-1)/N]. Results are OLS estimates, with clustered standard errors and significance levels shown at the 99% (***), 95% (**), and 90% (*) levels.
Source: Authors' calculations.

importables and exportables relative to nontradables. Using column (4) as our preferred model, the estimated coefficients imply that the cross-over level of per-capita income below which governments have tended to destabilize prices is $1,600 for importables and $2,400 for exportables. On average in those countries, over the full period of our data, actual domestic prices have been less stable than undistorted prices would have been.

TESTING POLITICAL ECONOMY THEORIES
OF AGRICULTURAL POLICY

The policy choices presented above could be driven by many different influences. What kinds of political economy models can best explain the patterns we see? In these models, observed policies are an equilibrium outcome to be explained, like a market price. If policy making were to operate with full competitive efficiency, a political Coase theorem would apply: Individuals would "buy" and "sell" their policy interests and thereby acquire a Pareto-optimal set of policies. But the policies we observe appear to impose costs on some people that exceed their gains to others, so our explanations all involve one or another mechanism that might prevent the competitive market sketched in Coase (1960) from applying. Each model posits a specific mechanism that prevents losers from buying out the gainers and thereby obtaining Pareto-improving reforms, and suggests certain variables that might therefore be correlated with the particular policies we observe. Identifying which kinds of political market failures have been most important could help policy makers circumvent these constraints through rules and other interventions that help shift the political-economy equilibrium toward Pareto-improving policy outcomes.

The following sections describe various possible mechanisms, drawing on the last half-century of political economy modeling. The theories are well known so we describe them only briefly, and focus on the empirical correlations between variables. Our results are organized into two sets: Regressions using aggregate national-average data are in Table 9.3 and those using product-level data are in Table 9.4. Note that none of our tests make any attempt to control for endogeneity. These are all exploratory regressions aimed at establishing correlations, comparing a large number of competing hypotheses in a common framework. Future work to test particular mechanisms would call for more specialized models and datasets.

Table 9.3. *Testing political economy hypotheses at the country level*[a]

Dependent variable	(1)	(2)	(3)	(4)	(5)	(6)	(7)
Total NRA for:	All Prods.	All Prods.	All Prods.	|All Prods.|	Exportables	Importables	All Prods.
Explanatory variables							
Income (log)	0.2643***	0.1234***	0.3175***	0.1913***	0.2216***	0.1142***	0.2461***
	(0.0230)	(0.0440)	(0.0242)	(0.0291)	(0.0184)	(0.0299)	(0.0248)
Land per capita	-0.4362***	-0.2850***	-0.4366***	-0.4263***	-0.7148***	-0.6360***	-0.4291***
	(0.0256)	(0.0467)	(0.0245)	(0.0277)	(0.0818)	(0.0338)	(0.0266)
Africa	0.0651	0.1544***	0.0964**	0.2612***	-0.1071***	-0.0628	0.0844**
	(0.0404)	(0.0489)	(0.0419)	(0.0522)	(0.0363)	(0.0575)	(0.0423)
Asia	0.1404***	0.2087***	0.1355***	0.1007**	-0.1791***	0.0217	0.1684***
	(0.0418)	(0.0515)	(0.0457)	(0.0504)	(0.0361)	(0.0564)	(0.0472)
LAC	-0.1635***	-0.0277	-0.1189***	-0.0947***	-0.2309***	-0.1780***	-0.1460***
	(0.0176)	(0.0242)	(0.0203)	(0.0189)	(0.0245)	(0.0311)	(0.0212)
HIC	0.4311***	0.2789***	0.4203***	0.3761***	1.0694***	0.8807***	0.4346***
	(0.0340)	(0.0456)	(0.0343)	(0.0390)	(0.1332)	(0.0604)	(0.0338)
Policy transfer cost per rural person		-0.0773*					
		(0.0422)					
Policy transfer cost per urban person		-1.2328***					
		(0.2830)					
Rural population			1.4668***				
			(0.1528)				

(continued)

227

Table 9.3 (continued)

Dependent variable	(1)	(2)	(3)	(4)	(5)	(6)	(7)
Total NRA for:	All Prods.	All Prods.	All Prods.	|All Prods.|	Exportables	Importables	All Prods.
Explanatory variables							
Urban population			-3.8016*** (0.3717)				
Checks and Balances				-0.0173*** (0.0063)			
Monetary depth (M2/GDP)					-0.0310*** (0.0041)	-0.0401*** (0.0073)	
Entry of new Farmers							-0.0737* (0.0407)
Constant	-2.0352*** (0.2024)	-0.9046** (0.3576)	-2.4506*** (0.2102)	-1.2465*** (0.2568)	-1.5957*** (0.1629)	-0.4652* (0.2696)	-1.8575*** (0.2210)
R^2	0.4180	0.45	0.437	0.294	0.373	0.397	0.419
No. of obs.	2269	1326	2269	1631	1629	1644	2269

[a] Dependent variables are the total NRA for all covered products in columns 1, 2, 3, and 7; the absolute value of that NRA in column 4, and the total NRA for exportables and importables in columns 5 and 6, respectively. For column 2, the sample is restricted to countries and years with a positive total NRA. Monetary depth is expressed in ten-thousandths of one percent. Results are OLS estimates, with robust standard errors and significance levels shown at the 99% (***), 95% (**), and 90% (*) levels.

Source: Authors' calculations.

Table 9.4. *Testing political economy hypotheses at the product level*[a]

Explanatory variables	Model					
	(1)	(2)	(3)	(4)	(5)	(6)
Income (log)	0.2605**	0.2989***	0.2363**	0.2159**	0.3160**	0.2804**
	(0.1089)	(0.0576)	(0.1039)	(0.0965)	(0.1230)	(0.1295)
Importable	0.0549	0.0048	-0.0061	0.1039	0.1106	0.0331
	(0.0753)	(0.0937)	(0.0901)	(0.0972)	(0.0882)	(0.1018)
Exportable	-0.2921***	-0.3028***	-0.2918***	-0.2868***	-0.3614***	-0.3414***
	(0.0697)	(0.0868)	(0.0749)	(0.0805)	(0.0728)	(0.0756)
Land per capita	-0.3066***	-0.3352***	-0.3478***	-0.3140***	-0.4738***	-0.1746**
	(0.0884)	(0.1080)	(0.1035)	(0.0950)	(0.1532)	(0.0760)
Africa	0.0553		0.1171	0.0901	0.0554	0.1236
	(0.1898)		(0.1956)	(0.1874)	(0.2207)	(0.2127)
Asia	0.2828		0.2998	0.2903	0.1833	0.2311
	(0.2250)		(0.2110)	(0.2140)	(0.2311)	(0.2355)
LAC	-0.0652		-0.0309	-0.0515	-0.1426	-0.0863
	(0.0880)		(0.0998)	(0.1053)	(0.1066)	(0.1151)
HIC	0.2605*		0.3388**	0.3136**	0.4837*	-0.0298
	(0.1395)		(0.1430)	(0.1393)	(0.2770)	(0.1762)
Perennials		-0.1315**	-0.1492***			
		(0.0540)	(0.0549)			
Animal Products		0.2589***	0.2580***			
		(0.0889)	(0.0892)			

(continued)

229

Table 9.4 *(continued)*

Explanatory variables	Model					
	(1)	(2)	(3)	(4)	(5)	(6)
Others		-0.1764**	-0.1956**			
		(0.0820)	(0.0795)			
Sugar				-1.0903**		
				(0.5398)		
Rice				-1.1926		
				(1.2711)		
Milk				-4.1447***		
				(1.0724)		
Wheat				-0.6149		
				(0.4403)		
Other Cereals				0.6198		
				(0.4822)		
Sugar*Income				0.1790***		
				(0.0620)		
Rice*Income				0.1502		
				(0.1663)		
Milk*Income				0.5476***		
				(0.1214)		
Wheat*Income				0.068		

230

Explanatory variables	Model					
	(1)	(2)	(3)	(4)	(5)	(6)
Other*Income				-0.0678		
				(0.0526)		
				(0.0471)		
Lagged Change in Border Prices					-0.0025***	
					(0.0006)	
Lagged Change in Crop Area						0.0083
						(0.0358)
Constant	-1.8516*	-2.0109***	-1.6685*	-1.5914*	-2.1625**	-2.0549*
	(0.9409)	(0.3957)	(0.8978)	(0.8445)	(1.0507)	(1.1023)
R^2	0.1950	0.2100	0.2240	0.2800	0.3020	0.1940
No. of obs.	25599	20063	20063	20063	15982	9932

[a] The dependent variable is the commodity-level NRA. Observations with a lagged change in border prices lower than -1,000% were dropped from the sample. Results are OLS estimates, with clustered standard errors and significance levels shown at the 99% (***), 95% (**), and 90% (*) levels.
Source: Authors' calculations.

231

Explaining the Data: Six Major Political Economy Theories

The simplest kind of explanation for observed policies is rational ignorance, by which individuals will not invest in learning or taking action about a policy if the policy's cost (or benefit) to them exceeds their cost of political organization. This mechanism could help explain why observed policies tend to generate highly concentrated gains that provide substantial benefits to a few people, thereby motivating them to act politically and obtain that policy. In many cases, the gains come at the expense of others who, if the cost per person is small, can be expected to remain on the sidelines. Such a focus on per-capita incidence is associated with Downs (1957) and could be the most powerful explanation for the patterns we observe. Influential applications to agriculture include Anderson (1995) who demonstrates how the concentration of gains and losses shifts during economic development.

Rational ignorance effects are tested in column 2 of Table 9.3, where the dependent variable is the value-weighted average of all commodity NRAs for the country as a whole, and the independent variable used to test for rational ignorance is its total cost (benefit) per capita in that sector. This test is applicable only to observations with positive total NRAs, so that a larger NRA imposes a greater cost (benefit) per urban (rural) person. Results show a large and significant pattern: When costs (benefits) per capita are larger, the percentage NRA levels are correspondingly smaller (higher). Furthermore, the effect is larger for people living in urban areas, perhaps because city dwellers are more easily mobilized than their rural counterparts, when controlling for other factors.

Column 3 of Table 9.3 tests a related but different explanation: the absolute size of each group. This may influence outcomes through free-ridership, if individuals in larger groups have more incentive to shirk as in Olson (1965). An opposite group-size effect could arise if larger groups are more influential, perhaps because they can mobilize more votes, political contributions, or other political forces. As it happens, column 3 of Table 9.3 shows that larger groups do obtain more favorable policies, perhaps because all of these groups are very large and have similar levels of free-ridership. Again the magnitude is larger for urban people than for rural people, suggesting that, on average, an additional urbanite has more political influence than an additional rural person.

Relative to the unconditional regression in column 1, the estimated coefficient on national income is markedly lower when controlling for rational ignorance in (2), and somewhat greater when controlling for group size in (3). In that sense, rational ignorance helps account for the development paradox, whereas group size is an additional influence. These regressions are not necessarily comparable, however, because of differences in the sample size.

A third kind of explanation is tested in column 4 of Table 9.3, concerning the rent-seeking behavior of political leaders themselves. This terminology is associated with Krueger (1974) and suggests that Pareto-inefficient policy choices will persist as long as government officials can avoid accountability. By focusing on policy makers' behavior, the rent-seeking approach explains the observed pattern of policy intervention in terms of the checks and balances that constrain policy makers differently across countries and across sectors. The clear prediction is that governments facing more checks and balances will choose policies that are closer to Pareto-optimality. In column 4 of Table 9.3, we test this view using the absolute value of NRA as our dependent variable, and a variable for "checks and balances" from the World Bank's Database of Political Institutions (Beck et al. 2001, 2008) as our measure of politicians' power. Results are significant, suggesting that after controlling for income, governments that impose more checks and balances on their officials do have less distortionary policies.

Columns 5 and 6 of Table 9.3 tests a fourth type of model, in which observed policies may be by-product distortions caused by measures chosen for other reasons, such as a tax revenue motive. Governments with a small nonfarm tax base may have a stronger motive to tax agricultural imports and exports, or conversely governments with a larger tax base may be less constrained by fiscal concerns and hence freer to pursue other political goals. Here, the variable we use to capture the extent of taxable activity is the country's monetary depth, as measured by the ratio of M2 to GDP. Since greater taxation of trade is associated with negative NRAs for exportables but positive NRAs for importables, this test is divided into two subsamples. What we find is that governments in more monetized economies have lower levels of NRA in both samples: They tax exportables more and tax importables less. On average in our sample, import taxes are associated with revenue motives (so they are smaller when other revenues are available), but export taxes are not.

The four major theories described above are tested in Table 9.3 using data at the national level, using value-weighted averages over all products; in Table 9.4, we test two additional kinds of theories that apply at the product level, with a much larger number of observations. This is done for the fifth and sixth kinds of theory, namely time consistency and status quo bias.

The fifth type of explanation tested at the product level involves time consistency and commitment mechanisms. Such theories are associated with Kydland and Prescott (1977), who show that current policy choices depend in part on how easily future governments can change those policies. Without an institution for credible commitment, introducing and sustaining a desirable policy may be impossible – particularly for products that are more dependent on irreversible private investments. Differences across products in the importance of irreversible investment thus allow us to test how much time consistency matters: If products with irreversible investments attract high taxation, then commitment devices that help governments maintain low taxes might be helpful. This idea is applied to help explain agricultural policy in Africa by McMillan and Masters (2003), who show that tree crops and other irreversible investments are more vulnerable to high taxation and simultaneously attract less public services. The same effect holds in these data: The results in columns 2 and 3 of Table 9.4 are consistent with such a time-consistency effect, as perennials are taxed more than annuals. Other differences across crops are also important. Column 4 of Table 9.4 shows that sugar and dairy are taxed more than other commodities at low incomes, and then as income grows, policies switch toward subsidization of these previously taxed commodities.

A sixth kind of political-economy mechanism is pure status quo bias, in which political leaders resist change as such, even if the change would be desirable in retrospect. Status quo bias could lead policy makers to resist both random fluctuations and persistent trends, even when accepting these changes would raise economic welfare. Several different mechanisms have been proposed to explain why change would be resisted *ex ante*, despite the desirability of reform *ex post*. An informal version of this idea that is specific to policy makers is described by Corden (1974) as a "conservative welfare function." A microfoundation for this idea could be individual-level "loss aversion," as formalized by Kahneman and Tversky (1979): People systematically place greater value on losing what they have than on gaining something else. Status quo bias can also arise for other reasons too. Fernandez and Rodrik (1991) show how Pareto-improving reforms may lack political support if those who will lose know who they are, whereas those who could gain do not yet know if they will actually benefit. If status quo bias leads policy makers to resist change in world prices, observed NRAs would be higher after world prices have fallen. NRAs could also try to resist changes in crop profitability more generally, and therefore be higher after acreage planted in that crop has fallen. We test for both kinds of status quo bias in columns 5 and 6 of Table 9.4. With our usual controls, we find support for status quos bias in prices, as there is a negative correlation between policies and lagged changes in world prices. However, there is no remaining correlation between policies and lagged changes in crop area.

A New Explanation: Demographic Influences on Political Pressures

The six political economy models tested above could all potentially explain the results we observe, and are often mentioned in the political economy literature. A seventh kind of explanation is more novel: It is based on exogenous but predictable changes in employment that affect whether other people are likely to enter the sector in the future. This could drive the level of political support in a dynamic political economy model, where individuals' incentives to invest in politics depend crucially on the probability of others' future entry to their sector and the resulting level of expected future rent dissipation.

A forward-looking model of lobbying effort driven by the entry of new agents has been suggested by Hillman (1982) and also Baldwin and Nicoud (2007), who used it to help explain why governments protect declining industries. In their models, declining industries invest more to seek policy-induced rents, because their secular decline creates a barrier to entry in the future. Agriculture experiences this kind of secular decline in its labor force only after the "structural transformation turning point," when total population growth is slow enough and nonfarm employment is large enough for the absolute number of farmers to decline (Tomich, Kilby and Johnston 1995). Before then, the number of farmers is rising, whereas after that point the number of farmers falls or remains constant.

The secular rise and then fall in the number of farmers could help explain NRA levels, to the extent that the entry of new farmers erodes policy rents obtained from lobbying. This would discourage farmers from organizing politically as long as new farmers are entering the sector, and facilitate organization once the entry of new farmers stops. Focusing on this dynamic of entry, as opposed to the absolute size of the group, could help explain the timing of transition from taxation to protection and also help explain the persistence of protection even where agriculture is not a declining industry. In many industrialized countries, for example, agricultural output grows but a fixed land area imposes a strong barrier to the entry of new farmers, helping incumbent producers capture any policy rents they may obtain through lobbying.

To test for an entry-of-new-farmers effect, we return to country-level data in Table 9.3, where the last column tests for the correlation with NRA of an indicator variable set to one if there is demographic entry of new farmers, defined as a year-to-year increase in the "economically active population in agriculture" reported by the FAO. The variable is set to zero when the number of farmers remains unchanged or declines. In column 7 of Table 9.3, with our usual controls, observed policies remain less favorable to farmers as long as the farm population is rising. This result is quite different from the predictions of other models and offers a potentially powerful explanation for the timing of policy change and the difficulty of reform.

This section has tested seven hypothesized mechanisms, using our generic stylized facts as control variables. One important question is whether these mechanisms are explaining the stylized facts or adding to them. As it happens, the specific mechanisms mainly add to the explanatory power of our regressions: Introducing them raises the equations' R-squared but does not reduce the magnitude or significance of the stylized factors with respect to national income, land abundance, or the direction of trade. There are, however, three important exceptions that account for some of the observed correlation with income: the effect of peoples' rational ignorance from having larger transfers per person, the effect of a government's revenue motive from having greater monetary depth, and the effect on rent seeking behavior of having more checks and balances in government. Variables specific to these effects capture a share of the variance in NRAs that would otherwise be associated with per-capita income, suggesting that they are among the mechanisms that might cause the development paradox, whereas other results are additional influences on governments' policy choices.

CONCLUSION

This chapter tests standard political-economy theories of why governments intervene to influence agricultural prices. Our key data source (Anderson and Valenzuela 2008) provides estimates for the tariff-equivalent effect on agricultural prices of all types of trade-related policies across around seventy countries from 1955 through 2007. Policy impacts are measured for seventy-two products, chosen to account for over 70 percent of agricultural value added in each country, resulting in a total of over 25,000 distinct estimates from particular products, countries, and years.

Our analysis begins by confirming three previously observed stylized facts: a consistent antitrade bias in all countries, the development paradox of antifarm bias in poorer countries and profarm bias at higher incomes, and the resource abundance effect toward higher taxation (or less subsidization) of agriculture in more land-abundant countries. We find strong support for a number of mechanisms that could help explain government policy choices. Results support rational ignorance effects as smaller per-capita costs (benefits) are associated with higher (lower) proportional NRAs, particularly in urban areas. Results also support rent-seeking motives for trade policy, as countries with fewer checks and balances on the exercise of political power have smaller distortions, and we find support for time-consistency effects, as perennials attract greater taxation than annuals. We find partial support also for status quo bias, as observed NRAs are higher after world prices have fallen, but there is no correlation between policies and lagged changes in crop area.

Three of our results run counter to much conventional wisdom. First, we find support for a revenue motive function of taxation only on importables, and the opposite effect on exportables. Second, we find no support for the idea that larger groups of people will have more free-ridership and hence less political success. Our results are consistent with the alternative hypothesis of a group-size effect in which larger groups tend to be given more favorable levels of NRA. Third, we find that governments in lower-income countries actually destabilize domestic prices, relative to what those prices would be with freer trade, over the full time period of our data. A given policy may achieve short-term stability, but on average these policies are not (or perhaps cannot be) sustained, leading to large price jumps when policies change.

An important novelty in our results is the finding that demographically driven entry of new farmers is associated with less favorable policies. This result is consistent with models in which new entrants erode policy rents, making political organizations depend on barriers to entry that allow incumbents to capture the benefits of policy change.

We find robust support for some theories and not others, but none of our regressions account for more than half of the variance across countries and over time. To explain the remainder would require deeper analyses of policies' institutional context in particular countries and commodities, and further econometric tests. Such research will also point the way toward improvements in data quality to reduce measurement error. The World Bank's project methodology aimed for much more consistency in data sources, definitions, and assumptions than is usually possible to achieve over such a large sample, but the data are inevitably noisy with random and also systematic variance in the NRA estimates. Future work could produce even more useful datasets, as well as further analysis of the hypotheses tested here.

References

Anderson, K. (1995), "Lobbying Incentives and the Pattern of Protection in Rich and Poor Countries," *Economic Development and Cultural Change* 43(2), January: 401–23.

Anderson, K., Y. Hayami and Others (1986), *The Political Economy of Agricultural Protection: East Asia in International Perspective*, London and Boston: Allen & Unwin.

Anderson, K., M. Kurzweil, W. Martin, D. Sandri and E. Valenzuela (2008), "Measuring Distortions to Agricultural Incentives, Revisited," *World Trade Review* 7(4): 1–30.

Anderson K., and W. Martin (eds.) (2009), *Distortions to Agricultural Incentives in Asia*, Washington DC: World Bank.

Anderson K. and W. Masters (eds.) (2009), *Distortions to Agricultural Incentives in Africa*, Washington DC: World Bank.

Anderson K. and J. Swinnen (eds.) (2008), *Distortions to Agricultural Incentives in Europe's Transition Economies*, Washington DC: World Bank.

Anderson K. and A. Valdés (eds.) (2008), *Distortions to Agricultural Incentives in Latin America*, Washington DC: World Bank.

Anderson, K. and E. Valenzuela (2008), *Global Estimates of Distortions to Agricultural Incentives, 1955 to 2007*, database available at http://www.worldbank.org/agdistortions

Auty, R.M. (ed.) (2001), *Resource Abundance and Economic Development*, London: Oxford University Press.

Baldwin, R.E. and F.R. Nicoud (2007), "Entry and Asymmetric Lobbying: Why Governments Pick Losers," *Journal of the European Economic Association* 5(5): 1064–93.

Bale, M. D. and E. Lutz (1981), "Price Distortions in Agriculture and Their Effects: An International Comparison," *American Journal of Agricultural Economics* 63(1): 8–22.

Beck, T., G. Clarke, A. Groff, P. Keefer and P. Walsh (2001), "New Tools in Comparative Political Economy: The Database of Political Institutions," *World Bank Economic Review* 15: 165–76.

Beck, T., P.E. Keefer and G.R. Clarke (2008), *Database of Political Institutions*, accessible at http://go.worldbank.org/2EAGGLRZ40

Coase, R. (1960), "The Problem of Social Cost," *Journal of Law and Economics* 3(1): 1–44.

Corden, M. (1974), *Trade Policy and Economic Welfare*, Oxford: Clarendon Press.

Dawe, D. (2001), "How Far Down the Path to Free Trade? The Importance of Rice Price Stabilization in Developing Asia," *Food Policy* 26(2): 163–75.

Downs, A. (1957), "An Economic Theory of Political Action in a Democracy," *Journal of Political Economy* 65(2): 135–50.

FAOSTAT (2007), FAOStat database, available online at http://faostat.fao.org/. Rome: Food and Agriculture Organization of the World Bank.

Fernandez, R. and D. Rodrik (1991), "Resistance to Reform: Status Quo Bias in the Presence of Individual-Specific Uncertainty," *American Economic Review* 81(5): 1146–55.

Hillman, A.L. (1982), "Declining industries and political-support protectionist motives," *American Economic Review* 72(5): 1180–7.

Isham, J., M. Woolcock, L. Pritchett and G. Busby (2005), "The Varieties of Resource Experience: Natural Resource Export Structures and the Political Economy of Economic Growth," *World Bank Economic Review* 19(2):141–74.

Kahneman, D. and A. Tversky (1979), "Prospect Theory: An Analysis of Decision Under Risk," *Econometrica* 47(2): 263–91.

Krueger, A.O. (1974), "The Political Economy of the Rent Seeking Society," *American Economic Review* 64(3): 291–303.

Krueger, A.O., M. Shiff and A. Valdés (1991), *Political Economy of Agricultural Pricing Policy*, Baltimore MD: Johns Hopkins University Press.

Kydland, F.E. and E.C. Prescott (1977), "Rules Rather than Discretion: The Inconsistency of Optimal Plans," *Journal of Political Economy* 85(3): 473–92.

Lindert, P. (1991), "Historical Patterns of Agricultural Policy," in C.P. Timmer (ed.), *Agriculture and the State: Growth, Employment, and Poverty in Developing Countries*, Ithaca NY: Cornell University Press.

McMillan, M.S. and W.A. Masters (2003), "An African Growth Trap: Production Technology and the Time-Consistency of Agricultural Taxation, R&D and Investment," *Review of Development Economics* 7(2): 179–91.

Olson, M. (1965), *The Logic of Collective Action*, Cambridge MA: Harvard University Press.

Penn World Table (2007), Penn World Table Version 6.2, available online at http://pwt.econ.upenn.edu. Philadelphia, PA: Center for International Comparisons, University of Pennsylvania.

Timmer, C.P. (1989), "Food Price Policy: The Rationale for Government Intervention," *Food Policy* 14(1): 17–42.

Tomich, T., P. Kilby and B. Johnston (1995), *Transforming Agrarian Economies: Opportunities Seized, Opportunities Missed*, Ithaca NY: Cornell University Press.

World Bank (2007), *World Development Indicators*, Washington DC: World Bank.

ANNEX 9.1. LIST OF VARIABLES AND SOURCES

Variable name	Definition	Source
Border prices	Price at which a commodity could be imported (cif) or exported (fob), as applicable, in each country and year.	Anderson and Valenzuela (2008)
Crop area	The area from which a crop is gathered. Area harvested, therefore, excludes the area from which, although sown or planted, there was no harvest due to damage, failure, etc.	FAOSTAT (2007)
Checks and balances	Measures the effectiveness of electoral checks on government decision makers or according to electoral rules that influence party control over members.	Beck, Keefer and Clarke (2008)
Entry of new farmers	Dummy variable that takes the value of 1 if the year change in the economically active population in agriculture is positive.	FAOSTAT (2007)
Exchange rate variation	Calculated as the standard deviation of the detrended ratio of the exchange rate between 1960 and 2004.	Penn World Table 6.2
Importable (Exportable)	Indicator variable for commodity-level NRAs, equal to 1 if the NRA is observed in a year when the commodity was imported (exported) and 0 otherwise.	Anderson and Valenzuela (2008)
Income	Real gross domestic product per capita, at PPP prices, chain indexed. Expressed in international dollars of 2000.	Penn World Table 6.2
Income growth variation	Calculated as the coefficient of variation of the growth rate of real GDP per capita between 1960 and 2004.	Penn World Table 6.2
Land per capita	Area of arable land as defined by the FAO, divided by the total population.	FAOSTAT (2007)
Monetary depth (M2/ GDP)	Money and quasi money comprise the sum of currency outside banks, demand deposits other than those of the central government, and the time, savings, and foreign currency deposits of resident sectors other than the central government.	World Bank (2007)
Policy transfer cost per rural (urban) person	The sum of each commodity NRA times the value of production at border prices, divided by populations as defined above. Results are shown as costs of policy, so NRAs per rural person are multiplied by -1.	Anderson and Valenzuela (2008)
Rural (Urban) population	Rural population estimates are based on UN Population Projection estimates of total population, minus urban population using varying national definitions of urban areas.	FAOSTAT (2007)

TEN

Why Governments Tax or Subsidize
Agricultural Trade

Kishore Gawande and Bernard Hoekman

Why governments choose the instruments they do to restrict or promote trade is not well understood by scholars in economics and political science (Rodrik 1995). That poor understanding helps explain why much of the theoretical and empirical work in international economics has failed to have much of an impact on policy makers, especially when it comes to agricultural trade policies. In practice, episodes of liberalization and reform are often made in the context of crises or under pressure from outside forces (e.g., trade negotiations) rather than from an internal consensus among policy makers about the efficiency gains from agricultural reform. There are significant differences across sectors, countries, and time, but when it comes to agriculture, government interventions across the world have been particularly widespread and persistent, with significant variance in the aim of policies and the types of instruments used.

This chapter is motivated by the question of what motivates governments to tax or subsidize imports and exports. This question, in turn, is important in understanding the constraints that governments perceive they face economically and politically, and in understanding the broader question of the choice of instruments to regulate trade.[1] Better understanding of this question should help in designing multilateral negotiations and agreements that will lead to real reform. A more informed view of the political economy forces that underpin status quo policies is critical in designing and implementing reform strategies. Top-down reform programs that fail to consider and understand the grassroots influences and constraints that

[1] We are therefore able to explore associations between political, institutional, and economic variables on the one hand and the preferences of policy makers on the other. De Gorter and Swinnen (2002) indicate the relevance of connecting institutions to agricultural policy outcomes. Olper and Raimondi (2010) is exemplary in this regard.

241

make government behave the way they do will frequently be doomed to fail. The lack of progress in the Doha round of multilateral trade negotiation during 2001–10 is an illustration of the consequences of underestimating the constraints governments face.

In this chapter, we seek to explore the determinants of effective taxation and subsidization of agriculture in developing and developed economies. We use the new agricultural price distortions database compiled by Anderson and Valenzuela (2008), which provides nominal rates of assistance (NRA) across a number of commodities spanning the last five decades for sixty-four countries. The NRAs measure the effect on domestic (relative to world) prices of a wide range of quantitative and price-based instruments used to regulate agricultural trade. The predominant instruments used by governments to regulate agricultural trade are border measures, and the dataset expresses those in ad valorem-equivalent terms as export taxes, export subsidies, import tariffs, and import subsidies (see Anderson et al. 2010, tables 8 and 9).

The focus of the present study is on the determinants of the binary choice of taxes versus subsidies for exported and imported products. We first pool the sample across the commodities distinguished in the dataset. The same results are then presented for each commodity. In addition, we present results for the applied rate of tax or subsidy. The determinants of the choice of type of trade policy (tax or subsidy) are thus differentiated from the determinants of the level of the trade tax/subsidy that is imposed.

Based on our findings, we develop a number of data-driven exploratory hypotheses concerning the economic and political/institutional determinants of the direction of policy toward agricultural trade. The findings go well beyond previous empirical studies and hopefully will be a useful input into further theoretical and empirical modeling of the choice of instruments used by governments to regulate trade.

The chapter proceeds as follows. The next section briefly surveys some of the relevant literature in this area. Then we describe the distortions estimates, which are sweeping in the extent of countries, commodities, and time period covered. They constitute a major advance over what has been available to researchers to date regarding agricultural trade policies around the world. An exploratory econometric model is then estimated, and aggregate as well as by-product results are reported and analyzed. The puzzle of instrument choice in agriculture is somewhat, though not fully, resolved, and the results suggest a number of hypotheses worthy of further exploration.

CONCEPTUAL ISSUES

Why do countries use the policies they do? This is the question with which we are concerned in this chapter. There is a huge, mostly theoretical, literature that analyzes the implications of the use of trade versus nontrade policies (e.g., the use of tariffs rather than more efficient production or consumption subsidy/tax instruments) to achieve specific objectives. Within the trade literature, there are numerous papers analyzing the equivalence or nonequivalence of instruments used to restrict trade, in particular tariffs versus quotas, under a variety of assumptions, beginning with the seminal papers of Bhagwati and Ramaswami (1963) and Johnson (1965). Rodrik (1986, 1992) has conjectured that developing country governments choose trade policy instruments such as import tariffs over more efficient policies or combinations of policies because they must deal with a great number of distortions as they prioritize their development agendas. A plan to industrialize can create a huge number of distortions that favor industry at the expense of other sectors such as agriculture. Labor market inflexibilities can present another set of distortions. Trade policies may be used because they are easier to implement and because it may be difficult, even impossible, to ascertain what the most efficient policies are in a world of many distortions. There are also administrative costs of implementing policies, and there is no guarantee that prevailing weak institutional structures will allow those policies to be executed as well as a single trade policy.

Our focus is limited to the direction of policy, that is, to the determinants of whether the set of policy instruments used by governments imply net taxation or subsidization of an importable or exportable agricultural commodity. We do not address the question of the choice of specific instrument to achieve the desired level of net support. This is not because we think this question is unimportant. Over twenty years ago, Deardorff (1987) noted his dissatisfaction with the then-already considerable economics literature is this area, arguing that the economically elegant literature failed to provide much concrete insight into what actually determines how governments choose their policies. In Deardorff's view, nontariff barriers were probably used not on the grounds emphasized in the literature, namely efficiency or inefficiency (welfare), profit-shifting motives, or large-country optimal tariff considerations. Instead, he argued, the real reasons were more down to earth, driven in part by constraints imposed as a result of multilateral trade agreements (such as tariff bindings and related disciplines on the use of tariffs, and prohibitions on the use of export subsidies),[2] and by the overriding concern of governments with protecting employment.

A noteworthy feature of the WTO is that its member governments are much less constrained in using trade policies that affect agriculture than they are with respect to nonagricultural sectors. It is only since the late 1990s that there have been effective constraints imposed through the WTO on the use of agricultural import quotas. The use of tariffs on farm products remains to a large extent unconstrained, and disciplines on farm subsidies often do not have any bite because the permitted levels of subsidization exceed applied levels, especially in developing countries. Thus agriculture is "special" in that the types of constraints identified by Deardorff that increase the incentives to use nontariff barriers rather than tariffs or subsidies apply to a much lesser extent than for nonfarm goods. That is, in the case of agriculture, the more general question of what determines the stance of governments (i.e., to tax or subsidize) is much less affected by international trade agreements.

From a policy perspective, a precondition for analyzing the specific choice of instrument is to understand the determinants of the direction (aim) of policy – whether and why a government seeks to tax or support agriculture in general, and within agriculture, tax or subsidize specific types of output or commodities. From a political economy perspective, an essential difference between agricultural policies of developed and developing countries is that in the former policy makers respond much more to private incentives and lobbies in forming policies, while policy makers in the latter intervene in agricultural markets for a different set of reasons (Anderson, Hayami and Others 1986, de Gorter and Swinnen 2002). Objectives of developing country governments include raising revenue, the pursuit of industrialization, and satisfying the median voter's demand for cheap food. One result of differences in motivation and initial conditions at any given point in time (such as fiscal constraints) is that export subsidies are predominantly found in developed countries (to satisfy export lobbies). This is because export subsidies are too expensive for developing country governments to provide, and are also less "needed" because these countries do not confront the issue of excess production stimulated by protection that can only be sold on world markets with a subsidy. However, developing countries may use subsidies to lower consumer prices of key

---

[2] Naoi's (2009) study of Japan's choice of trade instruments (VERs) focuses on the first of these considerations, namely the role of the GATT in curtailing flexibility in the use of other instruments.

food staples. Exports taxes are much more prevalent in poorer countries – agricultural export lobbies there often must swim against the tide. Import taxes satisfy both the protectionist motive of developed country governments in response to import-competing lobbies and the revenue needs of developing country governments. However, while the citizenry of developing countries may vigorously oppose higher import taxes on commonly consumed food products, the public in rich countries cares less because it spends a much smaller proportion of its income on food. Thus, protectionism in developing countries is probably politically easier to impose on goods that are consumed at the high end of the income distribution.

Average rates of protection for industries tend to decline across countries as the national capital-labor ratio increases. Industrialized countries with large capital stocks – both physical plant and equipment and human capital – relative to labor are more open to trade than countries with large stocks of labor relative to capital as in most developing countries (Rodrik 1995). However, rich countries tend to be much more protectionist toward agriculture, supporting domestic production and closing off markets against import competition. In contrast, poor countries tend to promote imports, either explicitly through import subsidies or implicitly by taxing domestic production.

Anderson (1995) argues that this can be explained as follows. In a poor country, food accounts for a large share of total household consumption, whereas in rich countries, food accounts for only a small share of expenditure. Moreover, agriculture is the main source of employment in a poor country, whereas it typically accounts for less than 5 percent of the labor force in a rich one. In poor countries, agriculture is also much less capital-intensive than in rich ones. If agriculture is protected in a poor nation, the resulting increases in food prices have a large impact on the demand for labor (given the size of the agricultural sector) and thus on economy-wide wages (because labor is mobile). The wage rise will be offset to a greater or lesser extent by the rise in domestic food prices, food being so important in consumption. At the same time, the wage increase puts upward pressure on the price of nontradables (services) and has a negative impact on industry by lowering profits. As the gains per farmer of protection are low, and the loss per industrialist is high, the latter will be induced to invest resources to oppose agricultural support policies. Supporting agricultural production in a poor country, therefore, may not make political sense. The converse applies to rich nations, where agricultural support has much less of an impact on wages (the sector being a relatively small employer), on the prices of nontradables, and on industrial profits. These stylized facts do much to explain the different policy stances that are observed in rich industrial and poor agrarian countries.

Anderson (1995) builds a simulation model that incorporates these basic differences between poor and rich countries and finds that a 10 percent rise in the relative price of manufactures in a poor nation would reduce farm incomes by only 2 percent while raising those of industrialists by 45 percent. In contrast, a 10 percent tax on industry in a rich country raises incomes of farmers by over 20 percent, while reducing those of industrialists by only 3 percent. These differences in costs and benefits for different groups in society – in conjunction with the differences in sizes of the various groups and hence in their costs of getting together to lobby collectively – help explain why farmers in rich countries are willing to invest substantial resources to obtain and maintain protection, and why industrialists and urban populations in developing countries are able to benefit at the expense of farmers.

Honma (1993) empirically investigates whether agricultural protection is determined according to the Anderson-Hayami (1986) framework of endogenous protection. Using panel data on fourteen industrial countries for the period 1955–87, Honma finds that the nominal rate of protection declines the higher the ratio of labor productivity in agriculture to that in industry, rises as the share in agriculture increases to 4.5 percent and falls beyond thereafter, and increases as the terms of trade of agricultural relative to manufactured goods decline.

DATA

The world's governments employ a multitude of price and quantity measures to regulate trade in agriculture. How these disparate instruments change relative prices is measured in great detail in the new agricultural distortions database compiled by Anderson and Valenzuela (2008), using the methodology described in Anderson et al. (2008). An achievement of the trade distortions database is to distill the use of multiple instruments into one ad valorem measure of distortions – the nominal rate of assistance (or NRA) for each covered commodity – for seventy-five countries annually since 1955 that collectively account for between 92 and 95 percent of global GDP, population, and agricultural output and trade. For the present study, we confine ourselves to estimates for sixty-four countries over the years between 1960 and 2004.

The NRA provided by the government of a country to agricultural good i, or NRA_i, is the tax equivalent of border and domestic measures used by the government (e.g., trade taxes and subsidies, any quantitative trade restrictions, plus domestic taxes or subsidies for farm outputs and inputs). This measure is our dependent variable. NRAs are disaggregated into four different border measures plus domestic market support or taxation on farm inputs and outputs. The largest component is due to output price distortions, and their predominant cause is border interventions. The de facto evidence is therefore that governments mostly use trade regulatory instruments in agriculture.[3]

The commodity coverage of the NRA data accounts for around 70 percent of the value of output of agriculture and lightly processed foods in each focus country (Anderson and Valenzuela 2008). It includes the major food items (rice, wheat, maize or other grains, soybean or other temperate oilseeds, palm or other tropical oils, sugar, beef, sheep/goat meat, pork, chicken, eggs, and milk) as well as cash crops such as tea, coffee or other tree crop products, tobacco, cotton, and wool).

One noteworthy feature of the data is that the sizes of the NRAs, whether positive or negative, are generally high in both developed and developing countries. That is, leaving agricultural prices undistorted is the exception, not the rule. A second feature of the estimated NRAs is that many developing country governments have effectively taxed producers of farm goods over many years. Argentina, Brazil, Bulgaria, Estonia, Ethiopia, Kenya, Madagascar, Malaysia, Mozambique, Nicaragua, Sri Lanka, Sudan, Tanzania, Thailand, Zambia, and Zimbabwe have lowered their domestic prices of farm products relative to world prices on average over the 1961–2004 period. While most countries in this group tax their exports, a few African countries (Mozambique, Tanzania, Zambia, and Zimbabwe) also subsidize staple food imports.

Averaging over the entire period hides the fact that there are frequent sign changes in the NRAs over time for each product. One reason for this large variation may be quantitative import restrictions that remain fixed in quantity terms and so cause large changes in NRAs as world prices change. A case in point is the year 1986, the year of the lowest real international food prices on record, owing to the US-EU farm export subsidy war. Countries insulating themselves from international price fluctuations

---

[3] This is consistent with the findings of Hoekman, Ng and Olarreaga (2004) and Anderson, Martin and Valenzuela (2006). Unlike manufacturing tariffs among GATT nations, which were negotiated multilaterally and maintained that way under GATT/WTO rules, agriculture remained excluded from the multilateral round agreements preceding the Uruguay round. Therefore, as noted above, agricultural policies have been largely unilaterally determined to date.

registered big NRA increases that year, which took time to dissipate. Also, the NRAs in many developing countries show rising agricultural protection of import-competing sectors. Even countries that began general trade and domestic economic reforms in the 1980s have their NRAs trending upwards (i.e., agricultural protection growth), around which the NRAs still fluctuate inversely with world prices.

Import-competing and exportable products are identified by the classification of farm products supplied in Anderson and Valenzuela (2008). For goods with predominantly one-way trade, such a classification is more readily possible than for goods with substantial two-way trade. For the latter, if the share of production exported is substantially above (below) the share of consumption imported, the sector is classified as exportable (importable). Otherwise, two-way traded goods are split into exportables and importables and their value of production is split according to those two shares in total trade. In the Anderson and Valenzuela sample, 40 percent of farm products are classified as exportables, 55 percent as importables, and 5 percent as nontradable. We exclude the nontradables from our sample, which then comprises 14,862 observations on importables (forty-three products pooled across countries and time) and 11,505 observations on exportables (fifty-eight products).

Dependent Variable

In most regressions the dependent variable is categorical, defined to equal 1 if the NRA is positive and -1 if the NRA is negative. In other regressions the level of the NRA is used as the dependent variable.

Independent Variables

Table 10.1 presents descriptive statistics for all the variables used in the empirical analysis. The NRA database has imports, exports, and output data, which we use to construct imports-to-output and exports-to-output ratios. We also employ a set of time-varying political economy regressors in our econometric models constructed from the World Bank's *World Development Indicators 2007* database and its Database on Political Institutions (DPI, see Beck et al. 2001, 2008). They include Rural Population Density, which measures whether land is a source of comparative advantage (the higher the density the greater the productivity of land), and the percentages of total land that is arable and that has access to irrigation (%Arable Land and %Irrigated Land). The latter is sometimes regarded as a

Table 10.1. *Summary statistics*

Source	Variable	Description	Full[a] exports sample			Full[a] imports sample		
			N^b	mean	sd	N^b	mean	sd
Distortions database	NRA	Nominal rate of assistance [approximates $(p-p^*)/p^*$]	9478	0.098	0.761	11111	0.535	1.026
Distortions database	NRA10	1 if NRA≥0, and 0 otherwise	9478	0.536	0.499	11111	0.801	0.399
WDI	%Arable Land	Arable land as fraction of total land area	9478	0.184	0.154	11111	0.206	0.143
WDI	%Irrigated Land	Irrigated land as fraction of total land area	9478	0.360	0.692	11111	0.521	0.759
WDI	%Rural Population	Rural population as fraction of total	9478	0.463	0.243	11111	0.418	0.201
WDI	Rural popn density	000 persons per square km. of arable land	9478	0.233	0.279	11111	0.301	0.313
Distortions database	Imports/ Output	Imports-to-output ratio				11111	1.245	3.916
Distortions database	Exports/ Output	Exports-to-output ratio	9478	0.457	0.598			
DPI	%Majority	Fraction of seats held by ruling party or coalition in legislature	5555	0.659	0.209	6481	0.621	0.181
DPI	EIEC	Index of competition for election to the executive	5555	6.164	1.641	6481	6.502	1.300
DPI	Undivided government	1 if executive and party in power are both from the same party and 0 otherwise.	5555	0.500	0.500	6481	0.414	0.493

Notes:

[a] Statistics for the abridged sample that includes DPI variables are close to those reported from the larger sample for non-DPI variables. The larger dataset is over 1961–2004; the smaller dataset is over 1971–2000. The sample pools data across 56 agricultural products and 64 countries.

[b] The samples are those used in the regressions.

Sources: Distortions database from Anderson and Valenzuela (2008); WDI=World Bank (2007); DPI= Beck et al. (2001, 2008).

measure of land quality and thus a source of comparative advantage but, as we shall see, this interpretation is at odds with the results. Imports/Output and Exports/Output ratios measure comparative costs (Baldwin 1985): the greater is the imports-to-output ratio, the higher are unit costs relative to sectors with lower ratios. The converse is true for the exports-to-output ratio: The greater this ratio, the lower are unit costs relative to sectors with lower ratios.

There is overwhelming evidence in the political economy literature that governments are not welfare maximizers. Where special interests are willing to participate in a political market, governments balance the potential welfare costs of distorting prices with the private monetary benefits they receive, either for what the monetary benefits are worth per se, or for how the monetary gains can help them stay in power (Grossman and Helpman 1994; Goldberg and Maggi 1999; Gawande and Bandyopadhyay 2000; de Gorter and Swinnen 2002; Gawande and Hoekman 2006). Even without special interests, their desire to get re-elected leads governments to adopt polices designed to attract the median voter (Mayer 1984; Dutt and Mitra 2002, 2005, 2006). To capture these political influences, we use a set of variables that measure political constraints, opportunities, and pressure. The share of the population that is rural (%Rural Population) indicates whether the median voter is rural. In developing countries, a rural worker is also poor, and so policies that are politically motivated may, at the margin, consider the rural voter to be pivotal. In order to investigate whether and how existing institutions condition policy outcomes, three political institutions variables are used: %Majority (the percent of total seats in the legislature held by the ruling party or coalition), the EIEC (an index of executive electoral competition), and Divided Government (which indicates whether the executive and the ruling party in the legislature are from the same party). These may be important determinants of the choice by governments to tax or subsidize trade in agriculture, especially in democracies where these institutions act as checks on the abilities of governments to serve their own interests rather than the public interest.

Since the regressors are not as completely available as the NRA data, the sample available is smaller than the full distortions database. For example, the political institution variables from DPI are available only from 1975. If the DPI variables are omitted, the sample size is 9,478 for export goods and 11,111 for import goods. Including those variables limits the samples to 5,555 and 6,481 observations, respectively. For this reason, we present results from both samples.

EXPLORATORY EMPIRICAL ANALYSIS

In this section we present results first for exports and then for imports, and in each case we first report the pooled sample results for all products in that group before providing disaggregated results by product.

Exports: Pooled Sample

Table 10.2 presents the country-fixed effects regression of the choice to tax (binary NRA=1) or subsidize (binary NRA=0) exportables in the full sample. The sample pools across three dimensions: countries, products, and time. The reported coefficients indicate the statistical significance of percent arable land, percent rural population, and rural population density. The signs on those coefficients imply that: The greater the percentage of land that is arable, the higher the probability that exports will be taxed; the higher the proportion of the population that is rural, the greater the likelihood that exports will be taxed; and the greater the rural population density, the greater the probability that exports will be subsidized.

Rural population density varies positively with land productivity up to the point where overcrowding leads to land degradation or overfragmentation. In a sophisticated survey of household response to rural population growth, Pender (1999) describes when rural population density can enhance land productivity and when it cannot. When higher levels of population density are combined with low wages and few off-farm opportunities, more labor-intensive methods are adopted in agriculture.[4] But while greater labor intensity increases land productivity, it reduces labor productivity unless the labor input is complemented by increased capital intensity or technical change. Unfortunately, data on capital use in agriculture are not available, and we leave this conditioning hypothesis to be tested in future studies. Another mechanism is that as rural populations increase, the fallow period is shortened in response to lower labor productivity, in order for farmers to have opportunities to work longer and keep their income from declining. As land becomes increasingly scarce, the increased labor intensity may either benefit land conditions or lower it. For example, more intensive farming can reduce the rate of deforestation and

---

[4] For example, "use of hoeing and hand weeding can replace burning to clear crop fields, both because vegetation is reduced by declining fallow periods and because the amount of labor available per unit of land is rising. Planting density may increase, as may the care given to planted crops through various labor-intensive methods to improve soil fertility, such as application of compost or mulch" (Pender 1999).

Table 10.2.   *Export regressions for tax/subsidy choice (binary NRA) and NRA levels (OLS with fixed effects)[a]*

Dependent Variable →	Binary NRA		NRA	
%Arable Land	−0.518	−0.627	−0.493	0.777
	[2.61]**	[1.42]	[1.37]	[0.93]
%Irrigated Land	−0.004	−0.006	−0.004	−0.006
	[0.18]	[0.15]	[0.09]	[0.08]
%Rural Population	−0.875	−1.506	−1.646	−2.467
	[7.56]**	[6.92]**	[7.95]**	[6.19]**
Rural Population Density	0.211	0.257	0.457	0.641
	[2.86]**	[1.96]*	[3.44]**	[2.66]**
Imports/Output				
Exports/Output	−0.004	0.012	0.192	0.248
	[0.59]	[1.55]	[16.17]**	[16.73]**
%Majority		0.117		−0.012
		[2.76]**		[0.16]
EIEC		0.02		0.017
		[3.36]**		[1.57]
Undivided government		0.026		0.005
		[1.50]		[0.15]
N	9972	5975	9478	5555
#countries	64	63	64	63
overall-R^2	0.24	0.27	0.11	0.19
Fraction of var due to FE	0.40	0.45	0.36	0.41
F-statistic for Ho: all FE=0	66.10	40.43	49.15	31.62

Notes:

[a] Absolute t-values in brackets; ** and * denote statistical significance at the 1 and 5 percent levels, respectively. Imports sample abridged at Imports/Output<50 percent. (Exports/output is always below that.) Country-fixed effects and year dummies included but not reported.

Source: Authors' calculations.

increase vegetative cover on the land. Adoption of labor-intensive soil fertility management practices may improve soil fertility, but they may not be able to offset the increased outflow of soil nutrients due to intensive farming. Finally, greater concentration of persons per square mile implies possible economies of agglomeration (urbanization), and the rural population density may measure the concentration of farming skills at a particular location. This may be especially true of developed countries: If the geographic size of the country is small relative to its population, we may expect that the productivity of land increases with population concentration.

The preceding discussion implies that rural population density should be correlated with the demand for export subsidization, since increasing land productivity confers a comparative advantage in agriculture (up to the point of overcrowding). The positive and statistically significant sign on % Rural Population Density supports this view.[5] The coefficient of 0.211 indicates that an increase of 233 persons per square kilometer (one standard deviation) would increase the probability of export subsidization (over taxation) by around 5 percent.

The coefficient of % RuralPopulation is perhaps better explained from the political economy perspective described in the conceptual section above. Since taxation of exports reduces the domestic price of food products, in countries where a high percentage of the population, and therefore the median voter, is rural, we should expect there to be a political motivation behind subsidizing rural consumption. An assumption, one that is satisfied in developing countries, is that the median voter spends a significant proportion of income on food. Even non-democracies that care less about their median voters, but have embarked upon industrialization programs, squeeze their farmers and rural populations by taxing agriculture. This provides food cheaply to their growing urban populations and also encourages migration into urban areas. Regimes that favor urbanization (either because urban residents are the median voters in democracies or because they are a critical component of the industrialization program, or both) might tax exports for those reasons.[6] We find that governments

---

[5] Including a quadratic Rural Population Density variable reinforced these results: The linear term is not statistically significant, but the quadratic term is positive and statistically significant in both samples.

[6] This is probably the more likely motivation, since even though export taxes may benefit rural consumers, to the extent that they are rural workers, the decline in the domestic price of the exportable diminishes their real wage. For urban consumers, there is only the benefit to be gained from lower prices on food products (unless they are migrant workers whose main source of income is from rural work and is supplemented by urban work off-season).

with greater rural populations tax exports more. The quantitative implication is significant: A country with a rural population that is 10 percent higher than another country is 8.75 percent more likely to tax exports (the numbers are almost twice as high in the smaller sample with the institutional variables).

If %Arable Land is a measure of comparative advantage, the Stolper-Samuelson theorem would predict that political pressure from landowners would lead to export subsidization (a positive coefficient on %Arable Land). An alternative explanation, where revenue-starved governments cannot commit to long-term low-tax regimes, is advanced in McMillan (2001): Once farmers incur sunk costs, they are sure to produce the exportable so long as their price covers marginal cost. The government then has an incentive to tax them, regardless of other promises they may have made in the past (to induce farmers to sink investment costs). In our context, sinking in the costs of making land arable commits landowners to producing if price covers variable costs of production. If %Arable Land proxies for sunk costs incurred by landowners, then the positive sign on its coefficient affirms McMillan's hypothesis. The %Irrigated Land variable similarly proxies sunk costs of irrigation, and we would expect it to have the same sign. This evidence is too weak to support the same hypothesis. McMillan's model, more generally, implies that specific factors are likely to be taxed in countries that are desperate for revenue. Add to this the political incentive to subsidize urban workers, as described above, and the motivation for an export tax becomes clear – it works to the government's benefit to penalize their rural sectors to benefit urban voters. To the extent land is specialized and farmers are inflexible in their production decisions, they will be forced to produce. If they are producing for exports, their taxation is further facilitated by the fact that government infrastructure is already set up to record and document the amount of exports. There is no place to hide their output from the grabbing hand.

The second model (see column 2 of Table 10.2) includes variables for political institutions and has a smaller sample, since the DPI data are recorded only from 1975 onwards. The coefficients on percent rural population and rural population density have the same sign as the smaller model. The %Arable Land variable is not statistically significant in this sample, indicating that McMillan's hypothesis may be less of a concern worldwide now than it was in the 1960s and 1970s (though it may continue to apply in specific countries, as she shows to be the case with a number of sub-Saharan African countries). The new findings in this extended regression are that: The greater the majority of the governing party or coalition in the legislature the greater the likelihood that exports are subsidized; and electoral competition for the office of the executive encourages export subsidization.

There are several possible reasons for these findings. With greater majorities, legislators are expected to favor special interests more since they are less worried about instituting polices that impose welfare losses on their public (e.g., export subsidies) than governments with thin or unstable majorities. At a deeper level, if pluralitarian systems are more likely to deliver greater majorities (as has been argued of winner-take-all systems) compared to a proportionate system of representation, the coefficient on %Majority implies that pluralitarian systems are more likely to award export subsidies.

Political theories of electoral competition with uninformed voters (Baron 1994, Grossman and Helpman 1996) indicate that the greater the electoral competitiveness, the more prone are candidates to satisfy special interests. This is because candidates need support (contributions) from special interests in order to sway uninformed voters. This is precisely what the positive coefficient on EIEC affirms.

The last two columns of Table 10.2 seek to explain the variation in the level of the NRA, using the same political economy and institutional variables as for the binary NRA regressions. An important difference in the two sets of results is that while the inferences about %RuralPopulation and Rural population density in the subsidize-or-tax choice regressions carry over to the subsidy/tax level regressions, political institutions are unimportant to the latter decision. The effect of some variables on the level of the tax/subsidy is dramatic. For example, the coefficient of 0.641 in the last column on Rural population density indicates that an increase of 279 persons per square kilometer (one standard deviation) would increase the level of the export subsidy by nearly 18 percentage points!

An additional factor that becomes an important determinant of the level of tax or subsidy is the exports-to-output ratio. Since the greater export-to-output ratios measure competitive cost advantage (Baldwin 1985), the positive sign indicates that industries that demonstrate great potential to export are subsidized. There is a possible endogeneity problem here, however, since the subsidization of exports may be the reason why those products have large export-to-output ratios.

Measures of fit are reported toward the bottom of Table 10.2. The country-fixed effects are statistically significant, and the explanatory power overall is quite admirable for a rather Spartan regression. Thus, within-country variation in the data is intuitively well explained by this set of political economy and institutional variables. The broad inference is that political and institutional considerations are important to a government's choice to tax versus subsidize exports, whereas economic considerations are more important determinants of the level at which governments decide to tax and subsidize. The greater the comparative cost advantage, the higher the subsidy, the greater the rural population, the greater the tax; and the greater the rural population density, the greater the export subsidy.

Exports by Product

Table 10.3 presents the tax/subsidy choice regressions for each exportable product with country-fixed effects. Of interest is the question of whether the inferences from the pooled sample carry over to the product-by-product regressions. Coefficients are lightly shaded if they share the statistical significance and the sign from the pooled sample, but are darker shaded if they are statistically significant but of the opposite sign. Coefficients reported in boldface font indicate that while they were not statistically significant in the pooled sample, they are so in the product regressions (regardless of their sign).

For example, the negative coefficient on %RuralPopulation is shared by the product regressions for apple, banana, barley, beef, coffee, egg, pig meat, potato, rice, and tomato. Thus, as the fraction of the rural population rises, governments tax exports of these products. However, for five products – rapeseed, rubber, sunflower, soybean, and wheat – governments subsidize exports as %RuralPopulation increases. There is no clear cash crop/food crop dichotomy that separates these opposite signs. For example, rubber and coffee are both cash crops, yet their signs are different.

The positive coefficient on rural population density is in evidence for just two products, rice and apples. It is negative for beef, cocoa, rapeseed, rubber, tobacco, and wheat. Thus, a small subsample dominates the pooled sample results. The heterogeneity across crops is clearer in these by-product regressions. It appears that exports of cash crops are more likely to be taxed when the rural population density is high. This finding goes against the Stolper-Samuelson prediction that the source of comparative advantage (here, land) will be subsidized, not taxed. Evidently, governments make more than welfare-maximizing calculations while setting policy. That is, it appears that the revenue motive trumps comparative advantage in agriculture when governments choose whether to tax or subsidize exports. It is highly likely that the heterogeneity across

Table 10.3. *Export regressions for tax/subsidy choice, by product, binary NRA dependent variable, without institutional variables (full sample, 1960 to 2004, OLS with fixed effects)*

	apple	banana	barley	bean	beef	cashew	cocoa	coconut	coffee	cotton
%Arable Land	2.769 [0.52]	-7.215 [1.06]	3.79 [1.07]	14.365 [1.13]	-1.558 [1.70]	-20.611 [0.47]	-3.647 [1.55]	-4.664 [0.43]	-1.407 [0.89]	1.398 [0.90]
%Irrigated Land	-1.847 [1.97]	0.592 [2.82]**	0.7 [1.12]	16.453 [1.97]	-0.252 [0.88]	0.675 [0.03]	-0.76 [4.08]**	0.559 [2.85]**	-0.182 [2.09]*	0.106 [0.56]
%Rural Population	-4.742 [3.34]**	-15.078 [5.91]**	-2.155 [2.01]*	22.365 [1.63]	-1.485 [1.99]*	2.436 [0.39]	0.503 [0.48]	1.982 [0.89]	-2.175 [2.69]**	-0.133 [0.30]
Rural pop. density	7.322 [2.18]*	0.156 [0.06]	3.381 [1.72]	2.364 [0.38]	-2.042 [3.16]**	-1.102 [0.36]	-0.898 [2.02]*	-0.395 [0.28]	0.117 [0.22]	0.315 [1.22]
Exports/ Output	-0.483 [5.44]**	-0.139 [1.50]	0.031 [0.22]	-7.324 [3.39]**	-0.061 [0.44]	0.369 [2.41]*	-0.127 [2.10]*	0.906 [1.27]	0.171 [3.24]**	0.019 [0.48]
N	170	168	255	60	477	57	242	117	456	610
#countries	5	5	17	4	28	2	6	3	14	18
R-squared	0.44	0.46	0.4	0.73	0.11	0.7	0.26	0.58	0.27	0.1

(continued)

Table 10.3 (continued)

	egg	grape	groundnut	maize	milk	oat	oilseed	orange	palmoil	pigmeat
%Arable Land	-0.06 [0.10]	15.357 [2.69]**	2.914 [0.69]	-0.379 [0.23]	0.047 [0.14]	-3.08 [0.76]	-1.495 [0.78]	5.351 [0.05]	-11.495 [1.17]	-2.345 [1.21]
%Irrigated Land	0 [0.00]	1.098 [1.18]	2.391 [4.00]**	0.383 [2.08]*	0.167 [2.24]*	-8.044 [2.44]*	60.111 [1.01]	-135.629 [0.30]	-1.541 [2.16]*	0.333 [1.98]*
%Rural Population	-1.3 [2.24]*	-0.289 [0.22]	-0.733 [0.49]	-0.794 [0.84]	0.072 [0.13]	-1.109 [0.52]	28.781 [1.24]	-31.094 [0.23]	-3.366 [1.40]	-1.973 [2.77]**
Rural pop. density	0.477 [0.89]	-0.657 [0.20]	-0.052 [0.03]	0.969 [1.09]	0.03 [0.09]	18.042 [1.25]	-1.212 [0.16]	44.86 [0.38]	0.328 [0.52]	0.357 [0.27]
Exports/ Output	-0.419 [2.57]*	-0.123 [2.62]**	-0.333 [1.17]	0.456 [2.99]**	0.009 [0.45]	0.277 [0.51]	0.177 [2.01]	-1.833 [0.59]	-0.158 [0.50]	-0.197 [1.30]
N	502	183	217	390	626	134	60	53	127	330
#countries	26	5	9	25	29	10	5	2	5	22
R-squared	0.37	0.38	0.4	0.17	0.1	0.48	0.53	0.95	0.51	0.28

	potato	poultry	rapeseed	rice	rubber	rye	sesame	sheepmeat	sorghum	soybean
%Arable Land	0.05 [0.08]	-0.471 [0.76]	-0.274 [0.06]	2.86 [1.95]	-5.372 [2.59]*	6.794 [0.79]	-10.367 [0.16]	2.805 [1.99]*	12.762 [1.25]	4.887 [0.85]
%Irrigated Land	-0.065 [0.67]	0.05 [0.66]	3.448 [2.49]*	-0.045 [0.42]	0.064 [0.37]	-36.079 [1.61]	8.965 [0.06]	0.365 [1.89]	-0.955 [0.98]	0.707 [2.12]*
%Rural Population	-1.102 [2.89]**	-0.742 [1.27]	15.014 [3.30]**	-2.944 [3.46]**	3.068 [2.43]*	32.036 [0.45]	26.144 [1.05]	0.025 [0.07]	-1.208 [0.98]	2.51 [2.16]*

	potato	poultry	rapeseed	rice	rubber	rye	sesame	sheepmeat	sorghum	soybean
Rural pop. density	0.646 [1.69]	-0.549 [1.05]	-41.264 [3.60]**	0.647 [2.89]**	-0.903 [2.26]*	55.873 [1.22]	37.588 [0.89]	0.09 [0.07]	6.945 [1.70]	0.266 [0.20]
Exports/ Output	-0.005 [0.10]	0 [0.00]	-0.155 [1.59]	0.035 [0.51]	0.586 [3.08]**	-0.734 [1.20]	0.02 [0.07]	-0.018 [0.17]	-0.016 [0.13]	-0.146 [0.42]
N	417	555	124	334	168	27	56	245	112	196
#countries	15	27	9	15	5	6	2	13	6	11
R-squared	0.4	0.16	0.43	0.21	0.43	0.88	0.77	0.31	0.49	0.42

	sugar	sunflower	tea	tobacco	tomato	vegetables	wheat	wine	wool
%Arable Land	-0.022 [0.02]	-1.623 [0.63]	3.525 [1.43]	-2.231 [0.51]	0.53 [0.13]	235.132 [1.13]	-1.156 [1.85]	9.983 [1.19]	-5.369 [0.66]
%Irrigated Land	0.11 [1.13]	0.591 [0.98]	0.103 [0.92]	0.359 [0.84]	-0.288 [0.99]	10.406 [3.09]**	0.034 [0.24]	1.111 [2.70]**	-0.185 [0.21]
%Rural Population	-0.402 [0.59]	6.027 [2.07]*	1.021 [0.75]	-1.567 [1.82]	-4.703 [2.67]**	0.143 [0.00]	2.067 [2.30]*	4.01 [1.65]	4.519 [0.50]
Rural pop. density	0.741 [1.21]	-3.228 [0.50]	0.116 [0.17]	-2.739 [2.77]**	6.572 [1.27]	8.514 [0.27]	-1.778 [3.03]**	0.062 [0.06]	-9.043 [0.32]
Exports/ Output	0.039 [0.93]	0.049 [1.23]	0.239 [4.69]**	0.042 [2.23]*	0.096 [0.73]	-0.495 [1.28]	0.013 [0.40]	0.195 [1.07]	0.111 [0.33]
N	430	166	218	176	143	64	614	127	86
#countries	21	13	6	5	8	2	30	5	2
R-squared	0.33	0.26	0.3	0.44	0.41	0.9	0.44	0.33	0.53

Absolute t-values in brackets; ** and * denote statistical significance at the 1 and 5 percent levels, respectively.
Source: Authors' calculations.

products in this result is driven by the institutional heterogeneity among countries that specialize in those products. In particular, countries specialized in those products may have weak systems of monitoring, collecting, and enforcing tax collection. This generates our first post hoc exploratory hypothesis:

H1: Exports of cash crops are more likely to be taxed the higher is rural population density.

The new results (compared to Table 10.2) are the statistical significance of %Irrigated Land and Exports/Output for a number of products. The negative sign on %Irrigated Land for cocoa, coffee, oat, and palm oil affirms the McMillan (2001) hypothesis that governments will take advantage of sunk cost commitments made by landowners and tax them for revenues. In fact, McMillan's analysis of sub-Saharan African countries affirmed her hypothesis using similar products in her sample. However, there is also evidence that governments can support landowner interests. The positive signs on coconut, groundnut, maize, milk, pig meat, rapeseed, and soybean indicate that the likelihood of government subsidizing exports increases with %Irrigated Land.

The statistical significance of Exports/Output implies that the likelihood of government taxation increases with exports for apple, bean, cocoa, egg, and grape. On the other hand, the likelihood of government subsidization increases with exports for cashew, coffee, maize, rubber, tea, and tobacco. This is the clearest demarcation of the heterogeneity of government policy on a cash crop/food crop basis. We advance the following exploratory hypothesis based on these results:

H2: Governments choose to subsidize cash crops as their exports-to-output ratio increases and tax food crops as their export-to-output ratio increases.

This hypothesis is in line with the idea that taxation of exports, in addition to providing revenue, is politically motivated by providing cheap food to the public. It should be noted, as we did earlier, that future studies that seek to confirm this result should take account of the inherent endogeneity problem in estimating the coefficient on the export-to-output ratio.

Table 10.4 presents the regressions by product for the smaller sample with institutional variables included. There are fewer conflicts with the corresponding results from the pooled sample in Table 10.2. We focus on just the institutional variables in order to draw exploratory hypotheses. The only products for which the %Majority is negative are soybean and rapeseed, while the positive sign is supported by banana, cashew, coconut,

Table 10.4. *Export regressions for tax/subsidy choice, by product, binary NRA dependent variable, with institutional variables (truncated sample, 1975 to 2004, OLS with fixed effects)*

	apple	banana	barley	bean	beef	cashew	cocoa	coconut	coffee
%Arable Land	-5.961	-22.299	3.148	-3.281	2.924	391.96	-4.564	-3.759	2.998
	[0.66]	[1.23]	[0.59]	[0.13]	[1.11]	[2.59]*	[0.90]	[0.17]	[0.86]
%Irrigated Land	-2.696	0.758	-0.614	27.517	0.228	34.39	-0.972	0.54	-0.119
	[1.78]	[2.55]*	[0.67]	[0.94]	[0.42]	[0.82]	[1.99]	[1.36]	[0.84]
%Rural Population	-6.715	7.189	-6.271	25.119	0.474	-36.564	0.894	11.494	-3.394
	[3.16]**	[1.54]	[3.98]**	[0.95]	[0.25]	[2.46]*	[0.25]	[1.93]	[2.23]*
Rural pop. density	10.498	-8.776	5.446	-8.554	-2.364	22.314	1.181	-2.396	-0.441
	[1.30]	[0.91]	[2.60]*	[0.85]	[2.12]*	[2.69]*	[1.41]	[0.82]	[0.56]
Exports/ Output	-0.288	-0.023	0.002	-7.759	0.199	0.245	-0.368	4.699	0.225
	[1.33]	[0.26]	[0.01]	[2.36]*	[0.87]	[1.39]	[3.60]**	[1.23]	[3.48]**
%Majority	-0.771	0.7	0.022	-0.293	0.264	3.758	-0.048	1.671	0.251
	[1.73]	[2.48]*	[0.08]	[0.55]	[1.59]	[2.45]*	[0.17]	[2.21]*	[1.96]
EIEC	-0.053	0.307	0.036	0.04	0.109	0.376	-0.071	0.233	0.023
	[0.73]	[6.93]**	[0.78]	[0.43]	[1.34]	[2.47]*	[1.80]	[3.33]**	[1.38]
Undivided govt.	-0.14	0.604	0.095	0.145	-0.022	-0.393	0	0.143	0.066
	[0.69]	[2.90]**	[1.03]	[0.47]	[0.28]	[1.83]	[.]	[0.31]	[1.02]
N	91	97	154	46	278	48	106	72	296
#countries	5	5	14	4	23	2	6	3	14
R-squared	0.49	0.76	0.53	0.71	0.13	0.83	0.39	0.67	0.26

(continued)

261

Table 10.4 (continued)

	cotton	egg	grape	groundnut	maize	milk	oat	oilseed	palmoil
%Arable Land	3.095	-0.667	8.519	8.965	-6.55	0.165	1.22	5.237	-26.156
	[0.83]	[0.80]	[1.02]	[1.03]	[1.63]	[0.28]	[0.11]	[0.95]	[1.41]
%Irrigated Land	0.486	0.108	2.049	3.765	0.476	0.031	-10.196	-72.718	-4.058
	[1.33]	[0.65]	[1.45]	[4.42]**	[1.45]	[0.30]	[2.03]*	[0.88]	[2.60]*
%Rural Population	0.591	-1.628	-1.389	-2.85	-4.567	-0.139	11.169	93.791	-0.496
	[0.80]	[1.58]	[0.74]	[1.23]	[1.96]	[0.16]	[1.06]	[1.67]	[0.10]
Rural pop. density	-0.238	0.111	-0.871	-1.793	-0.625	0.076	43.501	13.999	1.33
	[0.44]	[0.17]	[0.09]	[0.55]	[0.23]	[0.15]	[1.06]	[0.81]	[1.15]
Exports/ Output	0.052	-0.172	0.215	0.006	0.376	0.007	0.891	0.268	0.053
	[1.15]	[0.83]	[1.29]	[0.01]	[1.71]	[0.37]	[1.09]	[2.65]*	[0.13]
%Majority	0.617	-0.139	0.78	0.312	-0.201	0.129	0.007	0.406	0.111
	[3.60]**	[1.28]	[1.80]	[0.92]	[0.72]	[1.64]	[0.02]	[0.64]	[0.20]
EIEC	0.053	0.143	0.018	0.07	-0.078	0.487	0	0.093	-0.181
	[2.79]**	[5.02]**	[0.26]	[1.72]	[1.60]	[2.85]**	[.]	[0.62]	[1.13]
Undivided govt.	-0.055	-0.068	-0.209	0.216	0.205	0.017	-0.179	0.229	-0.645
	[0.90]	[1.56]	[1.30]	[1.52]	[1.50]	[0.70]	[0.51]	[0.39]	[1.19]
N	346	319	99	128	206	394	82	40	74
#countries	18	24	5	9	19	29	7	5	4
R-squared	0.15	0.34	0.48	0.49	0.22	0.12	0.53	0.63	0.63

	pigmeat	potato	poultry	rapeseed	rice	rubber	sheepmeat	sorghum	soybean
%Arable Land	-4.76	1.153	1.2	75.084	3.615	2.444	4.705	16.01	3.855
	[0.81]	[0.87]	[0.94]	[2.35]*	[0.89]	[0.58]	[0.97]	[0.75]	[0.48]
%Irrigated Land	-0.137	-0.191	0.207	1.504	-0.076	-0.392	0.43	0.048	0.957
	[0.39]	[0.86]	[1.65]	[0.70]	[0.33]	[1.34]	[0.91]	[0.02]	[2.32]*
%Rural Population	-6.239	-0.536	0.147	-17.352	-2.979	3.844	0.224	2.68	-0.905
	[3.47]**	[0.84]	[0.14]	[1.71]	[1.88]	[1.83]	[0.13]	[0.46]	[0.38]
Rural pop. density	0.629	0.932	-0.216	297.269	0.045	0.499	1.525	12.698	-0.183
	[0.28]	[1.42]	[0.25]	[3.83]**	[0.08]	[1.03]	[0.27]	[0.90]	[0.08]
Exports/Output	-0.301	0.021	-0.041	-0.452	0.045	0.605	0.057	-0.128	0.244
	[1.08]	[0.24]	[0.45]	[5.00]**	[0.48]	[3.09]**	[0.31]	[0.95]	[0.61]
%Majority	-0.464	-0.184	-0.292	-1.028	-0.01	1.049	0.283	0.08	-0.606
	[2.18]*	[0.96]	[1.95]	[3.10]**	[0.04]	[2.39]*	[1.53]	[0.09]	[2.52]*
EIEC	0.313	0.038	-0.118	0.777	-0.003	0.185	0.024	0.077	-0.033
	[1.58]	[1.26]	[3.11]**	[3.85]**	[0.05]	[2.72]**	[0.59]	[1.05]	[0.65]
Undivided govt.	-0.137	0.025	0.093	-0.348	-0.053	0.13	-0.111	0.829	0.1
	[1.42]	[0.45]	[1.73]	[3.41]**	[0.46]	[0.67]	[1.27]	[1.69]	[0.88]
N	203	261	364	68	180	112	124	62	138
#countries	18	15	25	6	11	5	10	5	10
R-squared	0.34	0.47	0.18	0.8	0.17	0.45	0.3	0.54	0.38

(continued)

263

Table 10.4 (continued)

	sugar	sunflower	tea	tobacco	tomato	vegetables	wheat	wine
%Arable Land	-1.528	2.964	0.49	-8.038	-17.082	-326.341	-0.301	2.071
	[0.42]	[0.91]	[0.15]	[0.82]	[1.18]	[0.92]	[0.23]	[0.14]
%Irrigated Land	-0.104	0.369	-0.229	1.165	0.494	6.225	0.159	-0.98
	[0.58]	[0.66]	[0.99]	[0.83]	[0.90]	[1.33]	[0.69]	[0.40]
%Rural Population	2.819	-1.114	1.237	-1.664	-1.502	145.309	0.437	6.435
	[2.20]*	[0.23]	[0.55]	[1.11]	[0.46]	[1.54]	[0.25]	[0.88]
Rural pop. density	-0.632	12.659	0.712	-2.076	3.957	-78.62	-0.875	-0.718
	[0.59]	[1.09]	[0.60]	[1.66]	[0.34]	[1.48]	[1.00]	[0.15]
Exports/ Output	0.121	0.005	0.185	0.035	0.186	-0.077	-0.005	0.344
	[1.86]	[0.10]	[2.86]**	[1.66]	[1.26]	[0.20]	[0.13]	[2.86]**
%Majority	-0.143	0.108	0.142	-0.068	-0.043	-6.495	0.135	-0.594
	[0.98]	[0.34]	[0.48]	[0.13]	[0.11]	[1.45]	[0.86]	[1.35]
EIEC	0.093	0.074	-0.07	0.075	0.217	-0.544	0.24	0
	[3.23]**	[0.35]	[2.04]*	[1.48]	[3.69]**	[1.45]	[1.89]	[.]
Undivided govt.	0.059	0.582	0.02	-0.034	0.587	0	-0.036	0
	[0.55]	[3.54]**	[0.17]	[0.40]	[3.66]**	[.]	[0.67]	[.]
N	244	94	134	115	90	46	384	61
#countries	16	10	6	5	5	2	29	4
R-squared	0.43	0.54	0.36	0.47	0.58	0.92	0.38	0.55

Absolute t-values in brackets; ** and * denote statistical significance at the 1 and 5 percent levels, respectively.
Source: Authors' calculations.

264

cotton, and rubber. While not unanimous, these results provide consider-able support for our next hypothesis:

H3: Legislatures in which the governing party or governing coalition has a comfortable majority are more likely to subsidize their exports rather than tax them.

A similar hypothesis applies to executive electoral competition. The positive sign on EIEC is evident for banana, cashew, coconut, cotton, egg, milk, rapeseed, rubber, sugar, and tomato, and is only contradicted by poultry and tea. We thus hypothesize that:

H4: Countries in which there is strong electoral competition for the office of executive are more likely to subsidize their exports than to tax them.

These two institutional variables indicate that democracies that feature legislative decision making and electoral competition are more receptive to special interest pressure from their exporters than are other govern-ments. It should be noted that the third institutional variable, undivided government, which was statistically insignificant in the pooled sample, is statistically significant for banana, rapeseed, sunflower, and tomato. However, that is not sufficient basis *per se* to advance an exploratory hypothesis about whether divided governments are more likely to tax or subsidize exports.

Imports: Pooled Sample

Table 10.5 presents the results from the pooled sample of imports. The first model, from the larger sample without political institutions variables, indicates the statistical significance of %Arable Land, %Rural Population, and Rural Population density. The results are strikingly similar to the cor-responding results from the exports sample: The signs on these coefficients are the same as in the corresponding Table 10.2 results. The coefficient estimate signs imply that: The greater the percentage of land that is arable, the higher the probability that imports will be subsidized; the higher the share of the population that is rural, the greater the likelihood that imports will be subsidized; and the greater the rural population density, the greater the probability that imports will be taxed.

In order to explain the negative sign on %Arable Land (which is puzzling if %Arable Land is taken to measure comparative advantage), we rely on an extension of McMillan's logic to imports. Governments that wish to keep domestic food prices low must also care less about protecting their grow-ers from imports. Thus, governments – especially in poor countries – take

Table 10.5. *Import regressions for tax/subsidy choice (binary NRA) and NRA levels (OLS with fixed effects)*

Dependent Variable →	Binary NRA		NRA	
%Arable Land	−1.1	−0.44	−2.379	−2.685
	[6.18]**	[1.23]	[5.23]**	[2.83]**
%Irrigated Land	−0.027	−0.092	−0.05	−0.153
	[1.24]	[2.32]*	[0.88]	[1.46]
%Rural Population	−0.713	−0.234	−3.01	−3.054
	[6.58]**	[1.17]	[10.79]**	[5.81]**
Rural population density	0.373	0.239	0.096	−0.371
	[5.98]**	[2.20]*	[0.60]	[1.29]
Imports/Output	0.003	0.001	−0.005	−0.002
	[3.62]**	[1.45]	[2.29]*	[0.86]
Exports/Output				
%Majority		−0.08		−0.299
		[2.09]*		[2.88]**
EIEC		0.043		0.06
		[6.62]**		[3.52]**
Undivided government		0.009		−0.075
		[0.52]		[1.67]
N	11409	6764	11111	6481
#countries	61	60	61	60
overall-R^2	0.01	0.03	0.02	0.01
Fraction of var due to FE	0.44	0.37	0.46	0.60
F-statistic for Ho: all FE=0	33.95	22.16	44.77	31.84

Notes:
[1] Absolute t-values in brackets; ** and * denote statistical significance at the 1 and 5 percent levels, respectively.
[2] Imports sample abridged at Imports/Output<50 (Exports/output always below that).
[3] Country-fixed effects and year dummies included but not reported.
Source: Authors' calculations.

advantage of the specificity of land to producing import-competing crops and effectively subsidize imports to get political support from their public by providing food, even imports, cheaply. The specificity of land is guaranteed once landowners commit to production by sinking costs into making land arable.

The reason imports are subsidized when %Rural Population is high is similar to why exports are taxed when %Rural Population is high, namely to keep the price low for their domestic consumers. In a democracy, the government's target may be groups from which legislators draw the median voter(s), and in non-democracies, the target may be urban groups that further the government's priorities (for example, a program of industrialization).

Finally, if rural population density is a measure of land productivity, then import-competing producers (land owners) will demand protection from imports. The positive sign indicates that governments are very likely to sell protection in return for contributions from special interests.

The extended version of this tax/subsidy choice regression with the institutional variables (and a smaller sample) produces some new results and calls into question others. As shown in column 2 of Table 10.5, %Arable Land is no longer statistically significant but %Irrigated Land is. The argument advanced about governments gaming the commitment by landowners to sink costs (into irrigation) and squeezing them to further their own political goals applies to this finding as well. The variable %Rural Population is also no longer statistically significant and neither is the import-to-output ratio in the smaller sample. The new findings are that %Majority and EIEC are important determinants of the tax-or-subsidize choice. The greater is the majority in legislature, the higher the likelihood that legislators will subsidize food imports (which is the opposite of what we found for exports). Perhaps the reason why the legislature enjoys a majority is in part the fact that they are able to keep food prices, even of imports, low for their publics. This mechanism perpetuates policies that continue to keep food prices low. The positive coefficient on EIEC (similar to the export sample) is in line with the theoretical argument of the electoral competition literature: The greater the electoral competition, the more the platforms of candidates are tailored to satisfy special interests in return for contributions (political support) that are used to enhance electability.

The NRA levels regressions (right-hand half of Table 10.5) are not qualitatively different from the choice regressions in the imports sample, in contrast to the exports sample. Thus, the institutional variables %Majority and EIEC are as important to the tax versus subsidy choice as they are to determining the levels of import taxes and subsides. The smaller model indicates that the higher the share of land that is arable the greater the import subsidy; the greater the percentage of the population that is rural the greater the import subsidy; the greater the rural population density the greater the level of protection to agriculture; and the greater the import penetration ratio the greater is the tax on imports.

Imports by Product

Table 10.6 presents the tax/subsidy choice regressions for each importable product with country-fixed effects. In order to draw exploratory inferences, we are interested to see whether inferences from the pooled sample are robust in the product-by-product regressions. The negative sign on %Arable Land is affirmed for barley, beef, maize, milk, poultry, soybean, sunflower, and wheat, and not contradicted in any product regression. Further, %Irrigated Land also has a negative and statistically significant coefficient for egg, maize, soybean, sugar, sunflower, and wheat. This robust finding deserves explanation. If both these variables are proxies for sunk costs by land owners, then McMillan's logic may be extended to explain why these products are likely to see import subsidization (rather than protection), all else held constant.

The idea here is that governments gain politically by squeezing landowners in order to satisfy their public's demand for cheap food. It is not surprising that most of these are food products, not cash crops. Thus, governments know that farmers and landowners are committed to production and exploit this commitment to satisfy a larger and politically more important constituency. In addition to satisfying the median voter in democracies or the urban consumer in industrializing non-democracies, by gaming landowners, governments are assured of at least some domestic output that lowers their costs of import subsidization. As we mentioned earlier, this is more of a developing country phenomenon, where tax systems are quite undeveloped or inefficient. We thus advance the following hypothesis:

H5: The imports of agricultural consumption goods are more likely to be subsidized the greater is the proportion of land that is arable or irrigated.

The variable %Rural Population has a negative coefficient for beef, egg, maize, milk, oat, soybean, sugar, and sunflower, mostly food crops or food products. However, it has a positive coefficient for cotton, potato, poultry, rice, and sheep meat, many of which are also food products. Thus, no obvious generalization may be made on the basis of %Rural Population. Rural population density has a positive coefficient for beef, egg, maize, milk, oat, sorghum, sugar, and wheat, but a negative coefficient for cotton, rice, and sunflower. It appears that whenever land (rural labor) is more (less) productive it is usually protected against imports (cotton, rice, and sunflower being the exceptions). This suggests the following exploratory hypothesis:

H6: Land (labor) as a source of comparative (disadvantage) advantage is more usually protected than not.

Table 10.6. *Import regressions for tax/subsidy choice, by product, binary NRA dependent variable, without institutional variables (full sample, 1960 to 2004, OLS with fixed effects)*

	barley	bean	beef	cotton	egg	groundnut	maize	milk	oat
%Arable Land	-1.632 [3.05]**	-6.089 [0.42]	-1.482 [2.23]*	-5.73 [0.08]	-1.501 [1.14]	20.52 [1.13]	-2.889 [4.34]**	-2.992 [2.30]*	0.257 [0.42]
%Irrigated Land	0.005 [0.06]	1.031 [1.42]	-0.066 [0.97]	-1.259 [0.40]	-0.701 [5.18]**	-124.374 [1.99]	-0.324 [4.21]**	-0.015 [0.16]	0.466 [4.05]**
%Rural Population	0.138 [0.29]	9.042 [0.90]	-1.012 [2.83]**	22.785 [2.61]*	-3.316 [5.95]**	-71.582 [0.84]	-3.201 [8.33]**	-0.859 [1.99]*	-1.641 [2.29]*
Rural pop. density	0.078 [0.19]	-3.045 [0.42]	1.024 [5.70]**	-16.783 [2.71]*	1.708 [3.73]**	-1.179 [0.10]	1.195 [6.91]**	0.694 [3.24]**	1.014 [2.03]*
Imports/Output	0.012 [2.42]*	-0.274 [0.64]	0.155 [3.32]**	-0.2 [1.50]	0.214 [1.93]	11.718 [2.75]*	0.004 [1.39]	0.076 [1.50]	0.01 [0.58]
N	617	68	845	65	328	45	1039	651	503
#countries	25	3	31	8	21	5	39	29	19
R-squared	0.24	0.77	0.23	0.74	0.33	0.83	0.21	0.15	0.54

(*continued*)

Table 10.6 (continued)

	oilseed	onion	palmoil	pigmeat	potato	poultry	rapeseed	rice	rye
%Arable Land	-17.147 [2.49]	-0.224 [0.03]	-1297.309 [0.32]	0.1 [0.19]	-2.451 [0.37]	-2.009 [3.38]**	-0.338 [0.93]	-0.591 [0.89]	-1.474 [0.39]
%Irrigated Land	103.07 [0.33]	0.194 [1.10]	-17.989 [0.53]	0.149 [2.08]*	0.202 [0.77]	0.021 [0.28]	0.012 [0.16]	0.113 [1.68]	4.142 [0.81]
%Rural Population	0.884 [0.02]	-3.449 [1.05]	100.137 [1.26]	0.081 [0.20]	2.037 [2.33]*	0.938 [2.27]*	-0.232 [0.54]	1.205 [2.84]**	-31.737 [0.76]
Rural pop. density	-16.517 [0.66]	0.852 [0.69]	-2218.571 [0.33]	0.316 [0.95]	-1.05 [1.25]	-0.313 [0.98]	0.013 [0.05]	-1.206 [5.18]**	-0.048 [0.00]
Imports/Output	-0.196 [1.69]	0.433 [2.25]*	0.086 [0.14]	-0.027 [0.33]	-0.068 [0.96]	-0.002 [0.24]	0 [0.03]	0.018 [2.68]**	0.068 [0.25]
N	28	82	34	782	172	704	421	891	44
#countries	4	3	3	30	8	34	14	27	6
R-squared	0.89	0.66	0.99	0.12	0.33	0.08	0.63	0.24	0.64

	sheepmeat	sorghum	soybean	sugar	sunflower	tobacco	wheat
%Arable Land	0.482	6.892	-8.506	-0.754	-6.095	-184.559	-3.358
	[0.89]	[1.82]	[4.26]**	[1.52]	[3.34]**	[0.62]	[2.84]**
%Irrigated Land	-0.031	-0.334	-0.991	-0.163	-0.583	-1800.832	-0.404
	[0.37]	[0.70]	[4.84]**	[2.24]*	[2.69]**	[0.68]	[3.10]**
%Rural Population	2.139	0.204	-2.928	-1.033	-4.45	-26.922	-0.37
	[4.17]**	[0.22]	[3.82]**	[2.85]**	[8.34]**	[0.79]	[0.72]
Rural pop. density	-0.31	2.876	-0.535	0.737	-4.828	-16.28	0.508
	[0.99]	[2.74]**	[1.01]	[5.34]**	[2.18]*	[0.29]	[2.17]*
Imports/Output	0.015	0.016	-0.001	0.008	0	0.063	0.008
	[1.13]	[0.37]	[0.37]	[4.16]**	[0.19]	[0.07]	[3.82]**
N	492	196	386	1097	240	50	900
#countries	15	9	18	43	11	2	40
R-squared	0.15	0.28	0.25	0.23	0.48	0.75	0.14

Note: Absolute t-values in brackets; ** and * denote statistical significance at the 1 and 5 percent levels, respectively.
Source: Authors' calculations.

271

An interesting and important finding is that the positive coefficient on the imports-to-output ratio continues to hold for beef, groundnut, sugar, rice, and wheat. Thus, the imports-to-output ratio is associated positively with the likelihood of protection or import taxation (we will also see a similar pattern with the smaller sample in the Table 10.7). We advance the hypothesis:

H7: Greater import penetration leads to a higher likelihood of governments protecting (rather than subsidizing) imports of important consumption products such as staple foods.

This positive coefficient on the imports-to-output ratio could also be caused by greater protection of these products. It is important that future studies resolve this endogeneity problem. Implicit in hypothesis H7 is the idea that the causality is far stronger in the direction implied.

The results with the institutional variable sample are presented in Table 10.7. The exceptional result is the positive coefficient on executive electoral competition (EIEC) for a number of products: barley, maize, milk, oat, sugar, sunflower, and wheat. Egg is the only contrary result. Overwhelmingly, this result supports the theory that greater competition to get elected leads candidates to favor special interests (Baron 1994, Grossman and Helpman 1996). Here, it means protecting import-competing producers or landowners. This leads to our last exploratory hypothesis:

H8: Greater electoral competition makes import protection more likely.

CONCLUSION

In this chapter, we have undertaken an exploratory econometric analysis of the association between economic and political/institutional factors that are commonly used in the empirical political economy of agricultural trade policy literature, and the observed stance of governments toward net taxation of agricultural exports and imports. The Anderson and Valenzuela (2008) dataset provides substantial empirical support for the cross-country pattern of relative protection/taxation of agriculture first observed in Anderson, Hayami and others (1986).

We also find significant support for the importance of political economy variables identified in the more recent literature. In particular, the data suggest that the greater the percentage of arable land and the higher the proportion of the population that is rural, the higher the probability that exports will be taxed. Our product-specific regression results suggest a number of hypotheses that can form the basis for subsequent research

Table 10.7. Import regressions for tax/subsidy choice, by product, binary NRA dependent variable, with institutional variables (truncated sample, 1975 to 2004, OLS with fixed effects)

	barley	bean	beef	cotton	egg	maize	milk	oat	onion	pigmeat
%Arable Land	-2.255 [2.02]*	-74.25 [1.37]	-0.836 [0.73]	-46.629 [0.36]	-7.964 [2.61]*	-2.408 [1.56]	-8.193 [2.98]**	-1.095 [0.88]	6.95 [0.57]	-2.261 [2.04]*
%Irrigated Land	0.061 [0.40]	-2.542 [0.82]	0.063 [0.41]	-1.043 [0.20]	-1.069 [4.08]**	-0.475 [2.49]*	-0.494 [2.69]**	0.372 [1.72]	0.009 [0.03]	-0.089 [0.68]
%Rural Population	3.333 [3.33]**	-17.747 [0.47]	0.354 [0.50]	33.24 [1.67]	-5.976 [2.75]**	-2.946 [5.00]**	-0.709 [0.89]	2.3 [1.73]	-2.435 [0.25]	1.527 [1.72]
Rural pop. density	-1.653 [2.47]*	-10.033 [0.20]	0.142 [0.39]	-22.292 [1.79]	2.679 [2.15]*	0.692 [2.11]*	1.557 [3.71]**	-0.712 [0.86]	1.54 [0.62]	-0.544 [0.88]
Imports/Output	0.002 [0.33]	-1.093 [2.41]*	0.278 [4.45]**	-0.26 [0.35]	0.086 [0.33]	0.005 [1.63]	0.35 [2.65]**	0.022 [1.15]	0.403 [1.74]	0.081 [0.63]
%Majority	-0.171 [1.18]	3.069 [2.29]*	-0.246 [1.69]	-0.051 [0.07]	-0.284 [1.28]	-0.107 [0.98]	0.11 [0.80]	-0.02 [0.13]	-0.346 [0.72]	-0.215 [1.42]
EIEC	0.401 [4.57]**	-0.219 [0.54]	-0.019 [0.66]	-0.768 [0.93]	-0.323 [2.82]**	0.056 [3.65]**	0.084 [3.01]**	1.144 [6.36]**	-0.013 [0.02]	0.002 [0.06]
Undivided govt.	-0.032 [0.48]	-1.781 [2.43]*	-0.047 [0.69]	-5.391 [1.46]	-0.058 [0.50]	-0.039 [0.86]	-0.014 [0.20]	-0.027 [0.41]	-0.424 [1.00]	-0.094 [1.43]
N	368	47	484	41	181	611	357	287	62	473
#countries	24	3	30	5	16	38	25	18	3	29
R-squared	0.16	0.85	0.22	0.75	0.35	0.17	0.22	0.74	0.68	0.1

(continued)

273

Table 10.7 (continued)

	potato	poultry	rapeseed	rice	sheepmeat	sorghum	soybean	sugar	sunflower	wheat
%Arable Land	-6.679 [0.55]	0.79 [0.61]	0.238 [0.60]	**4.113** [2.92]**	0.585 [0.67]	13.824 [1.80]	**-12.983** [4.31]**	0.245 [0.26]	-8.757 [2.53]*	0.62 [0.34]
%Irrigated Land	0.33 [0.50]	0.327 [2.24]*	-0.005 [0.07]	0.124 [0.97]	-0.297 [1.89]	-0.253 [0.27]	-1.037 [3.57]**	-0.343 [2.37]*	-0.32 [0.65]	-0.012 [0.05]
%Rural Population	**-22.829** [3.96]**	**3.02** [3.71]**	0.664 [1.19]	0.704 [0.93]	**2.345** [2.84]**	3.458 [1.22]	**-2.913** [2.69]**	**-1.338** [2.07]*	**-3.543** [4.52]**	0.57 [0.61]
Rural pop. density	0.718 [0.37]	-0.917 [1.84]	-0.2 [0.64]	-0.737 [1.98]*	-0.075 [0.16]	3.455 [1.87]	-0.832 [1.17]	1.183 [4.26]**	-4.148 [1.14]	-0.038 [0.09]
Imports/Output	-0.18 [1.59]	-0.002 [0.31]	0 [0.37]	**0.024** [2.07]*	**0.034** [2.02]*	0.011 [0.20]	-0.003 [1.32]	0.004 [1.34]	-0.003 [0.51]	**0.013** [1.99]*
%Majority	**-0.777** [3.07]**	0.124 [1.03]	-0.098 [1.84]	-0.214 [1.58]	0.137 [1.10]	0.002 [0.01]	0.201 [1.28]	-0.252 [2.21]*	-0.301 [1.38]	-0.306 [1.99]*
EIEC	0 [.]	0.03 [1.02]	-0.011 [0.23]	-0.005 [0.32]	0.087 [1.19]	-0.018 [0.24]	0.011 [0.27]	0.035 [2.31]*	0.082 [2.37]*	0.079 [3.58]**
Undivided govt.	0 [.]	**0.14** [2.23]*	0.009 [0.47]	-0.112 [1.88]	0.064 [1.37]	-0.246 [1.78]	0.042 [0.50]	**0.135** [2.84]**	-0.079 [1.32]	0.107 [1.47]
N	91	413	269	535	301	109	275	662	157	486
#countries	6	28	14	27	15	9	18	42	10	34
R-squared	0.59	0.11	0.14	0.2	0.2	0.37	0.25	0.19	0.46	0.16

Note: Absolute t-values in brackets; ** and * denote statistical significance at the 1 and 5 percent levels, respectively.
Source: Authors' calculations.

using the Anderson and Valenzuela dataset on NRAs. Some of these are intuitive and consistent with our priors. They include the result that countries with strong electoral competition are more likely to subsidize their exports and engage in import protection; that greater import penetration leads to a higher likelihood of governments protecting (rather than subsidizing) imports of important consumption products such as staple foods; and that the determinants of taxation of cash crops versus food crops differ.

Others results are less intuitive. For example, imports of agricultural consumption goods are more likely to be subsidized the greater the proportion of land that is arable or irrigated; land as a source of comparative advantage is protected; governments seem to choose to subsidize cash crops but tax food crops as their exports-to-output ratio increases; and legislatures in which the governing party or governing coalition has a comfortable majority are more likely to subsidize their exports. Clearly these results and the associated hypotheses call for more in-depth analysis that we hope will be taken up by researchers in future work.

References

Anderson, K. (1995), "Lobbying Incentives and the Pattern of Protection in Rich and Poor Countries," *Economic Development and Cultural Change* 43: 401–23.

Anderson, K., J. Croser, D. Sandri and E. Valenzuela (2010), "Agricultural Distortion Patterns since the 1950s: What Needs Explaining?" Ch. 2 in this volume.

Anderson, K., Y. Hayami and Others (1986), *The Political Economy of Agricultural Protection: East Asia in International perspective*, Sydney: Allen and Unwin.

Anderson, K., W. Martin and E. Valenzuela (2006), "The Relative Importance of Global Agricultural Subsidies and Market Access," *World Trade Review* 5(3): 357–76.

Anderson, K., M. Kurzweil, W. Martin, D. Sandri and E. Valenzuela (2008), "Measuring Distortions to Agricultural Incentives, Revisited," *World Trade Review* 7(4): 1–30.

Anderson, K. and E. Valenzuela (2008), *Global Estimates of Distortions to Agricultural Incentives, 1955 to 2007*, database available at http://www.worldbank.org/agdistortions

Baldwin, R.E. (1985), *The Political Economy of US Import Policy*, Cambridge MA: MIT Press.

Baron, D.P. (1994), "Electoral Competition with Informed and Uninformed Voters," *American Political Science Review* 88: 33–47.

Beck, T., G. Clarke, A. Groff and P. Keefer (2001), "New Tools in Comparative Political Economy: The Database of Political Institutions," *World Bank Economic Review* 15(1): 165–76.

Beck, T., P.E. Keefer and G.R. Clarke (2008), *Database of Political Institutions*, accessible at http://go.worldbank.org/2EAGGLRZ40

Bhagwati, J. and Ramaswami, V.K. (1963), "Domestic Distortions, Tariffs and the Theory of the Optimum Subsidy," *Journal of Political Economy* 71: 44–50.

de Gorter, H. and J.F.M. Swinnen (2002), "Political Economy of Agricultural Policy," pp. 1893–1943 in B.L. Gardner and G. Rausser (eds.), *Handbook of Agricultural Economics, vol. 2B*, Amsterdam, Elsevier.

Deardorff, A.V. (1987), "Why Do Governments Prefer Nontariff Barriers?" *Carnegie-Rochester Conference Series on Public Policy* 26: 191–216.

Dutt, P. and D. Mitra (2002), "Endogenous Trade Policy Through Majority Voting: An Empirical Investigation," *Journal of International Economics* 58: 107–33.

(2005), "Political Ideology and Endogenous Trade Policy: An Empirical Investigation," *Review of Economics and Statistics* 87: 59–72.

(2006), "Labor versus Capital in Trade-Policy: The Role of Ideology and Inequality," *Journal of International Economics* 69(2): 310–20.

Gawande, K. and S. Bandyopadhyay (2000), "Is Protection for Sale? A Test of the Grossman–Helpman Theory of Endogenous Protection," *Review of Economics and Statistics* 82: 139–52.

Gawande, K. and B. Hoekman (2006), "Lobbying and Agricultural Policy in the United States," *International Organization* 60(3): 527–61.

Grossman, G.M. and E. Helpman (1994), "Protection for Sale," *American Economic Review* 84: 833–50.

(1996), "Electoral Competition and Special Interest Politics," *Review of Economic Studies* 63: 265–86.

Hoekman, B., F. Ng and M. Olarreaga (2004), "Reducing Agricultural Tariffs versus Domestic Support: What is More Important for Developing Countries?" *World Bank Economic Review* 18(2): 175–204.

Honma, M. (1993), "Japan's Agricultural Policy and Protection Growth," in T. Ito and A.O. Krueger (eds.), *Trade and Protectionism*, Chicago: University of Chicago Press.

Johnson, H.G. (1965), "Optimal Trade Interventions in the Presence of Domestic Distortions," pp. 3–34 in R. Caves, H. G. Johnson and P. Kenen (eds.), *Trade, Growth and Balance of Payments*, Amsterdam: North-Holland.

Mayer, W. (1984), "Endogenous Tariff Formation," *American Economic Review* 74: 970–85.

McMillan, M. (2001), "Why Kill the Golden Goose? A Political-Economy Model of Export Taxation," *Review of Economics and Statistics* 83(1): 170–84.

Naoi, M. (2009), "Shopping for Protection: The Politics of Choosing Trade Instruments in a Partially-Legalized World," *International Studies Quarterly* 53(2), forthcoming.

Olper, A. and V. Raimondi (2010), "Constitutional Rules and Agricultural Policy Outcomes," Ch. 14 in this volume.

Pender, J. (1999), "Rural Population Growth, Agricultural Change and Natural Resource Management in Developing Countries: A Review of Hypothesis and Some Evidence from the Honduras," EPTD Discussion Paper 48, International Food Policy Research Institute, Washington DC.

Rodrik, D. (1986), "Tariffs, Subsidies and Welfare with Endogenous Policy," *Journal of International Economics* 21: 285–96.

(1992), "Conceptual Issues in the Design of Trade Policy for Industrialization," *World Development* 20: 301–20.

(1995), "Political Economy of Trade Policy," pp. 1457–94 in G.M. Grossman and K. Rogoff (eds.), *Handbook of International Economics*, Vol. 3, Amsterdam: North-Holland.

World Bank (2007), *World Development Indicators 2007*, Washington DC: World Bank.

ELEVEN

Impacts of Ideology, Inequality, Lobbying, and Public Finance

Pushan Dutt and Devashish Mitra[1]

Barring very few exceptions, international trade has never and nowhere been free, even though only under extraordinary circumstances are deviations from free trade optimal. To explain this puzzle, an entire literature on the political economy of trade policy has emerged over the last three decades. In this literature, one common feature is that trade policies are chosen not with the aim of maximizing national economic efficiency and aggregate welfare, but set by politicians and policy makers whose objective functions diverge from aggregate welfare. Trade policies, in this view, are often used as indirect tools to redistribute income to certain targeted groups. The identity of these groups depends on (a) the type of political economy framework (lobbying or majority voting) assumed, (b) the actual economic, political, and geographic characteristics of the various sectors in the economy that determine which of them are politically organized, and (c) the political and economic ideology of the government.

The objective of this chapter is to explain both the cross-country variations in agricultural protection and the within-country evolution of this protection over time. The general trend has been an increase in agricultural protection in developed countries over time as their per capita incomes have increased.[2] This protection has taken the form of tariff and nontariff barriers on imports plus substantial subsidies provided by governments to their farmers. While membership in the GATT/WTO has attempted to control the growth of such protection in developed countries, it has so far not succeeded in eliminating or reducing it. In fact, agricultural support

[1] The authors are grateful for very useful comments and discussions from seminar participants, particularly Johan Swinnen and Will Martin.
[2] For detailed theoretical and empirical analyses of the evolution of agricultural protection during the process of economic development, see Anderson, Hayami and Others (1986) and Hai (1991).

or protection is one of the primary reasons behind the current impasse in the Doha Round of trade talks. In developing countries, by contrast, the bias has been against agriculture and in favor of the manufacturing sector that has historically been highly protected. This has resulted in negative effective rates of protection for agriculture. This bias against agriculture has been reduced in recent times. It is these trends in agricultural protection in developed and developing countries and the differences in their levels across countries that we are proposing to explain. In doing so, we draw upon the vast theoretical literature on the political economy of trade policy.

To examine the political economy drivers of the variation in agricultural protection across countries and within countries over time, we set up a basic framework that allows us to put forth various testable hypotheses on the variation and evolution of agricultural protection. We find that both the political ideology of the government and the degree of income inequality are important determinants of agricultural protection. Thus, both the political support function approach as well as the median-voter approach can be used in explaining the variation in agricultural protection across countries and within countries over time. In other words, while the government's decision making has some partisan elements, the concerns of the majority are also important.

We find that our results are consistent with the predictions of a model that assumes that labor is specialized and sector-specific in nature. The predictions of a model in which labor is assumed to be a general, intersectorally mobile factor do not hold. Finally, some aspects of protection also seem to be consistent with predictions of a lobbying model in that agricultural protection is negatively related to agricultural employment and positively related to agricultural productivity. Public finance aspects of protection also seem to be empirically important. Moreover, lobbying considerations are relatively more important in high-income countries, while public finance aspects are empirically relevant for developing countries.

This chapter is organized as follows. The next section provides a review of pertinent literature review before we set up a theoretical framework where we lay out all the hypotheses that we are going to test. We then briefly discuss our data sources and econometric methodology and present the results before drawing some conclusions.

LITERATURE REVIEW

Political economy models of trade are of two main types. In the first type, called "median voter" models, the approach taken is one of majority voting.

The second type, "lobbying models," may be further classified (following the typology in Rodrik 1995) into four approaches: (1) the tariff-formation function approach, (2) the political support function approach, (3) the political contributions approach, and (4) the campaign contributions approach. Within these lobbying models, (1) and (2) adopt a black-box approach to the modeling of lobbying in trade policy, whereas (3) and (4) have much stronger microfoundations.

Under the tariff-formation function approach, the tariff is a direct increasing function of resources going into lobbying in favor of the tariff and a decreasing function of lobbying resources devoted against the tariff. No microfoundations are provided for the function itself. Examples of this approach include Findlay and Wellisz (1982), Feenstra and Bhagwati (1982), and Rodrik (1986).

In models using the political support function approach, the government maximizes an objective function where different groups in the general population are given different weights depending on their political importance to the incumbent government (Hillman 1989, van Long and Vousden 1991).

In political contribution models, policies are determined through contributions by lobbies to incumbent politicians (Grossman and Helpman 1994), whereas in campaign contribution models, political competition between parties is fully modeled and contributions are made to competing parties (Magee, Brock and Young 1989).

In the theoretical modeling of endogenous protection, Grossman and Helpman (1994) made the biggest advance in providing strong microfoundations to the behavior of lobbies and the government, where the government maximizes a weighted sum of contributions and aggregate welfare, taking as a given contribution schedules provided by lobbies in a prior stage. Mitra (1999) endogenizes the formation of lobbies within this framework and analyzes its implications for sectoral tariffs.

Empirical Implications of the Median-Voter Approach

In the median-voter approach to tariff formulation, preferences on tariffs are assumed to be "single peaked," and conditions are imposed such that the most-preferred policy of each individual is monotonic in a certain characteristic. Then, holding other individual characteristics constant across the population, the tariff chosen under two-candidate electoral competition is the median voter's most-preferred tariff. The median voter here is the median individual in the economy when all individuals in the economy are ranked according to the characteristic under consideration. Mayer (1984) applied this median-voter principle to the Heckscher-Ohlin and specific-factors trade models. In the Heckscher-Ohlin case, the political economy equilibrium tariff is the most-preferred tariff of the median individual in the economy-wide ranking of the ratio of capital to labor ownership. If this median individual's capital-to-labor ratio is less than the economy's overall capital-to-labor ratio, that is, if the asset distribution in the economy is unequal, the equilibrium trade policy is different from free trade and is one that redistributes income from capital to labor. Hence it is protrade in a labor-abundant economy and antitrade in a capital-abundant economy.

In the Heckscher-Ohlin version of the Mayer median-voter model, a simple comparative static exercise produces the following result which is the main hypothesis that is empirically tested in Dutt and Mitra (2002): *A rise in asset inequality will make trade policy more protrade in a labor-abundant economy and more protectionist in a capital-abundant economy.*

Dutt and Mitra (2002) estimate the following protection equation using cross-country data on inequality, capital-abundance, and diverse measures of protection:

$$t_c = \alpha_0 + \alpha_1 (K/L)_c + \alpha_2 (Inequality)_c + \alpha_3 (Inequality)_c (K/L)_c + \nu_c$$

where the "c" is an index for country c. The theory predicts that $\alpha_2 < 0$ and $\alpha_3 > 0$ such that the partial derivative of protection with respect to inequality is positive if K/L is above a threshold, and negative if K/L is below that threshold. Dutt and Mitra (2002) find empirical support for this hypothesis.[3] Besides running the above regression cross-sectionally, Dutt and Mitra also run the regression in time differences (difference between the 1990s and 1980s) and find strong empirical support. Thus, not only does the above median-voter prediction help explain variations in overall trade protection levels across countries, but it also can explain long-run policy changes within a country.

---

[3] In this context, it is also important to mention Milner and Kubota (2005) who use a median-voter approach to empirically investigate the relationship between democratization and trade reforms in developing countries. Dutt and Mitra (2005) also perform a cross-country empirical investigation of the role of political ideology in trade policy determination. They use a political support function approach within a two-sector, two-factor Heckscher-Ohlin model. See Milner and Judkins (2004) on this issue. Also, see Hiscox (2001), who performs a study of six western nations to look at how historically the nature and structure of partisanship on trade issues change over time and depend on the extent of intersectoral factor mobility. Hiscox (2002) looks at the same question exclusively for the U.S., analyzing major pieces of congressional trade legislation between 1824 and 1994.

Empirical Implications of the Special-Interest Approach

The special-interest approach has evolved from the simple Findlay-Wellisz (1982) "tariff-formation function" approach to the state-of-the-art Grossman and Helpman (1994) "political-contributions" model. The latter is a very significant advance in several directions. Firstly, it is multisectoral. Secondly, it provides strong microfoundations to the behavior of the different actors in the model. A "menu-auctions" approach is used in modeling policy bidding by interest groups. Multiple principals, namely the various organized lobbies, try to influence the common agent, namely the government. The government's objective function is linear in political contributions and aggregate welfare, while each lobby maximizes its welfare net of political contributions. The level of protection for each industry is derived as an econometrically estimable function of industry characteristics and other political and economic factors. Most importantly, especially from an empirical perspective, the model provides the following hypothesis: *Holding everything else constant, organized sectors are granted higher protection than unorganized sectors. Further, protection to organized sectors is negatively related to import penetration and the (absolute value of the) import demand elasticity, while protection to unorganized sectors is positively related to these two variables.*

The following protection equation comes directly from the theory:

$$\frac{t_i}{1+t_i} = \frac{I_i - \alpha_L}{a + \alpha_L} \cdot \frac{z_i}{e_i}$$

where t_i denotes the ad valorem tariff (export subsidy in the case of an exportable) to sector i, z_i represents the output-to-import ratio (output-to-export ratio in the case of an exportable) in that sector, e_i its import demand elasticity (export supply elasticity in the case of an exportable), α_L the proportion of the total population of the economy that is politically organized, and a is the weight placed by the government on aggregate welfare relative to political contributions in its objective function. I_i is an indicator variable that takes the value 1 if the sector is politically organized and 0 otherwise.

The predictions of the Grossman and Helpman (1994) model are very intuitive: If an industry is import-competing and is organized ($I_i = 1$) then it buys protection and receives a positive tariff. If an industry is an exporter and organized, it is able to "buy" an export subsidy. Next, a high import-penetration ratio (high volume of imports relative to domestic output of importables) implies that specific-factor owners have less to gain from the increase in domestic price induced by the tariff, and the economy has more to lose from protection. So we are likely to see lower levels of protection. Similarly, when the import elasticity is higher, the deadweight loss from protection is also higher, so the government will grant it lower levels of protection. Next, an unorganized sector gets negative protection according to this theory if $\alpha_L > 0$ and gets zero protection if $\alpha_L = 0$, which is the case where factor ownership and political organization are concentrated in the hands of a few people that form a negligible proportion of the population. Thus, this theory leads to the estimation of the following estimating equation:

$$\frac{t_i}{1+t_i} = \frac{1}{a+\alpha_L} \cdot \frac{I_i z_i}{e_i} + \frac{-\alpha_L}{a+\alpha_L} \cdot \frac{z_i}{e_i} + u_i$$

where this equation can be linearly estimated with $\dfrac{1}{a+\alpha_L}$ and $\dfrac{-\alpha_L}{a+\alpha_L}$ as the two coefficients that are directly estimated, and then a and α_L can be inferred from the two coefficient estimates. Alternatively, these parameters can be directly estimated by nonlinear estimation.

Goldberg and Maggi (1999) and Gawande and Bandyopadhyay (2000) estimate the Grossman-Helpman "Protection for Sale" tariff expressions using industry-level data from the United States. Using slightly different econometric specifications from each other, both papers confirm empirically the Grossman-Helpman prediction regarding the relationship of protection to import protection and import demand elasticity. Holding everything else constant, organized sectors are granted higher protection than unorganized sectors. Both these papers find that the weight on aggregate welfare in the government's objective function (a) is several times higher than that on contributions. This finding is somewhat puzzling and perhaps worrisome. Although the Grossman-Helpman model does not provide any indication on the expected magnitude of the parameter a, the higher the weight governments put on aggregate welfare, the less compelling seems the raison d'être for the entire political economy literature. Moreover, the estimates of the proportion of population who are organized are very high in both the Goldberg-Maggi and Gawande-Bandyopadhyay papers.

Mitra, Thomakos and Ulubasoglu (2002) and McCalman (2004) obtain similarly high parameter estimates of the Grossman-Helpman model for Turkey and Australia, respectively. An interesting result that comes out of the empirical exercise by Mitra, Thomakos, and Ulubasoglu is that the relative weight on aggregate welfare was higher in the democratic regime than under the dictatorial regime in Turkey for the period spanned by the dataset. Due to the panel nature of the dataset, this study is able to explain both the cross-industry as well as the time series variation in protection.

Gawande, Krishna and Robbins (2006) use a new dataset on foreign political activity in the United States and extend the "Protection for Sale" model to include foreign lobbies. In line with the Grossman-Helpman's prediction, they find that foreign lobbying activity has significantly reduced US trade barriers. As a result, foreign lobbying has increased consumer surplus and overall welfare in the United States. In another empirical application, through an extension of the Grossman-Helpman model, Gawande and Krishna (2006) investigate the effects of US trade policy lobbying competition between upstream and downstream producers. Their parameter estimates are a significant improvement over those in the earlier literature even though they do not completely resolve the puzzle.

Finally, the most relevant paper from the point of view of the present study is the recent paper by Gawande, Krishna and Olarreaga (2009). This paper looks at the cross-country and cross-industry variations in protection at the same time. The Grossman-Helpman tariff expression for an organized sector can be written as:

$$\frac{t_{ict}}{1+t_{ict}} = \frac{1-\alpha_{Lc}}{a_c + \alpha_{Lc}} \cdot \frac{z_{ict}}{e_{ict}}$$

where the subscript "*ict*" denotes industry i in country c at time t. Assuming ownership of specific factors and political organization to be fully concentrated among a negligible proportion of the population, we have:

$$\frac{t_{ict}}{1+t_{ict}} = \frac{1}{a_c} \cdot \frac{z_{ict}}{e_{ict}}$$

which in turn can be written as

$$\frac{t_{ic}}{1+t_{ic}} \cdot \frac{e_{ict}}{z_{ict}} = \frac{1}{a_c}$$

and can be estimated as

$$\frac{t_{ic}}{1+t_{ic}} \cdot \frac{e_{ict}}{z_{ict}} = \beta_c + \xi_{ict}$$

The variance of the disturbance term is allowed to vary by country, and the coefficient $\beta_c = \dfrac{1}{a_c}$ is a measure of a government's affinity for political contributions, and its inverse gives us the weight the government puts on aggregate welfare relative to contributions in its objective function. The ranking of countries on the basis of the estimates of *a* and 1/*a* obtained by Gawande, Krishna and Olarreaga is quite realistic. The Spearman rank correlation of this estimate with Transparency International's corruption index turns out to be 0.67. Several political variables from the Database on Political Institutions (Beck et al. 2001), such as constraints on the executive, competition for executive, party concentration, and number of government seats, do very well in explaining the variation in *a* and 1/*a*. In addition, institutional variables such as the nature of the legal system also perform well. This study, therefore, provides useful insights into the institutional and political variables that may potentially explain the variation in protection to agriculture both across space and over time.

Empirical Implications of the Political Ideology or Partisan Government Approach

Dutt and Mitra (2005) use a reduced form special-interest approach (earlier referred to as the "political support function" approach) to study how variations in political ideology of governments can explain international and intertemporal variations in protection. Ideology of the government is labeled as right, center, and left. Using the same Stolper-Samuelson intuition as in their median-voter paper, they arrive at the following testable hypothesis: *A more left-wing government (i.e., that attaches a higher weight to the welfare of workers/labor) is more protectionist in the case of capital-abundant countries but is less protectionist in the case of capital-scarce countries.* That hypothesis results in the following estimating equation:

$$t_c = \alpha_0 + \alpha_1 (K/L)_c + \alpha_2 (\text{Ideology})_c + \alpha_3 (\text{Ideology})_c (K/L)_c + \nu_c$$

Dutt and Mitra (2002) find support for their ideology hypothesis. In another paper, Dutt and Mitra (2006) combine both their ideology and their inequality (median-voter) hypotheses into the following umbrella model to show that protection is determined both by general-interest and special-interest concerns:

$$t_c = \alpha_0 + \alpha_1 (K/L)_c + \alpha_2 (\text{Ideology})_c + \alpha_3 (\text{Inequality})_c$$
$$+ \alpha_4 (\text{Ideology})_c (K/L)_c + \alpha_4 (\text{Inequality})_c (K/L)_c + \nu_c$$

Again, these models provide some guidance for the present study of agricultural protection.

Lessons from the "First Generation" Empirical Work

Unlike recent work described above, the early empirical literature, or what Gawande and Krishna (2003) call "first generation" empirical work on endogenous trade policy, is not driven by formal models. Nevertheless, we believe it does provide very useful insights and guidance for future research. It is important here to note that there were some important correlations revealed between tariffs and a number of political and economic variables by this early literature. For example Baldwin (1985) found that tariffs are higher for industries that are labor-intensive, have low wages, have a small number of firms and employ a large number of workers, and experience a high degree of import penetration. Also, he finds that tariff cuts from the GATT's Tokyo round were the lowest for the most unskilled labor-intensive industries.

Another well-known empirical piece from the early literature on the political economy of trade policy is by Trefler (1993), who finds that import penetration and other comparative advantage measures are more important in the determination of the nontariff barrier coverage ratios than industry concentration, scale, and capital measures.

Other important papers in the old literature include Caves (1976), Saunders (1980), Ray (1981), Marvel and Ray (1983), Ray (1991) and Trefler (1993).[4] The main finding of this early empirical literature is that protection is higher for sectors that are labor-intensive, low-skill and low-wage, for consumer-goods industries, for industries facing high import penetration when geographical concentration of production is high but that of consumers is low, and in sectors with low levels of intra-industry trade.[5]

Lessons from the Literature on Agricultural Protection

A large proportion of the theoretical research on the political economy of trade policy prior to the Grossman and Helpman (1994) model was on agricultural protection. Noteworthy in this literature is Swinnen (1994), who uses a Hillman-type of political support function approach within a fairly rich structure of the economy (three factors, of which one is mobile

---

[4] See Rodrik (1995) for a detailed survey of this literature.
[5] For an examination of the cross-national variation in average protection levels across industrialized countries, see Mansfield and Busch (1995). They find that nontariff barriers are increasing in country size, unemployment rate, and number of parliamentary constituencies and are higher for countries that use proportional representation as their electoral system.

and two are fixed), to study the relationship between agricultural protection and economic development.[6]

Honma (1993), who uses the Anderson and Hayami (1986) framework, finds support for the Anderson (1992) hypothesis that the shrinking of the agricultural sector makes opposition to agricultural protection more diffused and the lobbying for it more concentrated.[7] Honma uses panel data from fourteen industrial countries for the period 1955–87. He further finds that agricultural protection is inversely related to agricultural industry productivity and positively related to deterioration in its terms of trade.

Olper (1998) tries to explain cross-country variations in agricultural protection among the European Union (EU) countries in the 1970s and 1980s. Specifically, he looks at the Common Agricultural Policy (CAP) of the EU. He shows that agricultural protection is countercyclical to market conditions and is positively related to the extent of comparative disadvantage in agriculture. Also, agricultural protection is greater in countries with a smaller number of farms, finding evidence for the free-rider problem in lobbying.[8]

Finally, a recent paper by Gawande and Hoekman (2006) tests a modified version of the Grossman and Helpman (1994) "Protection for Sale" model for US agriculture. The modification is the uncertain outcome of lobbying, and the dataset they use contains both agricultural protection (tariffs and subsidies) and PAC contributions in the United States during the late 1990s. This is the first empirical piece in the agricultural protection literature that is completely structural in that the estimating equation is derived exclusively from theory.

THEORETICAL FRAMEWORK FOR THE PRESENT STUDY

In the theory we develop here, we recognize the existence of land as a factor that is of primary importance to agriculture. To do this, we make the extreme assumption that land is a factor of production specific to

[6] For an application, see Swinnen, Banerjee and de Gorter (2001). The literature on the political economy of agricultural protection until the early 1990s is comprehensively surveyed in de Gorter and Swinnen (2002).

[7] For a CGE study, based on a similar argument, trying to explain the bias against agriculture in poor countries and high agricultural protection in rich countries, see Anderson (1995).

[8] Also, see Olper (2007), where he looks at the interaction between ideology and inequality in the determination of agricultural protection. This work builds on Dutt and Mitra (2002, 2005, 2006).

agriculture. We develop our hypotheses under two scenarios: one where labor is intersectorally mobile and one where it is sector-specific.

Consider a two-sector specific-factors model. In the economy under consideration, assume there are two sectors, manufacturing and agriculture. The manufacturing sector uses capital (specific to manufacturing) and labor under constant returns to scale (CRS), while agriculture uses land (specific to agriculture) and labor, also under CRS. An unconditional prediction of this set of assumptions is that an increase in agricultural protection increases the real incomes (welfare) of landowners, while it reduces the real incomes of capitalists. In this framework, if labor is also sector-specific and immobile across sectors, then the prediction gets modified to the following: An increase in agricultural protection increases the real incomes (welfare) of landowners and agricultural workers, while it reduces the real incomes of capitalists and manufacturing workers. On the other hand, if labor is mobile across sectors, then the effect of agricultural protection on labor's welfare is ambiguous – it depends on labor's share of expenditure on agricultural products (food).

Political Ideology and Inequality

Clearly, in the mobile labor framework described above, a right-wing government (one that puts a higher weight on the well-being of capitalists) will try to keep protection as low as possible for agriculture. In such a framework, what will a left-wing government do? Remember that a left-wing government has an affinity for workers, which means they attach a higher weight to labor's welfare than to the welfare of others in the country. Protecting agriculture raises the overall demand for workers in the economy and increases their real wages in terms of the manufactured good, but lowers real wages when measured in terms of the agricultural good (food). Thus, if the share of expenditure on food is small enough, workers will be made better off through agricultural protection. A left-wing government will in such situations want to protect agriculture. There will be labor-land coalitions formed in such situations. The opposite will be the case when the expenditure share of food is high. Since the expenditure share of food varies inversely with per capita income, a left-wing government will want to protect agriculture in rich countries and not in poor countries.

In the immobile labor case, with a move from right-wing to centrist to left-wing governments, we will get an increase in agricultural protection if a large proportion of employment is in the agricultural sector. Since a left-wing government is pro-labor, it will support the sector that has relatively more workers. In general, the share of agriculture in employment is higher in poor countries. Therefore, the poorer a country the more likely it is that a left-wing government (relative to a right-wing or centrist government) will provide assistance to agriculture.

This brings us to **Competing Hypotheses 1:**

(a) *Mobile Labor Case: Countries with left-wing governments will exhibit higher levels of agricultural protection when per capita income is high. At high levels of income, agricultural protection goes up when the political ideology of the government changes from rightist to centrist to leftist.*

(b) *Immobile Labor Case: Countries with left-wing governments will exhibit higher levels of agricultural protection when per capita income is low. At low levels of income, agricultural protection goes up when the political ideology of the government changes from rightist to centrist to leftist.*

Majority Voting and Inequality

In a model where governments set policies that have the support of the majority of the population, agricultural protection will respond to income inequality. The predicted direction of response (to such changes in inequality) will once again depend on whether labor is intersectorally mobile or immobile.

In the mobile labor case, in a setting where the government tries to put in place policies that get majority support, agricultural protection will again be conditional on the food expenditure share. When this expenditure share is low, the majority, who are mainly workers, are likely to demand higher agricultural protection since this will increase the real incomes of workers in terms of their consumption baskets. When the expenditure share of food is low, which is the case when income is high, an increase in asset inequality will increase agricultural protection. This happens since, with an increase in inequality, the share of labor income in the incomes of the majority of the people goes up.[9] The opposite is the case when income is low and the share of food in overall expenditure is high.

In the immobile labor case, with an increase in inequality, there will be a demand for inequality reduction and we will get an increase in agricultural protection if a large proportion of employment is in the agricultural sector.

[9]   In the median voter model, it is common to assume that the median voter is labor-rich and asset-poor. From an empirical perspective as well, such an assumption seems plausible.

In general, the share of agriculture in employment is higher in poor countries. Therefore, the poorer a country the more likely it is that an increase in inequality will lead to an increase in assistance to agriculture.

Therefore, we have **Competing Hypotheses 2:**

(a) *Mobile Labor Case: Countries with higher levels of inequality will exhibit higher levels of agricultural protection provided income levels are high enough. Countries that experience an increase in inequality will increase their levels of agricultural protection over time, provided income levels are high enough.*

(b) *Immobile Labor Case: Countries with higher levels of inequality will exhibit higher levels of agricultural protection provided income levels are low enough. Countries that experience an increase in inequality will increase their levels of agricultural protection over time, provided income levels are low enough.*

Lobbying

With economic development and rising per capita incomes, agriculture's share in overall employment goes down. There are two main reasons for this. Firstly, in line with the traditional Engel effect, the share of expenditure on food goes down. Secondly, technological progress in agriculture means that fewer workers are required to produce a given level of output. As the employment share of agriculture goes down, agricultural workers and landowners will probably find it easier to organize and mitigate the inherent free-rider problem of lobby formation. As a result, a decline in the share of employment in agriculture is likely to be accompanied by an increase in agricultural protection. Second, if agricultural productivity goes up, lobbying becomes more beneficial and we are likely to see more agricultural protection.

This brings us to the following **Noncompeting (Complementary) Hypotheses 3:**

(a) *Countries with a lower share of employment in agriculture and higher agricultural productivity will exhibit higher levels of agricultural protection.*

(b) *Countries that experience a falling share of employment in agriculture and rising agricultural productivity will increase the levels of agricultural protection over time.*

Public Finance

During the initial stages of development, a country's tax infrastructure to raise revenues through direct taxes is weak. So revenues are raised through indirect taxes including tariffs on imports, which at that stage of development are mainly manufactured goods (but could include some agricultural goods). Over time, incomes increase and the returns to having a strong direct tax infrastructure rise, which results in government investment in an effective internal revenue service. Most of the revenue now comes from income taxes. Some of these revenues can now be used to give agricultural subsidies (especially since most rich countries have a comparative disadvantage in agriculture).

Thus, we have the following **Noncompeting (Complementary) Hypotheses 4**:

(a) *Countries with a small direct tax base (income taxes as a proportion of total tax revenues or government expenditure) will exhibit higher levels of agricultural tariffs.*

(b) *Countries whose direct tax revenues (as a proportion of total tax revenues or government expenditure) rise over time will exhibit a fall in their agricultural tariff rates and a rise in agricultural subsidies.*

EMPIRICAL RESULTS

To test these hypotheses we gather data on political variables from a variety of sources. Table 11.1 lists the data sources and the coverage for each of our explanatory variables.

We examine both the cross-country variations in agricultural protection as well as the within- country variation in agricultural protection over time. Table 11.2 shows the regressions that we run and the predicted coefficients on the independent variables to test our cross-country hypotheses as well as those which are within country and over time. To investigate cross-country variations, we use pooled ordinary least squares (OLS). For the within-country variation over time, we use panel data estimation techniques. This allows us to control for unobserved and time-invariant country-specific effects by using country-fixed effects.

Table 11.1. *Description of variables*

Variable	Years	Description
Relative Rate of Assistance to agriculture (RRA)	1955–2007	Anderson and Valenzuela (2008). (Methodology in Anderson et al. 2008.)
Nominal Rate of Assistance to agriculture (NRA)	1955–2007	Anderson and Valenzuela (2008). (Methodology in Anderson et al. 2008.)
Political Ideology	1975–2000	Political Ideology of chief executive (the President for Presidential systems and largest ruling party for Parliamentary system). *Source*: Database of Political Institutions 2004 (update of Beck et al. 2001).
Income Inequality	1960–1999	Gini coefficients from Dollar and Kraay (2002) and Deininger and Squire (1996, 1998). Data for the latter at http://www.worldbank.org/research/ inequality/data.htm
Land Inequality	One year	Land Gini from Li, Squire and Zou (1998).
Per capita GDP	1960–2000	GDP per capita on a PPP basis. *Source*: World Bank (2007).
Share of agriculture in employment	1960–2000	Total workers employed in agriculture as a proportion of labor force. *Source*: World Bank (2007).
Comparative Disadvantage in Agriculture	1960–2000	Measured as $(X - M)/(X + M)$, where X is exports of agricultural products and M is the imports of agricultural products.
Direct taxes (% of total taxes)	1970–2000	Direct taxes include income taxes, profits, and capital gains tax. *Source*: World Bank (2007).
Constraints on Executive	1960–2000	Extent of institutionalized constraints on the decision-making powers of chief executives, whether individuals or collectivities. *Source*: Polity IV Project, (Marshall, Jaggers and Gurr 2000).
Rural party	1975–2000	Dummy equals 1 if chief executive's party can be classified as rural. *Source*: Database of Political Institutions 2004 (update of Beck et al. 2001).

Source: Authors' compilation.

Table 11.2. *Hypotheses and predicted signs*

Hypotheses	Description	Predicted signs
1: *Political Ideology*	Regress agricultural protection on left-wing ideology and leftist ideology×per capita income	Mobile labor case: Negative on leftist ideology and positive on the interaction term.
		Immobile labor case: Positive on leftist ideology and negative on the interaction term.
2: *Inequality*	Regress agricultural protection on income inequality and inequality×per capita income	Mobile labor case: Negative on inequality and positive on the interaction term.
		Immobile labor case: Positive on inequality and negative on the interaction term.
3: *Lobbying*	Regress agricultural protection on share of agriculture in employment and agricultural productivity	Negative on employment share and positive on agricultural productivity
4: *Public Finance*	Regress agricultural protection on share of direct taxes in total taxes/ expenditure	Negative on direct tax share

Source: Authors' compilation.

Ideology, Inequality, and Agricultural Protection

To examine the role played by ideology and inequality in influencing agricultural protection, we first estimate the following equations:

$$agprot_{ct} = \alpha_1 (per\,capita\,income)_{ct} + \alpha_2 (\text{Ideology})_{ct} \\ + \alpha_3 (\text{Ideology})_{ct} (per\,capita\,income)_{ct} + \epsilon_{ct}$$

$$agprot_{ct} = \alpha_1 (per\,capita\,income)_{ct} + \alpha_2 (\text{Inequality})_{ct} \\ + \alpha_3 (\text{Inequality})_{ct} (per\,capita\,income)_{ct} + \epsilon_{ct}$$

where the subscript "c" is for country and "t" denotes time. "Agprot" stands for agricultural protection. For the within-estimates, we add country (as well as time) fixed effects to the above specification.

In Table 11.3, we see how political ideology and inequality affect the Relative Rate of Assistance (RRA) to agriculture. In column 1, the

Table 11.3. *Ideology and per capita GDP as determinants of RRAs*

	(1)	(2)	(3)	(4)
	RRA	RRA	RRA	RRA
Left–wing ideology	0.555*** (0.148)	0.726*** (0.177)	0.270** (0.124)	0.240* (0.133)
Ideology*per capita GDP	−0.064*** (0.017)	−0.082*** (0.021)	−0.030** (0.013)	−0.027* (0.014)
per capita GDP	0.528*** (0.046)	0.562*** (0.057)	0.385*** (0.054)	0.376*** (0.063)
Constraints on executive		−0.002 (0.002)		0.001** (0.000)
Presidential system		−0.091*** (0.018)		0.097*** (0.026)
Rural party in power		0.634*** (0.221)		0.446*** (0.144)
Constant	−4.444*** (0.408)	−4.687*** (0.508)	−3.328*** (0.513)	−3.265*** (0.576)
Observations	1261	1077	1261	1077
R^2	0.39	0.43	0.17	0.22
Number of countries	60	58	60	58
Country-fixed effects	No	No	Yes	Yes
Year-fixed effects	No	No	Yes	Yes

Robust standard errors in parentheses; * significant at 10%; ** significant at 5%; *** significant at 1%. The dependent variable is the relative rate of assistance (RRA) calculated as $((1+NRA_{ag})/(1+NRA_{nonag})-1)$, where NRA_{ag} is the nominal rate of assistance to tradable agricultural products and NRA_{nonag} is the nominal rate of assistance to tradable nonagricultural products. Ideology is coded as 1 for Right-wing governments, 2 for Centrist, and 3 for Left-Wing governments. We use the political ideology of the executive for Presidential systems; of the largest governing party in the parliament for parliamentary system and average of the Executive and largest party for mixed systems. Columns 1 and 2 present pooled OLS estimates; columns 3 and 4 present within-estimates with country and time-fixed effects.
Source: Authors' computations.

coefficient on the ideology variable is positive and significant, whereas the coefficient on the interaction of ideology with per capita income is negative and significant. The signs of the ideology term and its interaction with per capita income suggest that the intersectoral mobility of labor is quite low and so the immobile labor model is a better approximation to reality than the mobile labor model. Column 2 shows that this finding is robust to the addition of three political institution controls: Constraints on the executive, which captures checks and balances on the chief executive (higher in democracies); a dummy equal to 1 for Presidential systems; and a dummy equal to 1 if the ruling party can be classified as rural. Columns 3 and 4 present within-estimates, where again we see that political ideology influences agricultural protection. The signs of the estimated coefficients are compatible with the immobile labor scenario.

The coefficient of the ideology term divided by the absolute value of the coefficient of the interaction term gives us the critical per capita income at which the relationship changes sign. Per capita income is measured in natural logarithms, and the threshold is about 8.7 in column 1, which in levels is about $6,000. When we add country-fixed effects, we observe a decline in the magnitude of the coefficient estimates. However, the critical per capita income remains substantively unchanged in column 3 (equal to 9).

Table 11.4 presents regressions analyzing the effects of inequality. Columns 1–3 show pooled OLS estimates, whereas columns 4 and 5 present within-estimates. All columns use the income Gini coefficient as the measure of inequality, except column 2, which uses the land inequality measure from Li, Squire and Zou (1998). The estimated coefficient on the Gini coefficient is positive and significant, and its interaction with per capita income is negative and significant. As with political ideology, these signs are consistent with the immobile labor scenario. The threshold per capita income is only $3,000 in this case, except for column 2 (where the land Gini is used), where the threshold is even lower. The results hold for the within-estimates as well, with the critical per capita income rising to $3,500.

We next explore whether it is actually the relative size of agricultural employment that is driving these results. In Table 11.5, instead of per capita income, we use the share of agriculture in total employment. As expected from the first set of regressions, we now have the political ideology coefficient negative and significant. The coefficient of the interaction between political ideology and the share of agriculture in employment is positive and significant in column 1 (where no fixed effects are used) but insignificant in column 2 where country and year-fixed effects are used. When inequality is used in place of ideology in these regressions (columns 3, 4, and 5), the inequality variable is positive and significant, and the interaction of inequality with the share of agricultural employment is negative and significant, both in the absence and presence of country

Table 11.4. *Inequality and per capita GDP as determinants of RRAs*

	(1)	(2)	(3)	(4)	(5)
	RRA	RRA	RRA	RRA	RRA
Inequality	0.109***	0.054*	0.107***	0.049**	0.050**
	(0.020)	(0.029)	(0.021)	(0.023)	(0.023)
Inequality*per capita GDP	−0.014***	−0.008**	−0.014***	−0.006**	−0.006**
	(0.002)	(0.003)	(0.002)	(0.003)	(0.003)
per capita GDP	0.800***	0.792***	0.768***	0.484***	0.488***
	(0.084)	(0.237)	(0.088)	(0.110)	(0.111)
Constraints on executive			−0.004***		0.001
			(0.001)		(0.001)
Presidential system			−0.063**		0.037
			(0.025)		(0.028)
Rural party in power			0.068		0.205
			(0.187)		(0.227)
Constant	−6.308***	−6.091***	−6.031***	−3.680***	−3.944***
	(0.724)	(1.993)	(0.755)	(0.854)	(0.948)
Observations	450	43	441	450	441
R^2	0.46	0.67	0.46	0.31	0.30
Number of countries	62	43	62	62	62
Country-fixed effects	No	No	No	Yes	Yes
Year-fixed effects	No	No	No	Yes	Yes

Robust standard errors in parentheses; * significant at 10%; ** significant at 5%; *** significant at 1%. The dependent variable is the relative rate of assistance (RRA) calculated as $((1+NRA_{ag})/(1+NRA_{nonag})-1)$, where NRA_{ag} is the nominal rate of assistance to tradable agricultural products and NRA_{nonag} is the nominal rate of assistance to tradable nonagricultural products. Columns 1 and 2 present pooled OLS estimates; columns 3 and 4 present within-estimates with country and time-fixed effects. Column 2 uses Land Gini as the measure of inequality. All others use income Gini. *Source*: Authors' computations.

and year-fixed effects. In other words, these results hold in both cross-sectional and within-country, across-time variations in the data.

Lobbying and Agricultural Protection

As the employment share of agriculture goes down, agricultural workers and landowners will probably find it easier to organize, as a result of which protection to agriculture is likely to go up. In Table 11.6, the negative and

Table 11.5. *Ideology, inequality, and share of employment as determinants of RRAs*

	(1)	(2)	(3)	(4)	(5)
	RRA	RRA	RRA	RRA	RRA
Left-wing ideology	−0.119*** (0.040)	−0.036* (0.021)			
Ideology*share of agric. in emplt.	0.002** (0.001)	0.001 (0.001)			
Gini			−0.026*** (0.005)	−0.038*** (0.010)	−0.015** (0.007)
Gini* share of agriculture in emplt.			0.000*** (0.000)	0.002* (0.001)	0.000* (0.000)
share of agriculture in employment	−0.018*** (0.002)	−0.026*** (0.004)	−0.031*** (0.005)	−0.018*** (0.005)	−0.032*** (0.010)
Constraints on executive	−0.011*** (0.001)		−0.014 (0.016)	−0.055 (0.048)	0.009 (0.015)
Presidential system	−0.243*** (0.027)		−0.119*** (0.038)	−0.064 (0.074)	0.031 (0.040)
Rural party in power	0.784*** (0.282)		0.084 (0.240)	0.000 (0.000)	0.276 (0.271)
Constant	1.137*** (0.095)	0.749*** (0.108)	1.691*** (0.222)	2.065*** (0.480)	1.159*** (0.342)
Observations	645	645	284	27	284
R^2	0.25	0.31	0.37	0.63	0.33
Number of countries	49	49	50	27	50
Country-fixed effects	No	Yes	No	No	Yes
Year-fixed effects	No	Yes	No	No	Yes

Robust standard errors in parentheses; * significant at 10%; ** significant at 5%; *** significant at 1%. The dependent variable is the relative rate of assistance (RRA) calculated as $((1+NRA_{ag})/(1+NRA_{nonag})-1)$, where NRA_{ag} is the nominal rate of assistance to tradable agricultural products and NRA_{nonag} is the nominal rate of assistance to tradable nonagricultural products. Ideology is coded as 1 for Right-wing governments, 2 for Centrist, and 3 for Left-Wing governments. We use the political ideology of the executive for Presidential systems; of the largest governing party in the parliament for parliamentary system and average of the Executive and largest party for mixed systems. Columns 1, 3, and 4 present pooled OLS results; the rest present results with country and time-fixed effects. Column 4 uses Land Gini as the measure of inequality. Columns 3 and 5 use income Gini.
Source: Authors' computations.

Table 11.6. *Lobbying and RRAs*

	(1)	(2)	(3)	(4)
	RRA (all countries)	RRA (all countries)	RRA (OECD only)	RRA (OECD excl. Cairns group)
Employment in agriculture (% of total employment)	-0.913*** (0.134)	-2.712*** (0.406)	-2.991*** (0.821)	-3.423*** (0.894)
Agricultural productivity	0.069*** (0.021)	0.194*** (0.035)	0.261*** (0.082)	0.269*** (0.101)
Constraints on executive	-0.005* (0.003)	0.003* (0.001)	0.004 (0.003)	0.004 (0.003)
Presidential system	-0.134*** (0.022)	-0.005 (0.028)	0.020 (0.066)	0.023 (0.071)
Rural party in power	0.389*** (0.150)	0.385*** (0.095)	0.398*** (0.114)	0.405*** (0.121)
Constant	0.052 (0.198)	-0.908*** (0.330)	-1.577** (0.794)	-1.469 (0.967)
Observations	746	746	376	313
R^2	0.30	0.28	0.43	0.48
Number of countries	58	58	20	17
Country-fixed effects	No	Yes	Yes	Yes
Year-fixed effects	No	Yes	Yes	Yes

Robust standard errors in parentheses; * significant at 10%; ** significant at 5%; *** significant at 1%. Column 1 presents pooled OLS results; columns 2–4 present results with country and time-fixed effects. Columns 1 and 2 include all countries; column 3 includes only OECD countries; from which column 4 excludes the Cairns group of countries (Australia, Canada and New Zealand). *Source*: Authors' computations.

significant coefficient of the employment share of agriculture provides support for this hypothesis. This is true for all countries pooled together (column 1), when we restrict the sample to only OECD countries (column 2), and when we restrict the sample to OECD but exclude the Cairns group of countries.[10] We see that this variation is both cross-sectional as well within-country across time. The positive and significant coefficients of agricultural productivity in Table 11.6 provide support for the hypothesis that as agricultural productivity rises, lobbying becomes more beneficial,

---

[10] The Cairns countries are those who favor free trade and open market access in agriculture.

and we are likely to see more agricultural protection. The rise in the magnitude of the coefficient between columns 2 and 3 suggests that lobbying plays a more important role in rich OECD countries.

Revenue Motive for Agricultural Protection

In Table 11.7, the variable of interest is direct taxes as a percentage of total tax revenue. If the government has a well-developed tax infrastructure, it can raise revenue through direct taxes, and it can use some of this revenue to provide agricultural subsidies. In this case, there should be a complementarity between the government's ability to raise direct taxes and agricultural assistance. On the other hand, if the government is not able to raise direct tax revenues, it might have to resort to indirect taxation, which can take the form of import tariffs. If these tariffs are agricultural tariffs, then we might see some substitutability between direct taxes and agricultural assistance. Whether the ability to raise direct taxes negatively or positively affects agricultural assistance is therefore an empirical question. All but one of our regressions in Table 11.7 show a negative sign for the coefficient of direct taxes as a share of total tax revenues. This result holds both for nominal and relative rates of assistance to agriculture. For the latter, it is driven primarily by non-OECD countries.

CONCLUSION

Our main objective in this chapter is to identify the political economy drivers in the evolution of international trade policies with respect to agriculture. Understanding these determinants should not only help provide deeper insights into trade policy formulation in general, but also allow us to understand what makes agriculture a particularly contentious issue in recent trade talks.

We have set up a basic framework that allows us to put forth various testable hypotheses on the variation and evolution of agricultural protection. We find that both the political ideology of the government and the degree of inequality are important determinants of agricultural protection. Thus, both the political support function approach as well as the median-voter approach can be used in explaining the variation in agricultural protection across countries and within countries over time. The results are consistent with the predictions of a model that assumes that labor is specialized and sector-specific in nature. Some aspects of protection also seem to be consistent with predictions of a lobbying model in that agricultural protection

Table 11.7. *Revenue motive for agricultural assistance*

	(1) NRA	(2) NRA	(3) RRA	(4) RRA	(5) RRA (OECD only)	(6) RRA (non-OECD only)
Direct taxes (% of total taxes)	-0.002** (0.001)	-0.003** (0.001)	-0.002* (0.001)	-0.003** (0.001)	0.005 (0.009)	-0.004*** (0.001)
Revealed comp adv in agriculture		-0.047 (0.057)		-0.091 (0.057)	-0.182 (0.270)	-0.023 (0.051)
Constraints on executive		0.001*** (0.000)		0.001*** (0.000)	0.000 (0.000)	0.001** (0.000)
Presidential system		0.114*** (0.023)		0.172*** (0.027)	0.000 (0.000)	0.124*** (0.019)
Constant	0.223*** (0.055)	0.356*** (0.084)	0.132** (0.064)	0.285*** (0.069)	0.943* (0.477)	-0.049 (0.047)
Observations	554	301	531	285	100	185
Number of countries	64	50	64	49	19	30
R^2	0.13	0.14	0.13	0.14	0.51	0.34
Country-fixed effects	Yes	Yes	Yes	Yes	Yes	Yes
Year-fixed effects	Yes	Yes	Yes	Yes	Yes	Yes

Robust standard errors in parentheses; * significant at 10%; ** significant at 5%; *** significant at 1%.

The dependent variable in columns 1 and 2 is the nominal rate of assistance to agriculture. The dependent variable in columns 3–6 is the relative rate of assistance to agriculture (RRA) calculated as $((1+NRA_{ag})/(1+NRA_{nonag})-1)$, where NRA_{ag} is the nominal rate of assistance to tradable agricultural products and NRA_{nonag} is the nominal rate of assistance to tradable nonagricultural products. Direct taxes include income taxes, profits, and capital gains tax. Revealed comparative advantage in agriculture is defined as $(X-M)/(X+M)$, where X is exports and M is imports of agricultural products. All columns include country and time-fixed effects. Column 5 shows results with only OECD countries; column 6 shows results with only non-OECD countries.

Source: Authors' computations.

300

is negatively related to agricultural employment and positively related to agricultural productivity. Public finance aspects of assistance to agriculture also seem to be empirically important.

References

Anderson, K. (1992), "International Dimensions of the Political Economy of Distortionary Price and Trade Policies," pp. 290–310 in I. Goldin and L.A. Winters (eds.), *Open Economies: Structural Adjustment and Agriculture*, Cambridge and New York: Cambridge University Press.

(1995), "Lobbying Incentives and the Pattern of Protection in Rich and Poor Countries," *Economic Development and Cultural Change* 43(2): 401–23, January.

Anderson, K., Y. Hayami and Others (1986), *The Political Economy of Agricultural Protection: East Asia in International Perspective*, London: Allen and Unwin.

Anderson, K. and E. Valenzuela (2008), *Global Estimates of Distortions to Agricultural Incentives, 1955 to 2007*, database available at http://www.worldbank.org/agdistortions.

Anderson, K., M. Kurzweil, W. Martin, D. Sandri and E. Valenzuela (2008), "Measuring Distortions to Agricultural Incentives, Revisited," *World Trade Review* 7(4): 1–30.

Baldwin, R.E. (1985) *The Political Economy of U.S. Import Policy*, Cambridge MA: MIT Press.

Beck, T., G. Clarke, A. Groff and P. Keefer (2001), "New Tools in Comparative Political Economy: The Database of Political Institutions," *World Bank Economic Review* 15(1): 165–76.

Caves, R. (1976), "Economic Models of Political Choice: Canada's Tariff Structure," *Canadian Journal of Economics* 9(2): 278–300.

de Gorter, H. and J. Swinnen (2002), "Political Economy of Agricultural Policies,", pp. 2073–2123 in B. Gardner and G. Rausser (eds.), *Handbook of Agricultural Economics*, Volume 2, Amsterdam: Elsevier.

Dollar, D. and A. Kraay (2002), "Growth is Good for the Poor," *Journal of Economic Growth*, 7(3): 195–225.

Deininger, K. and L. Squire (1996), "A New Data Set Measuring Income Inequality," *World Bank Economic Review* 10(3): 565–91.

(1998), "New Ways of Looking at Old Issues: Inequality and Growth," *Journal of Development Economics* 57: 249–87.

Dutt, P. and D. Mitra (2002), "Endogenous Trade Policy Through Majority Voting: An Empirical Investigation," *Journal of International Economics* 58: 107–33.

(2005), "Political Ideology and Endogenous Trade Policy: An Empirical Investigation," *Review of Economics and Statistics* 87: 59–72.

(2006), "Labor versus Capital in Trade-Policy: The Role of Ideology and Inequality," *Journal of International Economics* 69(2): 310–20.

Feenstra, R. and J. Bhagwati (1982), "Tariff Seeking and the Efficient Tariff," in J. Bhagwati (ed.), *Import Competition and Response*, Chicago IL: University of Chicago Press.

Findlay, R. and S. Wellisz (1982), "Endogenous Tariffs, the Political Economy of Trade Restrictions, and Welfare," in J. Bhagwati (ed.), *Import Competition and Response*, Chicago IL: University of Chicago Press.

Gawande, K. and S. Bandyopadhyay (2000), "Is Protection for Sale? A Test of the Grossman–Helpman Theory of Endogenous Protection," *Review of Economics and Statistics* 82: 139–52.

Gawande, K. and B. Hoekman (2006), "Lobbying and Agricultural Policy in the United States," *International Organization* 60(3): 527–61.

Gawande, K. and P. Krishna (2003), "The Political Economy of Trade Policy: Empirical Approaches," in J. Harrigan and E.K. Choi (eds.), *Handbook of International Trade*, Malden MA: Basil Blackwell.

(2005), "Lobbying Competition over U.S. Trade Policy," Working Paper No. 11371, Cambridge, MA: NBER.

Gawande, K., P. Krishna and M. Olarreaga (2009), "What Governments Maximize and Why: The View from Trade," *International Organization* 63(3): 491–532, July.

Gawande, K., P. Krishna and M. Robbins (2006), "Foreign Lobbies and U.S. Trade Policy," *Review of Economics and Statistics* 88(3): 563–71.

Goldberg, P. and G. Maggi (1999), "Protection for Sale: An Empirical Investigation," *American Economic Review* 89: 1135–55.

Grossman, G.M. and E. Helpman (1994), "Protection for Sale," *American Economic Review* 84: 833–50.

Hai, W. (1991), *Agricultural Trade Protection and Economic Development*, unpublished Ph.D. Dissertation, University of California, Davis.

Hillman, A. (1989), *The Political Economy of Protection*, Chur: Harwood Academic Publishers.

Hiscox, M. (2001), *International Trade and Political Conflict: Commerce, Coalitions and Mobility*, Princeton NJ: Princeton University Press.

(2002), "Commerce, Coalitions, and Factor Mobility: Evidence From Congressional Votes on Trade Legislation," *American Political Science Review* 96: 593–608.

Honma, M. (1993), "Japan's Agricultural Policy and Protection Growth," pp. 95–114 in T. Ito and A. Krueger (eds.), *Trade and Protectionism*, Chicago: University of Chicago Press.

Li, H., L. Squire and H. Zou (1998), "Explaining International and Intertemporal Variations in Income Inequality," *Economic Journal* 108(446): 26–43.

Magee, S., W. Brock and L. Young (1989), *Black Hole Tariffs and Endogenous Policy Theory*, Cambridge and New York: Cambridge University Press.

Mansfield, E. and M. Busch (1995), "The Political Economy of Trade Barriers: A Cross-National Analysis," *International Organization* 49: 723–49.

Marshall, M.G., K. Jaggers and T.R. Gurr (2000), "Political Regime Characteristics and Transitions, 1800–2002," Polity IV Project, Center for International Development and Conflict Management, University of Maryland, College Park MD.

Marvel, H. and E. Ray (1983), "The Kennedy Round: Evidence on the Regulation of Trade in the US," *American Economic Review* 73(1): 190–7.

Mayer, W. (1984), "Endogenous Tariff Formation," *American Economic Review* 74: 970–85.

McCalman, P. (2004), "Protection for Sale and Trade Liberalization: An Empirical Investigation," *Review of International Economics* 12: 81–94.

Milner, H., and B. Judkins (2004), "Partisanship, Trade policy, and Globalization: Is There a Left–right Divide on Trade Policy?" *International Studies Quarterly* 48: 95–119.

Milner, H. and K. Kubota (2005), "Why the Move to Free Trade? Democracy and Trade Policy in the Developing Countries," *International Organization* 59: 107–43.

Mitra, D. (1999), "Endogenous Lobby Formation and Endogenous Protection: A Long Run Model of Trade Policy Determination," *American Economic Review* 89: 1116–34.

Mitra, D., D. Thomakos and M. Ulubasoglu (2002), "Protection for Sale in a Developing Country: Democracy vs. Dictatorship," *Review of Economics and Statistics* 84: 497–508.

Olper, A. (1998), "Political Economy Determinants of Agricultural Protection Levels in EU Member States: An Empirical Investigation," *European Review of Agricultural Economics* 25: 463–87.

(2007), "Land Inequality, Government Ideology and Agricultural Protection," *Food Policy* 32: 67–83.

Ray, E. (1981), "The Determinants of Tariff and Non-tariff Restriction in the United States," *Journal of Political Economy* 89: 105–21.

(1991), "Protection of Manufactures in the United States", in D. Greenaway (ed.), *Global Protectionism: Is The US Playing on a Level Field?* London: Macmillan.

Rodrik, D. (1986), "Tariffs, Subsidies and Welfare with Endogenous Policy," *Journal of International Economics* 21: 285–96.

(1995), "Political Economy of Trade Policy," in G. Grossman and K. Rogoff (eds.), *Handbook of International Economics*, vol. 3, Amsterdam: North-Holland.

Saunders, R. (1980), "The Political Economy of Effective Protection in Canada's Manufacturing Sector," *Canadian Journal of Economics* 13: 340–8.

Swinnen, J. (1994), "A Positive Theory of Agricultural Protection," *American Journal of Agricultural Economics* 76(1): 1–14.

Swinnen, J., A. Banerjee and H. de Gorter (2001), "Economic Development, Institutional Change and the Political Economy of Agricultural Protection: An Empirical Study of Belgium since the 19th Century," *Agricultural Economics* 26(1): 25–43.

Trefler, D. (1993), "Trade Liberalization and the Theory of Endogenous Protection," *Journal of Political Economy* 101: 138–60.

van Long, N. and N. Vousden (1991), "Protectionist Responses and Declining Industries," *Journal of International Economics* 30: 87–103.

World Bank (2007), *World Development Indicators 2007*, Washington DC: World Bank.

TWELVE

Agricultural Trade Interventions in Africa

Robert H. Bates and Steven Block

This chapter explores the political economy of agricultural trade protection in sub-Saharan Africa. It makes use of a new World Bank dataset of indicators of distortions to domestic prices of agricultural (and nonagricultural) commodities caused by government policies – trade taxes, nontariff trade barriers, subsidies, or currency distortions.[1] When greater than zero, the indicators suggest that government policies favor farming; when the relative rate of assistance is below zero, it suggests policies have an antiagricultural bias.

As indicated in Chapter 2, governments in Africa, like those elsewhere, have adopted less distorting/more neutral policies since the 1980s. Increasingly their policies impact farming and other industries in a less biased manner. However, policies in Africa continue to alter prices in ways that discriminate against farming, and more so than in other developing country regions.

In this chapter, we describe the levels of protection in our sample of twenty sub-Saharan African countries[2] and the manner in which they vary; and, drawing from the literature on the political economy of agriculture, we advance and test a series of explanations for the patterns we observe.

---

[1] Anderson and Valenzuela (2008), based on a methodology outlined in Anderson et al. (2008). See the Annex for specific definitions of these indicators.

[2] The sub-Saharan African countries in the sample are Benin (C), Burkina Faso (L), Cameroon (R,C), Chad (L), Cote d'Ivoire (C), Ethiopia (C,L), Ghana (C), Kenya (C), Madagascar (C), Mali (L), Mozambique (C), Nigeria (R,C), Senegal (C), South Africa (R,C), Sudan (L), Tanzania (C), Togo (C), Uganda (L), Zambia (R,L), and Zimbabwe (L). These countries account for no less than 90 percent of sub-Saharan Africa's population, GDP, farm households, and agricultural output. "C" indicates coastal; "L" indicates landlocked, and "R" indicates resource-rich. Note that for five of these countries (Benin,

PERTINENT FEATURES OF AFRICA

Agricultural policies in Africa vary substantially across the continent. In their recent study of Africa's economic performance in its first fifty years of independence, Ndulu et al. (2007) stress the importance of differentiating between countries whose economies are resource-rich,[3] landlocked, or coastal. These three different groups of economies behave as if possessing different production functions, they argue, and attempts to account for Africa's growth performance gain in explanatory power when taking this heterogeneity into account. The policies vary over time as well.

Figure 12.1 portrays the rate of protection of importable as opposed to exportable commodities, with negative numbers indicating a bias in favor

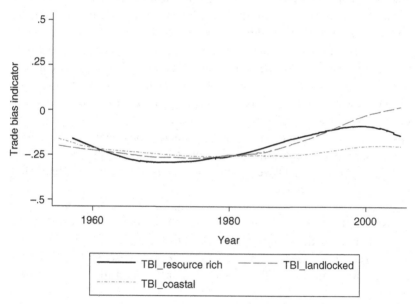

Figure 12.1. Trade Bias Index, Africa's resource-rich, landlocked, and coastal countries, 1955 to 2005.
Source: Based on national TBI estimates in Anderson and Valenzuela (2008).

Burkina Faso, Chad, Mali, and Togo), the data refer only to cotton. We include these countries only in our analyses of agricultural exportables and tradables.

[3] A country is classified as resource-rich if (i) starting in the initial year, current rents from energy, minerals, and forests exceed 5 percent of Gross National Income (GNI); (ii) a forward-moving average of these rents exceeds 10 percent of GNI; and (iii) the share of primary commodities in exports exceeds 20 percent for at least a five-year period following the initial year.

of import-competing crops and thus against agricultural trade. This bias reached a low point around 1980 and then subsequently lessened during the period of market-oriented reforms (the 1980s and 1990s). In recent years, those in landlocked countries have tended to exhibit the least bias against agricultural trade, whereas those in coastal states tend to exhibit the greatest.

The data in Figure 12.2 suggest that Africa's governments (with the exception of those in landlocked countries) have tended to protect food crops, raising the level of domestic prices above those prevailing in world markets, while taxing cash crops. The distortions introduced by government policies have eroded over time, with nominal rates of assistance for cash crops converging toward zero. Within the region, governments of resource-rich countries tend to provide the most favorable policy environment for producers of both food and cash crops,[4] while the governments of landlocked countries tended to impose the least.

Figure 12.3 illustrates the relative rates of policy support for agriculture versus nonagriculture (RRA, the relative rate of assistance to tradables), demonstrating that the bias against agriculture has abated since the 1980s but nonetheless remains. Here, too, the geographic distinctions are quite clear: Governments in all three types of the countries discriminate against agriculture, but those in landlocked countries consistently discriminate the most, whereas those that govern countries that are resource-rich discriminate the least, and governments in coastal economies consistently fall between these two extremes.

Figure 12.4 jointly summarizes the movement of these indicators. Constructed for each decade since the 1970s, the sequence of charts trace changes at the country level. Cells to the left of zero on the horizontal axis (TBI) reflect an antiagricultural trade bias, while cells below zero on the vertical axis (RRA) reflect an antiagriculture bias in sectoral policies.

The charts reveal that in the 1970s nearly every country in the sample implemented policies that were both antiagriculture and antitrade.[5] The dispersion of trade bias was relatively greater than the dispersion of relative rates of assistance to agricultural as opposed to nonagricultural commodities. Over time, however, the country averages tended to converge,

---

[4]   However, resource-rich countries still maintained a negative level of nominal assistance toward cash crops. See the Annex for details on the calculation of rates of assistance to food versus cash crops.

[5]   Exceptions include Kenya, which adopted policies favoring agricultural trade, and Nigeria, which maintained a slightly pro-agriculture stance until the current decade.

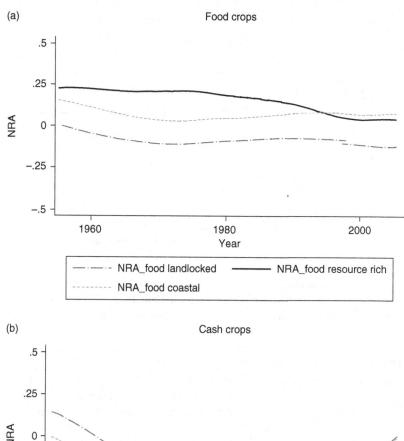

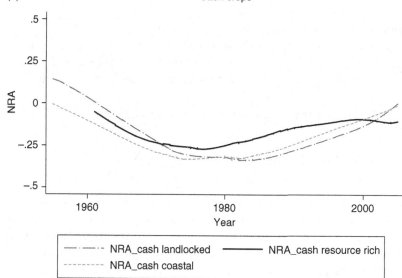

Figure 12.2. Nominal rates of assistance to food and cash crops, Africa's resource-rich, landlocked, and coastal countries, 1955 to 2005.

Source: Based on national NRA estimates in Anderson and Valenzuela (2008).

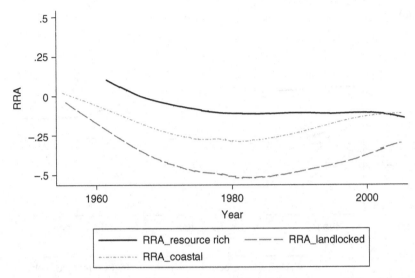

Figure 12.3. Relative rates of assistance to agricultural versus nonagricultural tradables, Africa's resource-rich, landlocked, and coastal countries, 1955 to 2005.
Source: Based on national RRA estimates in Anderson and Valenzuela (2008).

with the degree of convergence in trade bias exceeding that in the bias
against agriculture. Despite these changes, no countries emerged as both
pro-agriculture and pro-agricultural trade by the end of the sample period.
Indeed, most remained in the cell that captures biases against both agriculture and agricultural trade.

In the sections that follow, we seek to explain these patterns.

EXPLAINING POLICY CHOICES IN AFRICA: THEORETICAL CONSIDERATIONS

In accounting for variation in agricultural policies, researchers tend to
focus on the level of development, as signified by the degree of structural
transformation and corresponding differences in the level of per capita
income (Kuznets 1966; Chenery and Taylor 1968). When doing so, many
highlight the paradoxical position of agriculture in the political economy of development: When agriculture composes the single largest sector of the economy and farmers the single largest category in the labor
force, then governments tend to manipulate prices in ways that lower the
incomes of farmers; when, however, agriculture forms but a small portion

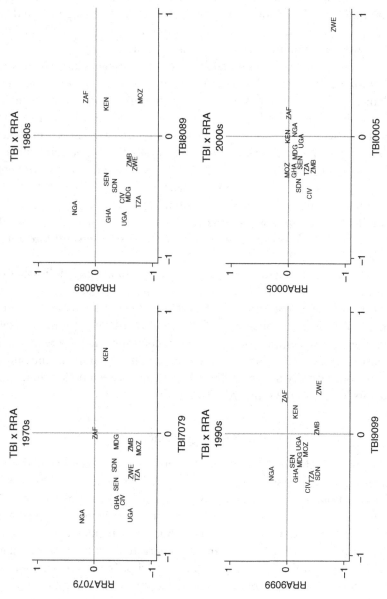

Figure 12.4. Relative rates of assistance and agricultural trade bias indexes, Africa, 1970 to 2005.

Source: Based on national RRA and TBI estimates in Anderson and Valenzuela (2008).

of the GDP and farming a miniscule portion of the labor force, then governments tend to adopt policies that favor the fortunes of farmers. As we commonly assume that political power tends to derive from income and numbers, the relationship between the level of development and the nature of government policy therefore poses a paradox – one that is fundamental in the political economy of development.

To begin to unravel this paradox, most turn to Engel's law, which holds that for a given rate of increase in consumer income, there will be a less than proportionate rate of increase in the portion of income spent on food. The empirical relationship between average income and the size of the agricultural sector conforms to this regularity. And so too would the reversal in government policy: When people are poor and spend a large portion of their incomes on food, they demand that governments protect their interests by adopting policies that lower the costs of food; as incomes improve and food forms a smaller portion of the consumption bundle, however, pressures for governments to lower food prices would tend to decline (Bates and Rogerson 1980; Anderson, Hayami and Others 1986; Lindert 1991).

Our sample is drawn from the lower portion of the global distribution of income and, as seen in the Annex, the within-sample variance is low. Our sample set of countries could therefore be expected to exhibit a common preference for policies that favor the interests of consumers. As we have seen, however, variation around this common tendency remains. By controlling the impact of per capita income, as it were, our data thus afford us the opportunity to explore the relationship between policy choice and factors left out of the standard account.

Our Arguments

One source of differences is variation in institutions. As changes in institutions mark the course of the recent history of Africa, they help to account for variations in policies over time. Differences in natural endowments constitute a second source of variation, with some being richly endowed and others not and many containing both rich regions and poor. Not being time varying, differences in these characteristics help to account for cross-country differences in agricultural policies. They do so, we argue, by influencing the politics of redistribution and revenue extraction, both of which shape the choice of public policies, particularly toward cash crops for export.

Political Institutions

By lobbying or voting, citizens affect the policy choices of governments. The voting size of the rural sector affects the way in which farmers can employ these channels.

Lobbying

When the rural population constitutes a large percentage of the national population, then agricultural production tends to lie in the hands of a large number of small producers, dispersed throughout the countryside. As no single producer can influence government policy, and as organizing so large and diverse a population is costly, the individuals' incentive to lobby is weak. In countries with large agricultural populations, agriculture should therefore constitute an ineffective interest group. In addition, when the portion of the population in agriculture is large, that which is urban is small. The number of nonrural consumers would then tend to be small and would be spatially concentrated.

Consumers should therefore hold a relative advantage as lobbyists in countries with large agricultural populations. And we therefore expect governments in countries with large agricultural sectors to adopt relatively adverse policies toward farming (Olson 1965, Bates 1981, Anderson 1995).

Voting

However, the very factors – size and dispersal – that render farmers weak lobbyists can render them powerful in electoral settings (Varshney 1995, Bates 2007a,b). Where representation is achieved through electoral channels, and where rural dwellers constitute a large segment of the voting population, politicians encounter powerful incentives to cater to the interests of farmers. In environments with electoral competition, politicians encounter electoral incentives that would impel them to resist the political pressures emanating from urban consumers.

Figure 12.5 captures the nature of political institutions in Africa. The 7-level scale depicted in this figure (described below) demonstrates the striking shift toward political competition over time. The index increases with the extent of electoral party competition (with level 7 being the most competitive). In the 1970s, over 80 percent of country-year observations fell at or below level 3 on this scale. In contrast, by 2000–2005, over 90 percent of observations were at level 6 or greater.

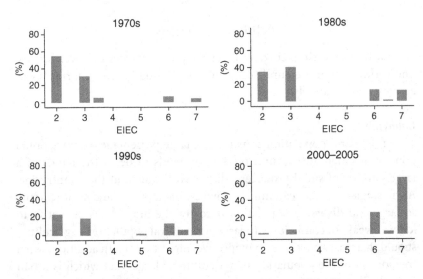

Figure 12.5. Index of Electoral Party Competition, Africa, 1970 to 2005.
Source: Webb et al. (2001, 2008).

In the sections that follow, we present statistical evidence relating the governments' choice of policy to (a) the size of the rural sector, as measured by the share of the population that dwells in rural areas, and (b) to the nature of political institutions and in particular to the presence or absence of party competition in the selection of the head of state.

Regional Redistribution

As noted by Ndulu and O'Connell (2007), a larger portion of Africa's economies are based on the extraction of natural resources than is the case in other regions of the world. One result is geographic inequality arising from differences in natural endowments. While in advanced industrial societies the politics of inequality takes the form of class conflict, in Africa it often assumes the form of conflict between regions.

Roughly 80 percent of Africa's economies possess within-country regions that appear significantly more prosperous than others,[6] and in roughly two-thirds of those cases these relatively prosperous regions include producers of cash crops. Examples include the coffee industry in the relatively wealthy Central Province of Kenya and the cocoa industry

---

[6] See, for example, the data gathered by Nordhaus (2006).

in the rich central districts of Ghana. Such regions may offer targets for those seeking resources to distribute to the poorer portions of the nation.

The impact of pressures for regional income redistribution depends, however, on the regional distribution of power. In Kenya, the long-serving head of state, Jomo Kenyatta, was from the agriculturally productive Central Province; when he was the president, he marshalled the power of the national government to defend the province's interests and resisted efforts to tax export agriculture (Bates 1989). In contrast, the political leadership in neighboring Tanzania came from the poor, semi-arid zones of the country and employed the power of the state to tax regions, such as Kilimanjaro, made wealthy from the production of cash crops. Policies toward cash crops thus depend not only on regional differences in income but also on the regional allocation of power.

The Revenue Imperative

For many nations in Africa, agriculture constitutes the largest portion of the economy and agricultural commodities figure prominently among the goods traded. And for most African countries, trade taxes constitute the single largest source of public revenue. Insofar as governments seek to raise revenues, they are therefore likely to tax agriculture. Only when other major sources of revenue – such as mineral or petroleum deposits – are available could one expect governments to deviate from this pattern. Governments endowed with ample revenue, moreover, are better able to fund programs that would enable them to lower food prices for consumers. We should, therefore, expect them to attempt to a greater degree than others to adopt policies designed to lower the domestic price of food crops.

Summary

Based on the preceding discussion, our expectations therefore are that:

- Agricultural taxation will decrease with declines in the rural population share.
- Electoral competition will mitigate the negative effects of rural population share.
- The presence of an economically privileged region, all else being equal, will reduce support (increase taxation) for cash crops but the

presence of a president from the privileged region will mitigate these effects.

- Resource-rich countries will impose less taxation on producers of agricultural exportables and simultaneously will impose less taxation on consumers of agricultural importables relative to those in international markets.

EXPLAINING POLICY CHOICES IN AFRICA: REGRESSION RESULTS

This section tests these hypotheses using both parametric and nonparametric methods. Of central interest are the correlates of the relative rates of assistance for agriculture versus nonagriculture (RRA) and the nominal rates of assistance for agricultural importables and exportables (Tables 12.1 to 12.3). Each table reports four sets of estimates, two (in columns 1 and 2) drawn from OLS models (with and without an interaction between rural population share and electoral competition); one drawn from a random effects model (column 3); and the last drawn from a system GMM model (column 4). The models include several control variables: per capita income (in logs), the extent of arable land, and the geographical situation of the country, with coastal location serving as the reference category.

Before commenting on the tests of our hypotheses, we first note the coefficients on the control variables. Those in Tables 12.1 and 12.2 confirm the absence of a relationship between the measure of per capita income, relative rates of assistance, and nominal rates of assistance for importables (most of which are food). In Table 12.3, by contrast, the coefficient on income is positive and significant in all models, indicating that, as will be discussed, the political economy of export crops differs from that of food crops. Consistent with Figure 12.3, the regressions in Table 12.1 indicate that landlocked countries substantially favor the interests of other sectors over those of agriculture. In addition, we find (in Table 12.2) that resource-rich countries tend to lower the domestic price of importables, that is, food, by comparison with the policy stance assumed in coastal economies. Viewing the share of land that is arable as a proxy for the overall importance of farming, the results in Tables 1 and 2 also suggest that the policy orientation of governments toward agriculture does indeed vary positively with the magnitude of this measure.

Table 12.1. *Determinants of relative rates of assistance, 1975 to 2004*

	(1)	(2)	(3)	(4)
	OLS	OLS	RE[a]	SYS-GMM[b]
Rural pop. share	−0.0002	−0.003	−0.003	−0.002
	(0.006)	(0.006)	(0.006)	(0.003)
Elecomp dummy	0.072	−0.414	−0.547	−0.475
	(0.052)	(0.298)	(0.268)**	(0.162)**
Log Real GDP	0.068	0.075	0.075	0.041
per cap	(0.070)	(0.073)	(0.065)	(0.040)
Landlocked	−0.263	−0.278	−0.285	−0.163
dummy	(0.118)**	(0.121)**	(0.120)**	(0.067)**
Resource rich	0.130	0.142	0.156	0.094
dummy	(0.098)	(0.102)	(0.105)	(0.062)
Arable land share	0.017	0.017	0.017	0.008
of total	(0.003)***	(0.003)***	(0.003)***	(0.002)***
Elecomp x rural		0.007	0.009	0.007
pop shr		(0.005)	(0.004)**	(0.003)**
RRA (t-1)				0.467
				(0.107)***
Constant	−0.934	−0.781	−0.737	−0.297
	(0.861)	(0.864)	(0.799)	(0.443)
Observations	375	375	375	373
R-squared	0.52	0.53	0.53	
Total Effect of:				
Rural pop. Share w/		0.004	0.006	0.005
comp. elections		(0.006)	(0.005)	(0.003)†
Comp. election, w/		−0.063	−0.100	−0.142
rural pop shr = 50%		(0.086)	(0.069)	(0.041)***
Comp. election, w/		0.182	0.213	0.090
rural pop shr = 85%		(0.105)*	(0.103)**	(0.063)

Robust standard errors (clustered by country) in parentheses.
* significant at 10%; ** significant at 5%; *** significant at 1%
† P = 0.113
[a] Random effects model
[b] One-step system GMM
Year Dummies not reported.
Source: Authors' calculations.

Table 12.2. *Determinants of NRAs for agricultural importables, 1975 to 2004*

	(1)	(2)	(3)	(4)
	OLS	OLS	RE[a]	SYS-GMM[b]
Rural pop. share	−0.016	−0.019	−0.017	−0.007
	(0.006)**	(0.007)**	(0.013)	(0.003)**
Elecomp dummy	0.198	−0.335	−0.438	−0.217
	(0.058)***	(0.541)	(0.560)	(0.277)
Log Real GDP per cap	−0.141	−0.133	−0.151	−0.054
	(0.100)	(0.105)	(0.121)	(0.038)
Landlocked dummy	−0.071	−0.086	−0.103	−0.032
	(0.123)	(0.128)	(0.166)	(0.055)
Resource rich dummy	−0.440	−0.426	−0.325	−0.120
	(0.116)***	(0.116)***	(0.184)*	(0.035)***
Arable land share of	0.034	0.034	0.027	0.008
total	(0.003)***	(0.003)***	(0.004)***	(0.002)***
Elecomp x rural		0.008	0.009	0.004
pop shr		(0.008)	(0.008)	(0.004)
NRA_ag importables				0.675
(t-1)				(0.087)***
Constant	2.102	2.269	2.285	0.834
	(1.096)*	(1.137)*	(1.736)	(0.428)*
Observations	375	375	375	374
R-squared	0.42	0.43	0.42	
Total effect of:				
Rural pop. Share w/		−0.011	−0.008	−0.003
comp. elections		(0.007)	(0.013)	(0.003)
Comp. election, w/		0.049	0.035	−0.0001
rural pop shr = 50%		(0.149)	(0.151)	(0.074)
Comp. election, w/		0.319	0.367	0.152
rural pop shr = 85%		(0.148)**	(0.163)**	(0.077)*

Robust standard errors (clustered by country) in parentheses.
* significant at 10%; ** significant at 5%; *** significant at 1%
[a] Random effects model
[b] One-step system GMM
Year Dummies not reported.
Source: Authors' calculations.

Table 12.3. *Determinants of NRAs for agricultural exportables, 1975 to 2004*

	(1)	(2)	(3)	(4)
	OLS	OLS	RE[a]	SYS-GMM[b]
Rural pop. share	0.007	0.006	−0.002	0.007
	(0.006)	(0.006)	(0.008)	(0.005)
Elecomp dummy	0.091	−0.092	−0.414	−0.109
	(0.059)	(0.411)	(0.392)	(0.334)
Log Real GDP per cap	0.270	0.273	0.227	0.268
	(0.085)***	(0.089)***	(0.094)**	(0.066)***
Landlocked dummy	−0.175	−0.181	−0.159	−0.178
	(0.087)*	(0.090)*	(0.094)*	(0.076)**
Resource rich dummy	0.116	0.121	0.005	0.142
	(0.113)	(0.117)	(0.151)	(0.118)
Arable land share of total	0.004	0.004	0.011	0.002
	(0.004)	(0.004)	(0.007)	(0.004)
Elecomp x rural pop shr		0.003	0.007	0.003
		(0.006)	(0.005)	(0.005)
NRA_ag exportables (t-1)				0.115
				(0.092)
Constant	−2.937	−2.879	−1.980	−2.714
	(0.959)***	(0.939)***	(1.205)	(0.627)***
Observations	375	375	375	374
R-squared	0.48	0.48	0.44	
Total Effect of:				
Rural pop. Share w/ comp. elections		0.008	0.005	0.009
		(0.006)	(0.008)	(0.005)†
Comp. election, w/ rural pop shr = 50%		0.040	−0.073	0.023
		(0.135)	(0.129)	(0.103)
Comp. election, w/ rural pop shr = 85%		0.133	0.165	0.116
		(0.098)	(0.099)*	(0.090)

Robust standard errors (clustered by country) in parentheses.

significant at 10%; ** significant at 5%; *** significant at 1%

† P = 0.113

[a] Random effects model

[b] One-step system GMM. Year Dummies not reported.

Source: Authors' calculations

Rural Population Share and Political Institutions

We have argued that collective action on the part of farmers is more difficult the greater their numbers, but that electoral competition transforms numbers into a political advantage. We thus expect government policies toward agriculture to be more adverse to the interests of producers the greater is the rural dwellers' share of the population, with this effect being conditional on the nature of the party system.

As an indicator of the country's party system, we employ a measure contrived by Ferree and Singh (2002) and subsequently amended and adopted by the World Bank for its Database of Political Institutions (Beck et al. 2001, 2008). The indicator (the Executive Index of Electoral Competitiveness, or EIEC) measures the level of competition that occurs during the executive selection process. To a greater degree than other measures (i.e., Gastil's political and civil liberties indices), the EIEC is based on observable characteristics rather than subjective judgments. Unlike the Polity measures, moreover, it is invertible: Given a score, an observer gains precise information regarding the political system. The indicator consists of seven levels as follows:

Level 1 – No executive exists.

Level 2 – Executive exists but was not elected.

Level 3 – Executive is elected, but was the sole candidate.

Level 4 – Executive is elected, and multiple candidates competed for the office.

Level 5 – Multiple parties were also able to contest the executive elections.

Level 6 – Candidates from more than one party competed in executive elections, but the President won more than 75 percent of the vote.

Level 7 – Candidates from more than one party competed in executive elections, but the President won less than 75 percent of the vote.

We deem a party system competitive when the EIEC score is greater than 6. Note that we omit all consideration of the "quality" of electoral competition, including whether elections have been deemed "free and fair."

As can be seen in the Annex, the mean share of the rural population in our sample is approximately 70 percent. The value of EIEC exceeded 6 in approximately 38 percent of country/year observations.

Estimation Strategy

Our generic specification is:

$$y_{it} = \alpha + \gamma_1 Elecomp_{it} + \gamma_2 Rurpopshare + \gamma_3 (Elecomp * Rurpopshare)_{it} \qquad (1)$$
$$+ X_{it}\beta + v_i + \epsilon_{it}$$

where y_{it} is one of our key policy indicators for country i in year t, *Rurpopshare* is the share of a country's population living in rural areas, X is a vector of the control variables from our baseline specification, and v_i captures unobserved time-invariant country-specific effects. The interaction term in equation (1) requires that we evaluate a linear combination of coefficients ($\gamma_1 + \gamma_3 * Rurpopshare$) in order to assess the impact of electoral competition (which we will evaluate at low and high levels of rural population share), and ($\gamma_2 + \gamma_3$) to assess the impact of rural population share when the electoral system is competitive. In selected cases, we also present semi-parametric results for key explanatory variables. For each left-hand side indicator, we begin by excluding the interaction term from equation (1) while still allowing the measures of rural population and electoral competition to enter separately.

In order to assess the robustness of our estimates, we employ a series of estimators to analyze this specification. We begin by employing OLS, initially constraining $\gamma_3 = 0$, then including the interaction term in our fully specified model.[7] We then exploit the panel structure of our data by employing two additional estimators. Most of the identifying variation lies in the cross-sectional dimension of the data: The "within" standard deviation in rural population share in our sample is only 3.6, as compared with the "between" variation of 10.7, relative to the mean of 70.6. As the fixed-effects estimator depends solely on within-country variation, we therefore employ a random effects estimator, a choice supported by the Hausman test. Lastly, given the tendency for hysteresis in policy choice, we also employ the system GMM dynamic panel estimator of Blundell and Bond (1998). Use of the GMM estimator helps alleviate concerns with endogeneity that might arise were rural population shares and the adoption of competitive electoral systems may depend on factors that influence the dependent variable as well, and that had been excluded from the model.

---

[7] All OLS estimates use robust standard errors, corrected for clustering at the country level.

Relative Rate of Assistance

Table 12.1 presents our results for RRA. As expected, the point estimate for the impact of rural population share in the absence of electoral competition is negative in all models and positive in the presence of electoral competition, although in no case is it statistically different from zero. Adding the interaction term permits a more nuanced analysis of the "shift" effect of party competition: At high levels of rural population share (85 percent, as compared with 50 percent),[8] in the OLS and RE models, electoral competition bears a positive and significant relationship with policy choices that favor the agricultural sector. While the coefficient for the GMM estimate does not significantly differ from 0, it is greater than the effect of party competition on policy choice at low levels of rural population share by a margin of 23 percent (P = 0.024), based on the GMM estimate.[9]

To probe these relationships more deeply, we relax that assumption of linearity and estimate semi-parametric (or "partially-linear") models of the form:

$$y_i = X_i\beta + g(Rurpopshare_i) + \epsilon_i \qquad (2)$$

where X includes all of the variables included above *except for* the rural population share and $g(.)$ is an unknown function relating the dependent variable to rural population share. We estimate this remaining non-parametric relationship for the subsamples with and without electoral competitiveness.

Figure 12.6 displays the semi-parametric relationship between RRA and rural population share while controlling for electoral competition. In the absence of competitive elections, relative assistance to agriculture declines rapidly as the rural population share increases above the sample mean. Competitive electoral systems appear to check the negative impact of larger rural populations.

Consistent with our hypotheses, we find in Table 12.2 that trade policy support for agricultural importables – largely consisting of food crops – declines as a function of rural population share. When the dummy variable for party competition enters without the interaction term (controlling

---

[8] Recall that the sample mean is roughly 75 percent.
[9] The bottom rows of each table describe "total effects." The total effect of rural population share with competitive elections (e.g., the partial derivative of the regression with respect to rural population share) asks whether the slope coefficient of rural population changes when there is party competition. Conversely, the total effect of party competition (e.g., the partial derivative of the regression with respect to party competition) asks whether the shift effect of party competition varies with the rural population share.

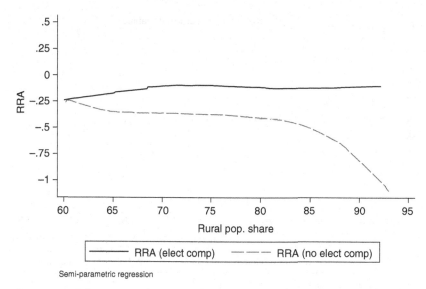

Figure 12.6. Relative rates of assistance by rural population share, Africa, 1970 to 2004.
Source: Authors' analysis, based on national RRA estimates in Anderson and Valenzuela (2008).

for average rural population share in column 1), it increases the nominal rate of assistance for agricultural importables by nearly 20 percent. When interacted directly with rural population share, the results reveal that the effect of electoral competition on nominal protection for agricultural importables depends critically on the level of rural population share. While not statistically different from zero at relatively low levels of rural population share, we find that electoral competition transforms high values of rural population share from a political liability into a political asset. At a high level of rural population share (85 percent), the estimates indicate a substantial and statistically significant benefit from electoral competition in all three models. Figure 12.7(a) captures graphically the relationship, while relaxing the assumption of linearity of the functional form.

Nominal Rate of Assistance to Agricultural Importables and Exportables

Table 12.3 suggests that rural population share bears no relationship with the level of nominal protection of agricultural exportables. As seen at the bottom of that table, at high levels of rural population share producers of agricultural exportables do benefit from electoral competition, but the impact is small and of little significance. Figure 12.7(b) confirms the first

Bates and Block

(a)   NRA for agricultural importables

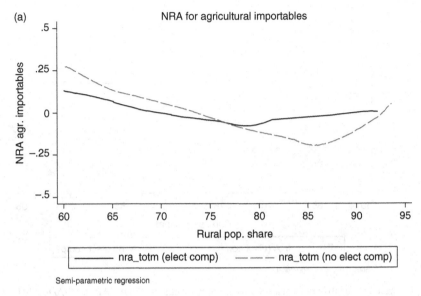

nra_totm (elect comp)   nra_totm (no elect comp)

Semi-parametric regression

(b)   NRA for agricultural exportables

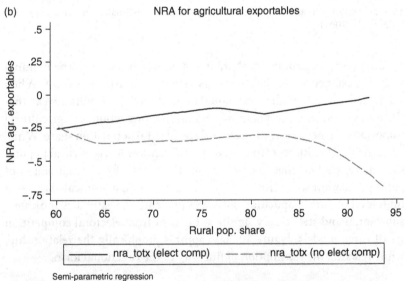

nra_totx (elect comp)   nra_totx (no elect comp)

Semi-parametric regression

Figure 12.7. Nominal rates of assistance by rural population share and trade focus, Africa, 1970 to 2004.

Source: Authors' calculations, based on national NRA estimates in Anderson and Valenzuela (2008).

finding that nominal assistance for agricultural exportables in the absence of competitive elections is not a function of rural population share, while suggesting that party competition can reduce the burdens based on agriculture when the rural share of the population is high.

In important respects, then, the findings for importables and exportables differ, which suggests that the political forces that shape government policies toward them differ as well. It is our argument, further elaborated in the following subsection, that the politics of cash crops is shaped by the forces of regionalism and revenue extraction to a greater degree than are the politics of food crops.

Regional Inequality and Presidential Origin

Data collected by the authors indicate that most African states contain rich regions and poor regions, and that in roughly 70 percent of the instances in which the country is marked by regional inequality, the region is prosperous in part because of the production of cash crops. Particularly in the case of cash crops, then, we would expect the politics of agricultural policy to be shaped by the politics of regional inequality, as poor regions seek to extract resources from rich, whereas rich regions seek to defend against their efforts.

To illustrate, consider the historic rivalries between the socialist systems of Tanzania and Ghana on the one hand and the "capitalist" systems of Kenya and Cote d'Ivoire on the other (Barkan 1994). In Tanzania, President Julius Nyerere drew his political support from the cities and the semi-arid lowlands; in Ghana, President Kwame Nkrumah drew his from the cities and the semi-arid north. Both seized a major portion of the revenues generated by the export of cash crops – coffee and cocoa, respectively – in order to finance projects designed to benefit their constituencies. In their neighboring states of Kenya and Cote d'Ivoire, by contrast, the Presidents' political constituencies lay in the richer regions. In Kenya, Jomo Kenyatta's constituency was the heartland of the coffee industry; in Cote d'Ivoire, Houphouet Boigny's lay within the cocoa zone. Rather than endorsing regional equality, Jomo Kenyatta and Houphouet Boigny employed the power of the state to defend the fortunes of their wealthy regions from those championing the fortunes of less well endowed.[10]

---

[10] Following the rapid rise of cocoa and coffee prices in the 1970s, Houphouet Boigny did launch a series of efforts to promote the fortunes of the north. Subsequent events suggest that the wisdom of these efforts as the diverging fortunes of the two regions exacerbated political tensions in Cote d'Ivoire.

The intuition imparted by these cases informs the models reported in Table 12.4. Our estimating equation in this case is similar to equation (1), but with the focus now on dummy variables indicating the existence of a privileged cash crop-producing region and indicating presidential origin from a privileged region:

$$y_{it} = \alpha + \gamma_1 cashregion_{it} + \gamma_2 pres\_origin_{it} + \gamma_3 (cashreg * pres\_origin)_{it} \\ + X_{it}\beta + \nu_i + \epsilon_{it} \tag{3}$$

where X includes all variables from the previous specifications.

In columns 1 and 2 of Table 12.4, the dependent variable is an indicator of relative policy support for cash versus food crops; positive values indicate relatively greater support for cash crops and negative values indicate a bias against cash crops in favor of food crops.[11] Both coefficients are negative, although only the first is statistically significant. When the president is from the privileged region, however, then the support for cash crops rises; the coefficients on the respective indicator are positive and significant. And as seen in the last row of columns 1 and 2, when the privileged region produces cash crops and the president is from that region, the coefficients are again positive and significant.[12]

In columns 3 to 6 of Table 12.4, we explore the correlates of the respective components of the CFBI index. In columns 3 and 4, the dependent variable is the nominal rate of assistance for cash crops, whereas in columns 5 and 6, it is the nominal rate of assistance for food crops. For each dependent variable, we report estimates based on OLS and GMM models, the latter to enable us to control for the impact of hysteresis in policy choice.

The coefficients in columns 3 to 6 of Table 12.4 reconfirm that the politics surrounding cash crops differ from those surrounding food crops. For food crops (columns 5 and 6), the larger the share of the population in agriculture, the greater the tendency of the governments to intervene in ways that lower domestic prices relative to those prevailing in global markets. In addition, governments tend to alter this policy when they must secure electoral majorities in order to secure power. Neither tendency characterizes the treatment of cash crops, however (columns 3 and 4). Rather, policies toward cash crops appear to be shaped by the politics

---

[11] See the Annex for the specific definition of this "cash-food bias indicator (CFBI)."

[12] The bottom row of Table 4 provides the partial derivative of the regression with respect to the dummy variable indicating that the president is from a privileged region. The question addressed in the last row is thus whether the shift effect of presidential origin differs when there is a privileged cash crop-producing region.

Table 12.4. *The role of a privileged cash crop region and presidential origin on protection of cash versus food crop protection, 1975 to 2004*

	(1)	(2)	(3)	(4)	(5)	(6)
	Dep Var: CFBI		Dep Var: NRA_cashcrops		Dep Var: NRA_foodcrops	
	OLS	SYS–GMM	OLS	SYS–GMM	OLS	SYS–GMM
Cash region	−0.255	−0.096	−0.218	−0.047	−0.021	−0.014
	(0.137)*	(0.058)	(0.078)**	(0.023)*	(0.078)	(0.043)
Pres. from privileged region	0.289	0.143	0.133	0.163	−0.087	0.008
	(0.159)*	(0.069)*	(0.110)	(0.029)***	(0.149)	(0.089)
Cash x pres from privileged region	−0.029	−0.025	−0.013	−0.126	0.085	−0.004
	(0.158)	(0.072)	(0.118)	(0.030)***	(0.204)	(0.122)
Rural pop. share	0.034	0.013	0.010	0.003	−0.019	−0.011
	(0.011)**	(0.006)**	(0.007)	(0.002)*	(0.006)***	(0.003)***
Comp. elections	−0.078	−0.066	0.040	0.002	0.111	0.081
	(0.074)	(0.041)	(0.074)	(0.025)	(0.039)**	(0.020)***
Log real GDP per cap.	0.377	0.146	0.116	0.024	−0.222	−0.134
	(0.206)*	(0.078)*	(0.156)	(0.035)	(0.074)**	(0.047)**
Landlocked dummy	−0.048	0.002	−0.088	−0.016	−0.051	−0.039
	(0.157)	(0.063)	(0.121)	(0.026)	(0.103)	(0.056)
Resource-rich dummy	0.571	0.229	0.021	−0.012	−0.491	−0.297
	(0.153)***	(0.087)**	(0.073)	(0.018)	(0.121)***	(0.057)***
Arable land shr of total	−0.026	−0.010	−0.000	0.001	0.026	0.015
	(0.005)***	(0.004)**	(0.003)	(0.001)	(0.006)***	(0.002)***
Lagged dep. var.		0.570		0.727		0.398
		(0.054)***		(0.062)***		(0.059)***
Constant	−5.414	−1.970	−1.981	−0.445	2.838	1.533
	(2.081)**	(0.809)**	(1.498)	(0.311)	(0.866)***	(0.478)***
Observations	249	247	249	248	249	247
R-squared	0.43		0.30		0.35	
Total effect of:						
Pres from prv if there is cash prv region	0.260	0.118	0.120	0.038	−0.001	0.003
	(0.110)**	(0.045)**	(0.083)	(0.020)*	(0.096)	(0.050)

Robust standard errors (clustered by country) in parentheses.
* significant at 10%; ** significant at 5%; *** significant at 1%
Year dummies not reported.
Source: Authors' calculations.

of regional inequality. In states in which cash crops are grown in "privileged regions," the government intervenes in ways that lower the incomes of farmers. The bias is reversed, however, when the President is from that region (as seen in the evaluation of the partial derivative in the last row of columns 3 and 4).

Revenue Imperative

Policies toward agriculture are also affected by the manner in which governments secure their revenues. Governments in Africa have long employed marketing boards and other instruments to extract revenues from the exports of cash crops; and they have expended revenues in efforts to accommodate the interests of domestic consumers of food crops (Bates 1981, Krueger, Schiff and Valdés 1991).

The coefficients on "cash region" in Table 12.4 are negative and significant in most models (columns 1–4). While consistent with a theory of revenue generation, these findings could also indicate efforts at regional redistribution. The coefficients on the "resource rich" dummy variable are less ambiguous. They suggest that governments with alternative sources of revenues do not differentially tax cash crops (see columns 3 and 4), but tend to favor them relative to food crops (columns 1 and 2) by conferring substantial subsidies on the consumers of food (columns 5 and 6).

While we might expect governments with additional sources of revenue to reduce the pressures they place on agriculture, the results thus suggest the contrary. As seen in columns 3 and 4 of Table 12.4, governments from resource-rich economies treat export agriculture no differently than do those in the coastal economies lacking such resources. And, as seen in columns 5 and 6, they adopt policies that lower the domestic prices for food crops. Governments that are wealthier because of presiding over economies abundantly endowed with natural resources are thus not inclined to reduce the burdens they place on farmers. Note that our data do not allow us to exclude an interpretation that treats governments as agencies of social welfare. If governments seek food security, the data might suggest those that are better endowed – that is, resource-rich – spend more on achieving food security. They may therefore confer subsidies on consumers. Without knowing the actual instruments employed, and whether they lower or increase the profits of farmers while lowering prices for consumers, we cannot discriminate between this interpretation and our own.

CONCLUSION

In this Chapter, we have explored patterns of variation in the content of agricultural policies in Africa. We have looked at the impact of the government's need for revenues, the incentives for farmers to lobby, and their capacity to affect electoral outcomes. We have also explored the political impact of regional inequality, especially insofar as it is generated by cash crop production. These factors operate in ways that deepen our appreciation of the political roots of agricultural policies.

Specifically, the implications we can draw from the above results are as follows:

- Policies toward agriculture are often the bi-product of other political concerns, so analysts should take into account the broader political setting when addressing agricultural policies.
- While policy analysts should continue to focus on normative and welfare issues, they should pay close attention as well to the incentives faced by policy makers.
- Precisely because they shape the incentives faced by politicians, institutions matter.
- The prospects for policy reform are greater in poor democracies than they are in poor countries that lack competitive elections.

References

Anderson, K. (1995), "Lobbying Incentives and the Pattern of Protection in Rich and Poor Countries," *Economic Development and Cultural Change* 43(2): 401–23.

Anderson, K., Y. Hayami and Others (1986), *The Political Economy of Agricultural Production: East Asia in International Perspective*, London: Allen and Unwin.

Anderson, K., M. Kurzweil, W. Martin, D. Sandri and E. Valenzuela (2008), "Measuring Distortions to Agricultural Incentives, Revisited," *World Trade Review* 7(4): 1–30.

Anderson, K., and E. Valenzuela (2008), *Estimates of Distortions to Agricultural Incentives, 1955 to 2007*, core database at http://www.worldbank.org/agdistortions

Barkan, J.D. (1994), *Beyond Capitalism vs Socialism in Kenya and Tanzania*, Boulder CO: Lynne Rienner.

Bates, R. (2007a), "Domestic Interests and Control Regimes," pp. 175–201 in B. Ndulu, P. Collier, R. Bates and S. O'Connell (eds.), *The Political Economy of Economic Growth in Africa, 1960–2000*, Cambridge: Cambridge University Press.

(2007b), "Political Reform," pp. 348–90 in B. Ndulu, P. Collier, R. H. Bates and S. O'Connell (eds.), *The Political Economy of African Economic Growth, 1960–2000*, Cambridge: Cambridge University Press.

Bates, R.H. (1981), *Markets and States in Tropical Africa*, Berkeley and Los Angeles: University of California Press.

(1989), *Beyond the Miracle of the Market*, Cambridge: Cambridge University Press.

Bates, R.H. and W.P. Rogerson (1980), "Agriculture in Development: A Coalitional Analysis," *Public Choice* 35(5): 513–28.

Beck, T., G. Clarke, A. Groff, P. Keefer, and P. Walsh (2001), "New Tools in Comparative Political Economy: The Database of Political Institutions," *World Bank Economic Review* 15: 165–76.

Beck, T., P.E. Keefer and G.R. Clarke (2008), *Database of Political Institutions*, accessible at http://go.worldbank.org/2EAGGLRZ40

Blundell, R. and S. Bond (1998), "Initial Conditions and Moment Restrictions in Dynamic Panel Data Models," *Journal of Econometrics* 87: 115–43.

Chenery, H.B. and L.J. Taylor (1968), "Development Patterns: Among Countries and Over Time," *Review of Economics and Statistics* 50(4): 391–416.

Ferree, K. and S. Singh (2002), "Political Institutions and Economic Growth in Africa: 1970–1995," in S. Chan and J. Scarritt (eds.), *Coping with Globalization: Cross-National Patterns in Domestic Governance and Policy*, Boulder CO: Frank Cass.

Krueger, A.O., M. Schiff and A. Valdés (eds.) (1991), *The Political Economy of Agricultural Pricing Policy, Volume 1: Latin America, Volume 2: Asia, and Volume 3: Africa and the Mediterranean*, Baltimore: Johns Hopkins University Press for the World Bank.

Kuznets, S. (1966), *Modern Economic Growth*, New Haven and London: Yale University Press.

Lindert, P. (1991), "Historical Patterns of Agricultural Policy," pp. 29–83 in P. Timmer (ed.), *Agriculture and the State*, Ithaca NY: Cornell University Press.

Ndulu, B., P. Collier, R. Bates and S. O'Connell (eds.) (2007), *The Political Economy of Economic Growth in Africa, 1960–2000*, 2 volumes, Cambridge: Cambridge University Press.

Ndulu, B.J. and S.A. O'Connell (2007), "Policy Plus: African Growth Performance 1960–2000," pp. 3–75 in B.J. Ndulu, P. Collier, R.H. Bates and S. O'Connell (eds.), *The Political Economy of Economic Growth in Africa, 1960–2000*, Cambridge: Cambridge University Press.

Nordhaus, W. (2006), *The G-Econ Database on Gridded Output: Methods and Data*, Yale University, New Haven. Available at http://gecon.yale.edu/gecon_data_%20 051206.pdf

Olson, M. (1965), *The Logic of Collective Action*, Cambridge MA: Harvard University Press.

Varshney, A. (1995), *Democracy, Development and the Countryside*, Cambridge: Cambridge University Press.

World Bank (2007), *World Development Indicators 2007*, Washington DC: World Bank.

ANNEX 12.1: POLICY INDICATORS AND OTHER VARIABLES USED

The principal indicators of trade interventions that we examine in this chapter draw on the World Bank's new Database of Agricultural Distortions (see Anderson and Valenzuela 2008 and, for the methodology behind it, Anderson et al. 2008). We propose models to explain agricultural distortions as indicated by nominal rates of assistance to agricultural tradables relative to nonagricultural tradables (the relative rate of assistance), as well as the nominal rates of assistance to agricultural importables and agricultural exportables (and the ratio derived from them, known as the Trade Bias Index).

For each commodity aggregate (x), the nominal rate of assistance when an ad valorem tariff is the sole intervention is calculated as:

$$(1) \quad NRA\_x = \frac{E \times P (1+t_m) - E \times P}{E \times P} = t_m$$

where t_m is tariff rate, E is the nominal exchange rate, and P is the dollar-denominated world price of the commodity. Anderson et al. (2008) provide a detailed discussion of how this basic formula is modified to incorporate additional distortions, such as taxes and subsidies on domestic production of the relevant commodities.

We also examine key ratios among these indicators. The relative rate of assistance captures the relative support given to agricultural versus nonagricultural tradables:

$$(2) \quad RRA = \left[\frac{1 + NRAag^t}{1 + NRAnonag^t} - 1 \right]$$

Thus, when agriculture is relatively favored (disfavored) by trade interventions in agriculture versus nonagriculture, the RRA is greater (less) than zero. Similarly, Anderson et al. (2008) provide an indicator of trade bias within agriculture by comparing the relative assistance to exportables versus importables (the trade bias index):

$$(3) \quad TBI = \left[\frac{1 + NRAag_x}{1 + NRAag_m} - 1 \right]$$

The TBI is negative when interventions are relatively unfavorable to agricultural exportables (interpreted as an antitrade bias).

Our analysis also makes reference to nominal rates of assistance to food crops and cash crops. To construct these aggregates, we use the nominal rates of assistance calculated by the World Bank dataset, weighting within each category by the share in the value of production of each commodity within that category. Our food crop aggregate includes cassava, maize, millet, tubers, sorghum, wheat, rice, and yams. Our cash crop aggregate includes cotton, cocoa, coffee, nuts, sugar, tobacco, and tea. Analogous to the TBI, we calculate a "cash-food bias index" (CFBI):

$$(4) \quad CFBI = \left[\frac{1 + NRA\,cashcrops}{1 + NRA\,foodcrops} - 1 \right]$$

As in the previous cases, this indicator is greater (less) than zero when cash crops are favored (disfavored) relative to food crops by trade policy interventions.

The various variables used in our analysis and their sources are as follows:

Variable	Units	Mean	Standard deviation	Source
NRA	Prop'n			Anderson and Valenzuela (2008)
___agricultural tradables		−0.148	0.275	
___non-ag tradables		0.148	0.160	
___agricultural importables		0.073	0.412	
___agricultural exportables		−0.255	0.280	
___foodcrops		−0.048	0.294	
___cashcrops		−0.288	0.339	
RRA	Prop'n	−0.198	0.276	Anderson and Valenzuela (2008)
Antitrade bias	Prop'n	−0.226	0.370	Anderson and Valenzuela (2008)
Competitive	0/1	0.317	0.466	Ferree and Singh (2002)
Elections				Beck et al. (2001, 2008).
Rural population share	Prop'n	0.756	0.126	World Bank (2007)

Variable	Units	Mean	Standard deviation	Source
Log real GDP per capita (constant 2000 US dollars)		7.090	0.610	World Bank (2007)
Landlocked	0/1	0.362	0.481	Ndulu et al. (2007)
Coastal	0/1	0.538	0.499	Ndulu et al. (2007)
Resource rich	0/1	0.176	0.381	Ndulu and O'Connell (2007)
Arable land share	Prop'n	0.11	0.092	World Bank (2007)
Cashcrop privileged region	0/1	0.723	0.448	Bates (2007)
President from privileged region	0/1	0.465	0.500	Bates (2007)

THIRTEEN

Trade Agreements and Trade Barrier Volatility

Olivier Cadot, Marcelo Olarreaga, and Jeanne Tschopp[1]

The economic analysis of of the politics of Regional Trade Agreements (RTAs) has largely focused so far on how they affect the *level* of trade distortions. On that count, the verdict is still out: Whereas early political economists held a dim view of their benefits (e.g., Grossman and Helpman 1995 showed that politically feasible RTAs were the most trade-diverting), recent papers (e.g., Ornelas 2005) have taken a more nuanced view, showing that RTAs can release trade-liberalizing forces. However, as noted by Braumoeller (2006), institutional arrangements like RTAs can equally importantly affect the volatility of trade barriers, and that aspect has been largely overlooked (with a few notable exceptions discussed below). We explore empirically here whether RTAs have reduced the volatility of agricultural trade protection rates, using the World Bank's new database on agricultural distortions (Anderson and Valenzuela 2008).

The issue of whether regionalism has dampened the volatility of agricultural trade restrictions is an important one. Volatility in food prices is more likely to trigger riots than volatility in the price of, say, shirts or home appliances. Indeed, Anderson (2009, Ch. 1) shows that border measures have been varied systematically by Asian countries to dampen the volatility of the domestic price of rice, a particularly sensitive commodity in that region. If changes in the level of border measures were used only to insulate domestic markets against terms-of-trade volatility, they could be justified on insurance grounds (Rodrik 1998). But they are also likely

[1] The authors are grateful for helpful comments from Jean Imbs, Jaime de Melo, Pascal St-Amour, and participants at the World Bank conference on Political Economy of Distortions to Agricultural Incentives held in Washington, DC in May 2008, the Geneva Trade and Development Workshop in September 2008, and the University of Lausanne's Doctoral Research Days for support from the Swiss Network for International Studies in Geneva (SNIS).

to have an "autonomous" discretionary component driven by the vagaries of local political processes. This discretionary policy volatility is likely to be welfare-reducing, because the welfare costs of distortions rise with the square of the wedge between domestic and world prices. It may also harm investment and growth if it creates an atmosphere of policy uncertainty (Sudsawasad and Moore 2006). If RTAs have the effect of reducing it through a commitment effect (whether based on rules-versus-discretion or strategic delegation), this is an important "nontraditional" argument in their favor, using the terminology of Fernandez and Portes (1998).

Whether volatility in protection rates is reduced by international institutions has been explored empirically in two recent papers: Rose (2004) on the WTO and Mansfield and Reinhardt (2008) on RTAs. Both papers use the volatility of trade flows (rather than protection rates) as the variable of interest and are based on variants of the gravity equation.

Rose (2004) starts from the observation that one of the stated goals of the multilateral trading system is to enhance the stability and predictability of the environment in which traders operate. The WTO's website, for instance, states that "just as important as freer trade – perhaps more important – are other principles of the WTO system. For example: non-discrimination, and making sure the conditions for trade are stable, predictable and transparent."[2] There are many mechanisms through which WTO rules could make the policy environment of WTO members more stable. For instance, binding tariffs reduces the scope for manipulating them. However, tariffs have been bound by developing countries at levels substantially above those applied: China bound its tariffs on imported agricultural goods at an average level of 16.5 percent even though the Nominal Rate of Assistance (NRA) that it applied at the time of its accession was only 7.3 percent; likewise, India, Pakistan, and Bangladesh bound their tariffs on agricultural imports at 114, 96, and 189 percent, respectively, against NRAs of 34, 4, and 6 percent (Anderson 2009). Similar arguments can be made about other aspects of WTO rules and about the effectiveness of its dispute-resolution system. Thus, whether the disciplines imposed by the multilateral trading system are sufficient to dampen volatility in trade protection rates – in agriculture or in other sectors – is an empirical question.

Rose's empirical strategy consists of regressing a measure of the long-term volatility of one-way bilateral trade flows (their coefficient of variation

---

[2] http://www.wto.org/english/thewto_e/whatis_e/10mis_e/10m02_e.htm, quoted in Rose (2004, p. 1).

over two successive twenty-five-year periods) on period averages of standard gravity regressors, as well as two binary variables marking WTO membership of the importer and exporter. The exercise can be thought of as a treatment-effect estimation with a treatment of variable intensity (zero, one, or two countries in the pair being "treated" by WTO membership). Using a variety of specifications (importer and exporter fixed effects, country-pair fixed effects, and so on), Rose consistently finds that WTO membership fails to reduce the volatility of trade flows, concluding that the multilateral trading system's disciplines are simply not strong enough to have a statistically traceable effect. The variety of specifications yielding the same negative answer makes it unlikely that Rose's result is merely a type-II error. However, the exercise highlights two difficulties: First, using the second moment of a time series as the dependent variable requires long series with lots of variation, especially if one looks at long-term volatility; second, as often in treatment-effect estimation, the treatment is here likely to be endogenous (since one of the stated purposes of the WTO is precisely to reduce trade protection volatility); at the same time, it is not immediately obvious what would be the right instrumentation strategy for something like WTO membership.

Mansfield and Reinhardt (2008) ask a similar question about regionalism, noting that the stated objective of a number of preferential agreements is to enhance security in market access, in accordance with Fernandez and Portes's "insurance" argument. As Abbott (2000) notes, RTAs are part of a general "trend toward higher levels of precision, obligation, and delegation in international trade that has been ongoing since the adoption of the General Agreement on Tariffs and Trade (GATT) in 1947" (Abbott 2000, p. 519). Precision, obligation, and delegation should all contribute to reducing discretionary volatility in border protection. Indeed, Abbott notes that "in regard to NAFTA, Canada insisted on adding precision to rules of origin and transformation with respect to automobiles and parts, because imprecise rules of CUSFTA had been interpreted by the United States to the detriment of Japanese investors in Canada. This U.S. interpretation created substantial uncertainty among prospective Japanese investors" (Abbott 2000, p. 528).

It is even more difficult to assess empirically the ability of RTAs to reduce discretionary volatility than in the case of WTO membership, because RTAs are diverse in nature and their effects can be asymmetric across their own member states. As to heterogeneity, Abbott shows in his detailed comparison of NAFTA and the European Union that the EU relied heavily on delegation to supranational institutions (the European

Commission and the European Court of Justice) to give substance to an initial text (the Treaty of Rome) that was imprecise. By contrast, NAFTA relies very little on delegation to supranational institutions, except in the areas of investment (where private agents can challenge the governments of partner countries at the World Bank's arbitration court, the ICSID) and antidumping. The reason for the EU's heavy reliance on delegation is that it was, at the outset, a political project meant to lead to political integration, whereas NAFTA never had that goal, and the U.S. Congress would have resisted any infringement on its sovereignty in legislative matters. However, the NAFTA treaty is very precise in its wording by the standards of preferential trade agreements. Thus the commitment mechanisms of NAFTA and the EU are different: rules versus discretion for the former, delegation for the latter.

As to asymmetry in the effects of RTAs, taking again the example of NAFTA, even though Article VI of the U.S. Constitution states that treaties are the supreme law of the land, the U.S. Congress "expressly denied the possibility of domestic direct effect for NAFTA in the legislation approving and implementing the agreement, and it may not be relied on as a source of rights in U.S. law" (Abbott 2000, p. 538). Thus NAFTA cannot be invoked directly by an importer to challenge a Customs decision; the legal basis of the challenge must be U.S. domestic law (presumably put in accordance with the NAFTA treaty though). By contrast, under the Mexican Constitution, the NAFTA Treaty has force of law and can be invoked directly in courts. This stronger commitment no doubt reflects the Mexican government's desire to use NAFTA to improve the country's image in terms of legal stability in order to encourage foreign direct investment. According to Whalley (1998), Mexican negotiators were mainly concerned with locking in domestic policy reforms rather than a bilateral exchange of concessions during NAFTA negotiations.

These two examples highlight both the potential for RTAs to act as commitment mechanisms (suggesting there should be an effect to look for) and the potential heterogeneity of their effect on domestic policy volatility (suggesting that the effect may be difficult to identify). Mansfield and Reinhardt (2008) explore empirically whether any effect is statistically traceable by estimating a system of two equations. In the first, the dependent variable is the level of bilateral trade in a standard gravity equation augmented, on the right-hand side, by the variance of the flows (that is, the equation is a particular kind of heteroskedastic regression where the variance of the dependent variable is among the regressors) and by "treatment variables" marking whether a bilateral trade flow is ruled by a preferential agreement or not and whether the trading countries are WTO members or not. In the second equation, the variance of trade flows is regressed on a number of control variables and the same treatment variables. Positive coefficients on the treatment variables in the first equation indicate that the treatments (RTAs and WTO membership) raise the level of trade conditional on its volatility; a negative coefficient on the variance indicates that volatility is, in itself, associated, *ceteris paribus*, with less trade (what the authors call a "volatility tax"). Negative coefficients on the treatment variables in the second equation indicate that they reduce the volatility of trade flows.

In contrast to Rose, Mansfield and Reinhardt find that both RTAs and WTO membership are associated with less volatility and with higher levels of trade flows, and that reduced volatility is itself associated with higher trade flows, giving a double bang on levels (directly and indirectly via reduced volatility). Because the thought experiences of Rose and Mansfield and Reinhardt are different, there is no immediate explanation for their conflicting results. One obvious difference is that the latter use short-term measures of volatility (year-on-year absolute values of log-differences or variances), whereas Rose used a very long-run approach (measured over a twenty-five-year span). There are other differences as well. By contrast, one common feature of these two studies is that neither treats the potential endogeneity of WTO and RTA membership, while both recognize – indeed, emphasize – that stability and predictability are among the stated objectives of the WTO and many RTAs, raising the suspicion that countries that adopt WTO or RTA membership may be those that suffer most from volatility (the argument is probably more important for RTAs than for the WTO). This creates a potential bias in the estimates.

We revisit the issue using World Bank's new panel database on agricultural distortions (Anderson and Valenzuela 2008), which gives, at the product level, the ad valorem equivalent of the wedge between domestic and world prices (what they call the Nominal Rate of Assistance or NRA) for seventy countries over half a century. For each product, we define volatility as the absolute value of the first difference in the NRA and take the simple average across all goods. This yields a gross measure of protection rate volatility for each country-year pair (our unit of observation), which we subsequently purge of the influence of world price volatility calculated the same way to retain only the discretionary component that is orthogonal to world price volatility. That is, we ask a question that is similar to Rose's and Mansfield and Reinhardt's but taking nominal rates of industry assistance rather than trade flows as our dependent variable and focusing on the agricultural sector's products. This means that our "WTO variable" (equal to one for WTO members after 1994) should be interpreted as picking up only the effect of the Uruguay Round's agricultural agreement, and nothing else. This also means that our measure of volatility is "multilateral" rather than bilateral: For each country, we measure the effect of membership in RTAs and the WTO on the volatility of an indicator of trade policy that lumps together all MFN and preferential border measures. This is important, because our measure picks up not only the effect of an RTA on the stability of the bilateral trade regime, but also on an aggregate of each member country's trade regimes vis-à-vis all its partners. Put differently, we measure whether membership in NAFTA reduces the volatility of Mexican trade barriers not just vis-à-vis the United States and Canada but also vis-à-vis Japan, by encouraging the susbtitution of rules for discretion in all areas of trade policy.

We also instrument our basic treatment variable (membership in RTAs), using the theoretical literature on determinants of trade agreements as a guide in the selection of potential instruments. Motives that we consider as potential instruments for signing trade agreements include the internalization of terms-of-trade externalities (Bagwell and Staiger 1999), market access insurance (Fernandez and Portes 1998), solving time-inconsistency problems in trade policy decisions (Maggi and Rodriguez-Clare 1998 and 2007), and the provision of public goods (Limão 2007).

Like Mansfield and Reinhardt, we find that RTAs are robustly associated with a decrease in agricultural NRA volatility across a variety of specifications. But we find that the effect of WTO membership is less precisely estimated, sometimes being insignificant, which seems to go some way toward reconciling their results with Rose's. Thus, as far as we can tell from our empirical experiment, in this particular instance the multilateral trading system and regional agreements work in the same direction, but the disciplines of the latter seem more readily identifiable than those of the former.

ESTIMATION

Let c denote a country, t denote time, σ_{ct} be the volatility of c's trade policy in year t, and TA_{ct} be a summary measure of the incidence of RTAs for country c in year t. The construction of σ_{ct} and TA_{ct} is discussed in the data section below. Let also WTO_{ct} be a dummy variable marking WTO membership, X_{ct} a vector of controls (whose composition is also discussed in the data section), α_t and α_c time and country fixed effects, and ε_{ct} an error term. The equation of interest is

$$\sigma_{ct} = \alpha_0 + \alpha_1 TA_{ct} + \alpha_2 WTO_{ct} + X\beta + \alpha_t + \alpha_c + \epsilon_{ct}. \tag{1}$$

where all continuous variables (including σ) are log linearized.

Because RTAs may be formed precisely in response to excessive trade policy volatility, OLS estimates of (1) will be biased downwards. We accordingly instrument TA_{ct} with a vector of instruments Z and estimate (1) by 2SLS and efficient two-stage GMM.

The existing theoretical literature on the determinants of trade agreements offers some guidance in finding valid instruments. First, large countries may want to sign trade agreements in order to overcome prisoner's dilemma situations where they unilaterally set tariffs too high because of terms-of-trade externalities. Moreover, the larger the country, the larger is the interest other countries have in securing access to that particular market.[3] In contrast, smaller countries may not be large enough to influence world prices or attract the interest of other countries. Therefore, we expect a positive relationship between the economic size of a country, measured by the level of its GDP, and its involvement in regionalism (the endogenous right-hand-side variable).

Second, Maggi and Rodrguez-Clare (1998) argue that governments with weak bargaining positions vis-à-vis interest groups are more likely to want to precommit because weak bargaining positions reduce the rents that

---

[3] This is nothing but Fernandez' "insurance" motive for the large country's partners. The argument gave rise to a lively debate on Dani Rodrik's blog. Commenting on Senator Clinton's proposal to submit trade agreements like NAFTA to five-year reviews, political scientist Dan Drezner wrote:

> Her campaign website proudly declares that as president, Clinton would restore America's standing in the world. Last week, however, she proposed that we reassess our trade agreements every five years and demand adjustments to them if necessary, starting with NAFTA.
>
> This proposal makes me wonder if Senator Clinton understands the value-added of these free-trade agreements, or FTAs. The dirty secret is that most FTAs do not have large effects on the American economy, but they do yield foreign policy dividends. These agreements cement ties with key allies. They offer a guarantee to these countries that their relationship with the United States – and their access to American consumers – will not be disrupted. Compare the unease and mistrust that characterized Mexican-American relations prior to NAFTA with the past 15 years. The effect can be dramatic.
>
> In short, trade agreements improve America's standing in the world. But Senator Clinton's proposal would strip these agreements of the very certainty that makes them attractive to our allies. How does Senator Clinton think our trading partners in the Middle East, Central America, and Pacific Rim will react to her proposal? How is this proposal any different from the unilateralism that Democrats have condemned for the past six years? (comment posted on October 18, 2007).

they derive from the political game. This suggests using domestic political institutions, a standard approach to instrumenting policy variables (see Besley and Case 2000 for a discussion). Maggi and Rodrguez-Clare also suggest that governments that are neither too sensitive, nor too impervious, to interest-group pressures are more likely to sign trade agreements. The argument is that a government that is too sensitive would not want to precommit for fear of losing the lobbies' contributions, while one that puts a large weight on social welfare would not need to precommit. To capture these nonlinearities, we include in the list of instruments the square of a measure of governments' weight on social welfare, taken from Grossman and Helpman's common-agency model.

Finally, as argued by Limão (2007), countries sign trade agreements to facilitate the provision of public goods. For instance, under the Andean Trade Promotion Act (ATPA) the United States offered duty-free access to Andean exports in return for cooperation in the war on drugs. Similarly, the European Union offers special preferential treatment to countries cooperating on "Singapore" and environmental issues under its GSP-plus.[4] Regional agreements can also reflect security concerns. This was certainly the case of Europe's Common Market, which was set up to reduce Franco-German tensions. Security concerns in the face of threats of Communist subversion have also been historical drivers of ASEAN. To proxy such security concerns, we use the number of military alliances to which each country belongs in a given year.

We use under-, over-, and weak-identification tests to assess the suitability of our instruments. All specifications control for heteroskedasticity and first-order autocorrelation in the error term, and in a robustness section we also control for the lagged level of trade distortions, conjecturing that the volatility of trade barriers may somehow be proportional to their level.

Dependent Variable Data

Data on the extent of domestic agricultural price distortions due to policy intervention are from the World Bank's Agricultural Distortions project (Anderson and Valenzuela 2008, the methodology for which is outlined in Anderson et al. (2008). Distortions are measured by the wedge between

---

[4] Note that both the ATPA and the GSP-plus run afoul of GATT Article XXIV and the Enabling Clause. The ATPA is accordingly being transformed into a reciprocal FTA with willing Andean partners, while the legal future of the GSP-plus is uncertain.

domestic and external price, that is, by NRA. Formally, let i be an agricultural product and, as before, c and t be country and year.

$$NRA_{ict} = \frac{p_{ict} - p_{ict}^*}{p_{ict}^*}$$

where p_{ict}^* is good i's CIF external price (that is, its world price plus transportation cost to country c) and p_{ict} its domestic price in country c. Therefore, the NRA is the ad valorem equivalent of the effect of all agricultural intervention measures. Border taxes and subsidies largely contribute to the nominal rate of assistance. Border policy instruments have the lowest contribution to the NRA (62 percent) in Latin America and the highest (94 percent) in high-income countries. In order to isolate the effect of border measures, we subtract from the NRA the part corresponding to domestic price support measures. The database provides NRA estimates, disaggregated at the product level, for sixty-eight countries over an average period of thirty-nine years. The countries and goods covered account for about two-thirds of global agricultural production.

The distribution of NRAs shows large variation across and within goods and countries. NRAs have been generally rising in high-income countries since the mid-1950s (the beginning of the database), with the exception of Australia and New Zealand. In developing countries, NRAs have also been rising, with export taxes rising between the 1950s and the 1980s and receding thereafter, and import taxes rising almost monotonically. Whether for export or import-competing goods, variations around the trend remain large over time. Clearly, NRA volatility is a common characteristic of both high-income and developing countries' agricultural policies.

We measure the volatility of NRAs in two steps: First, we take the absolute value of first differences in Anderson and Valenzuela's measure of the price wedge, product by product; next, we take the simple average of those absolute values across all goods in a given country and year. That is,

$$\sigma_{ct} = \frac{1}{M} \sum_{i=1}^{M} \left| NRA_{ict} - NRA_{ic,t-1} \right|.$$

Defining variability this way allows us to minimize the loss of observations in the time dimension.[5] In order to reduce the influence of outliers, we put σ_{ct} and all volatility variables in logs.

---

[5] Alternative measures include the square of the first differences (instead of the absolute value) or the variance calculated over blocs of n years. This last approach, however, entails

Independent Variable Data

The first regressor of interest is TA_{ct}. Many measures of the extent of a country's involvement in regionalism are possible. The proxy we use is the number of trade agreements (regional as well as bilateral) signed by country c and in force in year t. Computed this way, TA_{ct} weights all agreements equally regardless of their depth, number of partners, or economic size. (We explore various alternative measures in the robustness section below.) The second regressor of interest is WTO_{ct}, which marks membership in the WTO and therefore ratification of the Uruguay Round's Agricultural Agreement. WTO_{ct} is a dummy variable equal to one after 1994 for WTO members. It is, therefore, akin to a standard treatment-effect variable.

Our vector of controls is

$$\mathbf{X}_{ct} = \left[\sigma_{ct}^*, \sigma_{ct}^{GDP}, PRES_c, PARL_c, a_{ct} \right]$$

where σ_{ct}^* is the volatility of country c's external price (aggregated across goods), σ_{ct}^{GDP} that of its GDP (both in logs), $PRES_c$ and $PARL_c$ are dummy variables marking, respectively, presidential and parliamentary systems, and a_{ct} is the "revealed" weight on social welfare in a Grossman-Helpman (1994) governmental objective function (more on this later in this chapter).

The rationale for including the volatility of the external price is twofold. First, as discussed in the introduction, variations in border measures can be used to insulate domestic markets from terms-of-trade shocks, in which case variations in world prices would be negatively correlated with variations in trade barriers. Second, external-price variations translate mechanically into variations in the ad valorem equivalent of specific tariffs and quotas, two types of border measures widely used in agriculture. Putting the volatility of world prices on the right-hand side controls for both. The rationale for the volatility of GDP is to control for the use of trade policy to correct macroeconomic shocks (like Mexico's Tequila crisis of 1994, which triggered a round of tariff increases). We consider such tariff changes as different from purely discretionary interventions. Finally, following Besley and Case (2000), it has become customary to use political-institution variables to instrument for policy variables. We use the World Bank's Political Institutions Database (Beck et al. 2001, 2008) to identify systems other than pure parliamentary systems (the omitted

a substantial loss of observations, which would reduce our ability to estimate the autocorrelation parameter in the error term.

dummy), reasoning that (following the argument of Maggi and Rodrguez-Clare 1998) parliamentary systems are the weakest in terms of executive decision making. Because coalitions are typically less stable in parliamentary regimes, governments are likely to have less bargaining power and to be more sensitive to political pressure. Therefore, one might expect less trade-policy volatility under PRES than under PARL.[6]

We turn now to the construction of the weight on social welfare, a_{ct}. We adapt the tariff equation of Grossman and Helpman's common-agency model to an agricultural context following the empirical methodology of Gawande, Krishna and Olarreaga (2009).[7] In contrast to the existing literature, we assume that a sizable proportion of the population is politically organized. Relaxing the assumption of high concentration of the ownership of specific factors used in production makes it possible to generate import subsidies and export taxes in equilibrium, which is important in an agricultural context.[8] We calculate an aggregate weight on social welfare, overlooking possible differences between the case of export and import-competing goods. To recall, omitting the country subscript c, Grossman and Helpman's tariff equation is

$$\frac{\tau_{it}}{1+t_{it}} = \frac{I_{it} - \alpha_t}{a_t + \alpha_t} \cdot \left[\frac{y_{it}}{m_{it}} \right] \cdot \frac{1}{|e_{it}|} \tag{2}$$

where τ_{it} is the tariff on good i in year t; I_{it} is an indicator function equal to one if sector i is politically organized in year t; y_{it} is domestic production of good i in year t; m_{it} are imports of good i in year t; e_{it} is the import demand elasticity of good i in year t; α_t is the fraction of the total population of

---

[6] The PID's classification of political regimes can be considered too coarse. For instance, Olper and Raimondi (2010) show that autocracies and democracies behave differently in shaping agricultural policy. As a sensitivity check, we set autocracies apart and differentiated between presidential, assembly-elected, and parliamentary systems only for democracies. We also decoupled presidential, assembly-elected, and parliamentary democracies into majoritarian and proportional systems and distinguished them, again, from autocracies. Whichever definition of institutions we use, the incidence of trade agreements and of the multilateral trading system on agricultural trade policy volatility remains robust.

[7] In doing so, we abuse the model somewhat, as Grossman and Helpman's (GH) model did not include any bindings or commitment mechanism. What follows should, of course, not be constructed as a test of GH, but rather as a shortcut to proxy the vulnerability of governments to capture by special interests, a crucial element of any political economy analysis of trade protection.

[8] The database includes a large proportion of negative NRAs, in particular in its early years (roughly up to the 1980s). As the data in Anderson (2009) show, developing-country governments as a group have switched from taxing agriculture to protecting it only recently. For Latin America, for instance, average NRAs turned positive only in the 1990s.

voters who are represented by a lobby in year t; and a_t is the parameter we are interested in estimating (the weight given to social welfare in year t relative to political contributions in the government's objective function). Taking observables in (2) to the left-hand side, we can express it as

$$\frac{\tau_{it}}{1+\tau_{it}} \cdot \left[\frac{m_{it}}{y_{it}}\right] \cdot |e_{it}| = -\frac{\alpha_t}{a_t+\alpha_t} + \frac{1}{a_t+\alpha_t} \cdot I_{it} \tag{3}$$

where m_{it} are imports (exports) of good i in year t and e_{it} is the import demand elasticity (export demand elasticity) of good i in year t if product i is classified as importable (exportable). If the sector is organized, that is if $I_{it} = 1$, producers are able to buy protection and $\tau_{it} > 0$. If good i is imported (exported), τ_{it} is an ad valorem tariff (subsidy). If $I_{it} = 0$, $\tau_{it} > 0$; that is, if sector i is unorganized, its producers are penalized by an import subsidy if it is import-competing good and by an export tax if it is an export good. Letting $\beta_{1t} = -\alpha_t/(a_t + \alpha_t)$ and $\beta_{2t} = 1/(a_t + \alpha_t)$ and adding a normally distributed iid error term u_{it} we have

$$\frac{\tau_{it}}{1+t_{it}} \cdot \left[\frac{m_{it}}{y_{it}}\right] \cdot |e_{it}| = -\frac{\alpha_t}{a_t+\alpha_t} + \frac{1}{a_t+\alpha_t} \cdot I_{it} + u_{it} \tag{4}$$

$$= \beta_{1t} + \beta_{2t}I_i + u_{it}.$$

Formulating the problem this way allows us to remove any endogeneity issue between output, imports, and tariffs, as well as measurement-error issues for elasticities. As for I_{it}, it is not observable in general. Following Gawande and Hoekman (2010), we set $I_{it} = 0$ for all industries/countries such that $\tau_{it} < 0$ (import subsidies or export taxes) and $I_{it} = 1$ otherwise. This way we have really two equations:

$$\phi_{it} = \begin{cases} \beta_{1t} + \beta_{2t} + u_{it} & \text{if } \tau_{it} \geq 0 \\ \beta_{1t} + u_{it} & \text{otherwise} \end{cases}$$

where ϕ_{it} is the expression on the left-hand side of (4). In both cases, the right-hand side is a constant (up to the error term), so the OLS estimates of $\beta_{1t} + \beta_{2t}$ for the organized-industries subsample ($\tau_{it} \geq 0$) and of β_{1t} for the unorganized subsample ($\tau_{it} < 0$) are simply the respective averages of ϕ_{it}. Subtracting the second from the first gives $\hat{\beta}_{2t}$, and the parameter of interest $\hat{a}_t$ can then be retrieved as

$$\hat{a}_t = \left(1+\hat{\beta}_{1t}\right)\Big/\hat{\beta}_{2t}$$

while the estimate of the proportion of the population organized in interests'groups is given by

$$\hat{\alpha}_t = -\hat{\beta}_{1t}\big/\hat{\beta}_{2t}.$$

Import demand elasticities at the HS six-digit level are borrowed from Kee, Nicita and Olarreaga (2008, 2009). Table 13.1 gives descriptive statistics for all variables. For dummy variables, the mean is simply the proportion of countries/years for which the variable is equal to 1, that is, the incidence of the variable in question.

RESULTS

We begin by discussing the baseline results and then examine their robustness before turning to assess whether Latin America is different from other parts of the world.

Baseline Results

Estimation results of the basic specification are shown in Table 13.2. The first column shows OLS results, while the second and third column gives 2SLS and GMM results. In each case, standard errors are robust to heteroskedasticity and autocorrelation.

As expected, OLS estimates are biased downward and the bias is sizable, suggesting that, as conjectured, countries enter RTAs at least partly to overcome excess trade policy volatility. Whatever the estimation method, TA_{ct} significantly reduces volatility of NRAs. The point estimates of the coefficient on the count of trade agreements are very close under 2SLS and GMM (-0.140 and -0.122, respectively). That is, consistent estimation of the basic specification indicates that an additional trade agreement reduces agricultural NRA volatility by 12–14 percent (recall that our specification is a semi-log one).

Table 13.1. *Summary statistics*

Variable	Mean	(Std. Dev.)	Min.	Max.	N
Trade agreements (TAs)	3.136	(4.392)	0	26	1095
TAs (GATS' type)	0.832	(1.66)	0	9	1095
TAs (Partners and GATS' type)	3.561	(6.167)	0	27	1095

Variable	Mean	(Std. Dev.)	Min.	Max.	N
TAs *(Partners and OCDE countries)*	4.282	(6.622)	0	20	1095
TAs*(Partners, OCDE countries and GATS' type)*	3.389	(5.835)	0	20	1095
WTO	0.282	(0.45)	0	1	1095
Nominal rate of assistance	0.343	(0.626)	−3.4	4.476	1095
Nominal rate of assistance volatility	0.243	(0.346)	0	6.766	1095
Nominal rate of assistance volatility (in log)	−1.813	(0.972)	−12.822	1.912	1095
Price volatility	221.154	(447.641)	2.589	4824.143	1095
Price volatility (in log)	4.713	(1.039)	0.951	8.481	1095
Price inverse volatility	0.001	(0.002)	0	0.043	1095
Price inverse volatility (in log)	−7.429	(0.85)	−9.665	−3.148	1095
GDP (current bio USD)	292.394	(640.722)	1.664	5303.791	1095
GDP (current bio USD, in log)	4.257	(1.789)	0.509	8.576	1095
GDP volatility (current bio USD)	27.239	(69.446)	0.007	658.607	1095
GDP volatility (current bio USD, in log)	1.576	(2.042)	−4.974	6.49	1095
Government's social welfare weighting	9.061	(31.229)	0.007	246.405	1095
Government's social welfare weighting (in log)	0.54	(1.674)	−4.902	5.507	1095
Square of the government's social welfare weighting (in log)	3.092	(5.114)	0	30.327	1095
Presidential system	0.348	(0.477)	0	1	1095
Assembly-elected president system	0.064	(0.245)	0	1	1095
Parliamentary system	0.588	(0.492)	0	1	1095
Military alliances	3.688	(5.267)	0	31	1095

***, **, and * denote statistical significance at the 1%, 5% and 10% levels, respectively.
Source: Authors' compilation.

Table 13.2. *Explaining changes in agricultural NRAs*

Dependent Variable	OLS	2SLS	GMM
NRA volatility (in log)			
Regressors			
Trade agreements	−0.045***	−0.140***	−0.122***
	(0.014)	(0.043)	(0.042)
WTO	−0.101	−0.196**	−0.175*
	(0.083)	(0.094)	(0.093)
World price volatility (in log)	0.071**	0.080**	0.072**
	(0.031)	(0.032)	(0.031)
GDP volatility (in log)	0.030*	0.031*	0.031*
	(0.018)	(0.018)	(0.018)
Government's social welfare	−0.086***	−0.095***	−0.094***
weighting (in log)	(0.024)	(0.024)	(0.024)
Presidential system	−0.216*	−0.247**	−0.211*
	(0.116)	(0.120)	(0.118)
Parliamentary system	−0.122	−0.231*	−0.203
	(0.119)	(0.136)	(0.135)
Country and time fixed effects	yes	yes	yes
Observations	1095	1095	1095
R^2	0.216	0.159	0.178

Absolute standard errors are shown in brackets. ***, **, and * denote statistical significance at the 1%, 5% and 10% levels, respectively.
Source: Authors' calculations.

Ratification of the WTO's agricultural agreement also reduces agricultural NRA volatility (with a large effect of −19.6 percent and −17.5 percent under 2SLS and GMM, respectively) but the effect is significant at the 5 percent level in the former case and at the 10 percent only level in the latter case. The low level of significance of this effect is more in line with Rose's (2004) result than Mansfield and Reinhardt's (2008), who found a large and precisely estimated effect for WTO membership. It is not overly surprising, given the weak disciplines involved in the agricultural agreement. Note that we have not attempted to instrument for the WTO's agricultural agreement in the baseline specification. Instrumentation gives qualitatively similar results.

Except for macro shocks, controls behave as expected. World price volatility is significant, justifying the adjustment to purge the volatility of agricultural NRAs of the nondiscretionary component. The weight government

Table 13.3. *Explaining why countries sign trade agreements*

Dependent Variable	1st stage of 2SLS
Trade agreements	
Regressors	
WTO	−1.223***
	(0.443)
World price volatility (in log)	0.063
	(0.057)
GDP (in log)	1.475***
	(0.239)
GDP volatility (in log)	−0.054
	(0.054)
Presidential system	−0.046
	(0.257)
Parliamentary system	−1.012***
	(0.355)
Government's social welfare	−0.008
weighting (in log)	(0.058)
Square of the government's social welfare	−0.024
weighting (in log)	(0.019)
Military alliances	0.097***
	(0.036)
Country and time fixed effects	yes
Observations	1095
R^2	0.584

Absolute standard errors are shown in brackets. ***, **, and * denote statistical significance at the 1%, 5% and 10% levels, respectively.
Source: Authors' calculations.

puts on social welfare seems to be an important factor in explaining the dependent variable, as it statistically decreases volatility. While the effect of assembly-elected systems does not differ statistically from the one of parliamentary regimes, presidential systems, as conjectured, reduce volatility compared with parliamentary regimes.

Table 13.3 shows estimation results for the first-stage equation (determination of the number of trade agreements). Except for the weight on social welfare, the results are consistent with the conjectures. Large countries are more likely to sign agreements, and so are countries that are members of many military alliances.

Robustness

This section presents the results of two types of robustness checks, each including robust standard errors. The first type consists of using again the basic specification but controlling for the lagged level of assistance. In a model where changing trade policy implies political and economic adjustment costs (say a partial-adjustment model), the initial level of assistance will be a determinant of changes in trade policy. Also, one may assert that the relevant measure of volatility is not the percentage-point change in the rate of assistance, but rather the proportional change in the rate of assistance. Controlling for the lagged level of assistance addresses these concerns. Results of OLS, 2SLS, and GMM estimates are provided in Table 13.4.

Results of the first-stage estimation are available upon request. With the exception of the world price volatility in the second stage, the results are qualitatively the same to those reported in Tables 13.2 and 13.3. Adding the initial level of assistance causes the world price volatility coefficient to become insignificant. Also, the lagged level of assistance is statistically significant in the second stage while negative and statistically insignificant in the first stage.

The second set of robustness checks consists of using different measures of trade agreements. First, in order to proxy for the depth of agreements, we mark apart those with provisions on trade in services. This gives us a new variable TA_{ct}^{GATS}, with

$$TA_{ct}^{GATS} = \begin{cases} TA_{ct} & \text{if } c\text{'s agreements all have service provisions} \\ TA_{ct} - s & \text{if } s \text{ of } c\text{'s agreements do not have service provisions.} \end{cases}$$

Second, we recode TA_{ct}^{GATS} to take into account the number of signatories in agreements with service provisions. Let k be index agreements, S_{ct} be the subset of c's agreements at t with service provisions, and n_k the number of c's partners in k. Then

$$TA_{ct}^{GATS\,/\,PARTNERS} = \sum_{k \in S_{ct}} n_k.$$

Third, in order to account for the "borrowed-credibility" effect discussed in the introduction, we differentiate agreements by their number of OECD partners. Letting N_{ct} be the set of all of c's agreements at t (so $S_{ct} \subseteq N_{ct}$) and n_k^{OECD} the number of OECD partners in agreement k,

$$TA_{ct}^{OECD} = \sum_{k \in N_{ct}} n_k^{OECD}.$$

Table 13.4. *Explaining changes in assistance using lagged NRA*

Dependent Variable	OLS	2SLS	GMM
NRA volatility (in log)			
Regressors			
Trade agreements	−0.039**	−0.129***	−0.104***
	(0.015)	(0.042)	(0.039)
WTO	−0.205**	−0.284***	−0.261***
	(0.088)	(0.096)	(0.095)
Lagged nominal rate of assistance (in log)	0.098***	0.090***	0.090***
	(0.031)	(0.032)	(0.032)
World price volatility (in log)	0.044	0.051	0.040
	(0.031)	(0.032)	(0.031)
GDP volatility (in log)	0.032*	0.035*	0.034*
	(0.018)	(0.018)	(0.018)
Government's social welfare weighting (in log)	−0.058**	−0.071***	−0.075***
	(0.026)	(0.026)	(0.026)
Presidential system	−0.199*	−0.199*	−0.202*
	(0.107)	(0.111)	(0.111)
Parliamentary system	−0.090	−0.204	−0.175
	(0.121)	(0.139)	(0.138)
Country and time fixed effects	yes	yes	yes
Observations	998	998	998
R^2	0.255	0.199	0.225

Absolute standard errors are shown in brackets. ***, **, and * denote statistical significance at the 1%, 5% and 10% levels, respectively.
Source: Authors' calculations.

Finally, we interact the number of OECD partners and the presence of GATS provisions, which gives us

$$TA_{ct}^{GATS/OECD} = \sum_{k \in S_{ct}} n_k^{OECD}.$$

GMM results for the incidence of alternative measures of trade agreements are shown in Table 13.5. Deeper forms of trade agreements have stronger volatility-reducing effects. One additional RTA with a service-liberalization

Table 13.5. *Explaining changes in NRAs using alternative counts of trade agreements*

Dependent Variable	(1)	(2)	(3)	(4)
NRA volatility (in log)				
Regressors				
TAs (GATS' type) (1)	−0.238***			
	(0.077)			
TAs (Partners and GATS' type) (2)		−0.065***		
		(0.023)		
TAs (Partners and OCDE countries) (3)			−0.050*	
			(0.026)	
TAs (Partners, OCDE countries and GATS' type) (4)				−0.074***
				(0.027)
WTO	−0.190**	−0.123	−0.066	−0.121
	(0.089)	(0.090)	(0.094)	(0.091)
World price volatility (in log)	0.085***	0.083***	0.072**	0.082**
	(0.031)	(0.032)	(0.032)	(0.032)
GDP volatility (in log)	0.029	0.028	0.027	0.029
	(0.018)	(0.018)	(0.018)	(0.018)
Government's social welfare weighting (in log)	−0.089***	−0.102***	−0.106***	−0.103***
	(0.024)	(0.024)	(0.025)	(0.024)
Presidential system	−0.217*	−0.303**	−0.248**	−0.320**
	(0.118)	(0.129)	(0.126)	(0.134)
Parliamentary system	−0.093	−0.131	−0.060	−0.140
	(0.123)	(0.127)	(0.142)	(0.128)
Country and time fixed effects	yes	yes	yes	yes
Observations	1095	1095	1095	1095
R^2	0.219	0.203	0.187	0.199

Absolute standard errors are shown in brackets. ***, **, and * denote statistical significance at the 1%, 5% and 10% levels, respectively.
Source: Authors' calculations.

provision reduces volatility by 24 percent on average, against 12–14 percent in the baseline specification. The number of RTA partners, be it the number of OECD partners or the number of partners in service-including RTAs, also reduces agricultural trade-policy volatility significantly: -5 percent for an additional OECD partner (TA_{ct}^{OECD}), -6.5 percent for an additional partner in an RTA with a service provision ($TA_{ct}^{GATS/PARTNERS}$), and -7.4 percent for an additional OECD partner in an RTA with a service provision

($TA_{ct}^{GATS/OECD}$). Note that these coefficients are not directly comparable with those of the baseline specification, since the regressor of interest now counts partners rather than agreements (so the marginal effect is that of a partner country rather than that of an agreement, which means that the effect should be expected to be smaller). The number of partners alone does not seem to have any effect. This largely accords with intuition: Rules-versus-discretion effects are more likely to be present when a developing country with relatively weak institutions teams up with an industrial one having stronger institutions. The developing country can then "borrow the credibility" of the industrial one, pretty much like countries with weak inflation-fighting records in Europe borrowed the Bundesbank's credibility under the European Monetary System. This effect can be expected to be magnified with deeper agreements, which is what we find. The coefficients on political economy controls are largely unaffected by the choice of measure for RTAs.

Is Latin America Different?

Latin America is a region which has high degrees of NRA volatility, and one where regional integration has been quite active since the late 1970s with the creation of the Latin American Integration Association (LAIA). Of the 200 trade agreements that were active in 2006 and that had been notified to the WTO, 50 were signed by at least one Latin American country (25 percent, whereas Latin America represented around 10 percent of WTO's membership). It has been estimated that the share of trade in Latin America that occurs under regional trade agreements is above 50 percent (Grether and Olarreaga 1999). NRA volatility is also higher than in other developing regions. In our sample of agricultural products, Latin America is the region with the highest volatility among developing countries, followed by sub-Saharan Africa that has a 30 percent smaller degree of volatility. In order to disentangle any differences in the relationship between NRA volatility and regional trade agreements in Latin America, we introduced in (1) an interaction term between *TA* and a dummy that takes the value of 1 when the observation corresponds to a Latin American country. A positive coefficient on the interaction term would indicate that the negative impact of trade agreements on volatility is smaller in Latin America (or Latin American countries), whereas a negative coefficient would be evidence of a larger effect. Results are shown in Table 13.6 for the OLS, 2SLS, and GMM estimators. Standard errors are robust to heteroskedasticity and autocorrelation.

Table 13.6. *Exploring whether the Latin American region is different*

Dependent Variable	OLS	2SLS	GMM
Trade policy volatility			
Regressors			
Trade agreements	–0.045***	–0.138***	–0.120***
	(0.013)	(0.041)	(0.040)
Trade agreements in LAC	–0.032	–0.108**	–0.111**
	(0.028)	(0.050)	(0.050)
WTO	–0.092	–0.167*	–0.147
	(0.084)	(0.094)	(0.093)
World price volatility (in log)	0.071**	0.083***	0.079**
	(0.031)	(0.032)	(0.031)
GDP volatility (in log)	0.030*	0.029	0.032*
	(0.018)	(0.018)	(0.018)
Government's social welfare	–0.087***	–0.099***	–0.101***
weighting (in log)	(0.024)	(0.024)	(0.023)
Presidential system	–0.204*	–0.204*	–0.169
	(0.117)	(0.122)	(0.120)
Parliamentary system	–0.147	–0.314**	–0.278**
	(0.121)	(0.141)	(0.140)
Country and time fixed effects	yes	yes	yes
Observations	1095	1095	1095
R^2	0.216	0.157	0.176

Absolute standard errors are shown in brackets. ***, **, and * denote statistical significance at the 1%, 5% and 10% levels, respectively.
Source: Authors' calculations.

Under OLS, the interaction term coefficient is insignificant. However, once we instrument, the interaction term is negative and statistically significant. This additional effect for Latin American countries is economically as important as the one found on average for the full sample involving all regions. This implies that the average effect in Latin America is on average double the one estimated for the rest of the sample. Note that the impact of being a member of the WTO on NRA volatility becomes statistically insignificant, which can be partly explained by the fact that all Latin American countries are WTO members, and therefore part of the Latin American-specific effect was being captured by the WTO variable. This is now consistent with the results found by Rose (2004).

Given that, on average, trade agreements impose more discipline in Latin America than in the rest of the world, one may wonder which countries in

Latin America are driving these results: Is it Chile or Brazil, and what can explain these differences? Table 13.7 provides the results of the estimation where we added several additional variables that interact *TA* with country dummies for Latin American countries.[9]

The coefficients of the interaction terms for Argentina and Chile are negative and significant. They are also economically very large, with coefficients that are 2 to 4 times the average impact the rest of the sample, suggesting that trade agreements have been particularly successful in reducing agricultural NRA volatility in these countries. In the case of Argentina, one needs to note that it is a country that has historically experienced a lot of volatility in terms of not only trade policy but economic policy in general. The signing of the Mercosur agreement and the creation of a customs union with a much larger neighbor (Brazil) imposed an important constraint in terms of what can be done in the area of trade policy. In the case of Chile, the signing of bilateral trade agreements with large developed countries (Canada, European Union, United States) and large developing countries (Argentina, Brazil, Mexico, etc.) may partly explain the large reduction in NRA volatility. It can also be explained partly by the fact that Chile's tariffs became uniform at the time at which Chile engaged in an important number of trade agreements. Note, however, that nontariff barriers were not made uniform, and this is clearly an important determinant of agricultural trade policy.[10]

In the case of Colombia, the additional effect goes in the opposite direction, suggesting that in Colombia trade agreements reduce NRA volatility by less than that in the rest of the sample. Moreover, the magnitude of this additional effect is large enough to offset the impact predicted on average in our sample, which implies that Colombia's trade agreements had little impact on Colombia's agricultural NRA volatility. This may not be unexpected if one considers that, until 2002, Colombia was only part of LAIA and the Comunidad Andina de Naciones (CAN). These are agreements among developing countries that have been weakly enforced and have taken many different forms over the years.

Results for Brazil, Nicaragua, and Mexico suggest that the discipline imposed by trade agreements in those countries do not differ statistically from the rest of the world. For Nicaragua and Brazil, this may not be surprising as they are engaged either in weak agreements or, in Brazil's case,

---

[9] Note that the analysis is restricted by the database. Therefore, only six Latin American countries are part of the discussion.

[10] Indeed, according to estimates by Kee, Nicita and Olarreaga (2008, 2009), nontariff barriers explain 90 percent of the trade restrictiveness of Chile.

Table 13.7. *Exploring whether Latin American countries differ*

Dependent Variable	OLS	2SLS	GMM
Trade policy volatility			
Regressors:			
Trade agreements	−0.047***	−0.122***	−0.089***
	(0.014)	(0.039)	(0.033)
Trade agreements in ARG	−0.145	−0.357***	−0.384***
	(0.132)	(0.115)	(0.112)
Trade agreements in BRA	−0.154	−0.235	−0.192
	(0.102)	(0.151)	(0.142)
Trade agreements in CHL	−0.106**	−0.142**	−0.142**
	(0.050)	(0.064)	(0.059)
Trade agreements in COL	0.115*	0.134*	0.153**
	(0.060)	(0.079)	(0.077)
Trade agreements in MEX	−0.008	0.002	−0.009
	(0.028)	(0.041)	(0.040)
Trade agreements in NIC	−0.231	−0.396*	−0.229
	(0.158)	(0.235)	(0.225)
WTO	−0.089	−0.156*	−0.126
	(0.084)	(0.091)	(0.090)
World price volatility (in log)	0.076**	0.089***	0.087***
	(0.031)	(0.032)	(0.031)
GDP volatility (in log)	0.030*	0.031*	0.026
	(0.018)	(0.018)	(0.018)
Government's social welfare weighting (in log)	−0.085***	−0.091***	−0.078***
	(0.024)	(0.024)	(0.023)
Presidential system	−0.169	−0.167	−0.123
	(0.127)	(0.132)	(0.129)
Parliamentary system	−0.250*	−0.402**	−0.323**
	(0.135)	(0.168)	(0.157)
Country and time fixed effects	yes	yes	yes
Observations	1095	1095	1095
R^2	0.220	0.182	0.204

Absolute standard errors are shown in brackets. ***, **, and * denote statistical significance at the 1%, 5% and 10% levels, respectively.
Source: Authors' calculations.

with much smaller members. The outcome is more surprising for Mexico, which had at least three agreements in force for most of the time for which data are available. In 2002, twelve agreements were in force. Moreover, since 1994, Mexico is part of the NAFTA. One potential explanation as to why we do not observe additional effects for Mexico is that most of the bilaterals post-NAFTA were signed with other Latin American countries. Presumably, the exit costs of those bilaterals are not high enough to provide a credible threat in the case of deviations.

CONCLUDING REMARKS

This chapter looks at the volatility-reducing effect of RTAs on NRAs for agricultural products by taking as our dependent variable a direct measure of policy distortions rather than trade flows. In this sense, we differ from Mansfield and Reinhardt (2008) and Rose (2004), who looked at the effect of regionalism and WTO membership, respectively, on trade-flow volatility. This means that the effect we are looking for is at the same time more direct (since we consider directly the policy variable rather than an outcome variable whose volatility can pick up many other parasite influences) but also more diffuse, because our measure of policy distortions is a mixture of a country's bilateral and MFN trade policies. That is, we test whether a trade agreement between, say, Mexico and the U.S. stabilizes Mexican trade policy not just vis-à-vis the United States but also vis-à-vis all of its partners, preferential or MFN. In spite of these differences, our results are remarkably in line with those of Mansfield and Reinhardt: Regionalism significantly reduces the volatility of NRAs for agricultural goods, and the effect is quantitatively substantial (about 13 pecent less volatility for each additional RTA) and robust across a wide variety of specifications.

Our result concerning WTO membership (which means, in an agricultural context, ratification of the Uruguay Round's agricultural agreement) is less pessimistic than Rose's. Rose found no effect whatsoever, whereas we find a weakly significant but nevertheless identifiable volatility-reducing effect. One obvious difference between our exercise and Rose's is that we look at short-run volatility whereas he looks at it in the long run. Perhaps more importantly, in our equation that includes both WTO membership and various proxies for RTA membership, we instrument for the latter. Since most RTAs state, as one of their primary goals, the creation of a stable and predictable trading environment, countries that are most eager to form RTAs can be expected to be those that suffer from intractable policy volatility and therefore need to find outside commitment mechanisms. This means that OLS estimates are likely to be biased downward (indeed, this is what we find). Using fixed effects, as Rose does, certainly alleviates the problem by controlling for time-invariant country characteristics that may affect NRA volatility, but it may not be altogether neutralized.

More research is clearly called for to explain completely this difference in results.

We also find that deeper agreements and those involving "Northern" (industrial) partners seem to have more volatility-reducing effects. This accords with intuition. If the reduction in volatility is obtained by strategic delegation to supranational institutions, those are likely to be stronger if they are formed, like the EU, by countries with strong domestic institutions. Put crudely, Bulgaria is likely to get a stronger anchor for its trade policy by joining the EU than by forming an RTA with Romania, for example. If the reduction in volatility is obtained instead by substituting rules for discretion in an RTA with precise rules (like NAFTA), those rules will be stronger if they are backed by a country with strong and stable institutions. This is like countries with weak institutions (e.g., weak separation of powers) "borrowing" the credibility of countries with stronger institutions.

Results for Latin America, where regionalism and trade policy volatility have been predominant, confirm the overall picture. They suggest that the NRA volatility-reducing effect of regional integration agreements has on average been stronger in this region, although there is some interesting heterogeneity within the region.

Thus, by and large our results suggest that the reduction in NRA volatility should be counted as one of the "nontraditional" gains from regionalism. Inasmuch as policy volatility has harmful effects for investment and growth, this may be an important argument in support of regionalism.

References

Abbott, F. (2000), "NAFTA and the Legalization of World Politics," *International Organization* 54: 519–547.

Anderson, K. (ed.) (2009), *Distortions to Agricultural Incentives: A Global Perspective, 1955–2007*, London: Palgrave Macmillan and Washington DC: World Bank.

Anderson, K., M. Kurzweil, W. Martin, D. Sandri and E. Valenzuela (2008), "Measuring Distortions to Agricultural Incentives, Revisited," *World Trade Review* 7(4): 1–30.

Anderson, K. and E. Valenzuela (2008), *Global Estimates of Distortions to Agricultural Incentives, 1955 to 2007*, database available at http://www.worldbank.org/agdistortions

Bagwell, K. and R. Staiger (1999), "An Economic Theory of GATT," *American Economic Review* 89(1): 215–48.

Beck, T., G. Clarke, A. Groff, P. Keefer, and P. Walsh (2001), "New Tools in Comparative Political Economy: The Database of Political Institutions," *World Bank Economic Review* 15: 165–76.

Beck, T., P.E. Keefer and G.R. Clarke (2008), *Database of Political Institutions*, accessible at http://go.worldbank.org/2EAGGLRZ40

Besley, T. and A. Case (2000), "Unnatural Experiments? Estimating the Incidence of Endogenous Policies," *Economic Journal* 110: F672–94.

Braumoeller, B. (2006), "Explaining Variance: Or, Stuck in a Moment We Can't Get Out Of", *Political Analysis* 14: 268–90.

Fernandez, R. and J. Portes (1998), "Returns to Regionalism: An Evaluation of Non-Traditional Gains from Regional Trade Agreements," *World Bank Economic Review* 12(2):197–220.

Gawande, K. and B. Hoekman (2010), "Which Governments Tax or Subsidize Agricultural Trade?" Ch. 10 in this volume.

Gawande, K., P. Krishna and M. Olarreaga (2009), "What Governments Maximize and Why: A View From Trade," *International Organization* 63(3): 491–532, July.

Grether, J-M. and M. Olarreaga (1999), "Preferential and non preferential trade flows in world trade," in M. Rodriguez-Mendoza, P. Low and B. Kotschwar (eds.), *Trade Rules in the Making: Challenges in Regional and Multilateral Negotiations*, Washington DC: Brookings Institution.

Grossman, G. and E. Helpman (1994), "Protection for Sale," *American Economic Review* 84(4): 833–50.

 (1995), "The Politics of Free-Trade Agreements," *American Economic Review* 85(4): 667–90.

Kee, H.L., A.N. Nicita and M. Olarreaga (2008), "Import Demand Elasticities and Trade Distortions," *Review of Economics and Statistics* 90(4): 666–82.

 (2009), "Estimating Trade Restrictiveness Indices", *Economic Journal* 119(534): 172–99.

Limão, N. (2007), "Are Preferential Trade Agreements with Non-trade Objectives a Stumbling Bloc for Multilateral Liberalization?" *Review of Economic Studies* 74: 821–55.

Maggi, G. and A. Rodrguez-Clare (1998), "The Value of Trade Agreements in the Presence of Political Pressures," *Journal of Political Economy* 106(3): 574–601.

Maggi, G. and A. Rodríguez-Clare (2007), "A Political Economy Theory of Trade Agreements," *American Economic Review* 97(4): 1374–1406.

Mansfield, E. and E. Reinhardt (2008), "International Institutions and the Volatility of International Trade", *International Organization* 62: 621–52.

Olper, A. and V. Raimondi (2010), "Consitutional Rules and Agricultural Policy Outcomes," Ch. 14 in this volume.

Ornelas, E. (2005), "Trade-Creating Free Trade Areas and the Undermining of Multilateralism," *European Economic Review* 49: 1717–35.

Rodrik, D. (1998), "Why Do More Open Economies Have Bigger Governments?" *Journal of Political Economy* 106(5): 997–1032.

Rose, A. (2004), "Do We Really Know That the WTO Increases Trade," *American Economic Review* 94: 98–114.

Sudsawasad, S. and R. Moore (2006), "Investment Under Trade Policy Uncertainty: An Empirical Investigation," *Review of International Economics* 14(2): 316–29.

Whalley, J. (1998), "Why Do Countries Seek Regional Trade Agreements?" pp. 63–89 in J. Frankel (ed.), *The Regionalization of the World Economy*, Chicago IL: University of Chicago Press for NBER.

FOURTEEN

Constitutional Rules and Agricultural Policy Outcomes

Alessandro Olper and Valentina Raimondi[1]

The literature concerning political and economic determinants of agricultural protection tends to ignore the role that constitutional rules play in shaping agricultural policies. In contrast, the newly emerging field of comparative political economics places growing emphasis on the effect of political institutions on public policy outcomes. The inclusion of political institutions – such as electoral rules and forms of government – in formal political economy models has produced several testable hypotheses firmly motivated by theory. One of the most influential lines of research in this area is by Persson and Tabellini (2000, 2003), who look at how constitutional rules shape policy outcomes. Other recent contributions along the same research line are those by Grossman and Helpman (2005), who studied the effect of "party discipline" on trade policy, and by Persson (2005), Persson and Tabellini (2006, 2008), Besley and Persson (2008) and Acemoglu and Robinson (2000, 2008) who, among others, look at the economic and political effects of different forms of democracy and the origins of "State Capacity."

Evidence that links political institutions to agricultural policy outcomes (e.g., Beghin and Kherallah 1994, Swinnen, Banerjee and de Gorter 2001, Henning, Krause and Struve 2002, Olper 2001, Thies and Porsche 2007) provides a weak link with this "new generation" of political economy models, lessening our understanding of the mechanism in place and, consequently, its policy implications. Some contributions have tried to go further, closing the gap between theory and evidence (see Henning 2004, Olper and Raimondi 2004). However, questions still remain regarding the robustness and generalization of existing empirical

---

[1] The authors are grateful to Johan Swinnen for many discussions and insights, other project participants for helpful suggestions, and Mauro Vigani for research assistance.

findings. First, the low within-country variation in political institutions forces the researcher to look especially at the cross-country variation in the data, rendering the robustness of the inferences questionable. Second, actual evidence often refers to a broad definition of institutions, such as proxies for the degree of democracy or composite indices for institutions quality. Third, Glaeser et al. (2004) claim that it is hard to find rules-based measures of institutions systematically correlated with structural policies. To address this last point, conceptual studies and more recent empirical evidence stress that democratic details matter (see Persson 2005, Acemoglu 2005).

Starting from these considerations, the objective of this chapter is to find robust empirical regularity that maps constitutional rules into agricultural policy outcomes. The analysis takes advantage of the database on agricultural policy distortions developed by the World Bank (Anderson and Valenzuela 2008), covering a sample of more than seventy countries in the period 1955–2005. By exploiting the panel dimensions of the dataset, we investigate the effect of regime changes – autocracy versus democracy – on agricultural price distortions, as well as whether details of these forms of democracy, such as the nature of electoral rules and government types, systematically affect the extent of agricultural distortions.

From a methodological point of view, we follow the recent tendency of including democracies as well as non-democracies in the sample, to overcome the fact that established democracies do not display sufficient (time) variation in their constitutional features. This gives us the possibility of using a more robust empirical approach that can exploit the within-country variation in the data (see Papaioannou and Siourounis 2008, Giavazzi and Tabellini 2005).

The main results can be summarized as follows. First, we find a robust positive effect of transition into democracy on the level of agricultural protection: A shift from autocracy to democracy induces an increase in agricultural protection (or a reduction in taxation) of about 3–4 percentage points. Secondly, this average effect masks substantial heterogeneities across different forms of democracy. Indeed, what matters are transitions to proportional (as opposed to majoritarian) democracies, as well as to permanent (as opposed to temporary) democracies. Moreover, while we do not detect significant differences across alternative forms of government (presidential versus parliamentary), there is evidence that the effect of proportional systems is exacerbated under parliamentary regimes, but dampened under presidential ones.

PREVIOUS EVIDENCE

The first attempt to systematically study the effect of political institutions on agricultural protection in a broad context is that of Beghin and Kherallah (1994).[2] They look at how different political systems (no-party, one-party, dominant party, and multiparty systems) and civil liberties (Gastil index) affect the protection structure in twenty-five developing and developed countries. The results show that political institutions matter, and that their effect is nonmonotonic: Protection peaks with dominant party systems and then becomes nonincreasing despite further democratization.

A nonmonotonic relationship between democracy and protection in a larger cross-section of countries can also be found in Swinnen et al. (2000). Using the Gastil index of political rights, they found that moving from low to medium political rights reduces protection, but that any further increase in democratization does not necessarily result in substantial effects on agricultural protection. Clearly, this nonlinear behavior goes in the opposite direction to the previous one. Indeed, Beghin and Kherallah (1994) find an inverted U-shaped relation between democracy and agricultural protection, whereas Swinnen et al. (2000) find a U-shaped relation.

Motivated by this early evidence and by the growing literature linking institutions to economic growth and development (e.g., North 1990, Hall and Jones 1999, Acemoglu, Johnson and Robinson 2001), Olper (2001) uses alternative indices of democracy and composite indices measuring the quality of institutions that protect and enforce property rights.[3] The objective was to identify and separate the potential effects of these "different" institutional dimensions since, as suggested by several authors, focusing only on the level of democracy might be too simple to explain differences in performance and governance. The results strongly support this last prediction: Democracy displays a positive linear effect on protection, but it is not the level of democracy *per se* that seems to matter. Rather, Olper's study shows that the quality of institutions matters: Protection increases with institution quality at low levels of this dimension, but the relationship

---

[2] Important precursors of this kind of analyses can be found in the works of Bates (1983, 1989) on agrarian development in African countries. Moreover, the relationship between democracy and agricultural protection was first highlighted by Lindert (1991), who in a cross-country analysis found a positive relationship when democracy was associated with rapid agricultural decline.

[3] These composite indices come from two private international investment risk services, International Country Risk Guide (ICRG) and Business Environmental Risk Intelligence (BERI), and were first introduced in the growth literature by Knack and Keefer (1995).

turns negative once a moderate amount of institutional quality has been achieved.

The previous evidence relies largely on cross-section variation in the data. To date, the only study that uses a long time-series is that of Swinnen, Banerjee and de Gorter (2001), who look at the agricultural protection patterns in Belgium between 1877 and 1990. This paper, exploiting the within-country variation in protection, shows that only those political reforms that determine a significant shift in the political balance toward agricultural interests – for example, the extension of voting rights to small farmers in the early 20th century – induce an increase in agricultural protection. This result is important, first because it gives a logical interpretation to the democracy-protection nonlinearity discussed above, and secondly because it highlights the importance of drawing inferences from regime changes to more carefully capture the effect of democratization on protection (Swinnen 2010).

A major limitation of this first thread of evidence lies in its weak link with comparative political economy models. First attempts to link theory and evidence more closely were made by Henning, Krause and Struve (2002)[4] and Olper and Raimondi (2004). The former authors focus on the specific organization of legislative decision making, building on the political exchange model of Weingast and Marshall (1988) and on political science literature (Lijphart 1990). They show that agrarian interests are better represented in bicameralism systems due to the bias of the second chamber toward rural districts, and in the proportional electoral systems due to the bias of this system toward particular interest in organized minorities. Cross-country evidence on ten countries of Central and Eastern Europe supports these predictions.

In a similar vein, Olper and Raimondi (2004) test the prediction from recent political economy models that show how different electoral rules and forms of government systematically affect the level and composition of government spending (see also Persson and Tabellini 2000). In a sample of twenty-nine OECD countries, they show that, on average, presidential systems and majoritarian electoral rules are associated with smaller protection for the dairy industry (about 6–7 percent) than are parliamentary and proportional systems. However, this under-protectionist bias of presidential-majoritarian systems tends to reverse in countries where there is a strong geographical concentration of dairy farming, suggesting that the

[4] See also Henning (2004), where a similar model is used to explain the different levels of protection between the EU and U.S.

relationship between electoral rules, forms of government, and agricultural protection could be nonmonotonic.

A nonlinear relationship between agricultural protection and electoral rules in a cross-section of countries was also found recently by Henning (2008). Specifically, building on the probabilistic-voting model of Henning and Struve (2007), the author tests the prediction that in developed countries the relationship between agricultural protection and district magnitude would be an inverted U-shape. In other words, agricultural protection first increases and then decreases with district size. Developing countries, however, would have the same relationship reversed, or U-shaped. Empirical evidence from cross-country analysis supports this relationship, especially in developed countries.

Finally, Thies and Porche (2007) "extended" the previous evidence using a more heuristic approach and a larger set of political institution variables, including proxies for veto players, federalism, party structure, and also year of elections. Their econometric results find several of these political dimensions quite robust across different specifications, and in line with expectations.[5] For example, the authors show that having a federal system and higher party fragmentation increases protection. Interestingly, they also show a positive and significant effect of the electoral variable on protection. That result is consistent with the political business cycle literature (Alesina, Roubini and Cohen 1997).[6]

Overall, the empirical evidence summarized above is supportive of the important role political institutions play in shaping agricultural policy. At the same time, however, several shortcomings suggest that many aspects of the interaction between political institutions and agricultural protection remain unclear.

One concern is that, apart from some notable exceptions, the actual evidence is largely derived from a heuristic approach, where the link between political institutions and policy outcomes is not carefully derived from theory, thus reducing our understanding of the mechanism in place and, consequently, their policy implications. Secondly, several studies focus

---

[5] The authors also conclude that political variables are more robust explanatory variables than traditional structural-economic ones. However, a potential shortcoming of this result is that the specifications do not include, simultaneously, structural variables, such as agricultural labor or value added share, with the level of development, understandably omitted in the Thies and Porche's specifications.

[6] Other relevant institutional dimensions investigated by Olper (2007) are government ideology (left-wing versus right-wing) and land inequality. However, given our focus on constitutional rules, we do not further discuss this line of research. The relationship between ideology, inequality, and trade policy is developed by Dutt and Mitra (2002, 2005, 2010).

especially on the (cross-country) effect of democracy, adding further compliance to the analysis. This is because the definition of the degree of democracy is obviously a complex issue; furthermore, actual theory offers clear predictions, especially concerning the effects of the forms of democracy rather than the effect of democracy per se. Thirdly, and most importantly, several questions still remain with regard to both the identification of the causal effect of institutions on agricultural policies and the robustness of the empirical evidence. Indeed, given the low variation in political institutions, especially in developed countries, and the short time period involved by the majority of studies, actual inferences are drawn especially from cross-country variation in the data, limiting the ability of the researcher to control for unobserved characteristics that affect both political institutions and policy outcomes, such as history and culture.

CONCEPTUAL FRAMEWORK AND TESTABLE HYPOTHESES

Before presenting our hypotheses, we first examine further the relationship between democratization and agricultural protection and then the role of different forms of democracy.

Democratization and Agricultural Protection

One of the most fundamental features of political institutions is related to whether a country is a democracy or not, simply because this status is highly related to the credibility of constitutions (Acemoglu 2005). Thus, the first question that arises is whether democracies have agricultural policies different from autocracies, *ceteris paribus*. Theoretically, this relationship is complex and obviously linked to the more general effect of democracy on public policy.

As stressed by de Haan and Sturm (2003), economic theory does not give a clear answer to this question. Several authors point out that arguments exist for both a positive and a negative relationship (Przeworsky 1991, Banerji and Ghanem 1997). Others suggest that economic policies are, in a first approximation, the outcome of tradeoffs related to efficiency or to conflict among generations or among industries, and thus are not specific to particular institutions (Mulligan, Gill and Sala-i-Martin 2004).

According to Przeworsky (1991), one of the main differences between democratic and authoritarian regimes lies in the level, within the political process, of free participation by independent organizations. Authoritarian regimes abhor independent organizations and either incorporate them into centralized control or repress them by force. Starting from this consideration, we have two contrasting views about whether agricultural protection is more or less likely to occur under democratic or authoritarian regimes.

One view is that the voices of farmers may be better heard in an electoral democracy (Lindert 1991) where the interest groups are free to compete for political rents. By contrast, authoritarian regimes, which are better able to discourage rent seeking activities, tax or do not support their agricultural sectors. These arguments suggest that with democratization agricultural protection could be increasing, a view that fits the more general notion that democratization also induces redistribution (Acemoglu and Robinson 2000, 2008).[7]

Contrasting the previously mentioned view is the probability of governments adopting inefficient policies to benefit specific interest groups or "insiders," a probability that is actually higher under authoritarian regimes. In a well-functioning democracy, outsiders vote and impose some limits on what narrower interest groups can achieve, while in a less democratic environment, the government needs to worry only about groups that have real power (Banerji and Ghanem 1997). Thus it could be suggested that agricultural policy transfers are fewer in democracies, but this argument is also consistent with a nonlinear or nonmonotonic relationship.

A correlated argument stressed by de Haan and Sturm (2003) suggests that, at the beginning of liberalization, an authoritarian regime could be necessary, as the mass of voters often turn down economic reforms despite the fact that voters can see long-term benefits. Indeed, several policies popular in the long-run are often not implemented in democratic regimes.

From this brief discussion, it emerges that, conceptually, the net effect of democracy on agricultural protection appears, at best, of uncertain sign and inconclusive. Thus, to gain some insight from existing literature, we now focus attention on actual evidence linking democracy to public policies and economic development.

In a large sample of developing countries from 1970 to 1999, Milner and Kubota (2005) show that regime change toward democracy is associated with trade liberalization. Since an important component of agricultural distortions in developing countries is indirect and related to import-substituting industrialization policies (Anderson and Valenzuela 2008),

---

[7] Acemoglu and Robinson (2000) document how the extension of voting rights in several Western societies in the nineteenth century led to unprecedented redistributive programs. They also argue that these political reforms can be viewed as a strategic decision by the political elite to prevent widespread social unrest and revolution. The last argument is formally developed in Acemoglu and Robinson (2008).

this evidence suggests that transitions from autocracy to democracy could be positively related to agricultural protection.

More general evidence on the relationship between regime change and economic (trade) liberalization can be found in Giavazzi and Tabellini (2005) and Persson (2005). The former, using difference-in-differences estimation, shows that a transition to democracy induces a more liberal trade policy. The latter, using a similar estimation strategy, goes a step further and shows that what matters is not the simple dichotomy between democracy and autocracy, but the form of democracy. Specifically, Persson shows that the adoption of structural policies that promote long-term economic performance is more frequent in parliamentary-proportional democracies than in presidential-majoritarian ones. Such evidence is important because, by exploiting the within-country variation in the data, it leads to more robust results than cross-country evidence, overcoming the criticism of fragility advanced by several authors (e.g., Glaeser et al. 2004, Acemoglu 2005).

Finally, also relevant to our discussion are recent papers that study the effect of democracy on economic growth and development. The most robust stylized fact about agricultural protection patterns is the strong positive correlation with economic development (Anderson 1995, Swinnen 1994). The arguments as to why democracy can foster growth are similar to the arguments as to why democracy affects economic liberalization (see de Haan and Sturm 2003).

The relationship between democracy and economic performance, when studied in cross-section regressions, is ambiguous and inconclusive (Barro 1997, Glaeser et al. 2004). However, there is a growing literature exploiting the within-country variation in the data and difference-in-differences methodology (Papaioannou and Siourounis 2008, Rodrik and Wacziarg 2005, Giavazzi and Tabellini 2005, Persson 2005, Persson and Tabellini 2006). This literature, in combination with semi-parametric methods (Persson and Tabellini 2008), shows how the effect of democracy on growth tends to be positive and large in magnitude.[8] Thus, once again, these results appear supportive of a positive relationship between transition to democracy and agricultural protection. However, they also suggest that this positive effect could be conditional to the characteristics of reforming and nonreforming countries, and to the specific form of democracy.

---

[8] On the positive effect of democracy and growth, see also the recent contribution of Aghion, Alesini and Trebbi (2008), which stresses how political rights induce positive growth, especially in more advanced sectors.

Forms of Democracy and Agricultural Protection

From the previous discussion, it emerges that, while theoretically inconclusive, the effect of democracy on agricultural protection may also be related to the characteristics of democratic institutions. Thus, in this section, the focus is on two key aspects of any democratic institutions (Persson and Tabellini 2004): the electoral rules and the forms of government.

Electoral Rules and Economic Policy

There is a growing literature that has formalized how electoral rules influence the level and composition of government spending (Lizzeri and Persico 2001, Persson and Tabellini 2000, Milesi-Ferretti, Perotti and Rostagno 2002), as well as other public policies including trade policy (Hatfield and Hauk 2003, Roelfsema 2004, Grossman and Helpman 2005).

A first prediction from these models is that proportional elections tend to address government spending toward large programs benefiting large groups in the population (such as welfare programs), whereas majoritarian elections give the politicians a greater incentive to target transfers to geographically smaller constituency groups.

There are two main reasons at the root of these differences (Persson and Tabellini 2000, Ch. 8). In proportional elections, the legislators are elected from large districts and this gives the politician a strong incentive to get support from large coalitions in the population. By contrast, in majoritarian elections, the districts are small, creating a strong incentive for politicians to target policies towards key district constituencies. Furthermore, the electoral formula has a reinforcing effect. In proportional election, the voters choose a list of candidates, whereas in majoritarian elections, a single candidate is chosen. Thus, in the former case, the implemented policy is likely to reflect what is optimal for the party, often reflecting the national perspective and favoring broad forms of redistribution. The opposite applies in majoritarian systems, where the individual legislator tends to "look after" the interests of the represented district, thus favoring a more narrow distribution.

Several, but not all, models predict that the electoral rule also affects the level of government spending, with proportional elections normally associated with larger spending. Indeed, while Persson and Tabellini (1999) found greater overall government spending in majoritarian elections, both Milesi-Ferretti, Perotti and Rostagno (2002) and Kontopoulos and Perotti (1999) claim greater spending in proportional systems. The latter prediction was recently supported theoretically and empirically by Persson,

Roland and Tabellini (2007), who studied the effect of electoral rules on party and government structure in parliamentary democracies. They stress that proportional elections induce a greater incidence of coalition governments than do majoritarian elections, giving rise to a larger budget spending as minority interests are more represented in the legislature.[9]

A few recent papers have applied this kind of reasoning to trade policy, although the theoretical predictions and the empirical evidence appear mixed. For example, Roelfsema (2004) and Grossman and Helpman (2005) predict, *ceteris paribus*, higher average rates of protection in countries with majoritarian election, as an effect of the stiffer electoral competition in swing districts. Both Roelfsema (2004) and Persson (2005) find empirical support for the hypothesis that proportional democracies are associated with more open trade policies than majoritarian democracies. By contrast, both Rogowski and Kayser (2002) and Hatfield and Hauk (2003) obtain exactly the opposite result, namely that proportional systems have higher average tariffs than majoritarian systems. Wiberg (2006) tries to reconcile these apparent contradictions by incorporating an export industry producing for foreign markets. He argues and finds empirical support for the idea that trade policy is more (less) restrictive under proportional systems if marginal districts are populated by relatively more (less) factory owners with interests in the exporting sector.

Forms of Government and Economic Policy

Few formal models assess the effect of different forms of government on the level and composition of government spending. The classical distinction is between presidential versus parliamentary regimes. In the former, the appointment is direct, through citizen election, while in the latter it is indirect, through a vote of confidence from an elected parliament.

Persson, Roland and Tabellini (1997, 2000) compare these two forms, focusing on different features such as the separation of power over legislation (agenda setting) and the degree of "legislative cohesion." In parliamentary regimes, the government has stronger powers to initiate legislation than in a presidential regime, and thus it is easier for politicians to collude with each other at the voters' expense, resulting in higher taxes and spending. Moreover, in parliamentary systems, the vote of confidence induces

---

[9] Persson, Roland and Tabellini (2007) formalize the so-called common pool problem: If different groups have partial control over some component of government then none of them fully internalizes the fiscal costs. This problem is clearly exacerbated under proportional elections because, as suggested by political science literature (see, e.g., Lijphart 1990), proportional elections make coalition governments more likely.

more discipline within the government coalition. Thus, a stable majority tends to satisfy the broad interests of its constituents.

These models give clear predictions of the level and composition of government spending, thereby mimicking and reinforcing the previous discussion on electoral systems. Specifically, for presidential regimes, the prediction is for overall lower spending and taxation than for parliamentary regimes. Moreover, presidential regimes are also associated with target programs, whereas parliamentary systems tend to have broader spending programs (Persson and Tabellini 2000, Ch. 10).[10] The empirical evidence strongly supports the prediction of greater public spending and government redistribution in parliamentary regimes than in presidential. However, between these two forms of government, the empirical differences in the composition of government spending – narrow versus broad programs – are, in general, weak (Persson and Tabellini 2004).

Implications and Testable Hypotheses

The literature summarized earlier in the chapter leads us to develop three main hypotheses about the effect of political institutions on agricultural protection.

The link between democratization and agricultural protection, though inconclusive from the theoretical point of view, can be expected to be moderately positive, as several studies highlight a positive effect of democratization on indicators of openness, redistribution, growth, and agricultural protection itself. Moreover, in line with previous evidence, the magnitude of this effect is expected to be conditional to the form of democracy. Thus, our first hypothesis can be summarized as follows:

H1. Regime change and agricultural protection: The effect of a democratic transition on agricultural protection is positive, and its magnitude is conditional to the specific form of democracy.

The implications concerning the effect of the different forms of democracy, when translated to agricultural protection, need further qualification. The literature suggests two quite clear predictions about the *level* and the composition of government spending. The prediction about the level of spending could translate directly to agricultural policy, suggesting higher protection and support under parliamentary and proportional

---

[10] See also Grossman and Helpman (2008), who studied the budget formation in a model of separation of powers, where the ruling coalition in the legislature and the executive serve different constituencies.

democracies than under presidential and majoritarian systems. Differently, the predictions about the composition of government spending (targeted versus broad) is more complex and could go in either direction depending on the role agricultural voters play relative to other voters.

In developed countries, the farm group is small, representing a classic special interest group, whereas in developing countries, where the rural population often is a majority, the farm group represents the broad interests of the population. Thus, strictly speaking, the effect of regime types and electoral rules on agricultural protection should be conditional to the level of development, a hypothesis consistent with the recent model of Henning (2008).

Because our objective is to test predictions concerning the potential effect of a regime change into different forms of democracy, a transition that largely happens in developing countries, the above considerations suggest that in our context, agricultural protection represents a broad redistributive program.[11] The opposite should apply in a consolidated democracy. Keeping this qualification in mind, we put forward the following two hypotheses:

H2. Forms of government and agricultural protection: Reform toward a parliamentary democracy, as opposed to a presidential one, will, on average, result in a greater increase in agricultural protection.

H3. Electoral rules and agricultural protection: Reform toward a proportional democracy, as opposed to a majoritarian one, will, on average, result in a greater increase in agricultural protection.

In what follow, after a description on how democratic reforms are identified and classified, we present our econometric strategy for formally testing the above hypotheses.

DATA AND BASIC SPECIFICATION

The sample in Anderson and Valenzuela (2008) refers to seventy-four countries and comprises yearly estimates of agricultural protection from 1955 to 2007. Not every country is covered for the whole time period, but the average number of years of observation per country to 2005 is thirty-five. Overall, we worked with an unbalanced panel with more than 2,500 observations. As in Olper and Raimondi (2004) and other cross-country

---

[11] Indeed, in our dataset, the average and the median values of the share of agricultural population in countries undergoing transitions in and out of democracy are 55 percent and 57 percent, respectively.

studies, the European Union countries are considered as separate entities, given their different levels of farm support shown in many studies (Bureau and Kalaitzandonakes 1995, Anderson and Valenzuela 2008).

In classifying democratic reforms and other political institution variables, we follow the classification utilized in the preceding literature, particularly Persson and Tabellini (2003), Giavazzi and Tabellini (2005) and Persson (2005). The interested reader should refer to these papers for a deeper description of and justification for using those variables. Here we give only a summary of the key criteria and data sources.

Political Institution Variables

We classify countries into democracy or autocracy using the Polity2 index of the Polity IV dataset. The Polity2 index assigns a value ranging from –10 to +10 to each country and year, with higher values implying more democracy. Following Papaionannou and Siourounis (2008) and Giavazzi and Tabellini (2005), we code a country as democratic in each year that the Polity2 index is strictly positive, setting a binary indicator called *democracy* = 1 (0 otherwise). A reform into (or out of) democracy occurs in a country-year when this democracy indicator switches from 0 to 1 or vice versa. In order to render the before-after analysis plausible, it is also necessary that the outcome of interest, agricultural protection, be observed for at least two years before and after each reform episode.

Applying these criteria to the dataset, we reach sixty-six transitions into or out of democracy, of which forty-one are transitions into democracy and twenty-five are into autocracy. About 62 percent of the reforms occurred before 1985. As shown in column 1 of Table 14.1, the distribution of these reforms is not uniform across continents and time: 50 percent of the reforms are in Africa, 24 percent in Asia, 15 percent in Latin America, and 11 percent in high-income countries.

Following Persson (2005), we define other binary indicators for the forms of democracy. Among democracies, the countries are coded as presidential (*pres* = 1, and *parl* = 0) when the chief executive is not accountable to the legislature through a vote of confidence. In all other situations, we have a parliamentary system (*parl* = 1, and *pres* = 0).[12] Note that, following this logic, we have countries with a directly elected president, such

---

[12] As discussed in Persson and Tabellini (2003), this represents a quite crude classification, especially because the conceptual model also relies on separation of powers in the legislative process. However, using also this dimension to classify countries as presidential or parliamentary systems introduces difficulties that are beyond the scope of this study.

Table 14.1. *Number of political reforms and their distribution under different forms of democracy,[a] 1956 to 2005 (percent)*

	All	Into	Out	PARL	PRES	PROP	MAJ
Number of transitions	66	41	25	18	47	24	41
Share (%) of all transitions pre-1985	62	49	84	83	53	67	59
Regional shares (%) of all transitions:							
Latin America	15	17	12	0	21	33	5
Africa	50	46	56	39	53	25	63
Asia	24	24	24	28	23	13	32
Other countries	11	13	12	33	3	29	0
TOTAL	100	100	100	100	100	100	100

[a] Number of democratic transitions classified by forms of democracy and their relative distribution across time and continents (see text). The sum across different forms of government does not give the total number of transitions because one transition (Sudan in 1958) is unclassifiable.
Source: see text.

as Portugal and France, classified as parliamentary, and countries without a popularly elected president, such as Switzerland, coded as presidential. Moreover, countries are classified as majoritarian if their elections to the lower house rely strictly on plurality rule ($maj = 1$, and $prop = 0$). All the other electoral systems are classified as proportional ($prop = 1$, and $maj = 0$). The primary source for mapping the sample into this classification is the database of Persson and Tabellini (2003), supplemented by the Database on Political Institutions (DPI) of the World Bank (Beck et al. 2001), and the Comparative Data Set on Political Institutions (Lundell and Karvonen 2003).[13]

The number of transitions and their distribution across different forms of democracy is summarized in Table 14.1. Row 2 shows that 83 percent of reforms before 1985 are in parliamentary democracies, whereas reforms in presidential democracies, and in proportional and majoritarian democracies, are more equally spread before and after 1985.

[13] We wish to thank Krister Lundell for kindly providing the relevant variables used in this chapter. For our purposes, the main differences in these two datasets lie in the countries and time period covered. Specifically, the DPI data cover a larger set of countries but it is limited to the 1975–2004 period, while the dataset of Lundell and Karvonen (2003) covers only "democracies" but the data start in 1960, at least for the more consolidated democracies.

Some problems emerge with the distribution of reforms across continents. For example, reforms in presidential systems are over-represented in Africa, and reforms in proportional systems are over-represented in Latin America (lower part of Table 14.1). This suggests that the distribution of reforms is not random across continents. Thus, the econometric estimation strategy needs to avoid confounding this continent-specific incidence of reforms from continent-specific trends in agricultural protection (Persson 2005).[14]

Dependent Variable and Structural Controls

We test our hypotheses using two different dependent variables: the agricultural nominal rate of assistance (NRA) and the relative rate of assistance (RRA), both from the World Bank's Distortions to Agricultural Incentives Database (Anderson and Valenzuela 2008, methodological details for which are in Anderson et al. 2008). The NRA is measured as the weighted average of the nominal rate of assistance at the product level, using as a weight the industry's value share of each product. Differently the RRA to agriculture is calculated as the ratio between the agricultural and nonagricultural NRA.[15] One advantage of using also the RRA is that, especially in developing countries, one important source of indirect taxation to agriculture comes from protection of manufacturing sectors. Thus, the RRA is a more useful indicator in undertaking international comparison over time of the extent to which a country's policy regime has an anti- or pro-agricultural bias (see Anderson et al. 2008).

To simplify the interpretation of the regression coefficients, we express NRA (and RRA) as a percentage. Thus, the magnitude of the estimated coefficient on our political institution indicators measures the average percentage point changes in agricultural protection implied by a transition into (or out of) democracy.

In the empirical specification, we include additional structural controls that are likely to affect the level of agricultural protection, as suggested by many previous studies (e.g., Anderson 1995, Beghin and Kherallah 1994, Swinnen et al. 2000, Olper 2001). Specifically, our basic specification

---

[14] All the reform episodes discussed above, and their specific classifications, are listed in part (a) of the Annex to this chapter, while part (b) of that Annex reports the few (eleven) constitutional reforms that happen in permanent democracies.

[15] Specifically, RRA is calculated as $[(1 + NRA_{ag})/(1 + NRA_{nonag})-1]$, where NRA_{ag} is the nominal rate of assistance to agricultural tradables and NRA_{nonag} is the average nominal rate of assistance to nonagricultural tradable sectors.

always includes the following structural controls: the level of development, measured by the log of real per capita GDP; agricultural employment as a share of total employment; the log of agricultural land per capita; the log of total population; and, finally, given the high persistency of agricultural protection and for reasons discussed below, we always include the lagged dependent variable. All these variables are computed using FAO and World Bank (WDI) sources, or otherwise national statistics.

A Preliminary Look at the Data

Table 14.2 displays average levels of the nominal rate of assistance in the full sample and splits the sample across different forms of democracy and over time. Several interesting patterns emerge. First, autocratic countries have, on average, as well as in each time period considered, a negative NRA: agriculture in these countries is taxed at an average rate of -15 percent. The opposite applies in democratic countries, whose farmers are strongly protected at an average rate of 45 percent (although at a decreasing rate starting from the mid-1980s).

Table 14.2. *Average agricultural NRAs and political regimes,[a] 1956 to 2005*

	Full sample	Autocracy	Democracy	MAJ	PROP	PRES	PARL
1956–59	0.41	−0.13	0.66	n.a.	n.a.	n.a.	n.a.
1960–64	0.28	−0.16	0.54	0.13	0.98	0.73	0.49
1965–69	0.27	−0.13	0.51	0.10	1.02	0.53	0.51
1970–74	0.10	−0.24	0.46	0.04	0.90	0.48	0.45
1975–79	0.10	−0.23	0.44	0.04	0.75	0.37	0.48
1980–84	0.09	−0.22	0.38	0.12	0.60	0.12	0.51
1985–89	0.29	−0.06	0.59	0.16	0.85	0.30	0.75
1990–94	0.23	−0.14	0.41	0.09	0.59	0.24	0.53
1995–99	0.19	−0.13	0.28	0.03	0.38	0.21	0.33
2000–05	0.20	−0.08	0.26	0.04	0.35	0.20	0.31
All years	0.21	−0.15	0.45	0.08	0.71	0.35	0.48
Number of countries	74	39	67	28	46	35	40

[a] The figures report simple average of NRA across constitutional features and subperiods. The number of countries refers to "total presences" in each category in 1956–2005 (1960–2005 for forms of government), and changes over time due to entry and exit.

Source: Authors' estimations.

Another clear pattern emerges on comparing protection across electoral rules. Majoritarian countries consistently have a lower NRA than proportional ones. While the gap apparently decreases over time, in 2000–05, the relative differences are still stark and close to that of the 1960–64 period. The last two columns of Table 14.2 contrast presidential and parliamentary democracies. Here the pattern appears less clear: Until 1975, presidential democracies had an average NRA very close to parliamentary democracies, then we see a shift with consistently higher NRAs in parliamentary democracies.

Figure 14.1 displays a more formal test for unconditional differences in average NRAs across constitutional features. This is based on a smoothed nonparametric regression line with its correspondent 95 percent confidence interval. As evident from the figure, for both autocracies and democracies, and across electoral rules, the differences are stark. Consistent with the basic data reported in Table 14.2, for parliamentary and presidential systems, the 95 percent confidence interval of the two line overlaps for about half of the period, suggesting that the difference in the average NRA across forms of government is small.

Generally speaking, these patterns appear not in contradiction with the predictions discussed before. However, it is too early to come to any conclusions about the effect of constitutional rules on agricultural protection. This is because our key constitutional dimension, democracy, is also correlated to the level of development, which is itself a fundamental determinant of agricultural protection. Also, as shown earlier in the chapter and as explained in Persson and Tabellini (2003), the forms of democracy are not random but are correlated with other characteristics such as history and the continental location of a country. Thus, before any inferences are drawn concerning the effect of constitutions on policy outcomes, we need an econometric approach able to control for both observed and unobserved country characteristics.

ECONOMETRIC APPROACH AND RESULTS

Following recent tendencies in the comparative political economy literature (e.g., Rodrik and Wacziarg 2005 Giavazzi and Tabellini 2005, Persson 2005), we estimate the average effect of constitutions on policy outcomes using the difference-in-differences approach. This means running panel regressions with the following specification:

$$y_{i,t} = \beta D_{i,t} + \rho x_{i,t} + \alpha_i + \vartheta_t + \epsilon_{i,t} \tag{1}$$

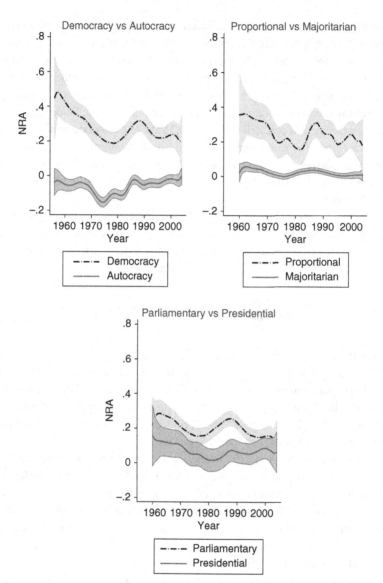

Figure 14.1. Average agricultural NRA and constitutional features,[a] 1956 to 2005 (percent).

[a] The figures show the evolution of the (smoothed) average *NRAs*, and their 95 percent confidence interval (computed using Stata's *lpolyci* using bandwith 3 and degree 4), calculated across democratic and autocratic regimes and across different forms of government. A country in a given year is classified as a democracy if variable Polity2 in the Polity IV dataset is greater than zero (see text).

Source: see text.

where $y_{i,t}$ denotes our measure of interest, namely agricultural protection, α_i and θ_t are respectively the country and year fixed effects, $x_{i,t}$ is a set of control variables, and $D_{i,t}$ is a dummy variable taking the value 1 under democracy and 0 otherwise. The parameter β is the difference-in-differences estimate of the reform effect. It is obtained by comparing average protection after a democratic transition, minus protection before the transition in the treated countries, with the change in protection in the control countries over the same period (Persson and Tabellini 2008). Here, the control countries are those that do not experience a transition into or out of democracy, thus those that have either $D_{i,t} = 1$ or $D_{i,t} = 0$ over the entire sample period.

We use regression (1) to estimate the average effect of democratization on agricultural protection. Moreover, as we are particularly interested in the (potential) heterogeneous effects induced by different forms of democracy, we follow Persson (2005) using also a multiple treatments specification:

$$y_{i,t} = \sum_{f=1}^{F} \beta^f D_{i,t}^f + \rho x_{i,t} + \alpha_i + \phi_t + \epsilon_{i,t} \tag{2}$$

where the $D_{i,t}^f$ is now a binary variable for a subset of the different forms of democracy $f = 1,...., F$, namely majoritarian versus proportional democracy or parliamentary versus presidential democracy. Once again, we compare the change in protection before and after the specific democratic transition with the change in protection of those countries that do not experience a reform over the sample period.

As stressed by Persson (2005), one problem with the interpretation of these specifications is the correct econometric identification. Specifically, the coefficient β^f identifies the causal effect of different democratic reforms only if countries in the various reform groups do not have trends in y which are different from those in the control group but unrelated to reforms. As discussed before, the frequency of transitions into democracy (autocracy) and different forms of democracy change quite a lot across continents. Thus, to avoid confounding such nonrandom incidence with continents-specific trends in agricultural protection, we ensure that the estimates of β^f are robust to the inclusion of a set of continent-time interaction effects.

A final econometric problem arises when the dependent variable displays a strong positive autocorrelation. In that circumstance, Bertrand, Duflo and Mullainathan (2004) show that the estimated standard errors with the difference-in-differences approach are strongly underestimated. To overcome this, we follow the most conservative method of estimating standard errors by clustering at the country level, allowing arbitrary country-specific serial correlation. Moreover, we always add to the specifications the lagged dependent variable. This transforms specifications (1) and (2) into a dynamic panel model where the lagged dependent variable allows for the strong persistence of agricultural protection.

Democracy and Protection: Econometric Results

Table 14.3 displays the results of specification (1) estimated across different samples. This corresponds to a standard difference-in-differences estimation on yearly data. The specification, other than country and year fixed effects and the controls reported in Table 14.3, always includes the log of country population, the agricultural employment share, the land per capita and the interaction effects between continent and year dummies. We start by making a couple of comments on the sign and significant level of the standard controls.

First, and not surprisingly, agricultural protection is positively and significantly associated with the level of development (GDP per capita) and displays strong persistency. In other words, current protection is a very good predictor of future protection. Moreover, protection is positively related to the log of population and negatively to both land per capita and employment share (results not shown). However, it is important to note that the last variables are insignificant in several specifications, suggesting that in the previous analyses they especially capture the cross-country variation in protection, here subsumed in the fixed effects.

Turning to the key variable of interest, democracy, and following Persson and Tabellini (2008), the regressions of Table 14.3 explore different assumptions about the treatments and the control group, testing the effect of a democratic transition on different samples.

Regression (1) imposes the assumption that the effect on protection of a transition to democracy is the same as the negativity of the effect of a transition to autocracy, thus exploiting the full sample. The coefficient on democracy is positive and significant at the 1 percent level, meaning that a transition into democracy induces an increase in agricultural protection of about 4 percent points. Thus, the effect is not only statistically significant, but also important from an economic point of view.

Regression (2) estimates only the effect of a transition into democracy, removing reforms to autocracy from the sample, and using as a control group only permanent autocracy. The democracy coefficient is again positive, but drops somewhat in magnitude and it is only barely significant.

Table 14.3. Average agricultural NRAs and democracy,[a] difference-in-differences estimates

Regression number	(1)	(2)	(3)	(4)	(5)	(6)	(7)	(8)	(9)	(10)
Dependent variable	NRA	NRA	NRA	NRA	NRA	RRA	RRA	RRA	RRA	RRA
Democracy	4.10***	3.20*	4.41***	2.31	5.38***	3.47***	2.73	3.70***	1.39	4.91***
	(1.24)	(1.86)	(1.44)	(1.62)	(1.48)	(1.20)	(1.67)	(1.38)	(1.87)	(1.48)
Lagged NRA (RRA)	0.77***	0.67***	0.78***	0.79***	0.68***	0.77***	0.70***	0.79***	0.77***	0.73***
	(0.03)	(0.05)	(0.03)	(0.03)	(0.04)	(0.03)	(0.06)	(0.02)	(0.04)	(0.04)
Dem*lagged NRA (RRA)					0.11***					0.06**
					(0.04)					(0.03)
Log GDP per capita	14.45***	15.12***	15.66***	16.79***	15.16***	11.71***	10.99**	12.79***	18.42***	12.32***
	(3.45)	(5.08)	(4.16)	(7.14)	(3.67)	(3.19)	(5.16)	(3.92)	(6.76)	(3.49)
Treatment (transition to)	Democracy autocracy	Democracy	Democracy	Autocracy	Democracy autocracy	Democracy autocracy	Democracy	Democracy	Autocracy	Democracy autocracy
Control group (permanent)	Autocracy democracy	Autocracy	Autocracy democracy	Democracy	Autocracy democracy	Autocracy democracy	Autocracy	Autocracy democracy	Democracy	Autocracy democracy
Continent-year dummies	Yes	Yes	Yes	Yes	Yes	Yes	Yes	Yes	Yes	Yes
Observations	2568	1191	2291	1517	2568	2314	1002	2064	1449	2314
Number of countries	74	38	73	52	74	69	33	68	51	69
R² (within)	0.73	0.77	0.75	0.74	0.73	0.74	0.78	0.75	0.72	0.74

[a] Robust standard errors clustered by country in parentheses. All regressions include: log of population, agricultural employment share, land per capita, year and country fixed effects, and interaction effects between continents (Africa, Asia, and Latin America) and year dummies (see text).
*** $p < .01$, ** $p < .05$, * $p < .10$.
Source: Authors' estimations.

However, a shortcoming of this regression is that we have only 11 countries that remain permanent autocracies across the sample period, and two of these – Chad and Togo – are somewhat problematic.[16] In regression (3), by adding also permanent democracies to the control group, the coefficient on the democracy dummy increases and turns out to be significant at the 1 percent level. Now the estimate implies that a democratic transition induces a greater NRA, by 4.4 percentage points.

Regression (4) estimates the effect of a transition out of democracy (or into autocracy), using permanent democracies as the control group. Here, the democracy coefficient is still positive, suggesting that the effect goes in the expected direction,[17] but it is low in magnitude and statistically not significant. Finally, in regression (5), we allow the coefficient for the lagged dependent variable to take on a different value across constitutional groups by interacting the democracy dummy with the lagged NRA. The interaction coefficient is positive and significant, showing that democracies display more persistence in agricultural policy than autocracies.

Columns (6) to (10) replicate the same battery of regressions using RRA as the dependent variable. As can be seen, the results are very similar: Only a slightly lower democracy effect is detected. Once again, the democracy coefficient is always positive and significantly different from zero when the treatment measures transitions toward democracy, and the control group also includes the permanent democracies, just as it is positive but insignificant when the treatment measures transition out of democracy, or the control group includes only permanent autocracies.[18]

Summarizing, this preliminary evidence suggests that the effect of transition to democracy induces an increase in agricultural protection of about 3–4 percentage points. Thus, agriculture, which is discriminated against and taxed in an autocratic country, will take advantage of a redistribution process after a democratic transition. This result is in line with the evidence reported in Acemoglu and Robinson (2000) and Swinnen, Banerjee and de Gorter (2001). Moreover, the fact that the same relation does not hold for transition out of democracy appears consistent with several stylized facts suggesting that, once implemented, agricultural policies tend to persist for

[16] A potential problem with these countries, as well as with Benin, Burkina Faso, and Mali, is that we only have protection data for one product, cotton. Thus, any specific shock to this sector could substantially affect the protection level of our benchmark in that regression. Note, however, that all these countries are not considered in the *RRA* sample.

[17] Remember that we are measuring the *negative* protection effect of a transition away from democracy.

[18] Note that by using *RRA*, we lose five countries from the full sample, as well as several observations as the *RRA* coverage is lower than *NRA*.

some time, even if changes in (external) factors make them "inefficient" or not politically justifiable (Olper and Swinnen 2008)

Forms of Democracy and Protection: Econometric Results

Table 14.4 tests Hypotheses 2 and 3, namely that forms of democracy should matter. This is done by interacting our democracy dummy with the respective dummies for government types and electoral rules, in order to disentangle their (potential) differentiated effect. Regression (1) contrasts parliamentary and presidential regimes. Contrary to our expectation, a reform to presidential democracy induces growth in agricultural protection that is slightly higher than a reform to proportional democracy, from 4.2 to 3.7 percent points, respectively. However, the two coefficients are not significantly different from each other. Thus, this preliminary evidence does not support the idea that reform into parliamentary democracy induces a higher NRA than reform to a presidential democracy.

Regression (3) of Table 14.4 contrasts the effect of reform to proportional democracy with reform to majoritarian democracy. Now the estimated differences are stark and in line with the prediction. The average protection effect of a transition toward a proportional democracy is 6.8 percentage points, thus about three time higher than a shift toward a majoritarian democracy, where the estimated coefficient is also barely significant. Not surprisingly, the F-statistic for the equality of electoral coefficients is strongly significant (results not shown), implying that what matters for democratic reform appears to be the choice of electoral rule.

Next, in regressions (2) and (4) of Table 14.4, we allow the coefficient for the lagged dependent variable to take on a different value across different constitutional features. Parliamentary and presidential democracies do not display differences in persistence. At the level of electoral rules, the differences are important, with proportional democracies showing higher persistence in agricultural protection than majoritarian democracies. Finally, regression (5) considers the distinction between permanent and temporary reforms. Not surprisingly, permanent democratization strongly increases the probability of a higher NRA, whereas temporary reforms have a lower and only slightly significant effect.

Table 14.5 replicates the same regressions using the RRA as the dependent variable. As we can see, all the qualitative and quantitative results discussed above remain substantially unchanged, suggesting that they are quite robust to small change in the sample size and country coverage, and in the definition of the dependent variable.

Table 14.4. *Forms of democracy and average agricultural NRAs,[a] difference-in-differences estimates*

Regression number	(1)	(2)	(3)	(4)	(5)
Dependent variable	NRA	NRA	NRA	NRA	NRA
PARL	3.69**	4.98***			
	(1.85)	(1.85)			
PRES	4.22***	5.66***			
	(1.39)	(1.83)			
PROP			6.76***	6.77***	
			(1.61)	(1.71)	
MAJ			2.38*	2.69	
			(1.42)	(1.80)	
Permanent					5.53***
					(1.40)
Temporary					2.96*
					(1.65)
Lagged NRA	0.77***	0.68***	0.77***	0.66***	0.77***
	(0.03)	(0.04)	(0.03)	(0.04)	(0.03)
PARL * Lagged NRA		0.11**			
		(0.05)			
PRES * Lagged NRA		0.12***			
		(0.04)			
PROP * Lagged NRA				0.14***	
				(0.04)	
MAJ * Lagged NRA				−0.04	
				(0.06)	
Observations	2511	2511	2511	2511	2568
Number of countries	74	74	74	74	74
Within R²	0.73	0.73	0.73	0.74	0.73

[a] Robust standard errors clustered by country in parentheses. All regressions include: log GDP per capita, log of population, agricultural employment share, agricultural land per capita, years and country fixed effects, and interaction effects between continents (Africa, Asia, and Latin America) and years dummies (see text).
*** $p < .01$, **$p < .05$, *$p < .10$.
Source: Authors' estimations.

Finally, Table 14.6 considers a more defined characterization of the forms of democracy, splitting the constitutional variables into the following four categories: *parl-prop, pres-prop, parl-maj*, and *pres-maj*. If the parliamentary-presidential distinction is independent of the proportional-

Table 14.5. *Forms of democracy and relative rates of assistance,[a] difference-in-difference estimates*

Regression number	(1)	(2)	(3)	(4)	(5)
Dependent variable	RRA	RRA	RRA	RRA	RRA
PARL	3.10*	5.13**			
	(1.92)	(2.17)			
PRES	3.64***	5.10***			
	(1.36)	(1.74)			
PROP			5.52***	6.40***	
			(1.68)	(2.08)	
MAJ			2.27	1.61	
			(1.49)	(2.08)	
Permanent					4.96***
					(1.39)
Temporary					2.49
					(1.69)
Lagged RRA	0.77***	0.71***	0.77***	0.69***	0.77***
	(0.03)	(0.05)	(0.03)	(0.05)	(0.03)
PARL * Lagged RRA		0.08*			
		(0.05)			
PRES * Lagged RRA		0.06**			
		(0.03)			
PROP * Lagged RRA				0.12**	
				(0.05)	
MAJ * Lagged RRA				−0.05	
				(0.05)	
Observations	2273	2273	2273	2273	2314
Number of countries	69	69	69	69	69
Within R^2	0.74	0.74	0.74	0.74	0.74

[a] Robust standard errors clustered by country in parentheses. All regressions include: log GDP per capita, log of population, agricultural employment share, agricultural land per capita, years and country fixed effects, and interaction effects between continents (Africa, Asia, and Latin America) and years dummies (see text).
*** $p < .01$, **$p < .05$, *$p < .10$.
Source: Authors' estimations.

Table 14.6. *Forms of democracy and nominal and relative rates of assistance, with alternative constitutional groups*[a]

Regression number	(1)	(2)	(3)	(4)
Dependent variable	NRA	NRA	RRA	RRA
PARL_PROP	9.64***	8.43***	7.50***	5.68**
	(2.48)	*(2.20)*	*(2.51)*	*(2.74)*
PRES_PROP	6.01***	5.39***	5.19***	4.66**
	(1.92)	*(1.68)*	*(1.83)*	*(1.83)*
PARL_MAJ	0.38	0.83	1.83	1.50
	(1.86)	*(1.71)*	*(2.09)*	*(1.92)*
PRES_MAJ	2.76	2.33	1.98	1.98
	(1.61)	*(1.56)*	*(1.66)*	*(1.68)*
Lagged NRA	0.76***	0.77***	0.76***	0.77***
	(0.02)	*(0.03)*	*(0.03)*	*(0.03)*
Log GDP per capita	13.45***	14.90***	11.29***	11.42***
	(3.43)	*(3.77)*	*(3.11)*	*(3.39)*
Continent-year dummies	No	Yes	No	Yes
Observations	2505	2505	2273	2273
Number of countries	74	74	69	69
Within R^2	0.69	0.73	0.70	0.74

[a] Robust standard errors clustered by country in parentheses. All regressions include: log of population, employment share, land per capita, year and country fixed effects. Interaction between years and continent dummies (Africa, Asia, and Latin America) included as indicated (see text).
*** $p < .01$, **$p < .05$, *$p < .10$.
Source: Authors' estimations.

majoritarian distinction, then the effects of the form of government and the electoral rule should be additive (Persson 2005). The evidence supports this hypothesis weakly and only for reforms into parliamentary-proportional democracy, where the respective estimated coefficients for *NRA* regressions, with values ranging from 8.4 to 9.6, are not far from the sum of the respective individual coefficients reported in Table 14.4. That is, there is some evidence that the effect of proportional election is dampened under presidential systems.

Summing up, in line with theoretical predictions, we find heterogeneity in the protection effect induced by different constitutional rules. Transition toward parliamentary-proportional democracy increases a country's agricultural NRA by about 8 percentage points, and by about 5 percentage points for presidential-proportional democracy. Instead, the protectionism bias of a transition toward parliamentary- or presidential-majoritarian democracy is virtually zero. This evidence suggests that agricultural protection is affected more by constitutional differences in electoral rules than by differences in the form of government. This evidence is in line with the predictions summarized in the theory section above, and are qualitatively similar to results obtained at a more aggregate level by Persson (2005) and Persson and Tabellini (2006), with the important qualification that at the aggregated level the form of government appears to matter quantitatively more than electoral rules.

CONCLUSION

Motivated by recent developments in political economy theory about the effect of rule-based political institutions on public policy outcomes, we have investigated how transitions into democracy affect agricultural protection. The empirical results highlight the important role played by the form of democracy in affecting agricultural policy distortions. In particular, using panel data and difference-in-differences estimation, we first documented a significant positive effect of a democratic transition on agricultural protection. We then showed that this average effect masks important heterogeneities across different forms of democracy. Indeed, what matters are transitions to proportional (as opposed to majoritarian) democracies, as well as to permanent (as opposed to temporary) democracies. Moreover, while we do not detect significant differences across alternative forms of government, there is evidence that the effect of proportional systems is exacerbated under parliamentary regimes but dampened under presidential ones. Finally, we find indications that different constitutional rules affect the dynamic adjustment of agricultural protection. Overall, these results support the notion that rules-based institutions do matter in affecting the adoption of structural policies.

Several further improvements should be made to better understand the interaction between institutions and agricultural policy distortions. For example, this analysis has assumed that electoral rules directly affect political incentives. However, there is evidence that electoral rules shape public policy only indirectly, through their effect on party and government structure (Persson, Roland and Tabellini 2007. At the same time, partial evidence detected concerning the differentiated effect exerted by different forms of government could simply suggest that other regime features, such as separation of powers, should matter. Extensions into these and other directions could improve our understanding of the interlink between constitutions and public policies.

References

Acemoglu, D. (2005), "Constitutions, Politics and Economics: A Review Essay on Persson and Tabellini's 'The Economic Effect of Constitutions'," *Journal of Economic Literature* 43(4): 1025–48.

Acemoglu, D., S. Johnson and J.A Robinson (2001), "The Colonial Origins of Comparative Development: An Empirical Investigation," *American Economic Review* 91(5): 1369–1401.

Acemoglu, D. and J.A. Robinson (2000), "Why Did the West Extend the Franchise? Democracy, Inequality and Growth in Historical Perspective," *Quarterly Journal of Economics* 115: 1167–99.

(2008), "Persistence of Power, Elites and Institutions", *American Economic Review* 98(1): 267–93.

Aghion, P., A. Alesina and F. Trebbi (2008), "Democracy, Technology and Growth," in E. Helpman (ed.), *Institutions and Economic Performance*, Cambridge MA: Harvard University Press.

Alesina, A., N. Roubini and G.D. Cohen (1997), *Political Cycles and the Macroeconomy*, Cambridge MA: MIT Press.

Anderson, K. (1995), "Lobbying Incentives and the Pattern of Protection in Rich and Poor Countries," *Economic Development and Cultural Change* 43(2): 401–23.

Anderson, K., M. Kurzweil, W. Martin, D. Sandri and E. Valenzuela (2008), "Measuring Distortions to Agricultural Incentives, Revisited," *World Trade Review* 7(4): 1–30.

Anderson, K., and E. Valenzuela (2008), Global *Estimates of Distortions to Agricultural Incentives, 1955 to 2007*, database available at http://www.worldbank.org/agdistortions

Banerji, A. and H. Ghanem (1997), "Does the Type of Political Regime Matter for Trade and Labor Market Policies?" *World Bank Economic Review* 11(1): 171–94.

Barro, R. J. (1997), *Determinants of Economic Growth: A Cross-country Empirical Study*, Cambridge MA: MIT Press

Bates, R.H. (1983), "Patterns of Market Intervention in Agrarian Africa," *Food Policy* 8: 297–304.

(1989), *Beyond the Miracle of the Market: The Political Economy of Agrarian Development in Kenya*, Cambridge and New York: Cambridge University Press

Beck, T., G. Clarke, A. Groff and P. Keefer (2001), "New Tools in Comparative Political Economy: The Database of Political Institutions," *World Bank Economic Review* 15(1): 165–76.

Beghin, J.C. and M. Kherallah (1994), "Political Institutions and International Patterns of Agricultural Protection," *Review of Economics and Statistics* 76: 482–9.

Bertrand, M., E. Duflo and S. Mullainathan (2004), "How Much Should We Trust Difference-in-difference Estimates?" *Quarterly Journal of Economics* 119: 249–75.

Besley, T. and T. Persson (2008), "The Origin of State Capacity: Property Rights, Taxation and Politics," NBER Working Paper No. 13028 (forthcoming in *American Economic Review*).

Bureau, J.C. and N.G. Kalaitzandonakes (1995), "Measuring Effective Protection as a Superlative Index Number: An Application to European Agriculture," *American Journal of Agricultural Economics* 77(2): 279–90.

de Haan, J. and J. Sturm (2003), "Does More Democracy Lead to Greater Economic Freedom? New Evidence for Developing Countries," *European Journal of Political Economy* 19(3): 547–63.

Dutt, P. and D. Mitra (2002), "Endogenous Trade Policy Through Majority Voting: An Empirical Investigation," *Journal of International Economics* 58: 107–33.

(2005), "Political Ideology and Endogenous Trade Policy: An Empirical Investigation," *Review of Economics and Statistics* 87(1): 59–72.

(2010), "Impacts of Ideology, Inequality, Lobbying and Public Finance", Ch. 11 in this volume.

Giavazzi, F. and G. Tabellini (2005), "Economic and Political Liberalization," *Journal of Monetary Economics* 52: 1297–1330.

Glaeser, E.L., R. La Porta, F. Lopez-de-Silane and A. Shleifer (2004), "Do Institutions Cause Growth, " *Journal of Economic Growth* 9(3): 271–304.

Grossman, G.M. and E. Helpman (2005), "A Protectionist Bias in Majoritarian Politics," *Quarterly Journal of Economics* 120(4): 1239–82.

(2008), "Separation of Powers and the Budget Process," *Journal of Public Economics* 92(3–4): 407–25.

Hall, R.E. and C. Jones (1999), "Why Do Some Countries Produce So Much More Output Per Worker Than Others?" *Quarterly Journal of Economics* 114(1): 83–116.

Hatfield, J.W. and W.R. Hauk (2003), "The Effect of the Electoral Regime on Trade Policy," SIEPR Discussion Paper No. 03–20, Stanford University.

Henning, C.H.C.A. (2004), "The Role of Institutions in Agricultural Protectionism,", pp. 137–51 in G. Van Huylenbroeck, W. Verbeke and L. Lauwers (eds.), *Role of Institutions in Rural Policies and Agricultural Markets*, Amsterdam: Elsevier.

(2008), "Determinants of Agricultural Protection in an International Perspective: The Role of Political Institutions," Working Paper, University of Kiel, February.

Henning, C.H.C.A., K.C. Krause and C. Struve (2002), "Institutional Foundation of Agricultural Protection: The Case of EU-Accession and Agricultural Policy in Eastern European Countries," Annual Meeting of AAEA, Long Beach, California.

Henning, C.H.C.A. and C. Struve (2007), "Postelection Bargaining and Special Interest Politics in Parliamentary Systems: The Case of Agricultural Protection," pp. 45–84 in M. Hinich and W. Barnett (eds.), *Topics in Analytical Political Economy, Volume 17 of International Symposia in Economic Theory and Econometrics*, Amsterdam: Elsevier.

Knack, S. and P. Keefer (1995), "Institutions and Economic Performance: Cross-Country Tests Using Alternative Institutional Measures," *Economics and Politics* 7: 207–27.

Kontopoulos, Y. and R. Perotti (1999), "Government Fragmentation and Fiscal Policy Outcomes: Evidence from the OECD Countries", in J. Poterba and J. von Hagen (eds.), *Fiscal Institutions and Fiscal Preference*, Chicago IL: University of Chicago Press.

Lijphart, A. (1990), "The Political Consequences of Electoral Laws, 1945–1985," *American Political Science Review* 84: 481–96.

Lindert, P.L. (1991), "Historical Patterns of Agricultural Policy", pp. 29–83 in C.P. Timmer (ed.), *Agriculture and the State: Growth, Employment, and Poverty in Developing Countries*, Ithaca NY: Cornell University Press.

Lizzeri, A. and N. Persico (2001), "The Provision of Public Goods Under Alternative Electoral Incentives," *American Economic Review* 91(1): 225–39.

Lundell, K. and L. Karvonen (2003), "A Comparative Data Set on Political Institutions," Department of Political Science Occasional Papers Series Nr. 19/2003, Abo Akademi University, Åbo, Finland.

Milesi-Ferretti, G-M., R. Perotti and M. Rostagno (2002), "Electoral Systems and the Composition of Public Spending," *Quarterly Journal of Economics* 117: 609–57.

Milner, H.V. and K. Kubota (2005), "Why the Move to Free Trade? Democracy and Trade Policy in the Developing Countries," *International Organization* 59: 107–43.

Mulligan, C.B., R. Gil and X. Sala-i-Martin (2004), "Do Democracies Have Different Public Policies Than Non-democracies," *Journal of Economic Perspective* 18(1): 51–74.

North, D. (1990), *Institutions, Institutional Change and Economic Performance*, Cambridge and New York: Cambridge University Press.

Olper, A. (2001), "Determinants of Agricultural Protection: The Role of Democracy and Institutional Setting," *Journal of Agricultural Economics* 52(2): 75–92.

(2007), "Land Inequality, Government Ideology and Agricultural Protection," *Food Policy* 32(1): 67–83.

Olper, A. and V. Raimondi (2004), "Political Institutions and Milk Policy Outcomes in OECD Countries," pp. 153–68 in G. Van Huylenbroeck, W. Verbeke and L. Lauwers (eds.), *Role of Institutions in Rural Policies and Agricultural Markets*, Amsterdam: Elsevier.

Olper, A. and J. Swinnen (2008), "The Political Economy of Instrument Choice in Agricultural and Food Policies," Working Paper, DEPA, University of Milan, February.

Papaioannou, E. and G. Siourounis (2008), "Democratization and Growth," *Economic Journal* 118, 1520–51, October.

Persson, T. (2005), "Forms of Democracy, Policy and Economic Development," Working Paper, Institute for International Economic Studies, Stockholm University, January.

Persson, T. and G. Tabellini (1999), "The Size and Scope of Government: Comparative Politics with Rational Politicians, 1998 Marshall Lecture," *European Economic Review* 43: 699–734.

(2000), *Political Economics: Explaining Economic Policy*, Cambridge MA: MIT Press.

(2003), *The Economic Effects of Constitution: What Do the Data Say?* Cambridge MA: MIT Press.

(2004), "Constitutions and Economic Policy," *Journal of Economic Perspectives* 18(1): 75–98.

(2006), "Democracy and Development: The Devil in the Details," *American Economic Review* 96: 319–24.

(2008), "The Growth Effect of Democracy: Is it Heterogeneous and How Can it be Estimated?" in E. Helpman (ed.), *Institutions and Economic Performance*, Cambridge MA: Harvard University Press.

Persson, T., G. Roland and G. Tabellini (1997), "Separation of Power and Political Accountability," *Quarterly Journal of Economics* 112: 310–27.

(2000), "Comparative Politics and Public Finance," *Journal of Political Economy* 108: 1121–61.

(2007), "Electoral Rules and Government Spending in Parliamentary Democracies," *Quarterly Journal of Political Science* 2: 155–88.

Przeworsky, A. (1991), *Democracy and the Market*, Cambridge and New York: Cambridge University Press.

Rodrik, D. and R. Wacziarg (2005), "Do Democratic Transitions Produce Bad Economic Outcomes?" *American Economic Review* 95(2): 50–55.

Roelfsema, H. (2004), "Political Institutions and Trade Protection," Discussion Paper Series 04–06, Tjalling C. Koopmans Research Institute, Utrecht University.

Rogowski, R. and M.A. Kayser (2002), "Majoritarian Electoral Systems and Consumer Power. Price-Level Evidence from the OECD Countries," *American Journal of Political Science* 46(3): 526–39.

Swinnen, J. (1994), "A Positive Theory of Agricultural Protection," *American Journal of Agricultural Economics* 76(1): 1–14.

(2010), "Political Economy of Agricultural Distortions: The Literature to Date," Ch. 3 in this volume.

Swinnen, J.F., A.N. Banerjee and H. de Gorter (2001), "Economic Development, Institutional Change, and the Political Economy of Agricultural Protection: An Econometric Study of Belgium Since the 19th Century," *Agricultural Economics* 26(1): 25–43.

Swinnen, J., H. de Gorter, G.C. Rausser and A.N. Banerjee (2000), "The Political Economy of Public Research Investment and Commodity Policy in Agriculture: An Empirical Study," *Agricultural Economics* 22(1): 111–22.

Thies, C.G. and S. Porche (2007), "The Political Economy of Agricultural Protection," *Journal of Politics* 69: 116–27.

Weingast, B. and W. Marshall (1988), "The Industrial Organization of Congress; Or, Why Legislators as Firms are Not Organized as Markets," *Journal of Political Economy* 96: 379–89.

Wiberg, M. (2006), "On the Indeterminacy of Trade Policy Under Different Electoral Rules," Working paper, Department of Economics, Stockholm University.

ANNEX 14.1: NATIONAL POLICY REFORM
EPISODES, 1955 TO 2005

(a) *Exits and entries in different forms of democracy*

Country	Year	Into or Out of Democracy	Form of government	Forms of elections
Argentina	1973	Into	Presidential	Proportional
Argentina	1976	Out	Presidential	Proportional
Argentina	1983	Into	Presidential	Proportional
Benin	1991	Into	Presidential	Proportional
Burkinafaso	1977	Into	Presidential	Proportional
Burkinafaso	1980	Out	Presidential	Proportional
Bangladesh	1991	Into	Parlamentary	Majoritarian
Brazil	1985	Into	Presidential	Proportional
Chile	1973	Out	Presidential	Majoritarian
Chile	1989	Into	Presidential	Majoritarian
Cote d'Ivoire	2000	Into	Presidential	Majoritarian
Cote d'Ivoire	2002	Out	Presidential	Majoritarian
Dominican Rep.	1978	Into	Presidential	Proportional
Ecuador	1968	Into	Presidential	Proportional
Ecuador	1970	Out	Presidential	Proportional
Ecuador	1979	Into	Presidential	Proportional
Spain	1976	Into	Parlamentary	Proportional
Ethiopia	1994	Into	Parlamentary	Majoritarian
Ghana	1970	Into	Parlamentary	Majoritarian
Ghana	1972	Out	Parlamentary	Majoritarian
Ghana	1979	Into	Presidential	Majoritarian
Ghana	1981	Out	Presidential	Majoritarian
Ghana	1996	Into	Presidential	Majoritarian
Indonesia	1999	Into	Presidential	Proportional
Kenya	1966	Out	Parlamentary	Majoritarian
Kenya	2002	Into	Presidential	Majoritarian
Korea	1963	Into	Presidential	Majoritarian
Korea	1972	Out	Presidential	Majoritarian
Korea	1987	Into	Presidential	Proportional
Madagascar	1991	Into	Presidential	Proportional
Mexico	1994	Into	Presidential	Proportional

(continued)

ANNEX 14.1(a) *(continued)*

Country	Year	Into or Out of Democracy	Form of government	Forms of elections
Mali	1992	Into	Presidential	Majoritarian
Mozambique	1994	Into	Presidential	Proportional
Nigeria	1966	Out	Presidential	Majoritarian
Nigeria	1979	Into	Presidential	Majoritarian
Nigeria	1984	Out	Presidential	Majoritarian
Nigeria	1999	Into	Presidential	Majoritarian
Pakistan	1970	Out	Presidential	Majoritarian
Pakistan	1972	Into	Presidential	Majoritarian
Pakistan	1977	Out	Presidential	Majoritarian
Pakistan	1988	Into	Presidential	Majoritarian
Pakistan	1999	Out	Presidential	Majoritarian
Philippines	1972	Out	Presidential	Majoritarian
Philippines	1986	Into	Presidential	Majoritarian
Portugal	1975	Into	Parlamentary	Proportional
Sudan[a]	1958	Out		
Sudan	1965	Into	Parlamentary	Majoritarian
Sudan	1970	Out	Parlamentary	Majoritarian
Sudan	1986	Into	Presidential	Majoritarian
Sudan	1989	Out	Presidential	Majoritarian
Senegal	2000	Into	Presidential	Proportional
Thailand	1974	Into	Parlamentary	Majoritarian
Thailand	1976	Out	Parlamentary	Majoritarian
Thailand	1978	Into	Parlamentary	Majoritarian
Turkey	1971	Out	Parlamentary	Proportional
Turkey	1973	Into	Parlamentary	Proportional
Turkey	1980	Out	Parlamentary	Proportional
Turkey	1983	Into	Parlamentary	Proportional
Taiwan	1992	Into	Parlamentary	Proportional
Tanzania	2000	Into	Presidential	Majoritarian
Uganda	1966	Out	Parlamentary	Majoritarian
Uganda	1980	Into	Presidential	Majoritarian
Uganda	1985	Out	Presidential	Majoritarian
Zambia	1968	Out	Presidential	Majoritarian
Zambia	1991	Into	Presidential	Majoritarian
Zimbabwe	1987	Out	Presidential	Majoritarian

(b) *Reforms in existing democracies*

Country	Reform	Type of reform
Bangladesh	1991	Government: presidential to parliamentary
France	1986	Election: majoritarian to proportional
France	1988	Election: proportional to majoritarian
New Zealand	1996	Election: majoritarian to proportional
Philippines	1998	Election: majoritarian to proportional
Philippines	2001	Election: proportional to majoritarian
South Africa	1994	Election: majoritarian to proportional
Sri Lanka	1979	Government: parliamentary to presidential
Sri Lanka	1989	Election: majoritarian to proportional
Taiwan	1996	Government: parliamentary to presidential
Ukraine	1998	Election: majoritarian to proportional

[a] Sudan's reform in 1958 is unclassifiable.

Source: See text.

APPENDIX

Coverage and Distribution of Assistance across Countries and Products, 1955–2007

Kym Anderson and Johanna Croser

The core global database that was developed as an integral part of the World Bank's research project on Distortions to Agricultural Incentives is publicly available at www.worldbank.org/agdistortions (Anderson and Valenzuela 2008). Case studies from which it is derived cover a total of seventy-five countries that together account for between 90 and 96 percent of the world's population, farmers, agricultural output, and total GDP. They also account for more than 85 percent of farm production and employment in each of Africa, Asia, Latin America, and the transition economies of Europe and Central Asia, as well as all OECD countries.[1] The only countries not well represented in the sample are those in the Middle East and the many small ones that together account for less than 5 percent of the global economy.

Nominal rates of assistance and consumer tax equivalents (NRAs and CTEs) are estimated for more than seventy different products, with an average of eleven per country. In aggregate, the coverage represents around 70 percent of the gross value of agricultural production in the focus countries and just under two-thirds of global farm production valued at undistorted prices over the period covered. Not all countries had data for all of the 1955–2007 period, but the average number of years covered is forty-one per country. Estimates for the transition economies of Europe start in 1992 and for China and Vietnam in 1981 and 1986, respectively. Estimates for three other large Asian countries start later, too (India in 1965, Indonesia and Thailand in 1970).

---

[1] A global overview of the results is provided in Anderson (2009), and the detailed country case studies are reported in four regional volumes covering Africa (Anderson and Masters 2009), Asia (Anderson and Martin 2009), Latin America (Anderson and Valdés 2008), and Europe's transition economies (Anderson and Swinnen 2008).

Of the 30 most valuable agricultural products, the NRAs cover 77 percent of global output, ranging from two-thirds for livestock, three-quarters for oilseeds and tropical crops, and five-sixths for grains and tubers. Those products represent an even higher share (85 percent) of global agricultural exports. Tables A.1 to A.5 provide further details of the above product and country coverage statistics. Figure A.1 shows the number of countries for which NRA and CTE estimates are produced for each of twenty-three key farm products, whereas Figure A.2 shows the share of global production of each of these key farm products covered by NRA and CTE estimates.

This book is focused primarily on explaining the differences across countries, products, and time of distortions to farmers' incentives, particularly as summarized by nominal rates of assistance. Figure A.3 summarizes the distributions and shows, for various regions of the world, a set of Box plots. The long bar in those plots shows the range within which 95 percent of the NRAs fall: 50 percent fall in the shaded area, and the vertical line within the shaded area is the median NRA for the sample time period. Then in Figure A.4, we provide similar Box plots of all the covered products for each focus country.[2] In both figures, the subperiods before and from 1985 are shown separately. A break in the mid-1980s roughly coincides with the time many developing countries and some high-income countries began to reform their agricultural and trade policies. Also, the earlier period coincides with that covered by the seminal World Bank study of eighteen developing countries by Krueger, Schiff and Valdés (1991), and the later period coincides with the time series of estimates of agricultural distortions in high-income countries by the OECD (2008). For a direct comparison of the Krueger, Schiff and Valdés estimates with those from the latest World bank study, see Anderson (2010).

---

[2]   We are grateful to Kishore Gawande for suggesting this type of plot be used to summarize the data.

Table A.1. *Summary of NRA coverage statistics, World Bank agricultural distortions project*

Number and size of countries	Number	2000–04 % of global	
		Popn.	Ag GDP
Africa	21	11	7
Asia	12	51	37
Latin America	8	7	8
SUB-TOTAL, all DCs	**41**	**69**	52
European transition econs	14	7	7
High-income countries	20	14	33
TOTAL	**75**	**92**	**92**
Number of years covered	**Maximum**	**Av. per country**	
Africa	51	43	
Asia	53	42	
Latin America	51	39	
SUB-TOTAL, all DCs	53	43	
European transition econs	47	17	
High-income countries	53	52	
TOTAL	**51**	**41**	
Number of products covered	**Maximum**	**Av. per country**	
Africa	44	8	
Asia	35	8	
Latin America	27	10	
SUB-TOTAL, all DCs	59	9	
European transition econs	25	12	
High-income countries	39	15	
TOTAL	**74**	**11**	
Total number of NRA ests. (years and products)	**Total**	**Av. per country**	
Africa	7318	348	
Asia	3546	296	
Latin America	2881	360	
SUB-TOTAL, focus DCs	13745	335	
European transition econs	2847	203	
High-income countries	13377	669	
TOTAL, focus countries	**29969**	**400**	

(continued)

Table A.1 *(continued)*

Number and size of countries	Number	2000–04 % of global	
		Popn.	Ag GDP
Share of global agric. prod'n of 30 key covered products, 2000–04	%		
Africa	5		
Asia	28		
Latin America	7		
SUB-TOTAL, focus DCs	41		
European transition econs	6		
High-income countries	29		
TOTAL, focus countries	77		

Source: Calculated from data in Anderson and Valenzuela (2008)

Table A.2. *Coverage of gross value of global agricultural production at undistorted prices, for 30 key products and 4 product groups, 2000 to 2004*

	Coverage of product's global GVOP, %	Product's share of global GVOP of 30 key products, %
Grains and tubers	85	31.4
Rice	92	9.5
Wheat	89	8.0
Maize	94	7.2
Cassava	41	2.4
Barley	83	1.6
Sorghum	70	0.7
Yam	77	0.8
Millet	29	0.6
Oat	61	0.3
Oilseeds	78	8.1
Soybean	96	4.0
Groundnut	34	1.2
Palmoil	90	1.0
Rapeseed	64	1.0
Sunflower	77	0.6
Sesame	9	0.3
Tropical crops	74	7.6
Sugar	87	2.5
Cotton	88	1.9

	Coverage of product's global GVOP, %	Product's share of global GVOP of 30 key products, %
Coconut	60	0.9
Coffee	75	0.7
Rubber	74	0.7
Tea	21	0.6
Cocoa	71	0.4
Chickpea	61	0.3
Livestock products	72	**52.9**
Pigmeat	91	12.4
Milk	83	12.0
Beef	69	10.5
Poultry	81	7.6
Egg	35	6.5
Sheepmeat	27	3.3
Wool	42	0.6
All above products	77	**100.0**

Note: Fruit and vegetables, which account for around 23 percent of global agricultural GVOP in 2001 (according to the GTAP database – see Dimaranan 2006), are not included in this table, even though several fruit and vegetables for selected countries are included in the analysis
Source: Calculated from data in Anderson and Valenzuela (2008).

Table A.3. *Coverage of national agricultural production in focus countries at undistorted prices, regional averages, 1980 to 2004 (percent)*

	1980–84	1990–94	2000–04
Africa	67	66	68
Asia	75	73	66
Latin America	65	69	70
SUB-TOTAL, focus DCs	72	72	67
European transition econs	62	61	63
High-income countries	73	73	72
TOTAL, all focus countries	**72**	**71**	**68**

Source: Calculated from data in Anderson and Valenzuela (2008).

Table A.4. *Derived shares of global agricultural production for 30 major covered products, by region, 2000 to 2004*

	Regional shares (%) of global gross value of agric production (GVOP)						Residual	World	Product share (%) of global GVOP of 30 products
	Covered products in focus countries								
	Africa	Asia	LAC	ECA	HIC	All			
Grains + tubers	11	40	5	6	23	85	15	100	31
Rice	3	81	2	0	5	92	8	100	9
Wheat	6	32	4	14	33	89	11	100	8
Maize	11	26	13	5	40	94	6	100	7
Cassava	39	2	0	0	0	41	59	100	2
Barley	0	0	1	25	57	83	17	100	2
Sorghum	26	13	14	0	17	70	30	100	1
Yam	77	0	0	0	0	77	23	100	1
Millet	29	0	0	0	0	29	71	100	1
Oat	0	0	0	28	33	61	39	100	0
Oilseeds	4	22	20	4	28	78	22	100	8
Soybean	0	15	37	0	43	96	4	100	4
Groundnut	17	17	0	0	0	34	66	100	1
Palmoil	8	81	2	0	0	90	10	100	1
Rapeseed	0	12	0	4	47	64	36	100	1
Sunflower	3	5	16	39	14	77	23	100	1
Sesame	8	0	0	0	0	9	91	100	0
Tropical crops	10	36	12	5	11	74	26	100	8
Sugar	5	43	17	6	16	87	13	100	2
Cotton	17	30	5	14	22	88	12	100	2
Coconut	0	60	0	0	0	60	40	100	1
Coffee	11	12	52	0	0	75	25	100	1
Rubber	0	74	0	0	0	74	26	100	1
Tea	11	10	0	0	0	21	79	100	1
Cocoa	68	0	3	0	0	71	29	100	0
Chickpea	0	61	0	0	0	61	39	100	0
Livestock products	3	21	6	7	36	72	28	100	53
Pigmeat	0	49	3	6	34	91	9	100	12
Milk	3	21	4	12	43	83	17	100	12

	Regional shares (%) of global gross value of agric production (GVOP)						Residual	World	Product share (%) of global GVOP of 30 products
	Covered products in focus countries								
	Africa	Asia	LAC	ECA	HIC	All			
Beef	6	1	16	5	41	69	31	100	10
Poultry	2	27	9	5	38	81	19	100	8
Egg	0	1	3	7	23	35	65	100	6
Sheepmeat	5	0	0	3	18	27	73	100	3
Wool	0	0	0	0	42	42	58	100	1
Total of above 30 products	6	28	7	6	29	77	23	100	100

Source: Authors' calculations based on FAO commodity balance to get volume of production data, and on the Agricultural Distortions database to convert this to value of production at undistorted prices so we can add up across commodities.

Table A.5. *Shares of regional agricultural production for 30 major covered products, by region, 2000 to 2004*

	Covered product shares (%) of regional gross value of agricultural production of focus countries					
	Africa	Asia	LAC	ECA	HIC	All
Grains + tubers	37.3	21.8	14.3	16.8	15.2	19.6
Rice	2.8	13.6	1.9	0.1	1.0	6.3
Wheat	4.7	4.6	3.0	10.2	5.6	5.3
Maize	8.4	3.3	8.3	2.7	6.2	5.0
Cassava	9.8	0.1	0.0	na	na	0.7
Barley	na	0.0	0.2	3.2	2.0	1.0
Sorghum	2.5	0.2	0.9	na	0.3	0.4
Yam	7.0	na	na	na	na	0.5
Millet	2.1	na	na	na	na	0.1
Oat	na	na	na	0.6	0.2	0.1
Oilseeds	3.3	3.1	14.5	2.2	4.8	4.5
Soybean	0.0	1.1	13.3	0.0	3.6	2.8
Groundnut	2.0	0.4	0.0	na	na	0.3
Palmoil	0.9	1.4	0.1	na	na	0.6

(continued)

Table A.5 *(continued)*

	Covered product shares (%) of regional gross value of agricultural production of focus countries					
	Africa	Asia	LAC	ECA	HIC	All
Rapeseed	na	0.2	na	0.2	1.0	0.4
Sunflower	0.2	0.1	0.9	2.0	0.2	0.4
Sesame	0.2	na	0.0	na	na	0.0
Tropical crops	7.9	5.1	8.1	3.5	1.7	4.2
Sugar	1.2	1.9	3.8	1.3	0.8	1.6
Cotton	2.3	1.0	0.9	2.1	0.9	1.1
Coconut	na	0.8	na	na	na	0.3
Coffee	0.8	0.1	3.3	na	na	0.4
Rubber	na	0.9	na	na	na	0.4
Tea	0.7	0.1	na	na	na	0.1
Cocoa	3.0	0.0	0.1	na	na	0.2
Chickpea	na	0.3	na	na	na	0.1
Livestock products	13.7	19.0	29.9	30.5	40.4	27.9
Pigmeat	na	10.6	3.0	6.6	8.9	8.3
Milk	3.5	4.5	4.4	11.8	11.1	7.3
Beef	6.8	0.2	14.7	4.6	9.1	5.3
Poultry	1.6	3.6	5.9	2.9	6.2	4.5
Egg	na	0.1	1.9	3.7	3.2	1.7
Sheepmeat	1.8	na	na	0.9	1.3	0.7
Wool	na	na	na	na	0.6	0.2
Total of above 30	62.2	48.8	66.7	52.9	62.2	56.2
All covered	68.2	66.1	70.3	60.9	72.4	68.3
Non-covered	31.8	33.9	29.7	39.1	27.6	31.7
All agric	100.0	100.0	100.0	100.0	100.0	100.0

Source: Calculated from data in Anderson and Valenzuela (2008).

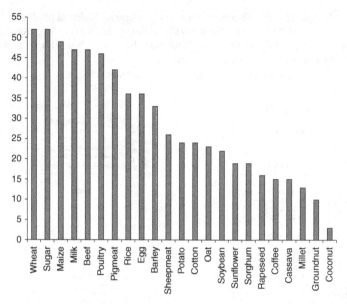

Figure A.1. Number of countries for which NRA and CTE estimates are provided for 23 key farm products.

Source: Drawn from estimates in Anderson and Valenzuela (2008).

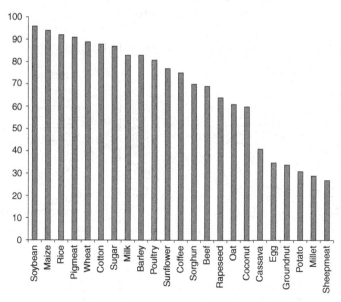

Figure A.2. Shares of global production of 23 key farm products covered in NRA and CTE estimates (percent).

Source: Drawn from estimates in Anderson and Valenzuela (2008).

Figure A.3. Box plot distributions of NRAs for 25 major agricultural products in each region of the world, 1955 to 2007 (long bar shows range within which 95 percent of the NRAs fall: 50 percent fall in the shaded area, and the vertical line within the shaded area is the median NRA for the sample period).

(a) All 21 focus African countries, plus Turkey (n = 7,988)

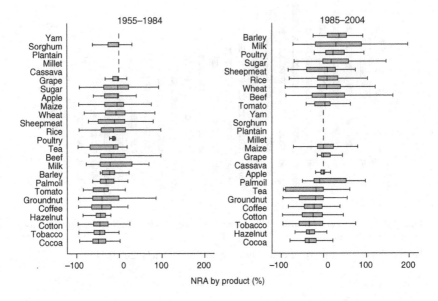

(b) All 12 focus Asian developing economies (excluding Japan) (n = 5,410)

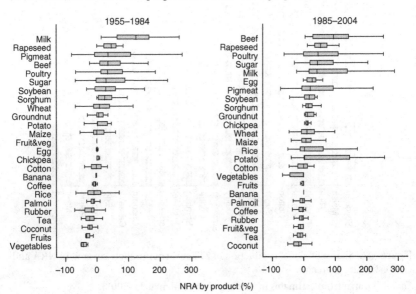

Figure A.3 *(continued)*

(c) All 8 focus Latin American countries (n = 4,180)

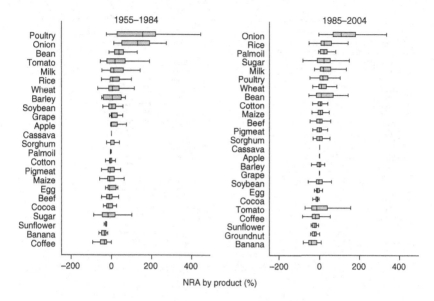

NRA by product (%)

(d) All 12 focus European transition economies (excluding Turkey) (n = 2,398)

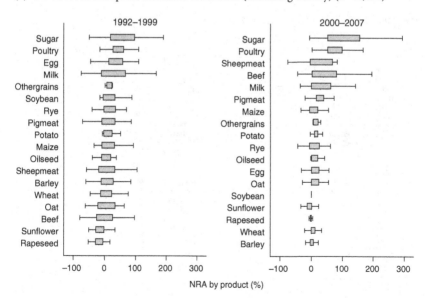

NRA by product (%)

Figure A.3 *(continued)*

(e) All 41 focus developing economies (including Turkey) (n = 14,392)

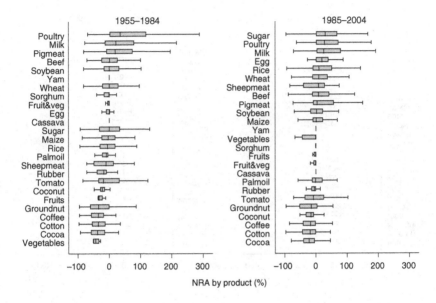

(f) All 20 focus high-income countries (n = 12,970)

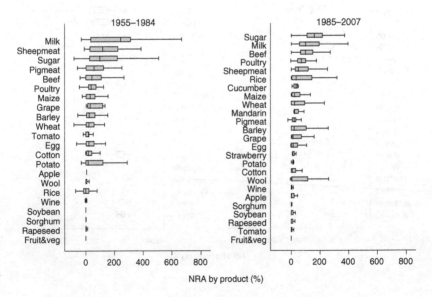

Figure A.3 *(continued)*
(g) All 73 focus economies of the world (n = 34,833)

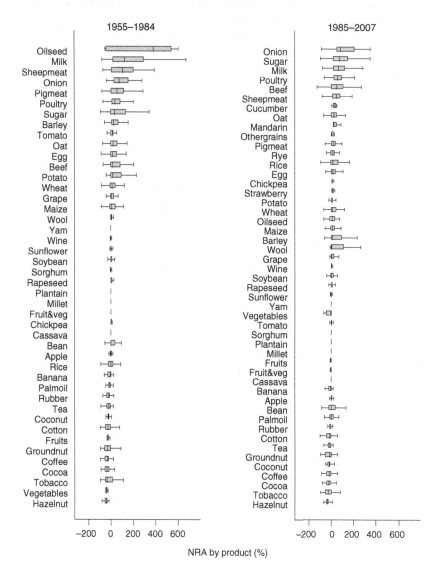

NRA by product (%)

Source: Drawn from estimates in Anderson and Valenzuela (2008).

Figure A.4. Box plot distributions of NRAs of all covered agricultural products for each focus economy, 1955 to 2007 (long bar shows range within which 95 percent of the NRAs fall: the shaded area has 50 percent of NRAs, and the vertical line within the shaded area is the median NRA for the available sample period).

(a) 16 African countries (excluding 5 cotton-dominant countries) and Turkey

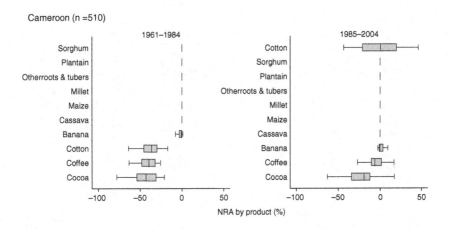

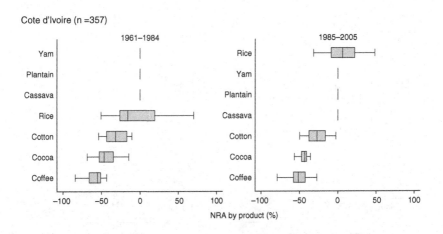

Figure A.4(a) *(continued)*

Egypt (n= 357)

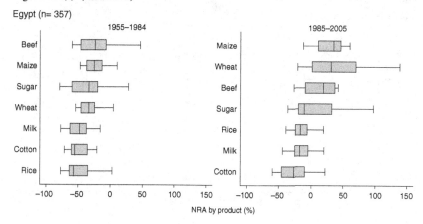

Ethiopia (n= 408)

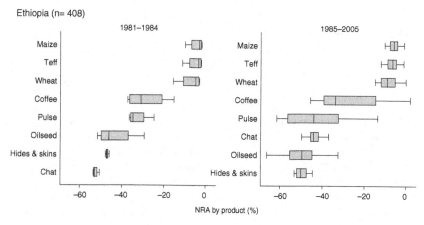

Ghana (n = 357)

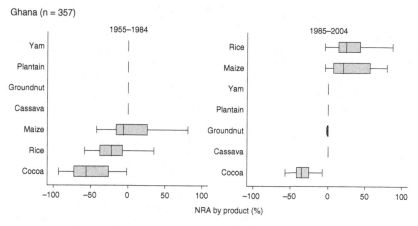

Figure A.4(a) *(continued)*

Kenya (n= 343)

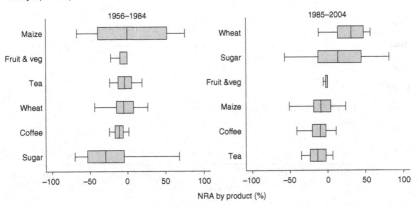

Madagascar (n= 510)

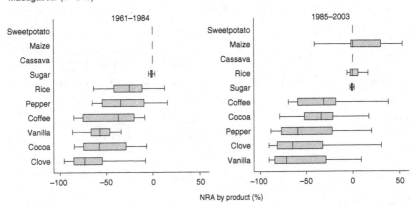

Mozambique (n = 668)

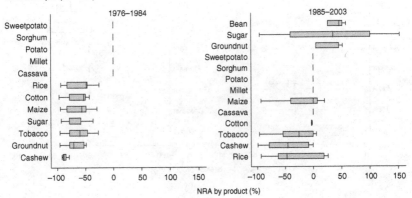

Figure A.4(a) *(continued)*

Nigeria (n = 510)

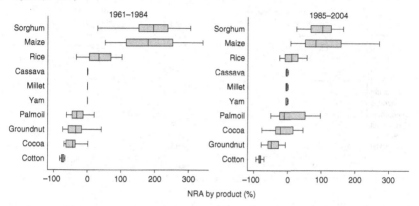

Senegal (n = 204)

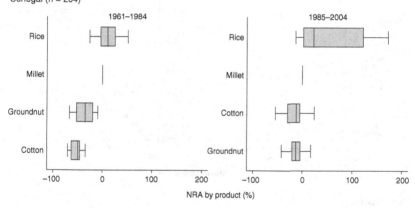

South Africa (n = 643)

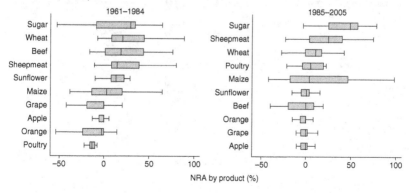

Figure A.4(a) *(continued)*

Sudan (n = 611)

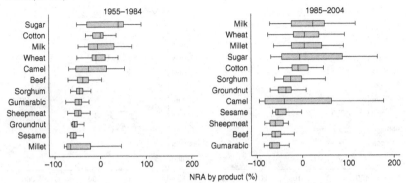

Tanzania (n = 918)

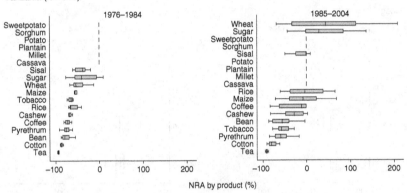

Turkey (n = 609)

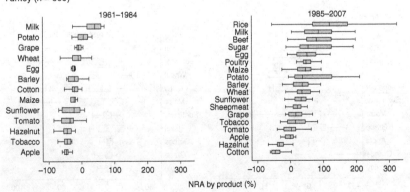

Figure A.4(a) *(continued)*

Uganda (n = 663)

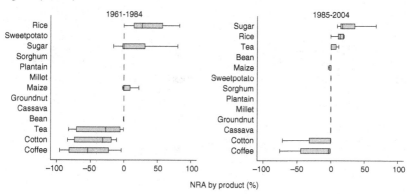

Zambia (n = 510)

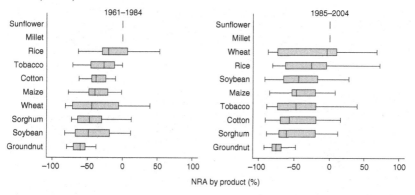

Zimbabwe (n = 408)

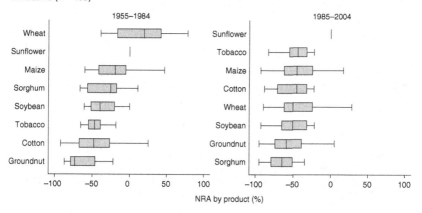

Figure A.4 *(continued)*
(b) 12 Asian developing economies

Bangladesh (n = 306)

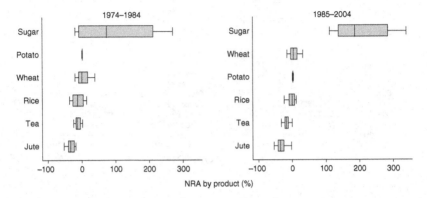

China (n = 561)

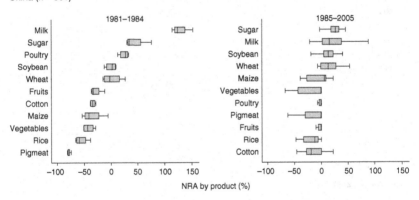

India (n = 663)

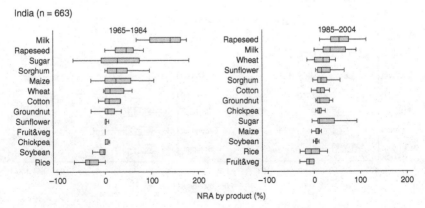

Figure A.4(b) *(continued)*

Indonesia (n = 510)

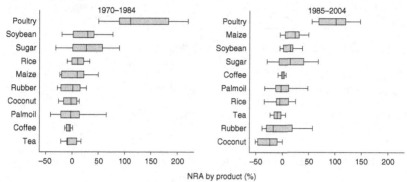

NRA by product (%)

Korea (n = 634)

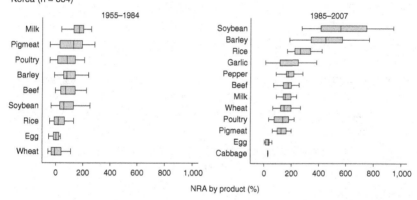

NRA by product (%)

Malaysia (n = 204)

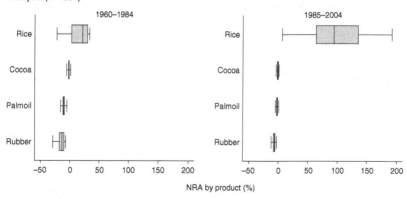

NRA by product (%)

Figure A.4(b) *(continued)*

Pakistan (n = 306)

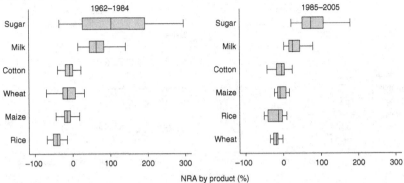

Philippines (n = 346)

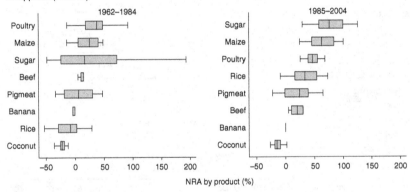

Sri Lanka (n = 357)

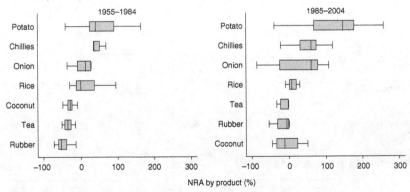

Figure A.4(b) *(continued)*

Taiwan (n = 357)

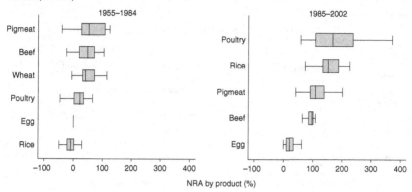

Thailand (n = 459)

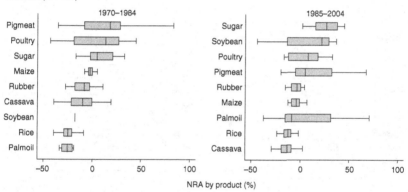

Vietnam (n = 306) (note: no data in 1955–85)

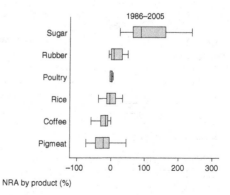

Figure A.4 *(continued)*

(c) 8 Latin American countries

Argentina (n = 306)

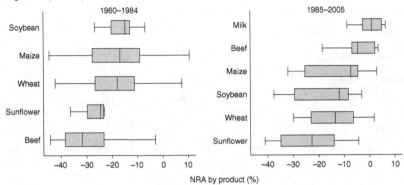

Brazil (n = 510)

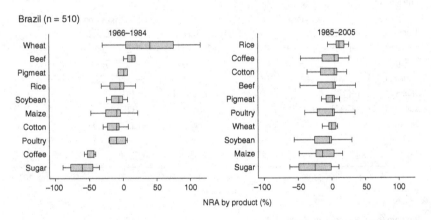

Chile (n = 357)

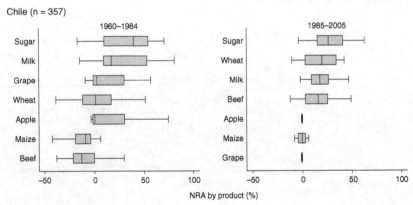

Figure A.4(c) *(continued)*

Colombia (n = 561)

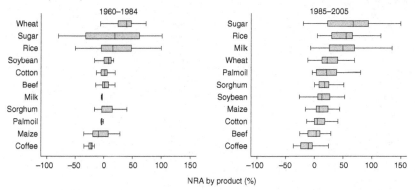

Dominican Republic (n = 510)

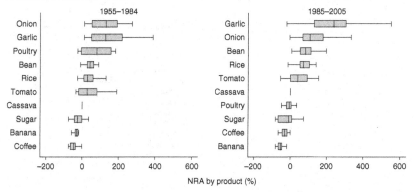

Ecuador (n = 561)

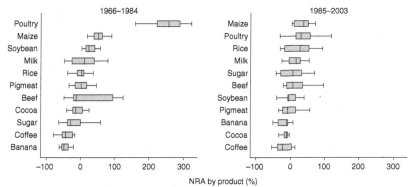

Figure A.4(c) *(continued)*

Mexico (n = 793)

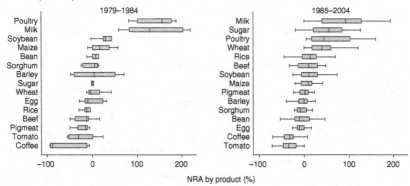

Nicaragua (n = 612) (note: no data prior to 1991)

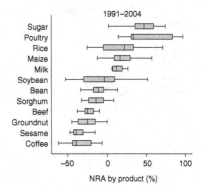

Figure A.4 *(continued)*

(d) 12 European transition economies

Bulgaria (n = 183)

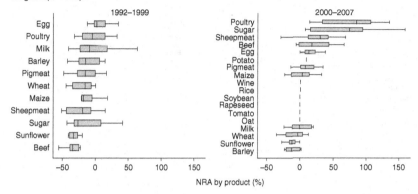

Czech Rep. (n = 165)

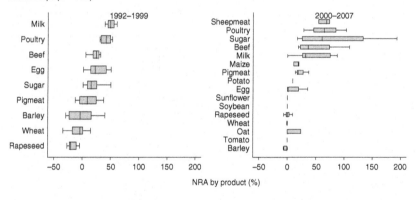

Estonia (n = 167)

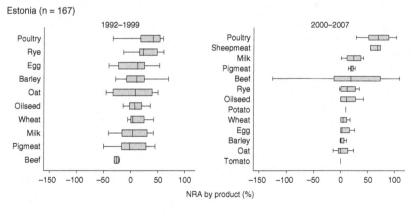

Figure A.4(d) *(continued)*

Hungary (n = 210)

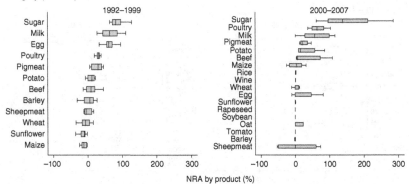

NRA by product (%)

Kazakhstan (n = 30)

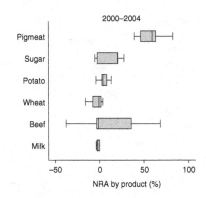

NRA by product (%)

Latvia (n = 181)

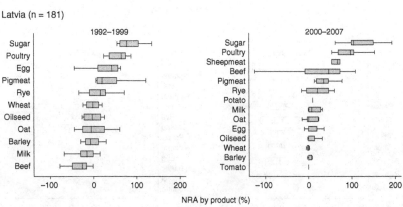

NRA by product (%)

Figure A.4(d) *(continued)*

Lithuania (n = 184)

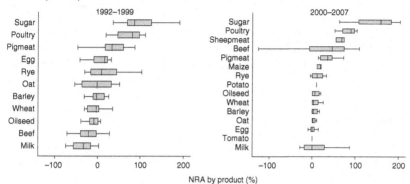

NRA by product (%)

Poland (n = 186)

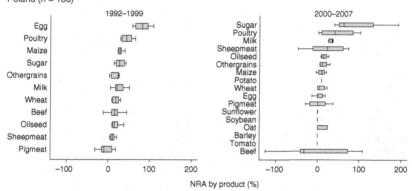

NRA by product (%)

Romania (n = 228)

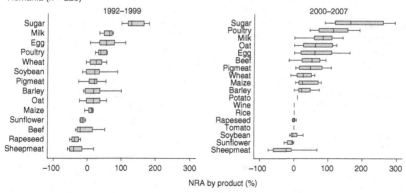

NRA by product (%)

Figure A.4(d) *(continued)*

Russia (n = 168)

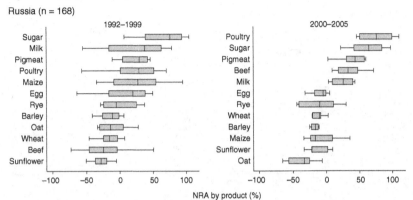

NRA by product (%)

Slovakia (n = 219)

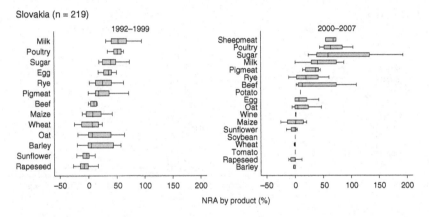

NRA by product (%)

Slovenia (n = 159)

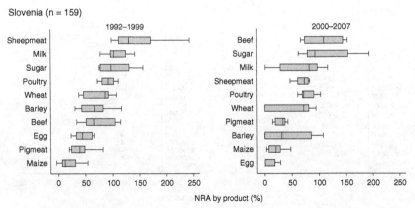

NRA by product (%)

Figure A.4(d) *(continued)*

Ukraine (n = 178)

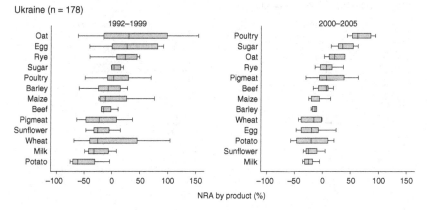

(e) 9 high-income economies (counting as 1 the EU member countries as of 1/1/2004)

Australia (n = 1317)

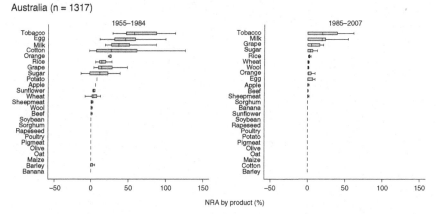

Canada (n = 630)

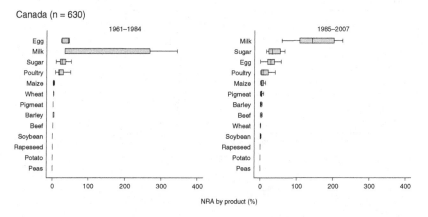

Figure A.4(e) *(continued)*

EU15 countries (as of 1/1/2004) (n = 8157)

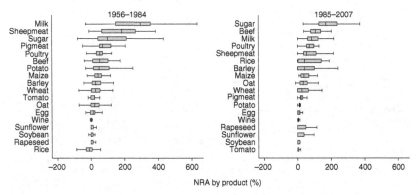

NRA by product (%)

Iceland (n = 203)

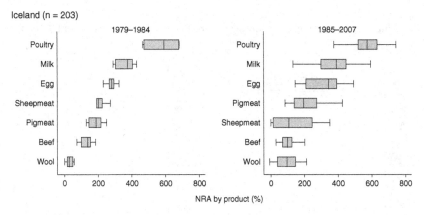

NRA by product (%)

Japan (n = 1007)

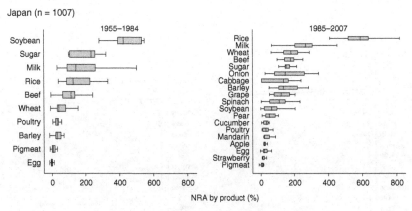

NRA by product (%)

Figure A.4(e) *(continued)*

New Zealand (n = 723)

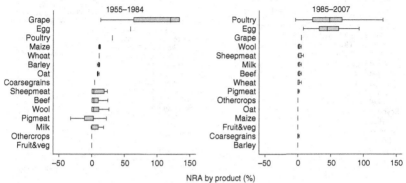

NRA by product (%)

Norway (n = 249)

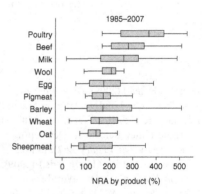

NRA by product (%)

Switzerland (n = 268)

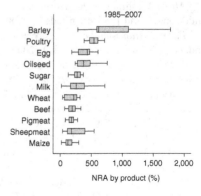

NRA by product (%)

Figure A.4(e) *(continued)*

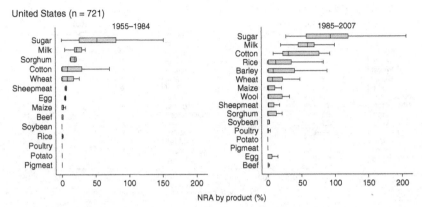

Source: Drawn from estimates in Anderson and Valenzuela (2008).

References

Anderson, K. (ed.) (2009), *Distortions to Agricultural Incentives: A Global Perspective, 1955 to 2007*, London: Palgrave Macmillan and Washington DC: World Bank.

Anderson, K. (2010), "Krueger/Schiff/Valdés Revisited: Agricultural Price and Trade Policy Reform in Developing Countries Since 1960", *Applied Economic Perspectives and Policy* 32(2): 195–231, Summer.

Anderson, K. and W. Martin (eds.) (2009), *Distortions to Agricultural Incentives in Asia*, Washington DC: World Bank.

Anderson, K. and W. Masters (eds.) (2009), *Distortions to Agricultural Incentives in Africa*, Washington DC: World Bank.

Anderson, K. and J. Swinnen (eds.) (2008), *Distortions to Agricultural Incentives in Europe's Transition Economies*, Washington DC: World Bank.

Anderson, K. and A. Valdés (eds.) (2008), *Distortions to Agricultural Incentives in Latin America*, Washington DC: World Bank.

Anderson, K. and E. Valenzuela (2008), "Estimates of Global Distortions to Agricultural Incentives, 1955 to 2007", World Bank, Washington DC, available on the Database page at www.worldbank.org/agdistortions.

Krueger, A.O., M. Schiff and A. Valdés (1991), *The Political Economy of Agricultural Pricing Policy, Volume 1: Latin America, Volume 2: Asia, and Volume 3: Africa and the Mediterranean*, Baltimore: Johns Hopkins University Press for the World Bank.

OECD (2008 and earlier years), *Agricultural Policies in OECD Countries: Monitoring and Evaluation*, Paris: Organization for Economic Cooperation and Development.

Index

Printed in the United States
by Baker & Taylor Publisher Services